T0249890

A crucial testimony to how issues of power and exploitation are negotiated and used while researching vulnerable groups and how more consideration of ethical issues turns the researched into co-researchers. An outstanding and thought-provoking book that provides an exceptionally powerful addition to the scarce literature on the needs of refugee professionals and the language teachers who work with them, whilst enhancing understanding of intercultural communication.

Dr. Mohammed Ateek, *Department of Languages, Cultures and Applied Linuistics Birkbeck, University of London*

This book tells a success story about refugees. It is a much-needed addition to the literature on language and intercultural communication which shows, through action research and an ethically motivated agenda, how displaced people can be helped to succeed in a new society by accessing key intercultural and linguistic skills that will help them integrate into the workplace. We need positive stories about refugees and asylum seekers.

Hans J. Ladegaard, *Professor and Head, The Hong Kong Polytechnic University*

Building Blocks of Tabletop Game Design

Second Edition

Building Blocks of Tabletop Game Design

An Encyclopedia of Mechanisms

Second Edition

Geoffrey Engelstein

Isaac Shalev

CRC Press
Taylor & Francis Group
Boca Raton London New York

CRC Press is an imprint of the
Taylor & Francis Group, an **informa** business

Second edition published 2022
by CRC Press
6000 Broken Sound Parkway NW, Suite 300, Boca Raton, FL 33487-2742

and by CRC Press
2 Park Square, Milton Park, Abingdon, Oxon, OX14 4RN

CRC Press is an imprint of Taylor & Francis Group, LLC

© 2022 Taylor & Francis Group, LLC
First edition published by CRC Press 2019

ISBN: 978-1-032-01583-5 (hbk)
ISBN: 978-1-032-01581-1 (pbk)
ISBN: 978-1-003-17918-4 (ebk)

DOI: 10.1201/9781003179184

Typeset in Adobe Garamond pro
by Deanta Global Publishing Services, Chennai, India

To Susan, for a wonderful 40 years, and to our children, Brian and Sydney, for always challenging my strategies across the game table and my ideas across the kitchen table.

Geoff

Much of the work of this second edition was done in the shadow of the COVID-19 pandemic. I would like to express my appreciation and gratitude to everyone who provided medical, food, and other essential services in this difficult and dangerous time. Thank you for helping us get back to the game table.

Isaac

Contents

2

3

4

5

7

11

12

Abbreviations

AI	Artificial Intelligence
CRT	Combat Results Table
FIFO	First In, First Out
KotH	King of the Hill
LIFO	Last In, First Out
PD	Prisoner's Dilemma
RPG	Role Playing Game
VP	Victory Point

Foreword

Eric Zimmerman

A game is a language.

In a way, when you sit down with someone to play *Chess*, *Poker*, or *Cosmic Encounter*, you are beginning a conversation.

Each move you make in the game is a way for you to express yourself to your partner—a way for you to make meaning. Every reckless aggression and coy bluff, every greedy power grab, and defensive stall for time is a word, a phrase, and a statement in the language of the game.

These conversations we have with each other, as we play games, can be awkward and confusing. Or deliciously cruel. Or wildly creative and unexpectedly beautiful. The kind of conversation that tickles parts of your mind that you didn't know were there, the kind of conversation that sticks with you, which turns acquaintances into bitter rivals and later into the best of friends.

But a game is not just a language.

It's more complicated than that. The moves we make as we play are a language built on top of yet another language. Beneath the meaning we express through the moves of the game is a kind of hidden grammar.

You move a pawn, pass a ball to a teammate, or maneuver your virtual avatar: all of them are statements made through gameplay. But what are the structures that make *those* meanings possible? The rules that permit action? The blood and bones and spirit that animate the body of the game as it is played?

That, exactly, is the subject of *Building Blocks of Tabletop Game Design*. So prepare yourself. Between these covers lies the hidden grammar of games. The structures behind the structures. The DNA of fun.

This book is a dictionary for the secret language of games.

You see, although games and play are ancient human endeavors (the Egyptian game *Senet* is at least 5,500 years old), it's only in the twentieth century that games shifted from folk culture to authored media. And as tabletop games, role-playing games, and video games have become industries of their own, we've done our best to understand them.

If you are reading this book, you are likely to be a serious game player. Like many others, you play games, discuss them, dissect them, and sometimes even design new ones. And for many years, many smart designers, critics, players, and scholars have been searching for the right way to talk about games, to understand how they work, and to figure out how best to approach the creation of new designs.

That's why *Building Blocks of Tabletop Game Design* is so significant. The incredibly detailed pages that follow, pages that crack open the inner components of tabletop games, constitute a kind of *Rosetta Stone* for game grammar.

Make no mistake. This book is a big deal.

Building on their own impressive accomplishments as designers, their relentless intellectual curiosity, and seemingly limitless connoisseurship of analog and digital games, Geoff and Isaac have put together a tremendously rigorous, wonderfully insightful, and astoundingly accessible encyclopedia of the elements that make tabletop games tick.

Why is this project so important? As someone who has studied, designed, and taught game design for 25 years, this volume is the sort of book I realize now I always needed. A manual for game mechanics. A foundation for structural analysis. An inspiration for new ideas. A sourcebook for teaching design.

On its surface, *Building Blocks of Tabletop Game Design* might seem like a deeply geeky endeavor, an obsession with rules and structures. The kind of overly formalist ludology that has (rightfully) gotten into so much trouble in recent years. And in part it is. But look deeper. In games, what seems like a pure abstract structure is inseparable from human experience. Chapter 4, on resolving game actions (those things players do to make meaning), begins in statistics and the mathematics of randomness. But then, it moves into the thorny terrain of the prisoner's dilemma, engaging with psychology and diplomacy, and even ethics—structures that help shape how people treat one another.

Reading any one of the dozens of modules in this book is like lifting up a big mossy rock in the forest. Underneath, there's an unexpected universe of complexity, a miniature ecosystem of moving parts, just waiting to be discovered.

The language of games is everywhere.

All of this gushing praise is well deserved. This book is a landmark in the study of games. But don't let that fool you. As enchanting as it is, *Building Blocks of Tabletop Game Design* is not a magic bullet that is going to suddenly let you understand exactly how every game works, to help you become a tournament winner, or to guarantee that your next design will be a hit.

The hidden grammars that this book describes, the structures behind the structures, are only part of the picture. *Building Blocks of Tabletop Game Design* doesn't investigate how games tell stories, impact the lives of their players, embody ideological values, fit into larger cultural landscapes, or even make a profit. That's just not what this book is about. And that's perfectly all right. Its titanic strength comes from its incredibly tight focus on the fundamental elements of games.

Despite these limitations, is this book still useful? Hell yes. I was recently trying to design a bidding structure for a game and found myself jaw-droppingly enlightened, reading Chapter 8 on Auctions, which details no less than 16 distinct bidding structures. Without a doubt, I will use this text in my classes. I am planning, for example, to assign a project by having each student turn to two random pages in this book and then create a game that combines both mechanics.

But there's more. The insights and ideas in *Building Blocks of Tabletop Game Design* can be applied outside of games.

How can we resolve an argument between two entrenched opposing positions? How should a winner in a multicandidate election be determined? What economic incentives lead to the best distribution of wealth? What's the right way to ensure fairness for all? These are dilemmas of modern society. And they are also the kinds of problems with which game designers wrestle on a daily basis. Believe it or not, the answers to these deeply important questions might begin to be answered by looking at the structures of this book.

Lastly, games are beautiful.

Don't get me wrong. I don't want to leave you with the impression that this book is valid only because it is useful. It doesn't matter that *Building Blocks of Tabletop Games* might be used to help teach classes or even make society better. This book is important because it is a heartfelt and soul-enriching love letter to games.

It is a lens to help us see the games we adore with fresh eyes. An advanced seminar in the complexity of systems. A spell book filled with recipes for creative play. *Building Blocks of Tabletop Game Design* unpacks the mystery of how these nerdy, knotty collections of rules—boxed up with cards, dice, and colorful tokens—produce something which is, in fact, the very opposite of rules.

For those ready to appreciate the beauty of games, the joy leaps off of every page. Isaac and Geoff have given us whole new ways to have conversations with the people and the games we love.

Happy reading.

Eric Zimmerman
Game Designer and Arts Professor
NYU Game Center
New York City, April 2019

Acknowledgments

Thank you to Erik Zimmerman and Doug Maynard for your excellent feedback and insightful comments on the manuscript. The readers thank you even more! Rob Daviau, Tim Fowers, Mark Herman, and Sen-Foong Lim provided key early enthusiastic support, without which we would not have embarked on this project.

This work would also not exist if not for those who blazed this trail and whose writings have shaped our thinking. Greg Costikyan's *I Have No Words & I Must Design: Toward a Critical Vocabulary for Games* (Tampere University Press, 2002) was Isaac's introduction to the world of critical thought about games. *Design Patterns: Elements of Reusable Object-Oriented Software* (Addison-Wesley, 1994) by Erich Gamma, John Vlissides, Ralph Johnson, and Richard Helm showed Geoff how design concepts could be broken down and built back up again. *Rules of Play* (MIT Press, 2003) by Katie Salen and Erik Zimmerman was another foundational text. We would also like to recognize the books, lectures, and blog posts by Jesse Schell, Bruno Faidutti, and Mark Rosewater, who continue to contribute to the growing body of thinking about games and game design.

Daniel Solis created delightful diagrams that illustrate each mechanism. His ability to concisely capture complex concepts is uncanny, and this book benefits greatly from his participation.

We are also indebted to Donald Dennis, Erik Dewey, Seth Jaffee, TC Petty III, Dirk Knemeyer, Adrienne Ezell, Sen-Foong Lim, Ben Begeal, Peter C. Hayward, Raph Koster, James Ernst, Eric Lang, Ralph Anderson, Stephanie Straw, Nicole Kline, Anthony Amato, Jr., Gil Hova, Ryan Sturm,

Mike Fitzgerald, Tom Vasel, Eric Summerer, all the fans and listeners of the *On Board Games* and *Ludology* podcasts, and our board game Twitter family. This work is, if nothing else, a memento of our relationships, conversations, and friendships. Thank you.

Finally, Sean Connelly and Jessica Vega at Taylor & Francis Group were absolutely stellar to work with and deftly handled two demanding authors.

Author Bio

Geoffrey Engelstein is the designer of many tabletop games, including *The Ares Project*, the *Space Cadets* series, *The Dragon & Flagon*, *The Expanse*, and more. He is the host of *Ludology*, a biweekly podcast about game design in its seventh year, and a ten-year contributor to the *Dice Tower* podcast with his biweekly "GameTek" segments discussing math, science, and psychology of games. He has published *GameTek: The Math and Science of Gaming* (2018), which was republished as *GameTek: What Games Can Teach Us about Life, the Universe and Ourselves* by Harper-Collins in early 2019. He is on the faculty of the NYU Game Center as an adjunct professor for board game design and has been invited to speak about game design at PAX, Gen Con, Metatopia, and the Game Developers Conference. When not talking about designing or playing games, Geoff runs Mars International, a product development firm focusing on consumer and medical device engineering. He has a BS in physics and a BS in electrical engineering from the Massachusetts Institute of Technology.

Isaac Shalev is the designer of board games including *Seikatsu*, *Waddle*, *Ravenous River*, and *Show & Tile*. He is also the co-host of *On Board Games*, one of the longest-running and most-respected tabletop game podcasts. Isaac also writes about game design at www.kindfortress.com, and his series on tabletop game design patterns is a favorite among game designers. Isaac's eclectic work in games includes advising publishers, editing rulebooks, consulting on game-based learning and gamification, lecturing about game design, and running board gaming fundraisers. When he's not playing games, making games, or talking about games, Isaac runs Sage70, Inc., a data strategy consultancy that works exclusively with nonprofit organizations. Isaac lives in Cary, North Carolina, with his wife, three kids, and a dog who is a very good girl.

Introduction

Geoffrey Engelstein and Isaac Shalev

There is no better time to be a tabletop board gamer. Hobbyists will debate whether the mid-1990s, which saw the rise of *The Settlers of Catan* and *Magic: The Gathering*, was the golden age of gaming or whether today is that golden age. No matter what your personal view may be, there is no doubt that modern tabletop gaming is in a period of exceptional fertility and is flourishing.

Games have come a long way since humans invented dice, pawns, and boards, and archeologists regularly turn up these artifacts at sites dating back 6,000+ years ago. The standard deck of cards has its beginnings over 1,000 years ago, and with the advent of the printing press, games became an ever-cheaper and more ubiquitous luxury. The history of the last century or so of games encompasses mass-market titles including *Monopoly*, *Scrabble*, *Clue*, and *Trivial Pursuit*, as well as the emergence of a whole new genre of tabletop games. The genre is so new that a single name has yet to meaningfully describe it, though suggestions have included hobby games, designer games, and other strange terms like TGOO ("these games of ours"). No matter what you call them, today's games feature higher levels of player agency, meaningful decisions, and substantially improved production values and offer something entirely new to players as compared to mass-market games.

Others have written about how war games developed into modern games in America and the countervailing rise of a European design sensibility in the post-World War II period that rejected war as a setting and direct conflict as a game dynamic. Our goal here is different. We'd like to address not how games evolved but how games are designed.

Even as gaming itself has taken flight, and even as thousands of new games are published each year to an ever-expanding audience of gamers, one critical aspect of gaming remains in a nascent stage: the art and craft of game design itself. Games have taken great advantage of modern communication networks and methods to spread, but we encounter challenges in spreading the knowledge and skills needed to design these games. In substantial part, this is because we do not yet have a strong shared vocabulary for discussing design.

In creative industries, from literature to films to video games, practitioners, participants, and critics develop a shared language, a common reference library, and a set of skills, approaches, and techniques for their fields. Film directors learn the difference between a jump cut and a dolly zoom and how different technical approaches produce different effects. Audiences and critics follow along, recognizing homages and allusions, and appreciating variations and innovations.

Tabletop game design is at a somewhat earlier stage, and this book is our attempt to begin to build a broader game design vocabulary and body of knowledge. Rather than attempting to formalize a specific game design language—an approach that is both daunting and perhaps premature—we've chosen to look at the building blocks of games themselves: the mechanisms or, if you prefer, the mechanics, as they're also frequently called by gamers. (We'll use the terms interchangeably through this book.)

The second-best piece of advice any new designer gets is to play more games. (The first piece of advice, by the way, is to create a physical prototype as quickly as possible.) Playing more games helps designers learn and grow by seeing, first-hand, a large variety of possible game experiences and mechanics. This is no different from any other creative field: every artist is enriched by experiencing the art and craft of other creators. Yet games, like books, can take a long time to experience, to master, and to fully appreciate, particularly for games that require large player counts, have long play times, or demand many repeated plays.

In an effort to accelerate the learning process, we present this book, which is a compendium of game mechanisms, grouped together thematically, that map the territory of modern gaming. Our goal is not to give a list of steps or instructions for how to design a game. To use a cooking metaphor, this is not a recipe book but rather a catalog of ingredients and how they can enrich a dish. We define close to 200 different mechanisms and variants, spanning topics like Movement, Game End and Victory, Economics, and more. Within each topic, we discuss how different mechanisms create different player experiences, what types of games these mechanisms give rise to, common pitfalls in implementing them, and even some of the physical user-interface issues raised by these mechanisms. With each mechanism, we present illustrative examples and games for further study, running the gamut from modern classics to contemporary new releases, as well as some lesser-known titles that nonetheless have much to teach. A good resource for learning more about the included examples is the website BoardGameGeek.com, which contains a massive game database featuring images and rulebooks that can assist in further inquiry.

Our hope is that this book serves many purposes. New designers can certainly benefit from reading this book and taking in many mechanisms in a short period of time, but this book can also be used as a reference. Whether you're an experienced designer looking for an overview of auctions, for example, or a gamer interested in exploring the worker placement genre, this book offers an easy way to review the topic and learn more. We feel this book will be of use to educators, students, professional and amateur designers, and anyone interested in reading about game design.

As important as what this book is, is what it is not: a comprehensive listing of all game mechanisms. Though we strove to be broad and inclusive, an exhaustive compilation of all game mechanisms was never our intention and is arguably impossible. While we do brush lightly on topics like narrative, dexterity, and pantomime, for example, there remains a lot of unmapped terrains. Similarly, while we do sometimes bring in examples from war-gaming, miniatures gaming, classic card games, and collectible card games, we largely center ourselves on modern board and card games. These lines are certainly artificial, and we have not sought to put forward a definition of what games are in drawing the lines as we did. Rather, we are eager to look to a future that continues to stretch, experiment with, and reconsider what games can be in light of new innovations in gaming.

We also do not mean to imply in any way that the well of new mechanisms has run dry. The opportunity for innovation in gaming is limitless.

Our intention is to make it easier for designers to learn to design, to talk with one another about design, and to mine the existing canon of board games for insight into how to design better games. We hope this collection is useful and inspirational to designers, and we look forward to playing the next generation of their games.

A Note on References in This Book

For your convenience, whenever we refer to another part of this book, we include a chapter reference, presented as an abbreviation. For example, the abbreviation ACT is for the chapter about Actions. A reference like ACT-02 means the second section of the Action chapter. This additional information may be helpful to you in understanding the context of the reference, even if you don't choose to look it up right away and may help in searching for references in digital versions of this text.

Introduction to the Second Edition

Geoffrey Engelstein and Isaac Shalev

As we were writing the first edition of *Building Blocks*, we swung back and forth between thinking it was a terrific idea and a horrible idea. Games are so varied, and the creativity and imagination that designers bring to the medium are so expansive that it seemed quixotic and hubristic for us to attempt to draw boundaries around gameplay and say here is something that is worth naming and learning about. Getting laughed out of the room was a distinct possibility.

Instead, we have been overwhelmed by the support this project has received since publication and gratified that it was accepted in the manner in which it was intended—as a stepping-stone to building a common vocabulary among game designers and not an exhaustive, definitive reference. It has been exciting to hear from teachers who have used it to give students a good grounding in core concepts, new designers looking for a place to start, and experienced designers brainstorming and drawing connections between mechanisms they may not have considered or may have simply forgotten about.

Shortly after publication, we were approached by BoardGameGeek.com, the premier online database of board game information, about incorporating the nomenclature of *Building Blocks* into their mechanism classification system. We were very pleased to work with them to develop that and also to review the classification of new games as a way to help us hone our definitions of certain mechanisms and identify new and overlooked mechanics, many of which have been incorporated into this new edition.

We were also approached by Matt Smith and Andrew Peterson of Ferris State University, who had incorporated the mechanisms into their curriculum and developed a card deck to help designers brainstorm and iterate through their designs. We were happy to support the project, which has since been published as *The Rapid Prototyping* Game by CRC Press.

We are also very grateful and pleased that *Building Blocks* has been translated into several foreign languages, with more languages on the way. Creating a common design language means reaching across and bridging many language and culture gaps, and we have been lucky to work with partners from around the world who are as passionate as we are about game design.

The success of the first edition has enabled the publication of this expanded and enhanced version. We have added many mechanisms which needed to be cut from the first edition due to space constraints, as well as incorporated color photographs of game elements to better illustrate certain mechanisms. We hope that you find this new version even more useful.

For those who are familiar with the first edition, these are the new mechanisms that have been added:

- ACT-19 Bingo
- ACT-20 Layering
- ACT-21 Slide/Push
- ACT-22 Matching
- ACT-23 Drawing
- AUC-17 Bids as Wagers
- AUC-18 Auction Compensation
- CAR-07 Deck Constructions
- CAR-08 Multi-Use Cards
- CAR-09 Tags
- ECO-20 Resource Queue
- RES-23 Hot Potato
- RES-24 Flicking
- RES-25 Stacking and Balancing
- RES-26 Neighbor Scope
- UNC-12 Deduction
- UNC-13 Induction
- UNC-14 Questions and Answers
- VIC-21 Ordering

In addition, many of the mechanisms have been updated and expanded with new examples and considerations.

We have also replaced some of the examples from the first edition in response to the revelations of unacceptable conduct and odious beliefs, including misogyny, violence against women, racism, homophobia, and transphobia among designers of many beloved and excellent games. When we wrote the first edition, we did not consider the impact of including these games in our discussion, and we now try to rectify that mistake. We have replaced references when we could find equivalent examples, but we did retain references that we felt we could not omit or substitute for because of their uniqueness or importance. This is an uncomfortable and imperfect compromise that we reached in consultation with a diverse group of advisers, including people directly impacted by the conduct in question. We hope we made an honorable and constructive decision, and we are grateful to everyone who guided us. This book is better thanks to their labor.

Thanks again to the gaming community that has supported this project and made it a success.

Isaac and Geoff

1

Game Structure

The first choice that designers make about a game is the game's basic structure. Who wins? Who loses? What is the overall scope of the game experience? Will it be just one game or perhaps a series of hands? Maybe, the game will encompass many scenarios, with game-state information persisting from play to play? The last 20 years of tabletop gaming have brought us enormous innovation in game structures, with no signs of slowing down.

Consideration of game structure raises the question of what it means to actually play the game. In a cooperative game, is the discussion among the players over which action to take the core of the gameplay, or is it the active player executing the action that is core? In games which limit communication, is the main gameplay overcoming the communication limits or solving the puzzle that the game presents? Designers need to be sensitive to participation issues in team games as well, because the game itself may force most of the action over to one teammate at the expense of another, which impacts player experience.

An increasingly popular trend is the inclusion of multiple game structures in the same box. For example, *Mage Knight* includes ways to play competitively, cooperatively, and solo. This extends the potential audience for the game.

In this chapter, we'll consider both the traditional structures like competitive and team games, as well as the latest ideas in scenario-based, legacy, and consumable games.

DOI: 10.1201/9781003179184-1   1

STR-01 Competitive Games

Description

A game with two or more players and a single winner.

Discussion

This is the most familiar game structure, the one we encounter as children in games like *Candyland* and *Snakes & Ladders*. Competitive games still make up the large majority of the market for tabletop games. They typically offer a symmetry of expectations: putting aside the impacts of unusual luck and skill, each player begins the game with a roughly equivalent chance of victory. When this promise is broken, the game is considered imbalanced and may even be tagged with the label "broken." As we'll discuss later (see "Variable Player Powers" in this chapter and "Variable Setup" in Chapter 6), players may have perfectly symmetric factions and starting conditions or highly asymmetric ones. But, in both cases, it's important that the game offers roughly even chances of victory to each player (Illustration 1.1).

In many games, there is an asymmetry that in-game balancing alone can't solve, like the first-mover advantage in chess or the service advantage in tennis. Competitive games often balance these advantages through meta-structures, like tournaments, that offer each player an equal number of chances to play from the advantaged position. In multiplayer games, this may be less practical. Instead, players may be offered other opportunities to balance any perceived or actual inequities, like the bidding in *Bridge*, betting in *Poker*, or the early alliances in *Diplomacy*.

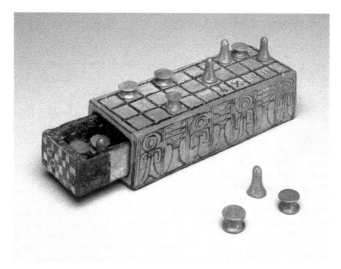

Illustration 1.1   The Egyptian game *Senet* is one of the oldest board games known, going back to 2600 BCE. This set dates around 1350 BCE.

The promise of balance in a competitive game gives rise to several related issues, like methods for determining victory and breaking ties. Tie-breaking (RES-18), in particular, is interesting because crowning a winner in a competitive game depends upon the game storing information that allows players to determine who played the better game. For many games, this information may not be available. Once we have to look beyond who scored the most victory points or who crossed some finish line first, there may not be relevant game-state information that could allow us to reasonably determine which of the tied players played best. And yet, in competitive games, many players disdain a game that ends in shared victory. Experience-oriented designers should consider that players tend to recall how a game ended more than the rest of the play experience, and hence the designers should seek to avoid an indecisive conclusion.

Sample Games

Acquire (Sackson, 1964)
Candyland (Abbot, 1949)
Chess (Unknown, ~1200)
Diplomacy (Calhamer, 1959)
Senet (Unknown, ~2600 BCE)
Snakes & Ladders (Unknown, ~200 BCE)

STR-02 Cooperative Games

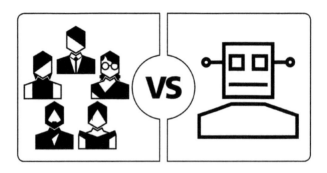

Description

Players coordinate their actions to achieve a common win condition or conditions. Players all win or lose the game together.

Discussion

Quite a few games call for cooperative play among players, including team games, one-vs.-many games, role-playing games, and games with secret traitors. These can be viewed as belonging to a hierarchical category of cooperative games. Some might even include solo games in this group. For our purposes, we'll treat each of these as separate categories and limit ourselves here to "pure" cooperative games in which all players play on one side and win or lose as a group.

Since 2008, when Matt Leacock released *Pandemic*, the genre of cooperative tabletop games has exploded. Earlier games like *Sherlock Holmes: Consulting Detective*, *Arkham Horror*, and *Lord of the Rings* laid a foundation and enjoy enduring popularity, but Leacock started a wave of innovation in cooperative gaming that continues to reshape modern gaming a decade and more later.

Cooperative gaming is accessible because it lowers barriers to entry for a game. Disparities in skill level can often make a competitive game a sour experience both for the expert and the newcomer. Complex competitive games can be intimidating to new players. Being coached by your opponent in such a game introduces some negative play dynamics because of the misaligned incentives of helping your opponent. The power imbalance between the players can also create awkward social dynamics. Cooperative games put players on the same team and foster comradery while allowing experienced players to help teach both the mechanics and strategy of the game, without facing conflicting incentives. For many new players, cooperative games are not only a gateway into gaming but a mainstay of their ongoing consumption of games.

Cooperative games can broadly be placed into two categories: those with artificial intelligence (AI) and those without. Cooperative games with an AI, like *Sentinels of the Multiverse* and *Mice and Mystics*, feature an opponent or opponents who behave according to a simple artificial intelligence, encoded by the designer. In *Sentinels*, the AI is driven by a deck of cards that governs the actions of the enemy villains and the players they will target. *Mice* has a simple algorithm that players use to control the play of enemy figures.

Non-AI games like *Hanabi*, the revolutionary Antoine Bauza title, and *Mysterium* present players with a puzzle to solve and limitations on time, resources, and interaction that players must contend with. However, these games have no villain or opposing force that drives the action and actively confronts the players.

Another consideration for the designer of cooperative games is keeping the difficulty consistent while scaling with a number of players. If each player has a set number of actions they may perform on their turn (as in *Pandemic*, for example), four players will have twice as many actions per round as two players. While there are many techniques, a very common design pattern is alternating between a player taking a turn and the game taking a turn—basically alternating "Good thing" (player actions) with "Bad thing" (game actions). This scales naturally as the number of players increases.

Another distinction between different kinds of cooperative games is whether each player retains agency over their in-game resources, actions, and choices or they seek consensus for all decisions, even if they nominally represent separate in-game characters. We might call the former game a partnership game and the latter a collaborative one. In general, cooperative games will tend to be played collaboratively unless the rules specifically and substantially impede this collaboration and force players to make independent decisions rather than build consensus. Examples include limits on communications, time, and focus.

For some players, collaborative play contributes to the "alpha player problem," also known as "quarterbacking," in which some player takes control of the group discussion and decision-making and creates a negative play experience by overriding other players. There are many possible reasons for the rise of an alpha player problem, many ways that problem can manifest, and a thicket of contributory social dynamics that are beyond the scope of this work. While some players and designers believe that the alpha player problem is a group-composition problem or a problem of unshared assumptions rather than a design problem, some design choices will make a game more vulnerable to alpha player takeovers. In particular, when all players share the same information and the game state is not too complex, alpha player behavior becomes likelier.

At the other end of the spectrum are games which cannot be taken over by an alpha player. *Magic Maze* and others of its type make player communication a game mechanism, such that players can't freely share information or advise one another on how to play. *The Mind* takes this to an extreme by forbidding players from having any kind of communication about which cards they hold. These types of communication limitations (UNC-06) may be presented like any other rule, but they do not actually create a bright line of which conduct is and is not permitted. Rather, these games can be played somewhat differently by each group, with the precise contours of allowable communication varying by tacit or overt agreement. This approach is deeply polarizing, and some players will utterly reject these kinds of games or cast doubt on whether they are games at all. That said, these communication restrictions have the potential to create incredible experiences that connect participants to one another on an almost mystical level.

Communication limitations are only one approach to preventing players from achieving consensus-based play. *Space Cadets*, *Space Alert*, and *FUSE* introduce a real-time element that forces players to make independent decisions because there is no time for players to collaborate. Other games attempt to strongly connect players to their roles, provide them with hidden information, or make operating their roles especially complicated. *Mechs vs. Minions* and *Spirit Island* both make it challenging for players to decipher each other's powers and possibilities. *Sentinels of the Multiverse* attempts something similar by providing each player with a unique preconstructed deck. Escape room games from *T.I.M.E Stories* to the *Exit* and *Unlock* series sometimes bar players from sharing information too specifically as well. The variety of challenges and puzzles these games offer, and even the various roles that players can take in the solving effort, all help ensure that every player finds a satisfying way to participate in the game.

Another notable trend in cooperative game design is the conversion of one-vs.-many, "overlord"-style games into co-ops with the assistance of an app. *Mansions of Madness: Second Edition* and *Star Wars: Imperial Assault* both introduced apps that allow the games to be played cooperatively. More generally, games are being released with cooperative and solo modes alongside competitive modes of play. Sometimes, as has been the case with *Orleans* and *Oh My Goods!*, cooperative modes have been introduced in expansions to competitive games.

The ongoing design exploration of cooperative games and their possibilities is one of the most exciting and fruitful trends in tabletop gaming today. Designers are encouraged to experiment with this popular and adaptable game structure.

Sample Games

Arkham Horror (Krank, Launius, Petersen, and Willis, 1987)
Exit: The Game (Brand and Brand, 2016)
FUSE (Klenko, 2015)
Hanabi (Bauza, 2010)
Lord of the Rings (Knizia, 2000)
Magic Maze (Lapp, 2017)
Mansions of Madness (Koneisczka, 2011)
Mechs vs. Minions (Cantrell, Ernst, Librande, Saraswat, and Tiras, 2016)
Mice and Mystics (Hawthorne, 2012)
The Mind (Warsch, 2018)
Mysterium (Nevskiy and Sidorenko, 2015)
Oh My Goods! (Pfister, 2015)
Orleans (Stockhausen, 2014)
Pandemic (Leacock, 2008), and the complete line of *Pandemic* games
Sentinels of the Multiverse (Badell, Bender, and Rebottaro, 2011)
Sherlock Holmes Consulting Detective: The Thames Murders & Other Cases (Edwards, Goldberg, and Grady, 1981)
Space Alert (Chvátil, 2008)
Space Cadets (Engelstein, Engelstein, and Engelstein, 2012)
Spirit Island (Reuss, 2017)
Star Wars: Imperial Assault (Kemppainen, Konieczka, and Ying, 2014)
T.I.M.E Stories (Chassenet and Rozoy, 2015)
Unlock! series (Various, 2017)

STR-03 Team-Based Games

Description

In team-based games, teams of players compete with one another to obtain victory. There are a variety of possible team structures, including symmetrical teams like 2v2 and 3v3, multiple sides like 2v2v2, and even One vs. All.

Discussion

Team-based play is an ancient human pastime and is prevalent in sports, classic card games, and war games. Thematic board games that model some conflict often have to deal with a bilateral narrative, whether in the conflict of good vs. evil like in *War of the Ring*, the eponymous conflict of *Axis & Allies*, or the entirely fabricated battle between villagers and their lycanthropic tormentors in *Werewolf*. Team games allow designers to faithfully recreate these two-sided conflicts while making space for more players at the table.

Most team games assign players to one team or another at the outset and allow collaboration and communication among partners. In some cases, partners may share territory and resources or even move each other's pieces around the board. Early editions of *Axis & Allies*, for example, featured Commander-in-Chief rules to model the historical reality of coordinating attacks by multinational armies.

Assigning players to teams in secret is a common trope in social deduction and betrayal-style games. In *Werewolf*, the werewolves know one another, but the villagers are left to deduce who is a fellow human and who might devour them in the night. In *Battlestar Galactica*, neither humans nor Cylons are revealed to one another, leading to intense suspicion and paranoia. *Battlestar Galactica* features a further twist: team assignments are not static, and a player might start the game as a human, only to become a Cylon in a mid-game loyalty phase that can potentially reassign players from the human to the Cylon side.

Some games support partnering at the meta-game level. In *Risk*, *Diplomacy*, and many other games, the rules specify that alliances can be formed and broken freely. There are even games that further encode these alliances into the rules. *Dune* provides for different end-game conditions for alliances with different numbers of factions, includes a specific phase when alliances may be formed, and has rules governing the conduct of allies (e.g., they may not attack each other). *Eclipse* establishes economic advantages for allying with other players, while limiting the number of these allegiances and enforcing in-game penalties on betrayers. There is a great deal of fluidity between games that allow for coordination in play and those that have explicit mechanisms to support that coordination.

Another common approach to team-based games is to assign players different roles in the game. This goes well beyond the distinct player abilities common to many co-op games. Party games from *Celebrity* to *Taboo* to *Codenames* feature one player in a clue-giving role, with one or more teammates in a guessing role. This structure is especially suitable for party games because of the concurrent play of the guessers and the ability for the game structure to support large numbers of players at any one time. It also allows players to easily enter and exit from a game without negatively impacting the overall play experience for other players.

It is not just party games that embrace role separation, though. *Space Cadets: Dice Duel* and *Captain Sonar* both have players crewing a ship as engineers, radar operators, captains, and weapons specialists. Each player plays a mini-game to model their function within the ship, and the broader game is the sum of these coordinated parts. Sometimes, these roles can be fixed for the whole game, sometimes, players will rotate through the roles every round, and sometimes, the game itself will force players to change roles. This last approach can be thematically interesting and appealing to experienced players but can be especially challenging for new players, who can easily be disoriented when forced to change roles. It also makes teaching these games much more difficult, since, in theory, every player needs to know every mini-game before the play can begin. Designers need to take this into account, perhaps by reserving role-changing cards and other triggers for advanced play only.

Somewhat less common are team games with more than two teams competing at once. Skirmish games like *Star Wars: X-Wing* can allow for these types of modes, but there are even more unusual examples. *Cyclades* with the *Titans* expansion enables a 2v2v2 mode, and *Ticket to Ride: Asia* also supports 2v2v2 play.

Team modes are fairly common in otherwise non-team games, and some team modes are attempts to enable a 1v1 game to scale to a higher player count. The aforementioned *Axis & Allies* and *War of the Ring* have team modes, but players may simply choose to play using the 1v1 rules and have teammates collaborate in decision-making instead of using the formal rules for team play.

Two other game genres feature partnerships. Card games, especially those in the trick-taking family, are one. The other partnership genre is dexterity games. *Flick 'em Up* has explicit partnership rules, and many flicking games like *PitchCar* and *Caveman Curling* are amenable to alternating play.

Another very popular game structure is One vs. All. This structure is especially suitable for hidden-movement hunting games, in which one player attempts to escape from a group of hunters, like *Scotland Yard*, *Specter Ops*, and *Hunt for the Ring*. It's also common in overlord-style games where one player controls the "bad guys" and the other players each control an individual hero. *Conan*, *Star Wars: Imperial Assault*, and *Level 7 [Omega Protocol]* all feature this style of play. Fantasy Flight Games has converted many of its overlord games into cooperative games by introducing an app to control the overlord player.

What distinguishes One vs. All most sharply from other team games is the asymmetric nature of the factions. In hunting games, each player typically controls only one character, but the characters tend to have very distinct abilities, and the victory conditions for the two sides are different too. In overlord games, the overlord usually controls a whole host of minions that they can deploy, whereas the other players control only one character. These games can be difficult to teach and learn because players need to learn how both factions work in order to play the game effectively. While the genre remains very popular, that challenge continues to bedevil designers and players.

Sample Games

Axis & Allies (Harris, Jr., 1981)

Battlestar Galactica: The Board Game (Konieczka, 2008)

Captain Sonar (Fraga and Lemonier, 2016)

Caveman Curling (Quodbach, 2010)

Celebrity (Unknown)

Codenames (Chvátil, 2015)

Conan (Henry, Bauza, Bernard, Cathala, Croc, Maublanc, and Pouchain, 2016)

Descent: Journeys in the Dark (Second Edition) (Clark, Konieczka, Sadler, and Wilson, 2012)

Diplomacy (Calhamer, 1959)

Dune (Eberle, Kittredge, and Olatka, 1979)

Eclipse (Tahkokallio, 2011)

Flick 'em Up (Beaujannot and Monpertuis, 2015)

Hunt for the Ring (Maggi, Mari, and Nepitello, 2017)

Level 7 [Omega Protocol] (Schoonover, 2013)

Mansions of Madness: Second Edition (Valens, 2016)

PitchCar (du Poël, 1995)

Risk (Lamorisse and Levin, 1959)

Scotland Yard (Burggraf, Garrels, Hoermann, Ifland, Scheerer, and Schlegel, 1983)

Space Cadets: Dice Duel (Engelstein and Engelstein, 2013)

Specter Ops (Matsuuchi, 2015)

Star Wars: Imperial Assault (Kemppainen, Konieczka, and Ying, 2014)

Taboo (Hersch, 1989)

War of the Ring (Second Edition) (Di Meglio, Maggi, and Nepitello, 2012)

STR-04 Solo Games

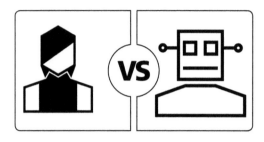

Description

A solo game is a game or game mode intended for play by a single player.

Discussion

Solo games can stretch the definition of what a game is, but solo games have been around for some time. *Patience*, or *Solitaire* card games, war games, interactive fiction (e.g., Choose Your Own Adventure® books), crossword puzzles, paper-and-pencil games, word searches, and many more single-player, game-like pursuits are very popular and have been there for years. What is new is the explosion of demand, and supply, for solo board games, whether as standalone games or as game modes in multiplayer games. Rather than quibbling over the definition, we choose to embrace the varieties and possibilities of solo gaming.

Solo games are closely related to cooperative games in the sense that the player plays against the game system itself, rather than a sentient opponent. Solo games can be considered as a special case of co-op games in which there is only one player—and thus, no alpha player problem. While most co-ops can be, and are, played solo, communications-based co-op games like *The Mind* typically can't be played solo at all. Cooperative Limited Card Games (a genre, i.e., a blend of collectible card games and deck-building games) are very popular among solo players, and the dungeon-crawl-style rogue-like game seems especially amenable to solo play. Players can usually brew their own unofficial solo game from these games or from many non-communication-based co-ops by playing more than one position in a co-op game, for example.

The modern solo design pushes beyond that basic approach to solo play. We can classify a few kinds of solo games: goal-based, record-based, and

AI-based. In goal-based games, players try to achieve some goal, usually a Victory Point (VP) total, within a certain number of turns, or a certain amount of time. This type of design is most similar to multiplayer cooperative games. These games might have an AI opponent of sorts, but typically the opponent is an asymmetric villain of some kind, or even an entirely abstract process, like a spreading fire in *Flash Point: Fire Rescue*. The AI is not an automated version of a human player who competes as another human player might.

Record-based games are those whose goal is to beat your previous high score. While this may seem like a mundane and dull victory condition, some games have developed large solitaire followings, complete with ladders and statistics that transform the game from a solo game to a community-based meta-competition. *Ganz schön clever* is one example of this type of game and community competition. Some goal-based games can also work as record-based games, as long as some scoring metric can be captured that adequately measures game performance. *Super Skill Pinball* uses this method to great effect, as the pinball metaphor naturally lends itself to players competing for the high score.

AI-based games attempt to recreate the multiplayer experience by introducing an automated player or players. Typically, this means some basic algorithm governs the moves of the AI player. These systems can be challenging to design and usually depend on decision flowcharts, as well as dice, cards, or other randomizers to create uncertainty about the AI player's choices. However, other approaches to AI opponents are also possible, as shown by Morten Monrad Pedersen's Automa system.

Pedersen's Automa system is more a philosophy and approach than an official system, and he and many other designers have used its principles to create Automas for games as varied as *Scythe*, *Anachrony*, *Baseball Highlights 2045*, and *Between Two Cities*. The key principles are that the solo game should feel as much as possible like the multiplayer game and that AIs should be representational, rather than procedural. The AI doesn't observe the rules and doesn't play the game as a player might. Rather, the AI focuses on the impact that an opponent has on the player's plans and emulates those—a kind of Potemkin player. In Pedersen's words, the AI is only the shell of a human player, and while the humans in a game of *Viticulture* have vineyards and grow grapes, the Automa players do not; they just give the impression that they do. In practice, Automas will claim action spaces, draft cards, block routes, and otherwise interfere with human players, but they will not collect resources, build buildings, or score victory points.

Another method for determining the behavior of an AI opponent is to have the player be the opponent as well. In this approach, the player wins or loses based on the fate of their primary faction, but they also play for the other factions in the game. At certain points in the game, the player may be required to change factions, typically switching from controlling their original faction to controlling the weakest of the other factions. Knowing that changes of faction control are part of the game gives the player incentive to keep all the factions relatively close, while putting their currently controlled faction in a position to grab victory. *The Peloponnesian War* is one of the earliest examples of this genre of solo play.

Solo games are enjoyed by a large, active, and growing community that continues to homebrew solo versions of multiplayer games, host contests, and challenges and enjoy an unexpected comradery despite the solitary nature of their pastime. Increasingly, including a solo mode is a desirable feature for published multiplayer games, and the success of a number of solo-only games, like *Friday* and *Hostage Negotiator*, has established that there is a market even for the loneliest of player counts.

Sample Games

Ambush (Butterfield and Smith, 1983)
Anachrony (Amann, Peter, and Turczi, 2017)
Arkham Horror: The Card Game (French and Newman, 2016)
B-17: Queen of the Skies (Frank and Shelley, 1981)
Baseball Highlights: 2045 (Fitzgerald, 2015)
Between Two Cities (O'Malley, Pedersen, and Rosset, 2015)
Flash Point: Fire Rescue (Lanzig, 2011)
Friday (Friese, 2011)
Ganz schön clever (Warsch, 2018)
Hostage Negotiator (Porfirio, 2015)
Lord of the Rings: The Card Game (French, 2011)
Mage Knight Board Game (Chvátil, 2011)
One Deck Dungeon (Cieslik, 2016)
Onirim (Torbey, 2010)
Robinson Crusoe: Adventures on the Cursed Island (Trzewiczek, 2012)
Scythe (Stegmaier, 2016)
Terraforming Mars (Fryxelius, 2016)
The Peloponnesian War (Herman, 1991)

STR-05 Semi-Cooperative Games

Description

A game which ends with either no winners or the players winning as a group but a single player being recognized as the individual winner as well.

Discussion

Semi-cooperative games are like cooperative games because players can all lose together to the game itself. However, if the players manage to overcome the game, one of the players will be crowned the individual victor, or a kind of most valuable player, based on some in-game achievement. A group's enjoyment of this style of the game depends on all members having the same answer to the question of whether a group win, coupled with an individual loss, is superior to a total group loss. If players are split on this question, those for whom an individual loss is as bad as a group loss will not seek optimal cooperative plays and may even sabotage the group while trying to secure a winning individual position. Players who prefer to win as a group, even if they lose as individuals, will be incensed by this conduct, and unhappiness will follow for everyone.

There's a strong connection between semi-cooperative games and role-playing games (RPGs). RPGs typically feature a similar dynamic: all players want to follow the main plot narrative and defeat the big bad, but each player has individual motivations that may sometimes work at cross-purposes, and in any case, each player is motivated to secure the greatest in-game rewards in terms of wealth, experience points, glory, etc. These competing motivations can help weave a complex and gripping narrative. In tabletop games, a semi-cooperative structure can create memorable moments of last-second betrayal and competitive jockeying for position.

Semi-cooperative games are fascinating as a design study because of how players engage with them. Many groups will play semi-cooperatives as co-ops, ignoring the individual win conditions or treating them as a means for recognizing a great performance by some players, rather than as a win condition to be claimed. Others will embrace the notion of an individual win and engage in brinksmanship in almost total violation of the cooperative element of the game. Despite the broad range of possible play styles, each group typically has a very narrow idea of the "right way" to play the game. In other words, it's unlikely that the same group would play *Arkham Horror* as a total co-op one night and then as a semi-co-op another night. Actually, you might be hard-pressed to find anyone who plays *Arkham Horror* with any care for the individual win condition. The game holds little attraction for players looking for that experience. Crafting a semi-co-op that is satisfying to play and that manages to incentivize both the individual and cooperative aspects of the game is like trying to land a jet plane in a phone booth.

Another route a designer can consider is introducing cooperative elements into a competitive game without creating a cooperative loss condition. Games like *Kingsburg* and *Survive: Escape from Atlantis* achieve this in different ways. In *Kingsburg*, all players must face a common foe at the end of each year. In *Survive*, players can share common resources like lifeboats to escape the ocean's dangers. These cooperative opportunities can enrich the game and create internal drama without confusing players as to their incentives or causing distress over what type of game players they thought they sat down to.

Note that this structure is not applicable to games where players sometimes cooperate and sometimes compete but where one player ultimately wins. The "everyone loses" condition is a necessary component of semi-cooperative games under our definition. Games that feature both cooperation and competition but only a single winner are not structurally distinct from competitive games (STR-01), though they often have explicit Negotiation mechanisms (ECO-18).

Sample Games

Archipelago (Boelinger, 2012)
Arkham Horror (Krank, Launius, Petersen, and Willis, 1987)
Castle Panic (De Witt, 2009)
CO$_2$ (Lacerda, 2012)
Defenders of the Realm (Launius, 2010)
Kingsburg (Chiarvesio and Iennaco, 2007)
Legendary Encounters family of deck-building games (Cichoski and Mandel, 2014)
The Omega Virus (Gray, 1992)
Republic of Rome (Berthold, Greenwood, and Haines, 1990)
Survive: Escape from Atlantis (Courtland-Smith, 1982)

STR-06 Single-Loser Games

Description

A game with three or more players in which players are not assigned to static teams and which ends with only one loser.

Discussion

Games with one loser flip the script by incentivizing players not to perform better than everyone else, but better than at least one other person. Like the old saw about not needing to outrun a ravenous bear, these games emphasize impeding other players more than advancing yourself. *Old Maid* is a well-known classic card with this structure. *Alcatraz: The Scapegoat* is a modern game in which all players, but one, escape prison. Alcatraz can end with all players losing, if they fail to break out of prison in time, which makes it a bit of a hybrid with a cooperative game.

Stacking games often feature a single-loser structure, because many of them end when a player knocks over the shared structure. *Jenga* and *Rhino Hero* are examples of this dynamic, though *Rhino Hero* does offer some rules for determining who the winner is among the surviving players. In practice though, groups often ignore this final scoring or even scoring of any kind.

Single-loser structures are not very common in modern games, perhaps because they encourage sharply confrontational "take-that" play in which players can directly impede or harm one another. These structures can also be susceptible to a bash-the-loser pattern, in which the player who falls behind becomes the most attractive target to all other players and has no chance to recover their position. This structure represents an innovation horizon for designers to explore.

Sample Games

Alcatraz: The Scapegoat (Cywicki, Cywicki, and Hanusz, 2011)
Aye, Dark Overlord (Bonifacio, Crosa, Enrico, Ferlito, and Uren, 2005)
Cockroach Poker (Zeimet, 2004)
Jenga (Scott, 1983)
Pairs (Ernest, Glumpler, and Peterson, 2014)
Rhino Hero (Frisco and Strumph, 2011)

STR-07 Traitor Games

Description

A traitor game can be seen as a kind of team game or as a cooperative game with a betrayal mechanism. The traitors typically win by triggering a failure condition for the players, though an affirmative win condition can also exist. For our purposes, a traitor game is characterized by traitors that begin the game with hidden identities.

Discussion

Traitor games sit at the overlap in the Venn diagram of social deduction games, team games, and cooperative games. The cooperative game engine sets the overall parameters for how players interact in the game, and those choices provide information that players can use and manipulate to deduce, accuse, and mislead. The team element provides coordination options for both sides, both out loud and in secret. These designs must add a layer of obfuscation to preserve uncertainty and mystery. Thus, in *Dead of Winter*, the cards contributed by players to meet the current crisis are shuffled prior to being revealed to hide which player contributed which card.

In designing traitor games, it's important to consider how the game plays at different stages of knowing the traitor's identity. The tension and suspense of not knowing who is on which side is great fuel for the beginning of the game, but once the traitor has been sussed out, is the game still fun? Does the traitor still have meaningful and interesting choices? Is catching the traitor a victory condition itself? *Betrayal at House on the Hill* is a traitor game with many story modules, each with its own mechanisms, that designers can treat it as a case study on this exact issue. *Betrayal* does not quite fit our definition of traitor game, in that the traitor is not determined at the start of the game. The initial part of the game, prior to the haunt that assigns the traitor role to one player, could perhaps be seen as an extensive gamified setup phase. In any case, the lessons from *Betrayal's* story modes apply to games that fall more firmly within our definition.

Another challenge facing traitor games is learnability. Like in team or One vs. All games, players have to learn how all the sides work to play properly. In traitor games with hidden identities, players can't readily ask questions or consult the rules without giving away their loyalties. Good player-aids and reference material need to be the areas of focus. These games also usually require that the traitor player knows the game well, to maximize the potential of their position. This emphasizes the need for an easily learned game. Good player-aids can go a long way too, especially when the player-aids for both factions help explain how the opposite faction plays too.

Sample Games

> *Battlestar Galactica: The Board Game* (Konieczka, 2008)
> *Betrayal at House on the Hill* (Daviau, Glassco, McQuilian, Selinker, and Woodruff, 2004)
> *Dead of Winter: A Crossroads Game* (Gilmour and Vega, 2014)
> *Saboteur* (Moyersoen, 2004)
> *Shadows over Camelot* (Cathala and Laget, 2005)
> *Werewolf* (Davidoff and Plotkin, 1986)

STR-08 Scenario/Mission/Campaign Games

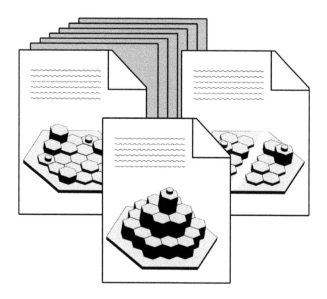

Description

This is a game system that can be applied to a variety of different maps, starting resources and positions, and even different win and loss conditions. These variable conditions can be assembled into a broader narrative or campaign, or they can be entirely disconnected from one another.

Discussion

The roots of scenario-based games are in storytelling, history, war games, and RPGs. The idea is that a rich experience can be woven out of multiple episodes, planned out to be experienced sequentially.

In war games like *Advanced Squad Leader*, the same core system, together with substantial supplements, enables players to model an enormous variety of possible conflicts. As players gain mastery, they can attempt more challenging and complex scenarios. At the other end of the spectrum, a war-themed game like *Memoir '44* gives players the opportunity to play the many battles and confrontations that made up the D-Day invasion with an intuitive ruleset that can be taught in ten minutes.

Scenario structures are popular in dungeon crawler games. Swap in a new dungeon map, a new boss monster, maybe some new mission types, and players can enjoy new challenges without learning new rules. Scenarios can also be completely detached from any narrative and simply allow players to face off against one another in a skirmish mode that provides some basic rules for force construction. Scenarios are also prevalent in cooperative settings, both for offering different levels of difficulty and for creating variety.

A "campaign" structure differs from the scenario in that the output from one scenario feeds into the next. Campaigns can have a specific set of scenarios that players go through in order or a tree-like structure where winning or losing a scenario determines which scenario is played next, or other structures. Typically, the impact of the past scenario on the next scenario is on the resources that players or enemy characters have access to (such as surviving units, character levels, or abilities). However, these are not the only options. In *Oath*, each game has different deck compositions, kingdom locations, and even victory conditions based on the prior game.

Recently, there has been an explosion in the types of games offering a scenario or campaign structure. *Catan* expansions going back as far as *Seafarers of Catan* have offered scenario play, but the hits like *The 7th Continent*, *Mechs vs. Minions*, *Near and Far*, and the card-based dungeon crawlers like *Pathfinder Adventure Card Game* and *Gloomhaven* have rocketed in popularity. It's also impossible not to mention *T.I.M.E Stories* and the various escape room game series like *Exit: The Game*, *Unlock!*, and *Deckscape*. Though each box is a self-contained experience, the play system is largely similar from box to box, and outside of the packaging and business model, these games are scenario-based in structure. One might even consider *Age of Steam* maps, *Power Grid* expansions, *Ticket to Ride* standalone variants from Europe to New York, *Pandemic: Iberia* and *Cthulhu*, and the *Mystery Rummy* series as follow-on scenarios, sold separately.

Sample Games

The 7th Continent (Roudy and Sautter, 2017)
Advanced Squad Leader (Greenwood, 1985)
Age of Steam (Wallace, 2002)
Dead of Winter: A Crossroads Game (Gilmour and Vega, 2014)
Deckscape (Chiachierra and Sorrentino, 2017)
Exit: The Game (Brand and Brand, 2016)

Mechs vs. Minions (Cantrell, Ernst, Librande, Saraswat, and Tiras, 2016)
Memoir '44 (Borg, 2004)
Near and Far (Laukat, 2017)
Oath (Wehrle, 2021)
Pandemic game system (Leacock, 2008)
Pathfinder Adventure Card Game (Selinker, Brown, O'Connor, Peterson, and Weidling, 2013)
T.I.M.E Stories (Chassenet and Rozoy, 2015)
Ticket to Ride (Moon, 2004)
Unlock! series (Various, 2017)

STR-09 Score-and-Reset Games

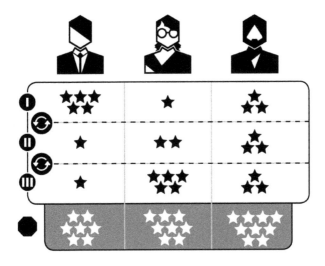

Description

This is a game in which players play until reaching a stopping condition, then record scores, reset the game, and play one or more additional rounds. The game concludes after some number of rounds, and the cumulative score is calculated to determine a winner.

Discussion

Score-and-reset is a very common game structure that is well represented among classic games from *Bridge* to *Backgammon*, and in modern games like *Red7*, *Ravenous River*, and *Incan Gold*.

Card games are especially amenable to this structure, which matches well with playing out a hand of cards, shuffling and redealing. Games with a strong turn-order advantage can take advantage of a score-and-reset structure by having players take turns in the lead position and using cumulative scoring to measure who played best over a series of rounds.

Stacking games like *Rhino Hero* use score-and-reset because once the shared structure is toppled, there's a need to collect up the cards and pieces anyway, and this represents a natural end point. Whether players do in fact record wins and losses or points is to some extent a matter of the dynamics of the game group itself. By contrast, dexterity games like *KLASK* and *BONK* reset after each goal, but scoring is rigorously tracked.

Score-and-reset structures can be somewhat informal. Players might play a series of games of *Hive* and declare a victor after one player reaches some total number of victories. There's not a sharp line between score-and-reset and round structure in general. *Amun-Re* features two ages, in which gameplay is identical, but the board itself does not fully reset. Pyramids built in the first age persist in the second age and influence the valuation of territories. In *Blue Lagoon*, the board is reset between the first and second half of the game, with the exception of the huts players lay out in the first half. However, the rules of placement change profoundly—where players were free to lay explorers on any sea space in the first half; in the second half, they must begin laying explorers adjacent to their huts.

Sample Games

Amun-Re (Knizia, 2003)
Blue Lagoon (Knizia, 2018)
BONK (Harvey, 2017)
Hive (Yianni, 2001)
Incan Gold (Faidutti and Moon, 2005)
KLASK (Bertelsen, 2014)
Ravenous River (Shalev, 2016)
Red7 (Chudyk and Cieslik, 2014)
Rhino Hero (Frisco and Strumph, 2011)

STR-10 Legacy Games

Description

A legacy game is a multisession game in which permanent and irreversible changes to the game state carry over from session to session.

Discussion

The first legacy game, Rob Daviau's *Risk Legacy*, came from the unlikeliest of places: Hasbro. Daviau, by his telling, half-shepherded, half-snuck the audacious design past the gatekeepers at the company and emerged with a genre-defining hit. Famously, the game was sealed with a sticker that had to be broken to open the box, and which warned ominously, "What Is Done Cannot Be Undone." This irreversible permanent change is what legacy games are all about (Illustration 1.2).

Legacy games are difficult to playtest, require generating quite a lot of content, and are tricky to produce and price properly. Curmudgeons will rightly point out that RPGs and campaign games are essentially legacy games, except that you don't have to destroy your game as you play. Yet that permanent destruction, the tearing of a card or writing on a board, generates a visceral response that those other games don't. Breaking this taboo and permanently altering a game can be a stressful and cathartic experience at the same time.

Illustration 1.2   The exterior seal in *Risk Legacy*. This helps place the player in the proper headspace for the game.

Legacy games aren't simply about destroying components and defacing boards. Another element common to these games is unlocks: gated content that can only be opened and accessed after some condition is met. We'll refrain from specific examples so as not to spoil these experiences for the uninitiated! Unlocks differ fundamentally from gated content in non-legacy games (see "Gating and Unlocking," ACT-15) in that unlocks usually occur at game-end, their impacts will only be felt in the next session, and these unlocks are typically not simply buffs and de-buffs to existing statistics, but rather, entire new mechanisms, characters, factions, maps, etc. These unlocks can also radically change the narrative or move the camera and offer players new perspectives and surprises.

Like campaign games, legacy games require a substantial commitment to complete, and they typically call for the same group to come together ten or more times. *Pandemic Legacy* can theoretically take 24 sessions to complete! Publishers, and thus designers, can feel trapped between offering a novel and essentially unrepeatable experience, on the one hand, while still providing sufficient re-playability to players, despite the consumable nature of the game. Most legacy games do allow players to keep playing the game even after the campaign is concluded, but anecdotally, it seems that few players do so.

It appears that the market is expanding to allow for a broader range of possible games such that at the right price point, even a single-play game like the *Exit* series can be a hit. Games like the *Harry Potter: Hogwarts Battle* deck-building game have used unlocks, but not destructibility, and are fully resettable. *Gloomhaven* takes a similar approach with reusable stickers to provide changes that are campaign-permanent but otherwise reversible. *Fabled Fruit* is even more easily reset, requiring nothing more than reordering a deck of cards. However, it is difficult to distinguish it structurally from, say, a deck-building game in which any given play session may include a completely different subset of cards.

Legacy games are a still-emerging category and definition. Elements we've identified may not exist in every game, and new elements may yet emerge, especially as legacy games and digital apps converge. Concerns about reusability and the environment do appear to have shifted designers away from requiring the destruction of components. In *Zombie Teenz Evolution*, a 2021 nominee for the prestigious Spiel des Jahres award, gameplay elements are mostly resettable, but a comic strip included in the rules is composed of sticker panels that are unlocked during gameplay. From a product design perspective, the game can be given to another group to play after one group completes it, but some aspects of the experience are only available to the purchaser of a new copy.

Sample Games

Betrayal Legacy (Daviau, Cohen, Honeycutt, Miller, Neff, and Veen, 2018)
Charterstone (Stegmaier, 2017)
Fabled Fruit (Friese, 2016)
Gloomhaven (Childres, 2017)
Harry Potter: Hogwarts Battle (Forrest-Pruzan Creative, Mandell and Wolf, 2016)
Legacy of Dragonholt (Valens, Clark, Flanders, and Mitsoda, 2017)
Pandemic Legacy: Season 1 (Daviau and Leacock, 2015)
Risk Legacy (Daviau and Dupuis, 2011)
Zombie Teenz Evolution (Lobet, 2020)

2

Turn Order and Structure

One of the elements that separates "games" from "play" is the introduction of structure. This takes many forms, including restrictions on how players perform activities and when they may perform them. Out of this arises the concept of a turn—an order or structure within which players take their actions.

The concept of taking turns is one of the first game-based concepts taught to young children. Many simple games, like *Candyland*, exist to teach how to wait your turn, among other early building blocks of playing games.

The turn structure of a game can set the tone for the entire experience, whether it is playful, strategic, or intense. Selecting the appropriate turn structure for the game is an important part of the design process.

This section includes a wide variety of these structures, including some that, while appearing unstructured, like Real-Time Games, actually contain their own internal structure, logic, and design challenges.

DOI: 10.1201/9781003179184-2

Terminology

For this book, we have adopted the following commonly used terminologies when describing turn structure:

> A **Turn** is typically one player taking a series of **Actions** or **Steps**, although sometimes other players may interrupt or otherwise participate.
>
> A **Round** is composed of multiple Turns taken by several players. This can be a fixed number of turns or variables depending on player actions or random events.

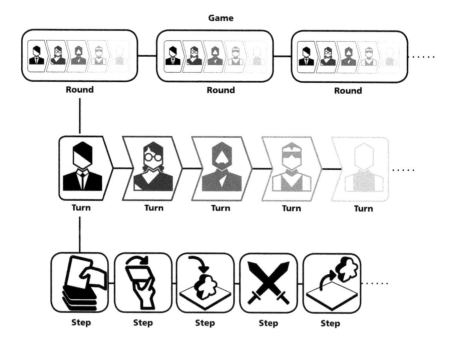

For example, *Agricola* consists of 14 Rounds. In each Round, there is a Start Player, who takes the first Turn. During that Turn, they perform two Steps: Placing a worker and performing the Actions designated by the space where the worker is placed. Players continue to take Turns in clockwise order until all workers have been placed. This concludes the Round.

There may be activities that take place at the beginning or end of a Round. For example, in *Agricola*, you may need to feed your workers or new Actions may be added to the available options.

Many games also introduce the concept of a **Phase**. Phases can be inserted at different places in the hierarchy depending on the needs of the designer. For example, a Round can consist of several Phases, and each Phase can have a series of Turns, or alternatively, a series of Rounds may make up a super-structure called a Phase. The section on Interleaved vs. Sequential Structures (TRN-15) discusses this in more detail.

The key distinguishing feature of Phases vs. Rounds or Turns is that there are usually multiple Phases, and each is named with a different and specific purpose. For example, there may be a "Feeding Phase" and a "Scoring Phase," and those can be radically different from each other. In contrast, Rounds and Turns are rarely distinguished in this way. They are identical in their basic structure. This is not to say that each Turn, for example, always consists of exactly the same Steps. Many games give players a choice of actions to perform. But a Turn performed by one player is typically very similar in structure, if not identical, to another player's Turn.

Some games also have levels above Rounds. These have a variety of names, from the generic Stage in *Die Speicherstadt* to the more thematic Age in *Through the Ages*.

This terminology is not written in stone, and there will be esoteric structures that may require different names. However, anything that is outside what players are expecting, or that inverts this customary order, will add cognitive load to the players, both in learning and playing. You can build a car that puts the windshield wiper controls underneath the radio instead of on a steering wheel stalk or make a new icon to represent the defrosters, but drivers will find it more challenging to drive. Eventually they will adapt, but the best approach is to keep to conventions unless there is a strong reason not to do so.

TRN-01 Fixed Turn Order

Description

Turn order is set at the start of the game and never varies. Each player takes a turn in the same sequence until the end of the game.

Discussion

A Fixed Turn Order is the most basic turn order, one that we are introduced to from the first games we play at a young age. In Western games, play generally proceeds from a starting player clockwise around the table; however, Asian games often proceed counter-clockwise. In this book, we will assume that games proceed clockwise (Progressive or Become First Player Action, for example). We recommend that the direction chosen by the designer match the cultural norm to reduce the cognitive load on players and to consider reversing turn order in localized editions of a game as appropriate.

Fixed Turn Order will often result in an imbalance favoring one of the player positions (typically the first player, but sometimes the last). To compensate, the designer may give a bonus to the other players. This can be extra or better resources, as in *Century: Spice Road*, bonus victory points, as in *Go*, or other advantages.

Another concern is ensuring players will have an equal number of turns. A common means for addressing this is using a token or indication of which player went first. When the game-ending condition is triggered, the round continues, the marker serving as a reminder of which players should still take a turn so that all players will have the same number of turns. *Century: Spice Road* uses this system, for example.

These systems may introduce additional complexity and design considerations, however. For example, some players may play their final turn not knowing it is their last turn, while others will know it is their last turn and will be able to optimize their play. Let's say there are five players: A through E, with A being the first player. If player C triggers the end of the game, D and E will get one final turn, then the game will end. This may give D and E an advantage over A and B, as D and E know this is their final turn and can execute accordingly.

Through the Ages uses a Fixed Turn structure, and keeps track of the first player. However, to help counteract the issue that some, but not all, players know what their last turn is, the game sometimes extends an extra round, depending on when the end is triggered. If game-end is triggered on the first player's turn, the current round would be the final round. If game-end is triggered on any other player's turn, the game goes on for another full round. This helps mitigate the situation, but it does add additional complexity to the rules.

Sample Games

Candyland (Abbot, 1949)
Century: Spice Road (Matsuuchi, 2017)
The Expanse Board Game (Engelstein, 2017)
Go (Unknown, 2200 BCE)
Monopoly (Darrow and Magie, 1933)
Parcheesi (Unknown, 400)
Snakes & Ladders (Unknown, ~200 BCE)
Splendor (André, 2014)
Through the Ages: A Story of Civilization (Chvátil, 2006)

TRN-02 Stat Turn Order

Description

The turn order within each Round is set by some statistic relating to the players' resources or position in the game.

Discussion

This Stat Turn Order mechanism gives the designer an additional tool to work with, particularly to implement a Catch the Leader mechanism (VIC-18). Frequently, the resource that is used as the basis for turn order is Victory Points (VIC-01), where the player in the last place goes first in the turn order, or possibly last. However, it can be other resources or board states. In *Civilization*, for example, it is based on the number of population tokens a player has on the board.

Turn order may also be variable for different phases of the game, based on different statistics. Both *Power Grid* and *Civilization* use this method. *Power Grid* always uses the number of connected cities as the ranking metric, but in some phases, the player with the most connected cities goes first, and in others, they go last. During the auction for power plants, the player in the lead must select and bid on the first power plant, which is disadvantageous. When purchasing resources and building power lines, the player in the lead goes last and is left with more expensive resources available to them for purchase or possibly getting blocked out of places to build. In *Civilization*, some phases are sequenced by Census (population tokens), while others are based on the victory track, either forward or reverse. This gives the designer fine-grained control over balance and the relative importance of different aspects.

It also allows players to manipulate turn order and gives the designer a tool to implement a Catch the Leader mechanism.

A word of caution is in order if Victory Points are used as the turn-order determinant, as in *Power Grid*, but many Victory Points are awarded at the end of the game or are otherwise not tallied on the Victory Point (VP) track immediately (VIC-06). Those "off-the-books" VPs are more valuable than VPs recorded on the VP track, because they do not hurt a player's turn-order positioning. If players who are ahead on the score track during the game are penalized by turn order, it will give increased weight to strategies that maximize end-game points, which the designer needs to consider for balance.

When the advantages of turn order are extreme, manipulating turn order may become a dominant feature of gameplay, which may or may not match the designer's intent. For example, in *Rise and Decline of the Third Reich*, a simulation of the European theater of World War II, turn order is determined by the production output of the sides (called Basic Resource Points, or BRPs). Typically, it is clear which side has more BRPs, and the turn order stays fixed. However, at critical points, the lead may change, resulting in a double turn, as the player that moved last in one turn moves first in the next. Players have some control over BRPs, as a portion of those not spent carry over to the next turn, and conquests, strategic warfare, and other effects may impact it, so paying close attention to this stat is vital.

This is clearly part of the design intent. In the early stages of the game, Germany will typically move first, but as the US enters the war and gains in economic strength there will inevitably be a transition resulting in Allied double move, which can strongly shift momentum in their favor. The Axis player tries to blunt this by controlling the timing of when this double move occurs, perhaps triggering it earlier than the Allied player wants and when they are not set up to take advantage of it.

Sample Games

Civilization (Tresham, 1980)
Power Grid (Friese, 2004)
Rise and Decline of the Third Reich (Greenwood and Prados, 1974)

TRN-03 Bid Turn Order

Description

Players bid for turn order. A variety of auction mechanisms may be used (see "Auctions" in Chapter 8 for more details).

Discussion

Adding an auction for turn order, or Bid Turn Order, helps improve balance by allowing the players to decide the relative merits of different turn orders at different times and situations. However, there are several drawbacks to this method. First, it will slow the game down. Auctions in general can add a lot of time to the game and can feel tacked-on when the auction is not integrated into the core game mechanism. This is normally the case with auctioning off turn order, which is usually a prelude to the main gameplay.

Age of Steam has a traditional Turn Order Until Pass auction (AUC-03). While the auction can be long, turn order in this game is very important, and the rules of the bid have additional tactical considerations, since players who drop out early get all or some of their bids back. In a tight economic game like *Age of Steam*, the bidding is extremely tense and important, and the experience more than makes up for the game length.

In *A Game of Thrones*, players bid for turn order via the Throne track. In addition to being the first player, the highest bidder on the Throne track also gains the ability to break any ties that occur in future auctions. Giving an extra benefit to the winner of the auction makes it more interesting to the players and raises the stakes of the bidding.

Another game that uses this mechanism is *El Grande*, where the playing of Power Cards determines the turn order. Each player has Power Cards numbered 1–20 and selects one to play. The selection is made based on the turn order of the prior turn. Each player may only play each Power Card once per game, and they may not play the same Power Card that another player has played earlier in the round. These rules speed the auction for turn order. In an example of elegant design, the Power Cards determine not just turn order but the number of pieces ("caballeros") that are made available to the player for the Area Majority competition (ARC-02) featured in the game. Power cards are designed to offer better turn order and fewer caballeros or vice versa. Timing their play is a critical part of *El Grande* and makes the turn-order auction step more engaging.

Auctions do suffer from another weakness, though. Auctions rely on players understanding the value of what they are bidding on. When bidding for resources or something tangible, it is easier for new players to judge relative worth. However, turn order is a much more nebulous concept for new players, and determining its value can be very tricky. This can lead to players over- or under-paying in the auction, which can lead to balance issues and lessened enjoyment. Therefore, if using a bid for turn order, it is recommended that designers give players guidelines for typical early game bids to help them bid appropriately.

Bid Order turn systems typically require a physical element to track turn order—a track, tokens, or cards, something to indicate the sequence. Because turn order does not go "around the table," this system can result in delays as players get confused, or need to check a secondary track, to determine whose turn it is.

Sample Games

> *Age of Steam* (Wallace, 2002)
> *El Grande* (Kramer and Ulrich, 1995)
> *A Game of Thrones* (Petersen and Wilson, 2003)

TRN-04 Progressive Turn Order

Description

One player has the First Player token. At the end of the round, the token passes to the player to the left who becomes the new First Player for that round. During the round, players take turns clockwise around the table.

Discussion

There are several advantages to the Progressive Turn Order system over the Fixed Turn Order (TRN-01) structure. First, it naturally rotates the first player marker through the players in a predictable way. This enables planning on the part of the players, and it introduces a timing element. If you are going second, you know that you will be going first in the next round and can plan accordingly.

Similarly, being first in a round is immediately followed by being last in the next round. This gives a nice rhythm to the game, as over a series of rounds you move closer and closer to going first and then slip to last place. It's a gradual build-up, followed by a sharp drop.

The above assumes, of course, that going first is the best position, and going last the worst. In some games, the opposite is true, like *Texas Hold'Em*

Poker. In this game, the first position is typically considered the worst, while the last, "the button," is the best, as seeing what other players do before you make your decision gives you more information to work with. Therefore, in *Texas Hold'Em* Poker, once the player is in the best position, the button, they gradually move closer and closer to the worst position, the small blind. Then the player jumps from being in the worst position to the best. (One might view the small blind as receiving some turn-order compensation for having the worst position, in that they must only stake half as much money as the big blind, which is the player following them in turn order.)

Progressive games can leave a large gap between player turns. For example, in a five-player game, when a player moves first, the next round he or she will move fifth. That means that it will be nine turns until the player gets to go again (eight opponent turns). Depending on the game, this can lead to serious downtime. For this reason, Progressive is most effective in games with short turns or where players take actions during other player turns. The latter is done in *Puerto Rico*, where the other players get to perform a less powerful version of the action selected by the main player (ACT-08).

Typically, games that use Progressive Turn structure are played to the end of the round in which the end-game condition is triggered. Therefore, the issue with players having an unequal number of turns does not arise as it does in Fixed Turn Order games. Sometimes, a mechanism is included to ensure that each player has the same number of opportunities to go first (often by setting the number of rounds equal to the number of players or a multiple of that number).

A less-used variant on Progressive Turn structure is Regressive, where the First Player token passes counter-clockwise, while turns are taken clockwise. Much of the discussion in Progressive applies here, in terms of psychology and gaps between turns. However, there is one important difference: in a Regressive structure, the player who goes last in one round will go first in the next. Players having two turns in a row can be extremely powerful, particularly when a player knows it is happening and can plan accordingly. The game needs to be designed and structured to either take advantage of that or blunt it in some fashion. For example, in *Dead of Winter*, a semi-cooperative potential hidden traitor game (STR-05), the hidden traitors would do well to reveal themselves to be the traitors in the round in which they go last, as they will have two successive turns in which to wreak havoc.

Regressive is unintuitive to players, because so many games go clockwise. Having a turn which moves clockwise, but a token which moves counter-clockwise, is an additional cognitive burden that should only be imposed for some specific design reason.

Sample Games

Progressive

> *The Little Prince: Make Me a Planet* (Bauza and Cathala, 2013)
> *Puerto Rico* (Seyfarth, 2002)
> *Quadropolis* (Gandon, 2016)
> *Terraforming Mars* (Fryxelius, 2016)
> *Texas Hold'Em* (Unknown)

Regressive

> *Dead of Winter: A Crossroads Game* (Gilmour and Vega, 2014)
> *Kepler* (Bariot and Montiage, 2012)
> *Viticulture* (Stegmaier and Stone, 2013)
> *Walk the Plank!* (Steely and Tinney, 2013)

TRN-05 Claim Turn Order

Description

In each round, there is a First Player, and turns are taken clockwise from the first player. There is an action that may be taken to claim a place in the turn order (typically, but not always, first) for the next round, with play proceeding clockwise from the First Player. If no one takes the action, turn order remains unchanged.

Discussion

Similar to Stat Turn Order (TRN-02), Claim Turn Order Action gives more control to the players over the turn order, as they need to do something to seize control over the first player marker.

Caution and finesse need to be employed by the designer when using this system, as there are a number of pitfalls. This technique is often used in Worker Placement (Chapter 9) or Action Drafting (ACT-02) games, and players will need to use one of their workers or actions to go first next time. This means that they are sacrificing their action now, effectively losing a turn, to gain that advantage. Balancing the cost can be tricky, as the value of going first can vary from situation to situation and player to player. The value of simply going first may not be that great, so players may avoid using an action to be the first player. In this case, the same player gets to remain the first player without losing an action. They simply remain the first player by default and reap the rewards at no cost.

Designers can sweeten the value of claiming turn order by including other resources or abilities with it. For example, in *Agricola*, the player who chooses the First Player action may also play a Minor Improvement (Illustration 2.1).

More importantly, the player to the left of the player who chooses to go first gets a great boon. They will get to play second, which, while not as good as going first, was obtained with absolutely no effort on their part. *Agricola* suffers quite a bit from this issue, as it is of great benefit to be to the left of the player who chose to go first and frustrating to be the player to the right, who will now go last, through no fault or action of their own.

First Class: All Aboard the Orient Express deals with this issue by giving bonuses to all positions when the First Player token is chosen as an action. In a four-player game, the player who chose to go first gains two coins, the third player may take a Train Card, and the fourth player may either take or upgrade a Train Card. The player who will now be going second receives no bonus—being able to go second in the round while not giving anything up is deemed sufficient compensation. The *First Class* system gives the designer a lot of flexibility in balancing the different player positions.

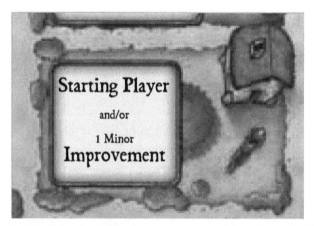

Illustration 2.1 In *Agricola*, a worker must be placed in this space to become First Player. When placing here you may also play a Minor Improvement.

Another pitfall to avoid is scripted play—obviously best moves by players. In earlier editions of the game *Twilight Imperium*, players chose an Action card on their turn to perform. One of them gave a Victory Point to the player choosing it, which was very powerful, and another let a player become First Player. Because the free Victory Point card was so strong, play almost always followed a scripted pattern. The first player to go would take the free Victory Point card, and the second player would take the card to become First Player, thus ensuring they would get the free Victory Point next turn.

Turn order ended up simply moving around the table, devolving into a Progressive turn structure. However, the presentation of turn order as a choice made it seem as if the game had more flexibility than it actually did. The forcing moves for the first two players made for a much less interesting play experience. A similar issue arises in *Stone Age*, where expanding fields and gaining workers are invariably the first two actions chosen in each round.

Sometimes, the action that determines turn order is tightly integrated into play. *High Society* has players bidding on objects, and the winner of an auction begins the bidding for the next auction. Trick taking games, where the winner of a trick takes the lead, are a similar example, which will be explored in more detail in Chapter 13. In both of these examples, play proceeds clockwise from the new start player.

A variant of this mechanism is seen in *Age of Empires III: The Age of Discovery* and other games. In these, players take an action to secure their place in the turn order, but more than one player can do this. The first player to do so becomes the first player in the next round, the second player becomes second, and so on. Players who do not take this action are moved to the back of the turn order.

This has similar issues to both the classic version of this mechanism and the Pass Order mechanism (TRN-06). Players must give up the opportunity for an action to improve their place in the turn order, and players that are currently early in the order have less incentive to spend an action there. Also, players that are early in the turn order have a better opportunity to keep it because they will have a first chance of using later round actions to maintain their turn position. However, it does mitigate some of the issues of the base version of this mechanism, as it puts more control into the hands of the players, albeit in an inequitable way.

Sample Games

Age of Empires III: The Age of Discovery (Drover, 2007)
Agricola (Rosenberg, 2007)
Bridge (Vanderbilt, 1908)
First Class: All Aboard the Orient Express (Ohley, 2016)
Hearts (Unknown, 1850)
High Society (Knizia, 1995)
Stone Age (Brunnhofer, 2008)
Twilight Imperium (Petersen, 1997)

TRN-06 Pass Order

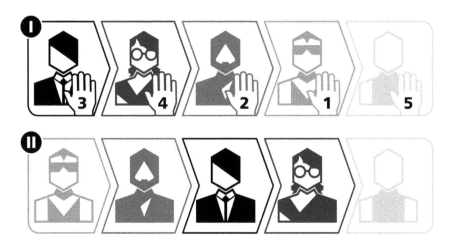

Description

On their turn, players may either take an action or pass. The first player who passes becomes the new first player for the next round. The second player who passes becomes the second player for the next round, and so on. Reversing pass order and turn order is also possible when going later in turn order is more advantageous.

Discussion

Pass Order attempts to address the issues created by more static turn-order mechanisms, or those which order all players based on the actions of a single player. With Pass Order, players are presented with a choice: take additional actions this turn or be earlier in the turn order for the entire next round. Players have to estimate whether continuing to take actions in the current round is worth more than having an earlier choice on actions in the following round.

A good place for this mechanism is in a game that features some type of drafting (CAR-06). In *Caylus*, players place workers on buildings ("Worker Placement," Chapter 9) to receive certain benefits. Each building can be occupied by only one player each round, so players are drafting from a limited pool of possible actions. Going earlier in turn order ensures players can select the buildings they desire most. But taking additional actions later in the turn order can yield additional benefits (Illustration 2.2).

Games in which players are very likely to take an equal number of actions in a round are a poor fit for this mechanism. For example, if players only have three actions in a turn, most likely they will all be passing after the same number of turns. If players take six or more actions in a round, the cost of losing later actions in the round is much reduced.

An important consideration with Action/Passing is the fate of the last player who has not passed. This is an issue that affects any game in which players end their round by choosing to pass. For example, in *The Networks*, players receive more money or victory points for passing early, rather than turn-order position. Nevertheless, because *The Networks* is a Rochester draft (see "CAR-06, Drafting" in Chapter 13), there are relatively few limits on the ability of the last player still active to sweep up whatever cards remain on the board. This can be quite powerful! Other games, like *Francis Drake*, limit the ability of the last player to gain too much advantage by requiring expending a limited pool of workers to activate the remaining buildings. *Caylus* addresses this issue in a different way, by making it increasingly expensive to place workers as more players pass. Finally, in *Sentient*, players who pass first go last, which actually provides them with the advantage of sweeping the board.

Designers using this structure should be careful to align the turn-order reward (first or last) with the game. The mechanism works best when turn-order preference is strong, when players act many times over the course of a single round, and when there is some hard limit on the total number of actions a player can take. Rewards other than turn-order advantage can be employed as an alternative or in addition.

Illustration 2.2   The pass track from *Caylus*, as illustrated in the instruction manual. The first player to pass places their disk in the rightmost slot, showing they will go first next turn. As players pass, they place their disks in each successive position.

Two final notes of caution. First, designers must provide some physical affordances for tracking who has passed and in what order. Ideally, these are combined so that when a player passes, they move some indicator to show that they have passed and when they will play in a future turn. Second, designers should also pay attention to the amount of downtime experienced by the first player to pass.

Sample Games

Caylus (Attia, 2005)
Francis Drake (Hawes, 2013)
The Networks (Hova, 2016)
Sentient (Kevern, 2017)

TRN-07 Real-Time

Description

There are no turns. Players play as quickly as possible, subject to certain constraints, until the game or phase is completed. Playing quickly confers some type of advantage.

Discussion

Real-Time Games bring a lot of excitement to the table, as players frantically work to completely execute their actions. However, they also bring a lot of challenges for the designer.

First, Real-Time Games need to be very simple. Anything that causes confusion requires the players to stop the action, resolve the issue, and then continue, or just carry on with a confused player who stops enjoying the experience or possibly violates the rules unwittingly. This can place very real constraints on what can and can't be done from a design standpoint.

The designer also needs to address timing issues if players are conflicting in actions they wish to perform. There are several ways to deal with this:

- Players play cards onto stacks. The sequence in the stack indicates the order.

- The player who touches a token first is allowed to manipulate it.
- Players do not interact during the real-time portion but only after it is completed, and interactions can be resolved at leisure.

The level of intensity and focus required from players in a Real-Time Game means that the game needs to be short. Twenty minutes is a reasonable maximum duration for a completely uninterrupted Real-Time Game.

Another consideration is dealing with mistakes and cheating. Some games, like *Pit Crew* and *Space Alert*, have specific rules for dealing with mistakes that give a penalty to the players or cancel the attempted action.

As players are absorbed in their own actions, cheating can also be an issue. In cooperative games like *Space Alert*, cheating is a different consideration. However, for competitive games, the designer may need to incorporate design techniques such as making sure that everything is in the open, that text on cards is large enough to be understood across the table rapidly, and that there is as little manipulation of components as possible (e.g., once a card or die is placed in a spot, it cannot be moved from that spot).

However, there have been several successful games that have not protected against mistakes and cheating, and it does not appear to have impacted their success. In *Captain Sonar* (more correctly classified as using a Punctuated Real-Time mechanism, TRN-08), each team writes and erases on laminated control panels behind a screen. It would be quite simple for a team to cheat behind the screen or make undetected mistakes. In practice, however, the social contract seems to hold and players are not concerned about this. This may open up more complex design opportunities for Real-Time Games, as long as the game is marketed toward an audience that accepts this stance regarding potential cheating.

Because of the nonstop nature of Real-Time Games, they are often structured with two phases: Action and Resolution. Action is when real-time action occurs. After a condition is met, typically a timer expiring, but possibly when a task is completed, or when a hand or deck of cards is exhausted, there is a Resolution phase. In this phase, results of the action phase are determined, without any time pressure. This two-mode approach allows for complex mechanisms that might otherwise not be possible.

There are typically two types of endings to a real-time phase. In the first, whenever the end-phase condition is met, the phase ends immediately. Players are informed that it is over, and that is that. *Spit* (aka *Speed* or *Blitz*) and *Pick-A-Polar Bear* are both triggered when one player reaches a particular game state (all cards gone from their deck in *Spit* and a player claiming to have no more legal options to take a card in *Polar Bear*). At that time, the phase instantly completes.

Some games use the phase-end trigger to set up "bonus time" for the other players, informing them that they have a set amount of additional time before the phase ends. For example, in *Show & Tile*, the first player to complete their artwork flips a sand timer. When that timer runs out, the artwork phase is over, and players proceed to the guessing phase. Other games flip this dynamic around and give players who finish early an additional bonus task that must be completed by the time all players finish the core task. In *Pit Crew*, when a team finishes the real-time task of repairing its car and getting it out on the track, the team switches to rolling a die to move the car, rolling over and over. Meanwhile, the other teams continue to repair their car and start rolling their own die if other teams are still working. The last team to finish does not roll its die but stops all other teams from rolling. This puts added pressure and tension on the teams who are still working on their repairs while others move around the track and add some narrative arc to the activity.

Games with an Elapsed Real Time ending (VIC-13), where they end after a fixed amount of time, also typically will fit into this mechanism (although not always—they may have a standard turn structure). Examples of this include "Escape Room" style games such as the *Unlock* series, where the players are under pressure to complete the game within a certain time frame.

Note that games without a turn order but that do not have time pressure, such as *The Mind*, do not fit into this classification.

Sample Games

> *Brawl* (Ernest, 1999)
> *Escape: The Curse of the Temple* (Ostby, 2012)
> *Falling* (Ernest, 1998)
> *Light Speed* (Ernest and Jolly, 2003)
> *Pick-A-Polar Bear* (Landsvogt, 2013)
> *Pit Crew* (Engelstein, 2017)
> *Show & Tile* (Loomis and Shalev, 2018)
> *Space Alert* (Chvátil, 2008)
> *Spit* (Unknown)
> *Unlock!: Escape Adventures (Carroll, Cauët, Demaegd, 2017)*

TRN-08 Punctuated Real-Time

Description

There are no turns. Players play as quickly as possible, subject to certain constraints, until the game or phase is completed. Play is also interrupted by specific player actions, which are resolved before resuming the real-time action.

Discussion

Punctuated Real-Time is a variation in real-time (TRN-07) and the difference is subtle. In a Real-Time Game, the action stops when some condition is met—a timer going off, or a deck exhausting—whereas in a Punctuated Real-Time Game, the action may be stopped at any time, at the discretion of a player, or upon taking a valid stopping action.

In *Space Cadets: Dice Duel* and *Captain Sonar*, players stop the action by shouting something ("Fire Torpedoes" or "Launch Mine"), and all players stop what they are doing to resolve the action.

To a certain extent, this mechanism is also present in the early twentieth-century game *Pit*, as players end the real-time trading portion by hitting a bell, after which the round is evaluated. Also dating back over a hundred years, baseball and American football are also exemplars of Punctuated Real-Time, where teams can plan, organize, substitute, and catch their breath prior to initiating the next pitch or play.

Punctuated Real-Time adds an additional layer of tension to the already tense mechanism of real-time. Players do not necessarily see the stoppage of play coming. In *Pit*, you don't know how close the other players are to winning the round. This mechanic also gives more flexibility to the designer on a number of levels. First, it allows for the inclusion of more complex mechanisms, as they can be resolved during the "stoppage time." Firing a torpedo in *Captain Sonar* falls into this category, as the resolution can include complexity that would normally be beyond what is reasonable in a Real-Time Game.

Second, Punctuated Real-Time allows the game to be longer, as the stoppage time gives players an opportunity to catch their breath or even get a snack or go to the restroom. In a fully Real-Time Game such as *Escape: The Curse of the Temple*, an action that continues more than 10–20 minutes or so risks exhausting and overwhelming the player. Punctuated Real-Time gives the designer a tool to create nonscheduled breaks to give the players a breather, allowing for a longer, more complex, and textured overall experience.

Sample Games

Captain Sonar (Fraga and Lemonier, 2016)
Escape: The Curse of the Temple (Ostby, 2012)
Merchants of Amsterdam (Knizia, 2000)
Pit (Cayce, Gavitt, and Parker, 1903)
Space Cadets: Dice Duel (Engelstein and Engelstein, 2013)

TRN-09 Simultaneous Action Selection

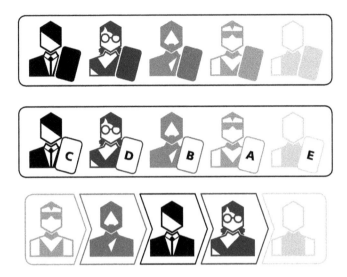

Description

Players plan their turn simultaneously and secretly. Then, they reveal their plans at the same time.

Discussion

A Simultaneous Action Selection Game has players selecting actions at the same time, but actions are generally resolved in turn order. The Action Selection mechanism will usually include a subsystem for determining the order by which the action resolution phase will be played. For example, in *Libertalia*, players choose a role card from their hand and play it face down. Then, all cards are revealed simultaneously, and the lowest-numbered card revealed is resolved first. Each player in *Libertalia* has the same role cards in their hands, so duplicate plays occur frequently. To resolve these ties, each card also shows a unique priority number. *Robo Rally*, a classic in the genre, uses a similar priority number mechanism to sequence the players once cards are revealed.

Priority numbers are not necessarily required for Simultaneous Action Selection. *Race for the Galaxy* has players simultaneously select which roles they would like to execute, but then the roles are always performed in a specific order. See the Role Order mechanism for more details (TRN-10).

Typically, cards are used to implement this mechanism, although other components, such as tiles or dice, can also be used. In *Incan Gold*, each turn, players simultaneously decide whether they are going to remain in the cave or return to camp. In the original version (called *Diamant*) players indicated this choice by either secretly holding their wooden adventurer figure in their hand or having an empty fist. Later versions replaced this mechanism by placing a "Stay" or "Go" card face down. In the *A Game of Thrones* board game, actions are planned using order tokens that are placed face down and then revealed by flipping them all face up.

This mechanism gives players the opportunity to try to anticipate what their opponents will do and to plan accordingly. The general term for mechanisms which have players trying to guess what their opponents will do is called "Yomi," a Japanese word. We discuss Yomi in more detail in UNC-01.

Simultaneous Action Selection can also speed up games and reduce downtime, as players are acting simultaneously. However, if the planning is extensive, as in *Diplomacy* and *A Game of Thrones*, it can give room for Negotiation (ECO-18) and increased strategy, which adds length.

Sample Games

    Diplomacy (Calhamer, 1959)
    A Game of Thrones (Petersen and Wilson, 2003)
    Incan Gold (Faidutti and Moon, 2005)
    Libertalia (Mori, 2012)
    Robo Rally (Garfield, 1994)

TRN-10 Role Order

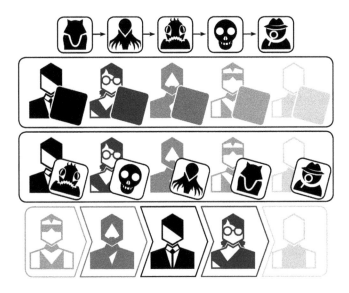

Description

Players secretly and simultaneously select an action, role, or priority. Then they are revealed, and the actions/roles revealed determine the order in which players act.

Discussion

Role Order is a subset of Simultaneous Action Selection (TRN-09). There are several ways to implement this mechanism. *Citadels*, for example, has players draft roles (like Thief or Assassin). There is one card for each role in a deck. Some of the roles are removed without any of the players knowing their identity. The first player then looks at the remaining roles, chooses one, and passes the remaining cards to the left.

After each player has selected a role, the first player calls out the roles from first to last, according to their number. Thief, for example, is number two. If a player has that role, he or she reveals it and takes that action.

Race for the Galaxy has a different approach. Each player simultaneously selects which of the roles (like Explore or Settle) they wish to play. Then all players reveal their choice. The roles are resolved in a defined order (e.g., Explore is always first). For each role that is chosen by at least one player, all players get to perform it, but the player(s) who chose it get to take a more powerful version of the action. More on this in the Follow mechanism (ACT-08).

If no one selects a role, it is skipped, so if players really want a specific role to occur, they can select it, or gamble that, based on the situation, other players are likely to select it, affording them the opportunity to choose something else. This introduces an element of Yomi (UNC-01), as players attempt to outguess each other.

In both of these games, players are not guaranteed that certain roles will occur. This is typical of implementations of this mechanism as a result of the hidden role selection—if all the roles were in play, players could readily deduce which roles were taken before them.

Using Role Order allows *Citadels* to introduce an interesting twist. The player who chooses the Assassin role names another role that will have to lose a turn. Note that it is the role that is targeted, not the player. Players losing their turn is an anti-pattern (TRN-16) that usually results in negative feelings because it frustrates the player's desire to play the game at all. However, in *Citadels*, the role is targeted, not a specific player. While the Assassin players may have an idea of who may be more likely to choose a role, they are not sure. Additionally, the role the Assassin names may not even have been selected that turn, rendering the ability moot.

Role Order allows the designers to control the order in which operations occur, while giving players a choice about which of those will happen. It also introduces a well-defined turn order that doesn't suffer from needing to have a mechanism to shift the first player. It happens naturally.

Sample Games

>*Citadels* (Faidutti, 2000)
>*Race for the Galaxy* (Lehmann, 2007)

TRN-11 Random Turn Order

Description

Representatives of play pieces or players are randomized and one is drawn at a time. That player or play piece takes its turn, and then a new random draw is made.

Discussion

Random Turn Order can introduce a lot of excitement and tension to a game, as players anxiously await which token will be revealed next. However, it also reduces the ability of the players to plan effectively, which makes it most effective in lighter games. Games are more tactical, as players need to react to the situation as it develops, because they can't predict when their turn will come.

There are ways to increase the ability for strategic planning when using a Random Turn Order. *Pillars of the Earth* is a Worker Placement game (Chapter 9), where workers are pulled from a bag. As with most Worker Placement games, going early is an advantage, as more and better options are available. When a player's piece is pulled, if that player wishes to place it, they need to pay a cost. This cost starts high and gradually drops throughout the turn. If a player does not want to (or cannot) pay the cost, the worker is placed to the side and is used to select an action at the very end of the turn. This presents players with an interesting strategic option of trying to judge the value of going early. The higher price of going early counteracts the luck of being drawn early.

In *Warrior Knights*, actions are represented by cards. Each player selects two cards from their personal deck that they wish to use that turn. The selections from all the players are shuffled together and then they are drawn one at a time and the player whose card is chosen performs the corresponding action.

The inability to create a perfect plan has made this a popular mechanism in war games. Rather than one player moving all pieces, and then the next player moving all of theirs, a random draw for who gets to activate next helps simulate battlefield uncertainty, while also reducing downtime for the players. *Firepower* implements this type of chit-pull system.

Random Turn Order also gives the war game designer flexibility in modeling superior and inferior units. For example, in the game *A Victory Lost: Crisis in Ukraine 1942–1943*, Activation Chits for units are placed into a cup. However, veteran units receive multiple chits, while new recruits may receive only one, modeling in a natural way the increased effectiveness of the veterans. This is a kind of Deck Building system (CAR-05).

Another technique is to include a wild card or category tokens, which give the player a choice of which unit to activate when they are pulled, as long as they correspond to the matching category. This also increases tactical flexibility and reduces the luck factor. *Battle Masters* is an example of a game that uses this approach.

Sample Games

> *Battle Masters* (Baker, 1992)
> *Firepower* (Taylor, 1984)
> *Pillars of the Earth* (Rieneck and Stadler, 2006)
> *A Victory Lost: Crisis in Ukraine 1942–1943* (Nakamura, 2006)
> *Warrior Knights* (Carver, Clequin, Faidutti, and Konieczka, 2006)

TRN-12 Action Timer

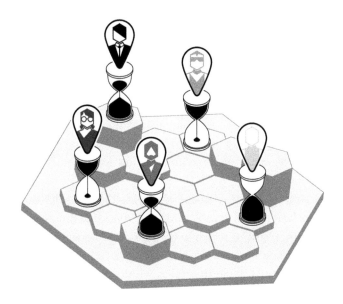

Description

Players place owned timers on action spaces and pieces and take an action. When the timer runs out, it may be moved to another location to take that action. There are no turns; players may move their own timers any time after they have expired.

Discussion

This Action Timer mechanism is typically implemented with sand timers. Timers allow for a real-time feel (TRN-07), while mitigating their frantic nature. It allows the game to flow naturally, while giving players some structure and breathing room to plan their next actions. As such, they can be used for longer periods of time than would be desirable in a traditional Real-Time Game.

Sand timers can be placed onto fixed spaces on the board to indicate what actions the players are allowed to take or onto specific pieces that move around. In *Time 'n' Space* (a remake of the classic *Space Dealer*), sand timers may be placed into a player's base for research and other actions or directly onto a spaceship to allow it to move. Similarly, in *War Time*, the sand timers are placed directly on the units, which allows them to move or attack.

Typically, the action is taken when the timer is placed. This allows the player to place the timer, then actually do the action (take cubes, gain a research card, perform an attack, move a unit, etc.) while the sands are running. This reduces overall downtime for the players. If you wait for the timer to end before doing the action, players will typically quickly move the timer to a new action to get it going, then go back and execute the original action, which can add some confusion.

In spite of this mechanism being real-time, it can have a fair amount of downtime for the players and feels sluggish at points as players watch the grains of sand, waiting to take their next action. To help mitigate this, players usually have multiple sand timers to use, to allow for action combos, and to move things along.

Some games also give players timers of varying durations. In *Wartime: The Battle of Valyance Vale*, players have 30-, 60-, and 90-second timers, and each can be used for any unit. Deciding which to use adds an additional tactical layer and also helps give the player more to do while waiting for other timers to run out.

TAMSK is an abstract game that takes a unique approach to using sand timers. The pieces are sand timers, and when they make a move the timers are flipped. A key element is that if a timer runs out of sand, it is locked into place. This gives players tactical options of how to use the timers and how much time they have to think about decisions. A piece that is moved again shortly after being moved will only have a little time remaining in the timer.

There are a number of physical issues that need to be dealt with in these games. First, when players interact with each other, there can be contention about which timer finished first and so which player might be able to take an action space or launch an attack first. This can be difficult to adjudicate in the midst of the game, as timers will continue to run.

Also, while a Real-Time Game can be stopped by mutual agreement of the players, this is harder with a sand timer game. The sand timers need to all be tipped over, which can take some time and also change the way the sand is distributed while they lie on their sides—to say nothing of their chances of rolling off the table!

Finally, there are manufacturing variations with sand timers that can lead to a timing difference of many seconds. A 30-second timer may take as long as 40 seconds to run. Indeed, the same sand timer may run faster or slower depending on the irregularity of the grains in it and how they happen to fall. Many timers have different run times depending on which side is up. These variations need to either simply be accepted or some type of manufacturing screening process needs to be implemented, which will add cost to production.

In spite of these issues, sand timer games have a unique feel that deserves further exploration by designers. Apps and other digital-analog hybrids hold some promise here as well.

Sample Games

Space Dealer (Stapelfeldt, 2006)
TAMSK (Burm, 1998)
Time 'n' Space (Stapelfeldt, 2013)
Wartime: The Battle of Valyance Vale (Guild, Lackey, Parks, and Tempkin, 2017)
Wok Star (Fowers, 2010)

TRN-13 Time Track

Description

There is a linear "Time Track" with many spaces. Each player has a marker on the track, which indicates where they are "in time." Markers farther on the track are further forward in time.

The player with the marker lowest on the track (furthest "back in time") takes the next action. Each action has a cost in time, and the player's marker is advanced a number of spaces according to that cost. Then, the next lowest marker on the track takes an action. It is possible that the same player takes multiple turns in a row.

Discussion

Time Tracks have a number of inherent advantages:

- Clarity: It is obvious who goes next, even though turn order jumps around a lot.
- Player Control: Players have some choice over who goes next, allowing for additional tactical play.
- Balance: The designer can include powerful actions but can give them a long time duration to compensate.

However, there are, of course, downsides to this technique. It can lead to players being out of the action for some time if they have taken long-duration options. Admittedly, they have chosen to do this, but an option available to players should not result in them having a less enjoyable experience.

To prevent this situation, designers typically do not include very long-duration activities. However, this compression of durations into a narrower range works against the benefits and promise of this system, as players usually are quite close together on the Time Track. *The Dragon & Flagon*, for example, has actions that range from one to four Time. Most of the actions in *Thebes* are in a similar range, although players can opt to dig for artifacts for up to 12 Time, which will give their opponents the opportunity to perform many actions before their turn comes around again.

Because of this tight-duration grouping, players frequently will share a space on the Time Track. These ties are usually resolved by having the player on top of the stack (the last piece to arrive there) move first. However, this "Last-in-First-out," or LIFO, system will give players guaranteed double moves in some situations. Depending on the game, this may not be an issue and may even be desirable. But for some, it may be too powerful and some mediation needs to happen. In *The Dragon and Flagon*, for example, Turn Order is randomly determined when multiple players share the same space.

Another alternative is to only allow one piece per space on the Time Track, forcing players who would otherwise occupy a space to move one or more spaces further forward until they find an empty space. This can add an extra layer of decision-making, as the actual cost of certain actions may vary based on the positioning of the opponent. When a game offers only a limited amount of time or creates triggers based on specific spaces on the track, the particulars of how ties are handled and whether players skip spaces become especially important.

Glen More and *Kraftwagen* use a Time Track combined with an Action Selection mechanism. Each space on the Time Track has an associated action. When players move to the space, they execute the action. The player furthest back on the track moves first, and two players may not occupy the same space. Players have the choice of moving far forward to guarantee a needed action but potentially giving their opponents multiple turns.

Sample Games

AuZtralia (Wallace, 2018)
The Dragon & Flagon (Engelstein, Engelstein, and Engelstein, 2016)
Glen More (Cramer, 2010)
High Rise (Hova, 2019)
Thebes (Prinz, 2007)
Tokaido (Bauza, 2012)

TRN-14 Passed Action Token

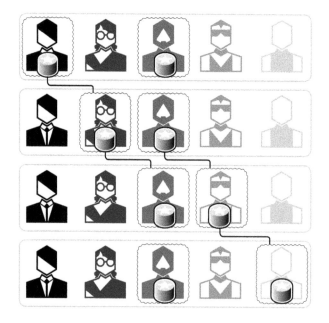

Description

Players possess one or more Action Tokens. Those who have an Action Token may take a turn, and then they pass the token clockwise, allowing the next player to perform an action. Actions are performed in real-time; there is no pausing and structure within the turn.

Typically, to prevent stalling and to keep the game moving, in games with multiple Action Tokens, if both tokens are held by the same player, they suffer a penalty.

Discussion

This mechanism is a cross between a real-time-based and a turn-based game. Similar to the Action Timer mechanism (TRN-12), it allows players to play at their own pace, and asynchronously, but still offers some structure. However, with the Action Timer mechanism, players are basically independent of one other and can operate simultaneously. Here, players are linked more closely, in that one player's turn can only start when the previous player finishes their turn. This helps solve the dilemma of players breaking rules (either inadvertently or deliberately) that are present in other real-time mechanisms. The inactive players can watch what the active players are doing and interrupt if necessary. This allows for more complex mechanisms within the game itself than is possible in traditional real-time games.

Generally, this mechanism requires that multiple Action Tokens are passed around the circle at the same time. The exception is if the round itself is timed in some fashion and having possession of the Action Token causes a player to lose. *Hot Potato* and *Catch Phrase!* are examples of this, where the player holding the item when time runs out loses (see Hot Potato, RES-23).

When using multiple Action Tokens, a key design consideration is what happens if multiple tokens end up with the same player. In *Camelot*, if another token would be passed to a player who already has one, it instead skips that player and goes to the person to his or her left. This is equivalent to losing a turn, as other players will get to act a second time before the affected player does. While we recommend against players losing a turn and classify it as an anti-pattern (TRN-16), in this case, the opportunity to avoid losing a turn lies with the player and is not luck-based or the result of targeting by other players. Therefore, it is an understandable and satisfying solution to use in this case. It forces players to move at a reasonable pace, at least comparable in speed to the other players.

While this solution encourages faster play, it does not mean that the faster players will always win. If a reasonably thought-out single move will beat a hasty double move, then playing as fast as possible will not be the dominant strategy. Players will need to balance optimal plays with "good enough" plays.

An alternative system to penalizing players for collecting a second Action Token is seen in *Diner*. In *Diner*, all players start with an Action Token and may continue to act simultaneously with others so long as they have at least one action token. After each action, players pass one action token to the left. Several Action Token can pile up in front of the same player, and they simply sit there until the player completes a move and passes a token to the next player. There is no "lapping" as there is in *Camelot*.

This can lead to slower and more conservative play, but in *Diner*, players are incentivized to play quickly in order to draft the best cards in a central tableau. Because players play simultaneously, playing slowly to accumulate several tokens will allow other players to grab more desirable cards.

It is also possible to use Passed Action Tokens as an overlay or subset of another structure. *Space Cadets* uses a real-time turn structure, but in certain situations, an Action Token (a small deck of cards in this case) is passed around to allow players to perform a special action beyond what they can normally do.

Eclipse, in a variant mode that can accommodate as many as nine players, uses two Action Tokens. The only distinction between the tokens is that one provides priority over the other for acquiring new technologies. The system is surprisingly effective at speeding along what would otherwise be an unplayable behemoth of a game.

Sample Games

Camelot (Jolly, 2005)
Catch Phrase! (Uncredited, 1994)
Diner (O'Malley, 2014)
Eclipse (rule variant) (Tahkokallio, 2011)
Hot Potato (Unknown, 1800's)
Space Cadets (Engelstein, Engelstein, and Engelstein, 2012)

TRN-15 Interleaved vs. Sequential Phases

Description

This describes two different meta-turn structures. In an Interleaved Phase structure (a), all players perform the first phase, then all perform the second phase, etc. In a Sequential Phase structure (b), each player performs all phases before moving on to the next player, who then performs all phases, etc.

Discussion

Interleaved structures in general are preferred in modern design, as they reduce downtime between player actions. War games in the 1970s and 1980s were notorious for their "I Go, You Go" structures, where one player would take a turn that could last for a very long time, with the other player wandering off to do some other activity. In the 1980s and 1990s, this started to shift, with designers moving to Interleaved turn structures to keep players more engaged throughout. However, there are plenty of games that stick to a Sequential turn structure for a variety of reasons.

The Russian Campaign, a simulation of the German invasion of Russia during World War II, uses a strictly Sequential turn structure. Each player performs all of these steps before the turn passes to the next player:

- Receive Reinforcements and Replacements
- Move All Units
- Combat
- Breakthrough Movement
- Breakthrough Combat

The Sequential structure of *The Russian Campaign* is integral to the strategy and experience of the game. Allowing one player to move and attack twice before the opponent gets to respond gives the game epic swings and devastating breakthroughs and does a particularly good job of capturing the early and late phases of the war, which featured large-scale encirclements and desperate breakouts.

In contrast, *Power Grid* uses an Interleaved turn structure. There are three main Phases in each Round:

- Buy Power Plants
- Buy Raw Materials
- Build Power Lines

In turn, all players perform Buy Power Plants, then in turn all players perform Buy Raw Materials, etc. There is little time between a player taking their next action.

Any turn structure can be used inside the meta-structures of Sequential and Interleaved. For example, *Power Grid* uses a Stat Order structure (TRN-02).

These structures are not mutually exclusive: some parts of a game may be interleaved and some may be sequential, and different Turn Order structures may be used for each. For example, Simultaneous Turn structure is frequently appropriate during upkeep or planning phases but the movement is usually sequential. As always, these different mechanisms are tools, and each has its place and circumstance.

Sample Games

Sequential

> *The Russian Campaign* (Edwards, 1974)
> *Through the Ages: A Story of Civilization* (Chvátil, 2006)

Interleaved

> *Orleans* (Stockhausen, 2014)
> *Power Grid* (Friese, 2004)

TRN-16 Lose a Turn

Description

This is a meta-mechanism that can be applied to a variety of turn structures. A player who "Loses a Turn" must skip their next opportunity for a turn.

Discussion

Losing a Turn was common in Roll and Move games of the nineteenth and twentieth centuries (MOV-02). In the current game-design philosophy, it is considered an anti-pattern to be avoided. It was frequently used as a possible outcome of landing on a particular space or drawing a card—actions which were, themselves, random and not the result of a player's choice. Losing a Turn keeps the player from enjoying and participating in the game and can be very frustrating if one player is disproportionately affected. Mostly though, it frustrates the intent of the player as a person seeking to engage in an activity. Players want to play a game, and losing your turn means not playing a game. Like the ads on the radio that interrupt the music, if it happens too often, players will "change stations" and play something else (Illustration 2.3).

There are other mechanisms where players are allowed to take a turn but may end up not doing anything, which can be equally an issue, that is functionally (and psychologically) and generally equivalent to Lose a Turn. An example may be having to win a Roll and Move game by "exact count," such as *Trouble* or *Snakes & Ladders*. In these games, players may only win by advancing to the final space by getting exactly what they need and can result in many turns of fruitlessly rolling a die or spinning a spinner. While

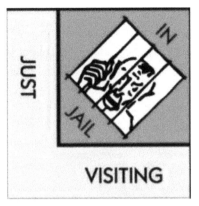

Illustration 2.3   The Jail space in *Monopoly* may cause players to lose up to three turns. Initially, this can be harmful to a player's position, but in the late stages of the game, it can be a respite from possibly landing on others' properties.

the players still get a turn, and there is some excitement in seeing if the player will win, it still can become frustrating if it lasts many turns.

Similarly, games like *Sorry!* require certain values to leave "Home" and, in essence, start the game. Again, this can result in many consecutive turns of inactivity, which leads to frustration and boredom. In *Monopoly*, players can be sent to Jail, where they will need to roll doubles to escape. *Monopoly* has some remediation to this "Lose a Turn" effect, as players may choose to pay to get out of Jail and will be let out after a maximum of three lost turns elapse. In later stages of the game, players may prefer (and hope) to remain in Jail to avoid the possibility of paying high rents for landing on properties with hotels.

There are other effects that are similar to losing a turn. In a Worker Placement game (Chapter 9), losing a worker for a round is equivalent to losing a turn. In an Action Retrieval system (ACT-03), the turn that the Actions are retrieved can feel like a lost turn to players. In a shedding card game where cards are shed one per turn (like *UNO*), having to draw cards is similar to "Losing a Turn" in terms of tempo, although it does not impinge on the player's participation in the game. Similarly, when some players gain extra turns, this is equivalent to the others losing a turn. However, due to psychological framing effects, these more modern takes do not feel as bad. Thus, giving extra turns to other players or removing resources can be a better solution for including "Lose a Turn" effects.

If the reason that a turn is lost is in control of the player, then this anti-pattern is remediated. If players choose to take a risky course or over-spend a resource that leaves them unable to take a turn, that can be an effective design, as turn loss results from player action and is not perceived as unfair by players. As an example, in the Passed Action Token game, *Camelot* (TRN-14), players who play too slowly may miss a turn if the other Action Token catches up to them. Instead of making a game slow and frustrating, this adds excitement, as players can see the Action Token getting closer and can speed up their play to avoid losing a turn.

Sample Games

Camelot (Jolly, 2005)
Monopoly (Darrow and Magie, 1933)
Snakes & Ladders (Unknown, ~200 BCE)
Sorry! (Haskell, Jr. and Storey, 1929)
Trouble (Kohner, Kohner, and Kroll, 1965)
UNO (Robbins, 1971)

TRN-17 Interrupts

Description

This is a meta-mechanism for Turn Order. Players may take an action that interrupts the normal turn flow.

Discussion

This mechanism can be used with almost any of the turn structures discussed. The ability to interrupt an opponent during their turn can be an important part of the design. The interruption can be a standard ability that players have and can be based on cards in their hands or other special tokens.

Squad Leader is an example of the "standard ability" style. During the Movement Phase, one player moves their pieces or stacks one-by-one, one space at a time. The other player (the "defender" for that turn) may, at any time, interrupt movement to take a Defensive Fire opportunity at the moving units. This is an option that is always available to units; no special ability is required.

Magic: The Gathering, by contrast, features cards that are labeled as Instants. These cards, but no others, can be played on the opponent's turn in response to an opponent's action. Other games frequently will call these cards Reactions. If you don't have a Reaction card, you will not be able to take a Reaction.

Incorporating Interrupts into the design has several positive features. First, it keeps players engaged. If players can interrupt their opponents and find the perfect opportunity to strike, they are incentivized to pay attention to the action at all times. This reduces downtime, or perceived downtime. Before *Squad Leader*, war games mostly had a strict "I Go, You Go" structure, which made it appealing for players to mentally check out when it was not their turn.

In *Squad Leader*, even if defenders never take a Defensive Fire shot, they were still engaged throughout their opponent's turn because they were always evaluating the option to fire. Similarly, in games where players can play reaction cards, players need to monitor the action continuously.

Interrupts add uncertainty and chaos to the game and undermine the ability of players to create a perfect plan. Players cannot be certain that their squad will make it across the street or that the monster will successfully attack. This can be positive or negative depending on the goal of the design.

Interrupts give a leg up to players who are more familiar with the game than new players. Understanding the range of possible opponent responses gives experienced players an advantage when formulating their plans. Even if they can't be perfect, they can plan contingencies for possible opponent responses.

Because of their asynchronous nature, Interrupts require rules and conventions around their play to give players the opportunity to react and also to adjudicate if multiple players want to react at the same time. In *Squad Leader*, for example, there is a specific rule that a player moving a stack of units must pause briefly after entering each space, to give an opponent the opportunity to announce Defensive Fire. This requires the cooperation of the players to keep these pauses long enough for players to decide but short enough not to unduly lengthen the game. Conventions may be developed, such as a player being allowed to request a few extra seconds to make a decision. Similarly, when playing reaction cards, there needs to be an opportunity for players to play them.

Some designs allow Interrupts to themselves be interrupted. Obviously, the system needs to prevent infinite Interrupts, such as requiring the play or discard of a card and/or resource(s) to execute an Interrupt.

There also needs to be a system to handle the order of resolving multiple Interrupts. *Magic: The Gathering* uses a LIFO system and an Instant stack. If a player wants to play an Instant in response to another Instant, they play the card on top of the earlier card. When all Instants have been played into this stack, they are resolved from the top down. The first card to be played will be the last to be resolved.

Some games will allow the Interrupt to change the turn order. For example, in *Mille Bornes*, a player may respond to a Hazard card being played on them by playing the matching Safety. If they do, the interrupting player—the one who played the Safety—immediately becomes the active player and takes a normal turn. The players between the old active player and the interrupting player are skipped, losing their turn (TRN-16).

Sample Games

Magic: The Gathering (Garfield, 1993)
Mille Bornes (Dujardin, 1954)
Squad Leader (Hill, 1977)

3

Actions

When watching a movie or seeing a play, the story progresses independent of the viewer. Games, however, require action by the player to move things forward. These actions may be based purely on luck, rely solely on the player's skill, or lie somewhere in between. But a fundamental differentiator of games from many other activities is that the players must act. While later chapters will discuss what those specific actions might be, this one describes different ways that the players are permitted by the designer to take actions and the way that those flow. Thus, the mechanisms discussed here should be viewed in conjunction with the Turn Structures of Chapter 2.

An *Action* is an atomic step or series of steps that a player chooses to perform. For example, moving a piece, picking up a cube, selling a share of stock, or initiating combat may all be Actions. An Action may also be compound, allowing a player to both pick up a cube and sell a share of stock, depending on the structure and metaphor of the game.

The selection and integration of Actions into the game can give play a specific feel. These Action systems control the complexity of the game, in terms of the number of Actions a player may perform consecutively and how they interrelate, the interaction between players, and other features. Manipulation of the Action system, as in a Rondel (ACT-10, Rondel Games) or Action Queue (ACT-06), can become the focus of the game itself and a key mechanism. Or it can simply provide a framework that fades into the background.

If a game is not interactive enough, or if it overwhelms players with too many choices, the root of the problem is frequently in how Actions are made available to the players. Looking closer at that part of the design may pay dividends.

DOI: 10.1201/9781003179184-3   77

ACT-01 Action Points

Actions: Action Points

Description

A player receives a number of Action Points on their turn. They may spend them on a variety of Actions.

Discussion

This is a broad mechanism that is isomorphic to a variety of game structures. However, some generalities can be discussed.

A common implementation is that a player receives a fixed number of Action Points on their turn and can spend them on any combination of Actions, each of which spends one of those points. *Pandemic*, for example, gives a player four Action Points each turn, which can be spent on several Actions, such as moving to another city or removing a disease cube.

Tikal takes a similar approach, but Actions may cost more than one Action Point. Each player gets ten Action Points for the turn, and the cost of Actions ranges from one to four. This can dramatically increase the decision space for players, so the designer needs to be cognizant of the additional weight this will add to the game (Illustration 3.1).

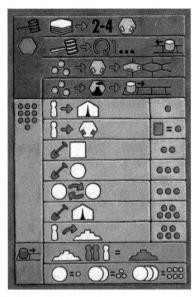

Illustration 3.1 The Action reference from *Tikal*. The cost of each action is indicated by the small red circles to the right. Players have ten Action Points to spend each turn.

A game may have multiple currencies of Action Points. *Through the Ages: A Story of Civilization* has two types of Action Points: Civil and Military. Each may only be spent on specific types of Actions.

Variations of this mechanism may also limit players to only performing an Action one time per turn. Some allow players to leave some Action Points unused to be carried over to the next turn, and others require that all be spent or lost.

Many games use this mechanism without explicitly awarding Action Points to the players. For example, the game may simply tell players that they may take two out of three possible Actions, or even one. In *Feudum*, each player simultaneously selects four out of eleven Action cards available in a personal pool to use each turn. This makes it obvious whether an Action can be performed multiple times, or just once, depending on how many copies of the same Action card are in the deck.

A variant Action Point system is found in *Starship Samurai*. Here, players select the Action they wish to perform from a limited menu. They must also use one of their order counters, which are numbered from one to four. The number determines the number of times the Action may be executed. For example, if players choose the Move Action and use their "3" token, they get to move 3 units.

Action Point systems give the players a lot of flexibility in how they approach their turn. The pace of the game can be controlled by the designer by changing the number of Action Points available each turn. Small values will lead to quicker turns. Larger values will lengthen turns but also open up more space for combos.

Sample Games

Android Netrunner (Garfield and Litzsinger, 2012)
Feudum (Swanson, 2018)
Forbidden Island (Leacock, 2010)
Kemet (Bariot and Montiage, 2012)
Pandemic (Leacock, 2008)
Starship Samurai (Vega, 2018)
Through the Ages: A Story of Civilization (Chvátil, 2006)
Tikal (Kiesling and Kramer, 1999)

ACT-02 Action Drafting

Description

Players select from an assortment of Actions in a shared pool. The available Actions are limited in quantity, and once a player has chosen an Action it may not be chosen again.

Discussion

This mechanism creates player interaction within the Action selection itself. While many games have Actions, typically if an Action is chosen by one player, that does not deny it to another. Action Drafting creates a market-place for Actions, with players competing to select them.

Action Drafting is a very common mechanism that goes by a variety of names, such as Role Selection or Worker Placement. In a Worker Placement mechanism, players place pawns ("workers") onto Action spaces on a board, perform the Actions, and deny the use of those Action spaces to their opponents. Because of the variety and importance of Worker Placement, we have dedicated Chapter 9 to exploring its considerations and variations. The issues discussed there, such as the strength of the first player advantage, apply to most of the mechanisms discussed here as well.

Citadels is an example of a Role Selection implementation of Action Drafting. In *Citadels*, the start player takes all the role cards (which show their associated actions), selects an Action card, and then passes the remaining cards to the player to the left. Because the card chosen is secret, this system generates information asymmetry (UNC-05). *Puerto Rico* and *Race for the Galaxy* are similar examples of Role Selection, as in each round, every player selects (drafts) a role and gets to perform associated actions. *Puerto Rico* allows all players to perform a less powerful version of the action the drafting player selected, only the player may select a given role each round (see "Follow, ACT-08" in this chapter). In *Race for the Galaxy*, players also can Follow with a weaker version of the action another player selected, but multiple players can select the same role and get the stronger version of the action.

Frequently this mechanism is implemented with a Dice Pool. At the start of the Action Selection phase, dice are rolled, with results corresponding to a specific action. In *La Granja*, for example, all the 4s rolled are placed into the "Take 4 Coins" action space. Once all dice are placed in their boxes, the players take turns selecting a die and performing the associated action. In a separate twist, there is an extra die left over after all players have selected two action dice, and every player gets to perform that final action.

An Action Drafting system based on a dice pool works against perfect plans, as players need to adapt to whatever actions are available. In addition, it forces players to consider not just their own plans but also what their opponents may need. Players may consider taking a sub-optimal selection in order to deprive their opponents of the option (so-called "hate drafting").

Another variant on this mechanic is found in *Dungeon Lords*. In this game, players secretly select three out of six possible Action cards, placing them face down in front of them in order. Each player then reveals their first card and places tokens on the corresponding spaces (with ties in order being broken by a Start Player token). The players who claim Action space earlier can perform more powerful versions of the Actions.

In *War of the Ring*, each player has their own pool of action dice and players take turns selecting one of their dice. These systems are not really drafting, in that players are not denying their opponent an Action. However, it does restrict the range of possible Actions, gives players flexibility, and an understanding of the possible Actions available to their opponent.

Sample Games

   7 Wonders (Bauza, 2010)
   Agricola (Rosenberg, 2007)
   Citadels (Faidutti, 2000)

Coimbra (Brasini and Gigli, 2018)
Dungeon Lords (Chvátil, 2008)
La Granja (Keller and Odendahl, 2014)
Puerto Rico (Seyfarth, 2002)
Race for the Galaxy (Lehmann, 2007)
War of the Ring (Di Meglio, Maggi, and Nepitello, 2004)
Yspahan (Pauchon, 2006)

ACT-03 Action Retrieval

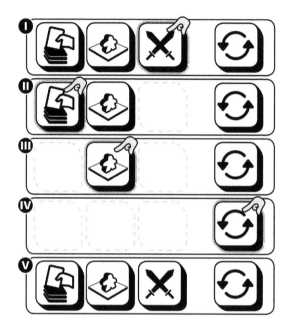

Description

Each player has a set of Actions available to them, represented by cards, tokens, or some other component. Once the Action is performed, the component is spent and the Action may not be performed again until the component is retrieved. Action Retrieval may be an Action taken as part of a turn or it may consume an entire turn.

Discussion

Action Retrieval rewards efficiency. Because retrieving the used cards takes an Action, players that retrieve more frequently will be at a disadvantage, as they will conduct fewer Actions that advance their cause.

The Actions available to players usually span a gamut of discrete options that affect different aspects of the game. For example, *Assault of the Giants* has the actions Move, Attack, Recruit, Make Alliance, and Leader. Once players use Move, they cannot play it again until they take a Retrieve turn, which restores all action cards used since the last Retrieve. This stops players from repeatedly selecting a specific Action over and over again, forcing them to adopt balanced strategies, and to plan several turns ahead. Therefore, a game that incorporates this mechanism will have a much more strategic feel. Action Retrieval also allows for additional tactical play, as your opponents will know, for example, that you do not have a Move action available and will not be able to respond to opponents moving to different areas (Illustration 3.2).

Many games introduce additional wrinkles to reward planning and sequencing. *Assault of the Giants*, for example, makes Actions more powerful as more Actions are played. For example, if the Move card is played as the first card after a Retrieve, only one unit can move. But if Recruit and Attack have been played before Move, then three units may move.

In *Champions of Hara*, cards have a "play" effect and a "retrieval" effect. An action is required to play them from the hand, which triggers the play effect. In a future turn, an action must be used to retrieve the card back into the player's hand, at which time, the card's retrieval effect is triggered.

Another variation on this mechanism is a mix of one-time and recoverable cards. *Gloomhaven* has some action cards that can only be used one time during a scenario. Others may be recovered by having a character Rest.

Illustration 3.2   When the Tribune card is played in *Concordia*, the player retrieves their action cards and gains a bonus. The more cards played prior to retrieval, the larger the bonus.

Sample Games

Assault of the Giants (Parks, 2017)
Century: Spice Road (Matsuuchi, 2017)
Champions of Hara (Barber, VanNest, and Zimmerman, 2018)
Concordia (Gerdts, 2013)
Gloomhaven (Childres, 2017)
Spirit Island (Reuss, 2017)

ACT-04 Action/Event

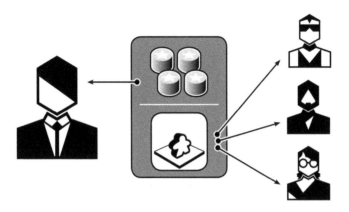

Description

On their turn, the player plays a card that shows Action Points and an Event. They must choose to either use the Action Points or perform the Event. If they choose to use the Action Points, typically the Event may be performed by another player.

Discussion

This mechanism builds on a basic Action Point system and allows designers to integrate a lot of flavors and special actions into a system to emphasize the theme. It was pioneered in historical simulations as a way of introducing historical events without unduly adding rules overhead. For example, *Twilight Struggle*, a simulation of the Cold War, has a card that can be used either for two Action Points or the Fidel event. If the Action Points are chosen, there is a standard list of Actions on which they can be spent (ACT-01) (Illustration 3.3).

Many games incorporate an Event Deck (ACT-17), which is another way to include special effects and deeper theming. However, the Action/Event system gives players another layer of choice, rather than simply imposing global effects.

Often, games using this system add another layer of player decision-making by having some or all events only eligible for specific players. For example, in *We the People*, a simulation of the American Revolution, certain events may only be performed by the Colonists and others by Great Britain.

FIDEL*

Remove all US Influence in Cuba.
USSR gains sufficient Influence in
Cuba for Control.

Remove from play if used as an event.

Illustration 3.3   The "Fidel" card in *Twilight Struggle* can
either be used for two Action Points (the number in the
upper left) or for the Fidel event. The Red Star icon shows
that the event favors the Soviet player and will trigger even
if the US player uses the card for its Action Points.

If a player is not eligible to use the event on a card, they must use the Action
Points. Similarly, some events are dependent on specific locations, control of
particular areas, the presence of certain characters, etc. In *Empires of the Void
II*, for example, events can be tied to specific planets, and if those planets
are not in play or the planet's condition does not match the event's prerequisites, the player may only use the card for its point value, rather than the
event. In *World War II: Barbarossa to Berlin*, there are prerequisite events that
must be triggered before other following events may be used. This helps prevent anachronisms in games that model historical events. It can also ensure
proper cause-and-effect in the narrative flow of a game.

Twilight Struggle takes this enforcement of sequencing even further by
automatically triggering your opponent's Event when you play a card featuring such an event for its Action Points. For example, the Warsaw Pact event
is a USSR event. If the US player plays the card, he or she must use the three
Action Points, but the USSR will still get to perform the Event. On the

other hand, if the USSR player plays the card, they must choose between the Event and the Action Points. Generally, used cards are recycled into the deck several times over the course of the game, but some cards are permanently discarded after their event is triggered. Once again, this helps with chronology—Anwar Sadat takes control of Egypt only once—but it also adds complexity to the choice of Action or Event and the sequence of play. It may be better to forgo playing your own Event, and using the Action Points instead, in hopes that the card will reappear in your opponent's hands and they will be forced to trigger it.

Twilight Struggle and *We the People* are two-player games. This system is extended to multiplayer in *The Expanse Board Game*, which supports up to four players, each of whom represents a faction. Between two and four factions are eligible for each event, and if a player uses the Action Points, the other players are given the option to perform it, in a priority order. In *1960: The Making of the President*, players may trigger their events when their opponent plays a card for its action points by spending a Momentum Marker. However, players may also pre-empt an event from being triggered by their opponent by paying two Momentum Markers when they play the card.

Sample Games

1960: The Making of the President (Leonhard and Matthews, 2007)
Empires of the Void II (Laukat, 2018)
The Expanse Board Game (Engelstein, 2017)
Hannibal: Rome vs Carthage (Simonitch, 1996)
Twilight Struggle (Gupta and Matthews, 2005)
We the People (Herman, 1993)
World War II: Barbarossa to Berlin (Raicer, 2002)

ACT-05 Command Cards

Description

Players have a hand of cards that allows them to activate and perform actions with a subset of their units.

Discussion

Players have a hand of cards that represent different geographic regions or unit types and must play one each turn. When a geographic region card is played, units in the region(s) indicated may take Actions. If a Unit Type card is played, only units of that type may take Actions.

In *Memoir '44* the cards represent the center, left flank, or right flank; or a set of units, for example, all Tank units. Players can plan their future actions based on the cards in their hands. Hand-size limits help define the information horizon and amount of look-ahead players can engage in. Players may try to build a bank of cards in a particular sector to orchestrate a multipronged attack, or they may riskily move a unit out of cover to take a better shot, despite not having another card in hand to move the unit to safety the next turn. Like in real battles, players may not be able to execute the tactics

Illustration 3.4   Command Cards from *Memoir '44*. While all are Recon cards, each may only activate units in the highlighted region.

they believe are best. The system is quite elegant as an abstraction of breakdowns in communication and command-and-control that occur in warfare (Illustration 3.4).

In a traditional war game, players can take actions with all of their units each turn. Command Card systems limit this to a subset of units, which reduces the length of turns and simplifies decision-making, giving the game a lighter feel.

Some games, such as *Risk: Star Wars Edition*, give players a range of one to three possible activation choices, building in greater flexibility and planning.

In the extreme limit, with one unit at a time being activated, this mechanism reduces to a Chit Draw system (TRN-11).

Sample Games

Battle Cry (Borg, 2000)
BattleLore (Borg, 2006)
C&C Ancients, Napoleonics, etc. (Borg, 2006–2018)
Combat Commander: Europe (Jensen, 2006)
Memoir '44 (Borg, 2004)
Risk: Star Wars Edition (D'Aloisio, Rucker, and Van Ness, 2015)

ACT-06 Action Queue

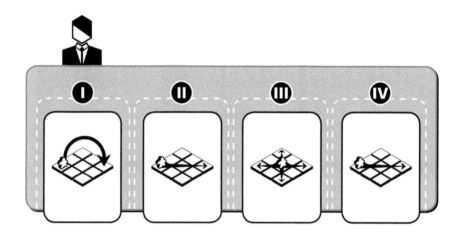

Description

Players create Action Queues and perform them in sequence.

Discussion

While this mechanism has many different implementations, at its core, the idea is that players must plan their actions and commit to a specific sequence of execution. For example, players may have to plot the movement of a robot by placing three Action cards in sequence that may, for example, cause the robot to move forward two spaces, then turn left, and then move one more space. The types of actions, the way they are revealed and resolved, and other specifics have several variations (Illustration 3.5).

Action Queues emphasize planning but can also introduce chaos as players commit to a course of action several steps or turns in advance, keep them hidden from the other players, and have limited opportunity to change the plan. This introduces Yomi (UNC-01), as players try to guess what other players will do and what the board state may look like in the future.

Actions are typically represented by cards, as they can contain a lot of information about the preconditions and resolutions. Tiles can also be used but need to be simpler. Queues can either be *Rolling*, where the Action at the head of the queue is revealed and performed as a new Action is added to the end, or *Batch*, where a set number of cards are added to the queue at one time and then all are resolved in order.

Illustration 3.5   A sample queue *Space Alert*. Coordinating the time step with other players is important, so players are allowed to leave blank steps—steps 2 and 5 in this example.

One of the earliest uses of a Rolling Queue is the 1965 game *Nuclear War*. In this game, each player has a queue of two cards in front of them. On their turn, they add a card to the end of the queue, and then turn up and execute the card at the queue head. In *Nuclear War*, the players start at peace and may perform certain peace actions, but when someone launches a missile, only war actions may be taken. The delayed Action Queue gives the game tremendous tension, as players need to decide if they can continue to perform peace actions or want to be the first to declare war.

RoboRally uses a Batch Queue. The players fully plan an entire series of actions and then resolve them using an Interleaved turn structure, with each player revealing and performing the action in the first slot, then each player doing the second action, etc. *Swashbuckler*, instead of using cards, has players record their actions on a record sheet, in blocks of six time steps. Players then resolve each time step.

RoboRally only allows players to queue Movement actions, with other actions (such as shooting) being done on the fly as the opportunity permits. In contrast, *Swashbuckler* allows players the full suite of movement, combat, and other actions.

Twin Tin Bots uses a Batch Queue approach, but the entire queue does not get replaced at once. Players may only replace one Action in the queue each turn. The others remain and are performed. This obviously adds more complexity to the programming step as players need to play further ahead about how they may change their queues. *Mechs vs. Minions* is a similar example of this system.

When queues get longer, and particularly when movement and rotation actions are included in the available actions, players need to visualize where they will be as they progress through the queue. Visualizing spatial relationships is cognitively taxing and tends to lead to a chaotic board state. This combination may not be well received by some players, because of the contrast between the cognitive effort expended and the seemingly unpredictable outcomes of the game. Some games, however, such as *RoboRally* and *Space Alert*, are built on this precise dynamic and experience.

Other games, such as *Colt Express*, address this challenge by limiting the size of the play area. In *Colt Express*, players can move to the head or rear of a short train of cars, or between the inside and the top of those cars. Each player can move to one of three spaces per turn, and the whole board is about ten spaces in a 2-by-5 array (depending on player count), increasing the likelihood of player collisions and interactions, while decreasing the cognitive load on players.

Root has a unique take on the Action Queue. One of the player-controlled factions must add a new Action to its queue each turn (in any position) and perform all the Actions in sequence. If an Action cannot be executed, the player loses victory points and all Action cards in the queue are discarded. Another variation is in *Valparaiso*. Players simultaneously plan their actions in a queue and then execute them in order. However, as the turn unfolds, they may pay gold to perform an action in their queue sooner than planned.

Sample Games

Rolling Queue

The Dragon & Flagon (Engelstein, Engelstein, and Engelstein, 2016)
Killer Bunnies and the Quest for the Magic Carrot (Bellinger, 2002)
Nuclear War (Malewicki, 1965)

Batch Queue

Colt Express (Raimbault, 2014)
Gunslinger (Hamblen, 1982)
Mechs vs. Minions (Cantrell, Ernst, Librande, Saraswat, and Tiras, 2016)
RoboRally (Garfield, 1994)
Root (Wehrle, 2018)
Space Alert (Chvátil, 2008)
Swashbuckler (O'Neill and Taylor, 1980)
Twin Tin Bots (Keyaerts, 2013)
Valparaiso (Malz and Malz, 2018)

ACT-07 Shared Action Queue

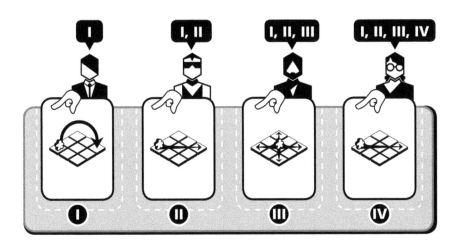

Description

All players add Actions to a central Action Queue. Actions in the Queue are performed by all players.

Discussion

This is a variation on the standard Action Queue mechanism. Here, on their turn, a player adds one or more Actions to the end of a queue shared by all players and then executes the full queue from start to finish. This system increases interactivity, as players plan actions not just for themselves but also for their opponents. It gives a different flavor of strategic options, as players attempt to plan actions that will benefit them more than their opponents. Sequencing may also play a role, as players may be out of position to execute an earlier action, a deficiency that cascades throughout the queue, as the effectiveness of later actions depends on having executed the earlier actions.

The two-player game *Major General: Duel of Time* takes this a step further by including two actions on each card played, one for each player. It is also unique in that actions may be placed anywhere in the queue, not just at the end. After playing an action, the player executes actions from the end of the queue closest to them. On their opponent's turn, they will resolve the actions in the opposite order and using the other actions on the cards.

Each turn in *Mottainai*, a player plays a card in front of them that allows the taking of a particular action. However, before performing it, the player first performs the actions in front of each opponent, going clockwise and ending with themselves. This is similar to Follow (ACT-08), except that the opponent's chosen actions are executed on your turn, not on the opponent's turn.

A variation on a Shared Action Queue is used in *Kraftwagen*, which has a queue of action tokens, trailed by a queue of player markers. The player at the end of the queue may move to any position and execute the Action of the token in that position. However, the farther ahead the person moves, the longer it will be until they are once again at the end, and in position to take a new action. *Kraftwagen* blends a Shared Action Queue with a Time Track (TRN-13).

Sample Games

Impulse (Chudyk, 2013)
Kraftwagen (Cramer, 2015)
Major General: Duel of Time (Liu, Moorman, Yeong, and Zhao, 2017)
Mottainai (Chudyk, 2015)

ACT-08 Follow

Description

One player selects an Action. Other players may then perform that Action or a modified version of it. This is closely related to Action Drafting (ACT-02) and Role Selection (TRN-10) and is often implemented alongside those systems.

Discussion

Follow mechanisms are a form of Action Selection that has a high degree of player involvement. *Puerto Rico* is a good example. On their turn, a player selects one of the available roles and executes the action associated with it. Then, in turn, each player gets to execute the role. The player who selected the role also gets a bonus for their action. For example, the player who selects Builder gets a discount on the cost of construction and performs the action first. The other players then each perform the Builder action, paying the normal cost.

This mechanism forces players to consider not just what they want to do but what will be good for their opponents. Does someone really need to build? Perhaps picking Builder is not the best choice. Can someone only build if they get the discount? Then selecting Builder, even if it helps other players too, may be the best option. Players need to look holistically at everyone's position, not just their own.

A variation on this mechanism can be found in *Glory to Rome* and *SPQF*. In these games, Actions are taken by playing a card from the hand, which are in certain suits. Other players may echo the action if they play one or more cards matching the suit. In this way, the players that are echoing may end up performing more powerful versions of the actions by discarding several cards. It also means that if players cannot match the action card's suit, they may not echo it. Since players' hands are hidden in these games, this makes determining the best option somewhat of a guessing game. But careful attention will show what may be useful to other players and what cards they may have collected.

Follow systems of this sort introduce a cost to the follow action. In *Eminent Domain*, players may Follow by discarding cards of the same suit, which further powers the action. Because the game is a deck-builder, the cards spent from hand are only an opportunity cost, as they will eventually be shuffled back into the player's deck. In *Tiny Epic Galaxies*, players must spend a Culture resource to follow, which is a more concrete cost.

In *Mottainai*, players, on their turn, may perform the actions that the other players played on their prior turn. Unlike other Follow mechanism implementations, this one calls for a batch execution of the sequence of actions, rather than an Interleaved system.

Generally, Follow systems are excellent at keeping players engaged on every turn, since players act, or have the potential to act, on every turn. However, they may also slow down play, since players have to decide on every single turn whether they wish to Follow and how. Designers are encouraged to include some physical tokens to keep track of who the active player is, too, since the interleaving of player actions inside each active player's turn can lead to turn-order confusion.

Sample Games

    Ceylon (Zinsli and Zinsli, 2018)
    Eminent Domain (Jaffee, 2011)
    Glory to Rome (Chudyk, 2005)
    Mottainai (Chudyk, 2015)
    Puerto Rico (Seyfarth, 2002)
    SPQF (Rodiek, 2018)
    Tiny Epic Galaxies (Almes, 2015)

ACT-09 Order Counters

Description

Players place Order Tokens into regions, indicating what they want to do in that particular region of the board. After all the tokens are placed, they are executed in sequence.

Discussion

This mechanism combines an Interleaved Turn Structure (TRN-15) with an Action Queue. Players are in essence creating multiple Interleaved Action Queues during a planning step and then resolving them. The tokens are typically placed face down, so opponents know where you are planning to act but not which actions you will take. If more than one order may be placed in a location, tokens are stacked to indicate their sequence.

Because players alternate placing orders into different areas, they must balance a variety of factors. Which actions do they wish to perform early? Will committing to a region alert an opponent to your intentions to operate there? What actions are the opponents planning?

The resolution of the Order Token stacks can be performed in several ways. First, they may either be resolved from the top down, so that tokens that were placed last are resolved first (LIFO, Last-In-First-Out), or the token stack may be flipped over, so that the earliest tokens are resolved first (FIFO, First-In-First-Out). Some games (such as *A Game of Thrones: The Board Game*) don't consider the placement order of the tokens and simply turn them all over and resolve them in turn order, over the course of three phases. Only tokens of particular types may be resolved in each phase, so in the Raid phase, only Raid tokens may be executed, and players who have not played any Raids are skipped in the turn order (Illustration 3.6).

Resolution order has a great impact on the strategy and feel for placement. LIFO gives the game a "chicken" feel, as players want to be the last into a region with key actions so that they are executed first, but it also increases cognitive load, as players need to remember the reverse order of tokens in the stack and modify their plans as they go. With a FIFO structure, players can gradually just build up their plans in their minds as they proceed, which is less cognitively taxing.

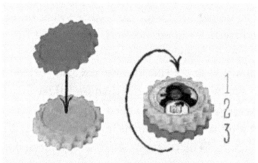

Illustration 3.6   In *Victorian Masterminds*, players place order tokens face down in different areas, stacking them on top of other tokens already there. When there are three tokens in an area (image 2), the stack is flipped over, and they are resolved in a first-in-first-out order.

Either way, this is a moderately complex mechanism, which is best reserved for heavier strategy games.

Sample Games

Forbidden Stars (Bailey, Kniffen, and Konieczka, 2015)
Francis Drake (Hawes, 2013)
A Game of Thrones (Petersen and Wilson, 2003)
Starcraft: The Board Game (Konieczka and Petersen, 2007)
Victorian Masterminds (Bauza and Lang, 2019)

ACT-10 Rondel

Description

The available Actions are represented as pie wedges in a circle. Each player has one or more tokens on Rondel's wedges. On their turn, they may move their token around the Rondel and perform the Action indicated by the wedge where they stop. It is typically more costly to move further around the Rondel.

Discussion

This mechanism is related to a basic Action Point system (ACT-01), as the Rondel represents a menu of available actions. However, the cost of the actions varies for each turn, for example, to move more than one space typically incurs some cost (money or some other currency). If a player wishes to move one space at a time, they incur a little cost but may not be most efficiently performing the actions (Illustration 3.7).

Rondel systems emphasize trade-offs, planning, and efficiency as players need to balance taking the action that they want to do now, and paying a cost, with waiting and paying no or a reduced cost.

There are several variations on this mechanic. In *Finca*, players have several tokens on the Rondel and may choose one of them to move. The distance that it may move is based on the number of tokens in the starting wedge, and the power of the action is determined by the number of tokens in the ending wedge. This makes for a highly interactive, yet, relatively simple system and also begins to blur with a Mancala mechanism (MOV-12).

Illustration 3.7   The Rondel in *Imperial*. Players may select an action that is up to three spaces away from where their marker currently is at no cost. If they wish to move further, they must pay to do so.

Sample Games

Antike (Gerdts, 2005)
Concordia (Gerdts, 2013)
Finca (Sentker and zur Linde, 2009)
Imperial (Gerdts, 2006)
Navegador (Gerdts, 2010)

ACT-11 Action Selection Restrictions

Description

Players are restricted in which actions they may choose.

Discussion

There are a wide variety of mechanisms that have been used to force players to choose less than optimal actions or even ones that are detrimental. Some of the more popular mechanisms have been included in their own section: Action Drafting, Action Retrieval, Rondels, and Command Cards are all examples. However, there are many approaches to this that have been used in only one game. Several of these are collected in this section.

In *Kemet*, the possible actions are laid out in a pyramid. Players must select at least one option from each pyramid level. In *Goa*, action tiles are laid out on a grid. The start player places a marker on the grid, taking that tile. Each player in turn then places their marker adjacent to the previous one played, onto another tile, either orthogonally or diagonally. Players need to consider how they may be helping their opponent by placing next to a tile they need.

In *Noria*, players place action tokens on concentric wheels. Only tokens in certain portions of the wheels may be used, and the wheels rotate at different speeds. *Tzolk'in: The Mayan Calendar* also uses rotating gears, and the longer workers remain on the gears the more powerful the actions they can perform. In *Calimala*, players place disks between two actions on a grid and can perform both connected actions.

Manitoba has a tower of disks of different colors, and the active player selects part of the stack which controls what map regions and tracks may be used for actions.

In *Keyforge: Call of the Archons*, in each turn, a player picks what "house" they will use, and only cards (actions) that belong to that house may be used. Looking for novel ways to limit the actions that players can take is a constant source of innovation in game design.

Warpgate gives players a hand of Action cards, each of which has two possible Actions that can be performed. When playing a card, the player may select which half to use. It has the additional twist that cards become more powerful the later they are played in the round.

Bonfire and *Honey Buzz* combine action selection with tile placement. Both games have players selecting tiles with multiple actions on them and placing them on a player board. In *Bonfire*, the actions are triggered on placement, and action placed adjacent to the same action tile gain a bonus. In *Honey Buzz*, if the hexagonal tiles completely surround a single empty space, the action on all six surrounding spaces is triggered.

Sample Games

Bonfire (Feld, 2020)
Calimala (Lopiano, 2017)
Forum Trajanum (Feld, 2018)
Goa (Dorn, 2004)
Honey Buzz (Salomon, 2020)
Kemet (Bariot and Montiage, 2012)
Keyforge: Call of the Archons (Garfield, 2018)
Manitoba (Conzadori and Pranzo, 2018)
Noria (Wagner, 2017)
Tzolk'in: The Mayan Calendar (Luciani and Tascini, 2012)
Warpgate (Nichipurov, 2018)

ACT-12 Variable Player Powers

Description

Each player has special Actions that only he or she can perform or that modify standard actions.

Discussion

This is a meta-mechanic that can modify Action and other systems, such as Resolution. We are placing it here, as it can give players additional actions that they can perform or it modifies standard actions or procedures.

Typically, each player has a unique player power that sets them apart from the other players. This is an excellent way to include asymmetry, as well as emphasize the theme, as in *Dune*, where the factions are highly differentiated through different actions and abilities and are quite evocative of the source material. For example, the Fremen faction, who resides on the planet, can build units anywhere and is better able to deal with the hazards on the planet. The Guild faction, which controls all space travel, gains money each time a non-Fremen player moves forces from orbit to the planet surface.

Variable Player Powers also increase replayability, as players will want to return to the game to try out different factions and see how they play, and, in some cases, this will feel like they are playing a completely different game.

These unique powers also increase complexity and cognitive load on the players, however. In addition to the standard rules, the special exceptions for each player need to be taught. The most successful of games where Player Powers are at the forefront are based on very simple frameworks. *Cosmic Encounter* is all about the player powers, which can radically change the way players play the game. The simple structure of *Cosmic Encounter* is well-suited to support this complexity. Combat is resolved by each player playing a number card and adding the number of tokens they have in the battle. The highest number wins. That simple framework allows the designers to take the special powers in a dizzying array of different directions. The designer has reserved most of the design space in this mechanism for the interactions of the unique player powers.

Another feature of player powers is that they may make a particular strategy optimal for that player. For example, a faction may be very good at fighting, which will encourage a military strategy. This can be positive, as it gives players identity and immediate strategic direction for new players. But it also limits players' strategic choices, and they can feel as if there is one "correct" way to play for a faction.

There are several options for conveying the details of a Variable Player Power to the players. One is to state the rules explicitly through a player mat or shield, as in *Cosmic Encounter* or *Spirit Island*, where they are all clearly presented to the player at the start of the game through a player mat or a limited number of cards. Alternately, they can be spread out among a large number of components, typically a deck of cards, such as in *Sentinels of the Multiverse*. The advantage of the latter is that it makes it simpler to teach the game, as the base rules are the same for all, and the differences only need to be taught when they arise. It also gives the players a sense of discovery, as they see cards and abilities they did not know existed. On the negative side, this can make it difficult for new players to take full advantage of a specific character and so may lead to an unsatisfactory initial play with a specific faction or character.

Sample Games

Cosmic Encounter (Eberle, Kittredge, Norton, and Olatka, 1977)
Dune (Eberle, Kittredge, and Olatka, 1979)
Pandemic (Leacock, 2008)
Root (Wehrle, 2018)
Sentinels of the Multiverse (Badell, Bender, and Rebottaro, 2011)
Sidereal Confluence: Trading and Negotiation in the Elysian Quadrant (Deichmann, 2017)
Spirit Island (Reuss, 2017)

ACT-13 Once-Per-Game Abilities

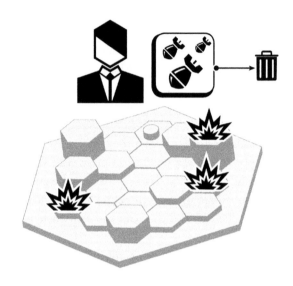

Description

Players have a special ability that they can use one time per game.

Discussion

While there are exceptions, Once-Per-Game Abilities are usually different for each player or character. Because they can only be performed once, the designer has great latitude to make them very powerful.

These two characteristics combine to make this mechanism potentially be player- or character-defining. The threat of using the ability, the decision of when to actually use it, and identifying the correct moment can dominate the play of the game as players maneuver for advantage and can elevate the available strategies and tactics. It also adds another dimension of consideration for players—timing—that is not present with always-on special abilities. In *Warmachine/Hordes*, each side has one Warcaster who has an extremely powerful single-use ability called a Feat. When and how to use the Feat is a critical part of the game. As such, when characters have wildly varying special abilities as in *Warmachine/Hordes*, it is important that players understand exactly what their opponents are capable of doing. This rewards veteran players and puts a burden on new players to understand the full extent of the special Action.

Some games give players a set of special Action tokens at the start of the game, which are usable one time during the game. These may be the same for each player, such as *Finca*. Often, if tokens are not used, they give bonus Victory Points to the player at the end of the game.

Sample Games

Battles of Westeros (Kouba, 2010)
Battlestar Galactica: The Board Game (Konieczka, 2008)
Drakon (Jolly, 2001)
Finca (Sentker and zur Linde, 2009)
Warmachine/Hordes (McVey, Snoddy, and Wilson, 2003)

ACT-14 Advantage Token

Description

One player has a token that permits them to perform a special Action or modify an Action. Once used, the token passes to another player.

Discussion

This is a meta-mechanism of Action Selection, as it determines what Actions may be available to a player. Originally introduced in the 1981 game *Storm over Arnhem* as the "Tactical Advantage" token, it represents the ebb and flow of a conflict. In *Storm*, the controlling player could use it to re-resolve combat or to force a turn to continue when it would otherwise end. After being used in this way, it is passed to the other player, who receives the same options.

This introduces another consideration for the player, as the value of using the Tactical Advantage must be weighed against its loss and the possible use of it by the opponent. Similar to Once-Per-Game Actions (ACT-13), a timing dimension is added to the decision-making. Normally, Variable Player Powers (ACT-12) are always on, so if you can use them, you should. But that is not the case with this mechanism.

Twilight Struggle uses this mechanism more thematically than *Storm over Arnhem* in the guise of *The China Card*, an actual card that is passed between players when it is used. It is a powerful card that is even more powerful when used to perform actions in Asia, but after use, it is given to the opponent. Again, consideration must be given to the timing and whether to use the card or simply hold on to it and deny its use to the opponent.

Advantage Tokens can also be used to give ongoing benefits to the owning player that do not require surrender. In *Storm*, for example, the player controlling the token gets to go first in a turn and decides the order of resolution of conflict situations.

Many games use this system less overtly for tie-breaking. In a Sealed Bid Auction for example (AUC-04), ties may be broken by a Priority Token. Then, the token is given to the player who lost the tiebreaker. This is different from the standard implementation of this mechanism, as the transfer is not controlled by the player. It simply designates who wins a tie, and its transfer is never a choice. In another variant of this mechanism, the *A Game of Thrones* board game features an Iron Throne token that is awarded to the winner of the turn-order auction. The holder of the Throne determines how all noncombat ties among all players are to be decided. The recurring turn-order auction is the means by which possession of the token moves around, rather than by its use.

The Advantage Token mechanism gives the designer an opportunity to give the players more control over certain random aspects of the game, such as combat resolution in *Storm over Arnhem* or card draw in *Twilight Struggle*. As such, it can make a game feel more strategic, without a lot of rules overhead.

Sample Games

> *Breakout: Normandy* (Greenwood and Stahler, 1992)
> *The Fog of War* (Engelstein, 2016)
> *A Game of Thrones* (Petersen and Wilson, 2003)
> *Storm over Arnhem* (Allen, 1981)
> *Twilight Struggle* (Gupta and Matthews, 2005)

ACT-15 Gating and Unlocking

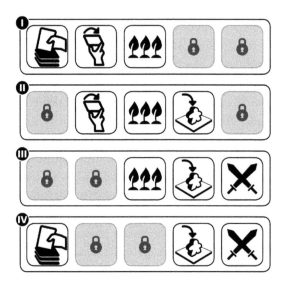

Description

At certain points in the game, new actions are made available to the players. Actions may become available by a variety of means, including reaching a certain turn or game stage. Depleting a shared pool or bringing some track past a threshold level through the cumulative effects of the actions of all the players is another common approach to triggering unlocks. The mechanism is not limited to gating actions. Game events and narrative breaks may also be gated and unlocked through this type of triggering mechanism

Discussion

This is a meta-mechanism of Action Selection, as it affects the availability of Actions, rather than how they are selected. It may be used with any of the Action Selection mechanisms.

The newly available Actions can introduce new resources, offer better or more efficient options than the older Actions, and introduce completely new mechanics. *Agricola* does all three of these. After each round, a new Action card is added to the game board. Some of these introduce new resources, such as Cattle or Boar, some provide a larger quantity of a resource than previously available Action cards, and others introduce a completely new Action, such as Family Growth.

Adding available actions as the game progresses can help the designer control complexity. Early in the game, actions can be simple and limited, giving the players a chance to understand the system without being overwhelmed. As the game progresses, more complex actions and combos can be introduced. Good candidates for this approach are actions that are difficult or impossible to perform early in the game or are tactically inappropriate. This helps give players a positive first experience by preventing them from making poor early choices or pursuing the wrong goals.

In addition to controlling complexity, adding actions also gives a sense of forward momentum and narrative arc. New options are introduced to the players, giving the game a progressively more advanced feel as it goes. Adding spaces that grant more resources or that allow earlier actions to be performed more efficiently accelerates player progress and makes player turns more powerful.

The 18xx series of railroad games, such as *1830*, has a strong gating system that is a critical part of the player strategy. Trains must be bought in order of power. As train levels are exhausted, a variety of game effects are triggered. Upgraded and more powerful track tiles become available, and older trains disappear. Understanding and predicting the timing of these transitions is a critical skill in 18xx games and is one of the reasons they are unforgiving for new players as these transitions accelerate as the game progresses, so timing can be tricky.

Through the Ages has the players' progress through a variety of Age decks, with upgraded technologies, abilities, and leaders. As each deck is exhausted, players must discard cards from older Ages and increase their per-turn food upkeep costs. Like in *1830*, the timing and anticipation of these transitions become a skill for players to master. *SpaceCorp* also has three Ages (called Eras), but the transition is more extreme as each is played on a completely separate board, with only some advantages carrying over from one Era to the next.

Gating and unlocking is a useful mechanism for scaling power curves. This is particularly true in the context of cooperative game engines. For example, in *Forbidden Island*, the pace at which island tiles are flooded each turn is controlled by "Waters Rise" cards drawn from a deck of artifact cards. With each Waters Rise card drawn, a marker is advanced on a track. After a few track advances, the number of island tiles that get flooded each turn increases by one, accelerating the sinking of the island and the danger facing the players.

Pairing a player power unlock with a penalty or disadvantage is another common pattern for this mechanism. In *Zombie Teenz Evolution*, players can unlock character powers such as the ability to build a blockade or to reroll a die. However, on that character's turn, players must also roll an additional die that can summon more zombies onto the board. More generally, legacy games take the fullest advantage of gating and unlocking to introduce new powers, mechanisms, threats, opportunities, and narrative developments, whether during the course of a single game or in between sessions of the same campaign.

Sample Games

1830 (Tresham, 1986)

Agricola (Rosenberg, 2007)

The Expanse Board Game (Engelstein, 2017)

Lords of Waterdeep (Lee and Thompson, 2012)

Mechs vs. Minions (Cantrell, Ernst, Librande, Saraswat, and Tiras, 2016)

SpaceCorp: 2025-2300 AD (Butterfield, 2018)

Through the Ages: A Story of Civilization (Chvátil, 2006)

ACT-16 Tech Trees/Tech Tracks/Track Bonuses

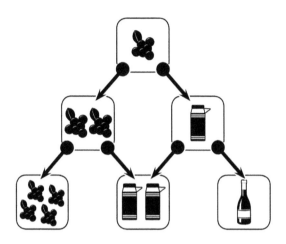

Description

During the course of the game, new Actions become available to specific players, or existing Actions are improved.

Discussion

This is similar in many ways to the meta-mechanism of Gating and Unlocking (ACT-15). New actions and abilities are introduced as the game progresses.

The differences in this mechanism are subtle but important. First, these new and upgraded Actions are typically only available to a single player. It is possible that multiple players can earn the same additional Action, but it needs to happen individually.

Some games allow other players to take advantage of another's personal Actions, either by paying the owning player some fee, obtaining the ability by force or trade, or by having the owner's monopoly on them expire after a number of turns, making them available to all.

These upgrades frequently do not make entirely new Actions available to a player. Instead, they make specific Actions more efficient or powerful.

Whereas Gated upgrades usually trigger on a timed or global schedule (as in *Agricola's* one new Action space per turn system) in a Tech system players need to accumulate and spend some resources in order to gain them. This can be a general currency, such as money, as in *Civilization*, or a specialized "research" currency as in *Eclipse* or *Through the Ages: A Story of Civilization*. There are games where techs are given out freely, although these still have an opportunity cost as players must forgo other choices.

Technologies do not have to be themed as research to use the mechanism. In many games, hiring people or building certain structures unlock new or advanced abilities. *Puerto Rico* is one of many examples of this. Growing, evolving, building, and training are other common metaphors for research.

Upgrades may have prerequisites that need to be satisfied or may be easier to obtain if you have an earlier tech. This results in a Tech Tree. For example, in *Stellar Conquest*, if you have researched Industrial Technology, it is less costly to then obtain Robotic Industry.

Tech Trees may also be expressed as Tracks. As players advance their markers along one or more tracks, they may pass certain spaces, which gives improved actions or abilities. *Orleans* and *Russian Railroads* both utilize this mechanism. There may also be physical markers placed along these tracks so that the first player to reach those spaces gains those markers and a special bonus. Other players will still receive bonuses printed on the track.

Tech Trees may be disguised thematically. In *Titan*, players recruit creatures into legions. The creatures that may be recruited into a legion depend on their current composition. Three Ogres may recruit a Troll, and three Trolls may recruit a Colossus. These creatures are more and more powerful, and some have special abilities such as flying (Illustration 3.8).

This type of system gives the designer fine-grained control over Actions available to players and gives a path to offer different strategic options, as players can choose which Actions and Abilities to invest in. Having a limited number of these Techs also forces player interaction and competition.

Sample Games

   Agricola (Rosenberg, 2007)
   Civilization (Tresham, 1980)
   Clash of Cultures (Marcussen, 2012)
   Eclipse (Tahkokallio, 2011)
   Kemet (Bariot and Montiage, 2012)

Orleans (Stockhausen, 2014)
Puerto Rico (Seyfarth, 2002)
Russian Railroads (Ohley and Orgler, 2013)
Stellar Conquest (Thompson, 1975)
Through the Ages: A Story of Civilization (Chvátil, 2006)
Titan (McAllister and Trampier, 1980)
Twilight Imperium (Petersen, 1997)

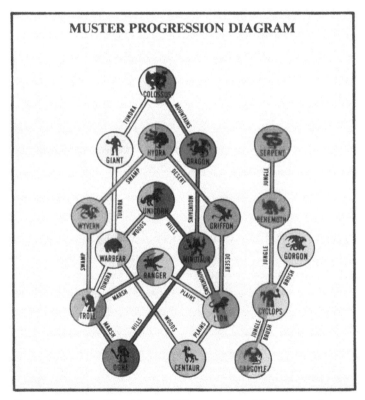

Illustration 3.8   The Muster Diagram from Titan, showing
which creatures may recruit other creatures. The creatures
at the bottom (Ogre, Centaur, Gargoyle) are the basic ones.
They may recruit creatures one level above them in the
terrain type shown. The separation of the Gargoyle–Serpent
tree from the other creatures creates interesting tactical and
strategic options for players.

ACT-17 Events

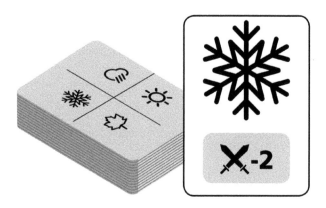

Description

Actions occur outside the control of players that cause an immediate effect, change the state of the game, or impact subsequent actions.

Discussion

Events can add variety and themes to a game. Many gamers' first exposure to events comes through *Monopoly*, in the form of Chance and Community Chest cards. These may immediately affect one or more players. This type of event is also found in *Empire Builder*, a railroad building game where cards may cause derailments, or floods wipe out tracks crossing rivers.

However, their usefulness is multiplied by affecting the overall game state for an extended period of time. Other events in *Empire Builder* may cause blizzards, which affect train movement near mountains, or storms that affect certain regions. This forces players to reevaluate their plans to try to avoid or take advantage of the changed circumstances. Sometimes this can be interesting for the players, but if it is too random and negative, it can feel punishing.

Events can also affect the global game state. In *Evo*, the overall temperature strongly impacts which dinosaurs will survive. Each turn, a die is rolled to determine how the temperature changes. The new environment affects all players. Similarly, in night missions in earlier editions of *Warhammer 40,000*, dice are rolled each turn to determine how far units can see.

Core Worlds: Galactic Orders delays the implementation of Events. Each round an Event is drawn, and all players can see what it is. However, it does not go into effect until the end of the round. This gives all players an opportunity to adjust to take advantage. Events in *Robinson Crusoe: Adventures on the Cursed Island* have an immediate effect and may further impact play unless the players resolve them in some way over several turns.

Terra Mystica gives players broader visibility to an Event of a sort—random scoring tiles. At the start of the game, tiles are placed that show what will give bonus points for each round. Players can see what is coming up and plan their strategy accordingly.

A delayed Event mechanism is used in *Through the Ages: A Story of Civilization*. In this game, players play Event cards into a stack that may, for example, give a bonus to the player with the strongest military. While the player who added that card to the stack knows it will be drawn in the future, the way that the events are played from stacks makes it very uncertain how many turns will elapse before it is drawn. While a player may have had the strongest military when they played the event into the stack, they may not by the time it is actually drawn.

Sample Games

Core Worlds: Galactic Orders (Parks, 2012)
Empire Builder (Bromley and Fawcett, 1982)
Evo (Keyaerts, 2001)
Monopoly (Darrow and Magie, 1933)
Robinson Crusoe: Adventures on the Cursed Island (Trewiczec, 2012)
Terra Mystica (Drögemüller and Ostertag, 2012)
Through the Ages: A Story of Civilization (Chvátil, 2006)
Warhammer 40,000 (Chambers, Johnson, Priestly, and Thorpe, 1993)

ACT-18 Narrative Choice

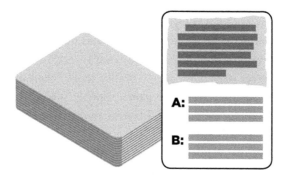

Description

Multiple action options are presented to the players via a narrative format.

Discussion

With the rise of *Dungeons & Dragons* in the 1970s, game designers looked for new ways to incorporate storytelling into game design. One of the earliest to do this was the late-1970s *Choose Your Own Adventure* book series, which began with *The Cave of Time*. In this series, at the end of short chapters, the reader would be presented with a series of choices, which would lead to other pages, and ultimately a good or bad conclusion.

This system has been adopted as part of more traditional tabletop games, with an early example being *Tales of the Arabian Nights*. In this game, after moving to a space, players are directed to read a numbered paragraph in a large book to reveal what adventure the character is experiencing. These vignettes offer choices of actions for the players, for example, "Bribe the Guard" or "Fight Your Way In." These lead to other numbered paragraphs, which give the result, and their impact on the game state.

Frequently, these systems use Stat Checks (RES-02) to determine the outcome. For example, if you choose to "Fight Your Way In," you may need to make a check against Strength or some other ability. You will proceed to different paragraphs depending on the outcome. Sometimes, not all the actions will be available to you unless you previously found some item or built up some stat to a sufficient level.

The strength of this mechanism is in the ability to bring a more structured narrative and flavor to the game, without the players needing to create a narrative from abstract game elements. However, the weakness of Narrative Choice systems is that the adventures they present can be disconnected from the main course of the game and thus can lack context. *Arabian Nights* ties the adventure to the player through the use of different environments (sea, desert, etc.) and player status (married, despondent, cursed) that impact the adventures. But the adventures themselves do not combine into a single coherent narrative.

Dead of Winter: A Crossroads Game attempts to deal with this contextual issue by the Crossroads mechanism. The player to the right of the active player draws a Crossroads card that applies to that turn. The card begins with an action trigger, such as entering a certain location, which is not revealed to the phasing player. If the player takes the trigger action, the Crossroads card-holder interrupts the action and presents the mini-adventure to the player. This means that the game designer can write an adventure knowing, for example, that it will specifically take place at a certain location. This mechanism has two different implementations that are worth noting. In the tabletop version, the Crossroads cards were written so that players were told what the outcome of each choice would be prior to making the choice. In a digital implementation, the outcome of each choice is hidden from the players. This is another example of input vs. output randomness, but in the context of making a meaningful narrative choice, hiding the mechanical, in-game outcomes creates a more character-driven experience.

Games such as *Ambush!* and *Action Castle* maintain narrative cohesion at the expense of replayability. In these games, players are presented with specific triggers or situations. For example, in *Ambush!*, moving into a specific space during a certain stage of the mission will always trigger the same paragraph to be read. *Action Castle* emulates computer adventure games and has players interact with the game via short phrases (such as "take sword"), but the same phrases will always work the same way in the same situation.

Other games strive to maintain cohesion by locking narrative choices so they only appear at specified times. In *Near and Far*, some of the narrative passages are tied to the game's campaign mode to preserve a more cohesive story. *Risk Legacy* uses a gating mechanism (see "ACT-15" in this chapter) to ensure that specific story beats are only revealed once players have progressed the campaign sufficiently to make the story fit.

Legacy of Dragonholt, a role-playing-style game, is built nearly entirely on the Narrative Choice mechanism. A tracker sheet for both the characters and the scenario allows for lots of stat-checking to determine progress. Scenarios often come with a map of areas to visit. Each area, when visited, will have different options open to the players based on a few factors. If you come to a store at night, the store will be closed. If you go to market on market day, there will be lots to explore. In addition to tracking time of day and day of the week, players also track when they complete specific story points, as instructed by the game book. These story points create a kind of memory for the system, so options presented to players may depend on their having marked a specific story point. If, for example, the innkeeper goes missing, the game will instruct players to mark, say, story point B7. Later options might direct players to read different texts if point B7 is marked, to ensure that there is story continuity and that the innkeeper who went missing isn't behind the bar the next morning. *Legacy of Dragonholt* shares more in common with pencil-and-paper interactive fiction books than with traditional tabletop board games, but it is an excellent example of how flexible the Narrative Choice mechanism can be.

Sample Games

Above and Below (Laukat, 2015)

Action Castle (Soren, 2009)

Ambush! (Butterfield and Smith, 1983)

The Cave of Time (Packard, 1979)

Choose Your Own Adventure: House of Danger (Uncredited, 2018)

Dead of Winter: A Crossroads Game (Gilmour and Vega, 2014)

Dungeons & Dragons (Arneson and Gygax, 1977)

Legacy of Dragonholt (Valens, Clark, Flanders, Mitsoda, and Spyridis, 2017)

Near and Far (Laukat, 2017)

Risk Legacy (Daviau and Dupuis, 2011)

Tales of the Arabian Nights (Freeman, Goldberg, Kaufman, Maroney, and Rolston, 1985)

ACT-19 Bingo

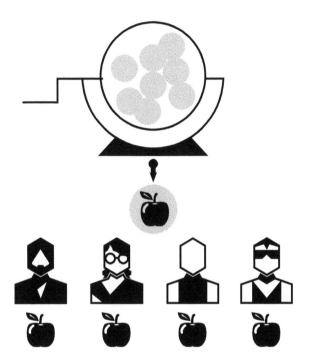

Description

Game elements are selected at random, and each player needs to use the elements for their own actions.

Discussion

This mechanism will be familiar to most players due to its use in the eponymous and popular Bingo. As such, it can be applied to a wide range of complexity levels, from low to high.

Bingo has the useful property of being able to take luck out of randomness. All the players are using the same sequence of random numbers, so if players are taking actions based on the random selection, it makes them perceive that there is less luck in the game. This typically is not strictly true, as players still must take risks based on a certain element being chosen in the future, but it still has this psychological effect.

A classic example that uses this mechanism is *Take It Easy*. In this game, each player has the same set of numbered hexagons, each of which has three colored lines on it. One player is designated as the "caller" and each turn draws one tile at random. They then announce the tile number to the other players, and each retrieves their copy and places it on their board. Players score based on making continuous lines of a single color. *Take It Easy* has no direct player interaction, but, because each player is using the same random sequence, there is a competition to see who will do better with that sequence.

This mechanism is at the heart of many "roll & write" games, where a dice roll or card flip is shared by all players, who then mark something on their player sheets. Examples of this include *Cartographers*, *Railroad Ink*, *Welcome To...*, and *Super-Skill Pinball*. Again, in these usages, the common random sequence somewhat reduces luck by giving all players the same random sequence, turning the random into the strategic.

As mentioned, both card (or tile) draws and dice rolls are used for this mechanism. Cards or tiles, unless shuffled frequently, will give a more strategic edge to the game, as players can make decisions based on a diminishing pool of possibilities. Dice, on the other hand, present the same possibilities at all points during the game. If the designer wishes to give more control with a dice-based Bingo game, they may consider luck mitigation systems such as special limited-use abilities to add or subtract from rolls, or to take specific "wild" results. Allowing players to earn these over the course of the game will give more of a sense of progress and narrative arc to the game.

On a high-level basis, Bingo systems are used in some tournament formats such as Duplicate Bridge. In Duplicate Bridge, each partnership in the tournament plays the same randomly generated deals. Using a Bingo mechanism in this case preserves the random nature of Bridge deals, while allowing partnerships to be compared to each other directly with how they performed with the same randomness.

Sample Games

Bingo (Unknown)
Cartographers (Adan, 2019)
Duplicate Bridge (Vanderbilt, 1908)
FITS (Knizia, 2009)
Railroad Ink (Hach and Silva, 2018)
Rise of Augustus (Mori, 2013)
Super Skill Pinball (Engelstein, 2020)
Take It Easy (Burley, 1983)

ACT-20 Layering

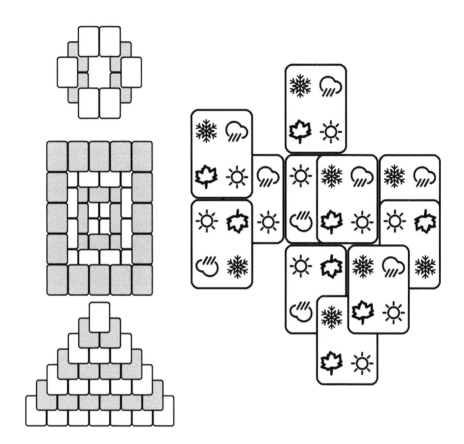

Description

Components are placed above other components and can overlap in various ways. Only the topmost visible icons/areas are active.

Discussion

This mechanism is usually implemented with cards, because they afford easy stacking. To organize the layering, the cards are laid out with grids. *Patchistory* and *Circle the Wagons*, for example, use a 4×4 grid.

As cards are added to a player's tableau, they may overlay cards that were played previously. Some games have specific rules about overlap—such as at least two squares must be overlaid—while others are more freeform.

The rules for overlapping are typically driven by how the visible icons are used. In *Patchistory*, for example, the icons give you resources or actions. The most efficient way to build would be to not overlap at all, as that will leave the most visible icons. Therefore, there is a rule that you must overlap, with certain rules about overlapping (e.g., water squares may not be built on) and maximum grid size that create interesting decisions for the players.

In *Circle the Wagons*, the player scores by having contiguous groups of the same color, so just sprawling outwards is rarely the best play. By cleverly overlapping the cards, players can form large groups. Therefore, there are very few rules governing how cards can be placed.

While cards to be placed are usually the same size, sometimes they are not. *Smartphone Inc.* has players overlap two 2×3 grids of icons (cleverly themed to look like apps on a phone screen) to determine which actions they will perform. Some icons, such as raise or lower prices, cancel each other, so careful orientation is important. During the game, players may earn Improvements, which are small extra tiles with a 1×2 grid of icons that can be placed over the main grids. This gives the players more flexibility and an upgrade path, while preserving the central nature of the main grids (Illustration 3.9).

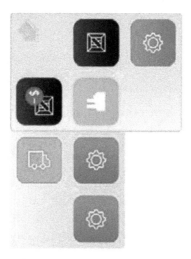

Illustration 3.9   A sample action configuration formed by overlaying two cards in *Smartphone, Inc.* The visible icons are executed.

The layering mechanism, tile placement, and jigsaw puzzles appeal in similar ways. All have a spatial element that involves twisting and matching up pieces, and all give the players the feeling that there is an answer and a "best" placement. However, layering is typically more complex than tile placement, as there are more options for placement, and the overlapping can be more challenging to visualize than, for example, the edge matching in most tile games, such as *Carcassonne*.

The physical implementation of this mechanism requires careful consideration. Cards are typically best because they are easiest to stack in uneven and irregular patterns and are unlikely to become unbalanced and topple over. However, even cards have a thickness, and the stacked tableau can get messy. Cards can slide and shift once the stack goes above three or four cards deep. Thicker cards or tiles will have even more of an issue as they are stacked.

The sample games discussed so far are about building up the layers as the game progresses. However, a game can start with layers already built, and gameplay then proceeds with removing cards. There are many traditional solitaire games, such as *Klondike* (Patience) and *Pyramid*, that start with the cards layered on top of each other. The player is only allowed to remove cards that have no other cards covering them.

This mechanism is also used in *7 Wonders Duel*, where the cards are laid out in a pyramid, and *Dragon Castle*, which has Mahjong-style tiles placed in a stack, with only the top-most ones available for play. In this implementation, layering limits the Actions available to players. Where the tableau is shared, it also presents a level of interaction, as removing an item will uncover other items for your opponents.

Another expression of this system uses transparent cards so that icons on earlier cards are still visible and have an effect. *Gloom* and *Mystic Vale* are examples of this technique.

Unlike the earlier games discussed, transparent cards are typically layered exactly on top of each other, not rotated or staggered. Icons are placed strategically at specific locations so newly placed cards can cover or leave revealed certain symbols.

In *Mystic Vale*, these transparent cards are placed into plastic sleeves, to combine into a single playable card. They are "constructible" in that players can choose how to combine the transparent elements to form very powerful single cards. The horror game *Hecatomb* has pentagonal creature cards with transparent edges. Players stack the cards to create hybrid Abominations that combine powers.

In *Gloom*, players try to make their own characters as unhappy as possible, while cheering up those of their opponents. The transparent cards can be used to cover up undesirable icons while leaving desirable ones behind. Cards are not removed, so the stack of cards can be looked at after the game, as they preserve a history of that character's life. This meshes nicely with the game's intended experience of having players generate stories about these characters and their odd lives.

Transparent cards are more expensive to produce and the printing on them is not as bright. Care has to be taken to ensure visibility through whatever stack depth is required for your game.

Splaying is a subset of Layering. In Splaying, cards are typically arranged so that one side of a lower card pokes out of the side of a card above it, revealing icons along that edge. This can give the player a choice of which edge they wish to have exposed (related to CAR-08 Multi-Use Cards), or the main power of the lower card (located in the center) is covered up, leaving a residual power along the edge.

Innovation cards have icons on three edges, and deciding which to splay out is a key strategy. Similarly, the letter cards in *Paperback Adventures* have symbols on both right and left sides, and when spelling and playing a word, the player needs to decide whether to splay to the left or right, gaining the effect of the revealed icons. In *...and then, we held hands*, players must re-splay their entire tableau to match their position on the board: if they are on the left side of the board, they may only see and use the left side of their tableau and vice-versa. In *Lotus*, cards are splayed in sets to look like flowers, which achieves a beautiful visual effect, albeit without any gameplay effects.

A distantly related implementation of this mechanism can be found in the game *Fold-It*. Each player has a cloth with a 4×4 grid of food items on each side. A target card is flipped, which shows three or four food icons. Players must then race to fold their clothes along the grid lines to be able to only have those exact icons showing. The players, in essence, are using folding to create layers that hide the icons they do not want to show.

Sample Games

...and then, we held hands (Chircop and Massa, 2015)
7 Wonders Duel (Bauza and Cathala, 2015)
Circle the Wagons (Aramini, Devine, Kluka, 2017)
Dragon Castle (Hach, Ricci, Silva, 2017)
Fold-it (Goh, 2016)

Gloom (Baker, 2005)
Hecatomb (Elliott and Tweet, 2005)
Innovation (Chudyk, 2010)
Klondike Solitaire (Unknown, 1783)
Lotus (Goddard and Goddard, 2016)
Mystic Vale (Clair, 2016)
Paperback Adventures (Fowers, Larsen, 2022)
Patchistory (Jung and Kim, 2013)
Pyramid Solitaire (Unknown)
Smart Phone, Inc. (Lashin, 2018)

ACT-21 Slide/Push

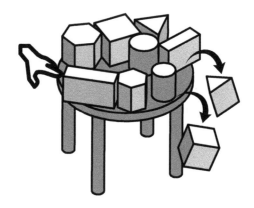

Definition

Players slide a token, and other tokens ahead of it are pushed.

Discussion

Slide/Push can be broadly broken up into two main categories: quantized and freeform. Quantized slides have the pieces move to specific locations, while freeform allows the pieces to move anywhere on the play surface.

The classic abstract *Abalone* is a good example of a quantized slide mechanism. Marbles are placed onto a hexagonal grid, and a turn consists of pushing a marble in a chosen direction. The marble will push other marbles ahead of it. Marbles always settle into specific grooves, marking a delimited play area with a set number of spaces.

Another example of quantized sliding is *Masters of Renaissance: Lorenzo il Magnifico – The Card Game* (quite the game name!), which has a 4×3 tray grid where differently colored marbles are placed. Each turn, the active player selects a row or column and gains resources based on the colors. They then take a spare marble and push it in the chosen row or column, changing the configuration for the next player. The player needs to consider not just what they want but also the position it will leave for the next player.

There are several gameplay considerations for slide mechanisms. The first we will look at is the number of pushing axes that are used.

Being on a hexagonal grid, *Abalone* has three axes of slide movement. *Masters of Renaissance*, sliding on a rectangular grid, has two axes of slide movement. There are also games that have a single axis of slide movement, with pieces pushing in a line, almost as a queue. An example of this is *Panamax*, which is about transiting the Panama Canal. In this game, players control container ships attempting to move through the canal. In the narrow canal zones, ships may not pass each other. Therefore, when a ship at the back of the line is moved, it also moves the ships ahead of it. Positioning your ships so that other players will move them for you by pushing their ships behind yours is a key strategy.

In general, increasing the number of axes increases player options. This can make decision-making more complex and adds to the weight of the game.

These three examples also illustrate very different features that Slide/Push can bring to player interaction. In *Abalone*, the players may push in a variety of directions and can become intricately entangled. The goal is to push the opponent's marbles off the edge, so keeping marbles in the center of the board is important, and in general, tactical placement considerations are paramount.

In *Masters of Renaissance*, the player interaction is indirect, and each time the grid is pushed, a marble will fall off and be recycled. The removal of a marble is very transient—it will be reintroduced into the grid the next turn. This creates a lower-key interaction than *Abalone*, as it is not the player's pieces that are being slid. The mechanism creates a constrained way for players to impact resource collection. A similar approach can be found in *Ulm*, where players slide action tiles into a 3×3 grid and take all three actions in the row or column they pushed into, including the tile they added. The tile that is pushed out of the grid does not activate.

Finally, the player interaction in *Panamax* is progressive in that it pushes another player's ship forward, which is always beneficial to that player and helps the ship progress towards scoring by providing it a free move. This interaction gives *Panamax* a bit of a taste of playing "Chicken," as players try to make their opponents' actions benefit them too. In *Abalone*, by contrast, sliding is never intended to benefit the other player, and making such a move is a blunder. Note, however, that this is a function of the zero-sum nature of a two-player game, rather than an inherent characteristic of the mechanism.

A key design decision that impacts the nature of the slide mechanism significantly is what happens to pieces that are pushed off the grid. Often, these pieces are eliminated or scored. However, it is possible to reintroduce them back into the grid immediately into the now-vacated position (a wrap-around effect) or on a future turn. In *Ulm*, for example, players can collect these tokens and reintroduce them to the grid later or spend them for other benefits as part of a different subsystem in the game's economy.

Freeform Slide does not have a specific grid where pieces move. Instead, there is an open surface where pieces can be pushed, collide, and react in a freeform way. Many bear a similarity to the arcade "penny pusher" machines, where a coin or token is dropped onto a surface and a mechanical arm pushes them forward, and the player keeps any coins that get pushed off the edge.

An early example of this is *Niagara*. In this game, the player's canoes are placed on acrylic disks onto a "river" track with raised sides. As more disks are added, the canoes move closer to the waterfall at the edge of the track and eventually will fall off. More recent examples are *Kabuto Sumo* and *Redcap Ruckus*, where disks of various sizes are pushed onto a raised platform. Players are attempting to knock their opponent's disks off the platform.

Another is *Via Appia*, where players push disks of different sizes into a quarry. They then gain resources based on the disks that fall off the edge.

A key design feature of these games is to introduce uncertainty into the pushing. You cannot be sure what is going to fall off the edge, and this can lead to a lot of excitement and surprising situations. The figure showing *Via Appia* illustrates this nicely. Note that the sides of the quarry flare outwards as they near the edge of the platform. This adds a healthy dose of uncertainty to what will fall off, far more than a straight chute would provide (Illustration 3.10).

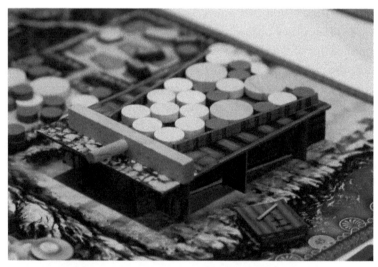

Illustration 3.10   The Quarry in *Via Appia*. Players insert a disk into the narrow end and get all disks that fall out the wide end. The angled sides make the outcome less predictable. Photo by Daniel Danzer.

The designer needs to take care to create physics that emphasize these features. Having pieces of various sizes, shapes, and weights; having uneven or curved edges; and constraining how players introduce new pieces onto the platform (e.g., with pushing sticks, at certain entry points) will all help to enhance the uncertainty. Physical prototyping will be more important than usual with this style of Slide/Push.

Sample Games

Quantized

Abalone (Lalet, Levi, 1987)
Black Angel (Dujardin, Georges, Orban, 2019)
Masters of Renaissance: Lorenzo il Magnifico – The Card Game (Luciani, Mangone, 2019)
Panamax (d'Orey, Sentiero, Soledade, 2014)
Ulm (Burkhardt, 2016)

Freeform

Kabuto Sumo (Miller, 2021)
Niagra (Liesching, 2004)
Redcap Ruckus (Ude, 2021)
Via Appia (Feldkötter, 2013)

ACT-22 Matching

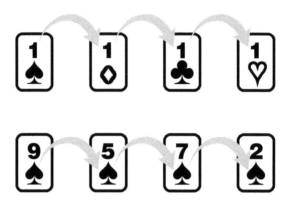

Description

A player is limited to playing a card or token that matches some feature on the card or the token played just prior. In some instances, several cards or tokens from previous plays will be visible and available to match against.

Discussion

The purest implementation of this mechanism, and the one that many players encounter very early in their lives, is in *Crazy Eights* and *Uno*. Play proceeds around a circle, and each player must play a card into the discard pile that matches either the value or color/suit of the card currently on top. Another example that may be familiar from childhood is *Dominoes*, in which players match numbers, rather than suits, and each tile features two values, one on each side, to facilitate matching. The simplicity of determining which plays are valid makes this an ideal mechanism for a lower-complexity game or for a subsystem in a high-complexity game.

Games that feature matching as the core mechanism are often shedding games, where the objective is for a player to get rid of all their cards.

The key design criterion that drives this mechanism, and makes it interesting, is to have multiple axes of matching or to make a single card have multiple matching opportunities. These axes can be thought of as tracks or paths that a player can use to play. *Crazy Eights* has two tracks—the suit track and the value track. The suit track is much larger—13 cards on 4 tracks, while the value track is the opposite—4 cards on 13 tracks. These intersect to give players different paths to navigate through the hands to discard all cards.

The designer needs to balance the number of crossing points at the different tracks and the size of each. Too many, and there will be little challenge in finding a match. Too few, and the game will lock, and many turns may be spent drawing cards or whatever the mechanism is to "unjam" the system.

Matching can also be used as a subsystem or for bonuses on matches. Trick taking (CAR-01) is a matching mechanism, as players are restricted to following suit if possible. In *Nightfall*, cards have linking colors. Effect cards can be played in a chain, with each one linking to a color in the chain. After no more cards are added to the chain, the cards are resolved. Playing cards in chains is a key tactic in the game, as it allows for combo effects.

This linking concept is used in the road game *Geography*, where players take turns naming a place, but it must begin with the last letter of the previous player's place. Players are not allowed to duplicate an answer already given, and the play continues until a player cannot come up with an answer. This game underscores the fundamental nature of this mechanism—restricting the domain of possible actions, hopefully to the one in which your opponent cannot.

The game *We the People* uses matching as a combat resolution mechanism. At the start of each battle, players draw cards that show tactics. The attacker leads, and the defender must match the tactic played by the attacker or lose the battle. The defender may then attempt to seize the initiative and lead the next card, or else the attacker does.

The definition of "matching" can also be extended to a category or rule, with interesting results. For example, in the difficult-to-internet-search-for game *The Game*, players play cards to pile some of which must have higher cards played on them, and some of which require lower cards. The "match" space shrinks during the course of the round, giving a narrative arc.

Many tile games, such as *Carcassonne*, require players to match sides to place tiles. These are discussed in SET-02, Tile Laying.

Finally, some games require the players not to match but react to matches. This mechanism is most often found in speed games, such as *Snorta!* and *Jungle Speed*. In these games, players take turns flipping the top card of their personal draw piles. If the card flipped matches one showing for another player, the players involved must be the first to react. In *Jungle Speed*, players need to be the first to grab a wooden totem in the center of the table. In

Snorta! each player has an assigned animal, and players must make the animal noise of the player they matched.

Several party games use a match, or sometimes anything-but-a-match mechanism. Some games leverage the Stroop Effect, including the eponymous *Stroop*. The Stroop Effect refers to the way our mental gears lock up when a word's visual presentation differs from its meaning, e.g., the word "green" written in red text. In *Stroop*, players must play a word that visually looks like the textual definition on the previous card. *Cockroach Salad* has players playing salad ingredients, naming the cards as they play them. However, if a player matches the same card as played just previously, they must "lie" and claim the card being played is something else. Similarly, if a player plays a card that matches the claim of a previous player, even if it does not match the card just played (e.g., in the case where the previous player lied), they must lie too. These party games work because they subvert our expectations, both psychological and ludological, about how matching typically works.

Sample Games

Carcassonne (Wrede, 2000)
Cockroach Salad (Zeimet, 2007)
Crazy Eights (unknown)
Dominoes (unknown)
The Game (Benndorf, 2015)
Geography (unknown)
Jungle Speed (Vuarchex, Yakovenko, 1997)
Nightfall (Gregg, 2011)
Snorta! (Childs, Richardson, 2004)
Stroop (Chaffer, 2017)
Uno (Robbins, 1971)
We the People (Herman, 1993)

ACT-23 Drawing

Definition

Players draw a picture and other players guess what the picture is intended to depict.

Discussion

The classic example of this mechanism is *Pictionary*. In *Pictionary*, players play in teams. One person on a team draws a picture to get their teammates to guess a word or phrase.

Note that we are using the term "drawing" here to imply some type of representation. There are games where you draw lines such as the classic paper and pencil game *Dots & Boxes*, or more recent games such as *Doodle Quest* and *VOC*. These are not included in this mechanism. However, we do intend to include games in which representation is created through collage or assembly of shapes and icons, such as in *Concept* or *Show & Tile*.

A key objective for most designs in this category is to level the playing field in terms of artistic talent. Many games use time pressure to achieve this. Some, such as *Pictionary*, achieve this through an actual timer. Others pit players against each other to create a sense of urgency. *Pictionary* also includes this mode ("All Play"), as well as *Pictomania*. In *Pictomania*, all players draw and guess what other players are drawing at the same time. When a player is done with both drawing and guessing, they grab a bonus token from the center of the table. When the last token is taken, the round ends immediately. Since there are fewer tokens than players, that forces a sense of urgency.

Another way to limit the utility of artistic talent is to use a Targeted Clues (RES-17). In this mechanism, the person drawing wants some but not all players to be able to guess. If the drawing is too good, it is a disadvantage. An example of a drawing game that uses this mechanism is *A Fake Artist Goes to New York*. In this game, one player is the Question Master, who secretly gives the same word to each player except for one, who is the Fake Artist. Players then take turns adding lines to a drawing to try to let the other "real" artists know that they know the target word. At the end of the round, the artists vote on who the Fake Artist was. If they are correct, they win—maybe. If they out the Fake Artist, then the Fake Artist has the opportunity to guess what the secret word was. If they are correct, they win anyway. As a result, players who know the word need to make a drawing that gives a hint of the target word but without being too obvious.

This concept can be extended beyond drawing by giving players other things to combine to represent the target. This levels the playing field by giving all players the same limited tool set to work with. In *Show & Tile*, players receive tangram tiles and have a set amount of time to create a shape that will help players guess a specific word. There are many other variations on this idea:

- *Squint* gives players cards with various lines and squiggles on them.
- *Pantone: The Game* gives players access to identically sized rectangular cards but in a rainbow of colors.
- *Imagine* uses transparent cards that have icons on them that players can overlay in various ways.
- *Concept* goes a step further and has a board with a variety of icons that players can indicate in different ways.

All of these are specific implementations of Action Selection Restrictions (ACT-11) and Communication Limits (UNC-06).

Sample Games

Concept (Beaujannot, Rivollet, 2013)
A Fake Artist Goes to New York (Sasaki, 2012)
Imagine (Fujita, Nakashima, Ohki, Oikawa, 2015)
Pantone: The Game (Rogers, 2018)
Pictionary (Angel, 1985)
Pictomania (Chvátil, 2011)
Show & Tile (Loomis and Shalev, 2018)
Squint (Boss, 2002)
Telestrations (Uncredited, 2009)

4

Resolution

In Chapter 3, we discussed Actions and the different ways that players can choose or plan Actions. Sometimes, the outcome of an Action is specific and definite. No chance is involved. For example, in *Chess*, if you take the Action of moving your knight, it will happen exactly as you plan.

However, some Actions have uncertain outcomes. Some are related to performative uncertainty, as in a dexterity game, where you may not succeed in performing your planned action. Others relate to chance interfering with your plans, which we call Output Randomness (see Chapter 6). For example, in *Risk*, you may declare an attack on Kamchatka (the Action), but the result of that Action is not known when it is declared. You may win without losing a single army, lose all your armies, or some result in between.

Because Output Randomness is most often associated with conflict, many of the examples here are from war or battle games. However, there are plenty of Actions that require some form of resolution, such as trying to sell at a market, finding a hidden object, upgrading a technology, or approving a budget in a political-economic game. This chapter discusses different ways of determining the outcomes of Actions.

RES-01 High Number

Description

Each player is represented by a numeric "strength," and the higher strength wins the conflict.

Discussion

This is a basic and common way of resolving conflicts. The base strength can be represented by a fixed value for the piece, as in *Magic: The Gathering*, or by the position on the board, as in *Cosmic Encounter*, where each defending token adds 1 to the total defender strength. Sometimes, strengths may be determined randomly. In *War*, players flip cards to compare strengths. Many games include a "roll-off" mechanism, where each player rolls a die and the high roll wins the contest.

Frequently, base strength can be modified by some factor. In *Magic: The Gathering*, there are a variety of cards that impact the Power and Toughness of creatures (comparable to an Attack and Defense strength). In *Cosmic Encounter*, each player secretly plays a number card which is added to the number of tokens on their side, including allies.

Modifiers need to be carefully considered by the designer. Their inclusion increases the complexity of the resolution, particularly if they come from multiple sources. For example, a game may grant the defenders a +2 modifier because they are defending in the mountains and a –1 modifier because they are infantry defending against artillery. While the math seems simple, having a long list of modifiers for the players to apply can be burdensome. It is better to have these factored into intrinsic strengths, or through card play or dice pools whose outcomes model the probabilities desired.

The dungeon-crawler *Descent: Journeys in the Dark* uses a High Number mechanism combined with a Dice Pool. The characters, weapons, and situation add or remove dice from the attacker's and defender's pools. They then each roll their dice and count hits (for the attacker) or shields (for the defender). The higher number prevails. If the hits exceed the shields, the defender takes damage based on the difference.

This attrition-style mechanism, where damage is based on the delta between the final strengths, is common. A less common alternative is Winner Takes All, where the losing side is completely eliminated at no cost to the winner. The game *4000 AD* implements this mechanism, which can lead to tension and wide swings, as a 10-strength fleet will completely eliminate both a 1- and a 9-strength fleet at no loss to itself. The lack of realism can impact theme and immersion.

An Ordered High Number system is used in the *Risk* series of games. In these games, Attacker and Defender typically roll multiple dice. The highest roll of the Attacker is compared to the highest of the Defender, second-highest Attacker roll to second-highest Defender roll, etc. Because of the simultaneous ordering of the rolls from highest to lowest, this system has lower variance than just making N independent rolls. It also offers a much simpler way to give an advantage to the player with greater numbers without resorting to modifiers. If a player has a 3:1 numerical advantage, they simply roll three dice versus the opponent's one, which is much simpler than gaining modifiers to the die roll.

An interesting twist on this system is to switch whether the high or low number is the winner within the same game. For example, in *Battleball*, a simulation of futuristic football, players are represented by dice of different sides—six-sided, eight-sided, twelve-sided, or twenty-sided. When moving, rolling higher is better. High rolls allow a player to move farther. The D20 wide receivers are great at dashing down the field. The D6 linesmen are much less mobile. But when trying to tackle, both players roll their die against each other, but now, the low number wins. So, linesmen will usually tackle wide receivers. However, this system leaves open the possibility for surprises in both running and tackling.

In numeric comparison systems, some means to deal with ties need to be included. In combat simulations, these ties typically are awarded to the defender; however, any tie-breaking mechanism can be used.

High Number and Stat Check mechanisms can be combined for a more nuanced mechanism. See the Stat Check section for more details.

Sample Games

> *4000 AD* (Doherty, 1972)
> *Battleball* (Baker, 2003)
> *Cosmic Encounter* (Eberle, Kittredge, Norton, and Olatka, 1977)
> *Descent: Journeys in the Dark* (Wilson, 2005)
> *Magic: The Gathering* (Garfield, 1993)
> *Risk* (Lamorisse and Levin, 1959)
> *War* (Unknown)

RES-02 Stat Check

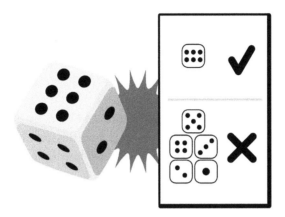

Description

There is a target number required to succeed at some tests. A random number is generated (by card draw, die roll, etc.), which is compared to the target. If it meets or exceeds the target, the action succeeds.

Discussion

This mechanism goes by a variety of names, including Task Check, Skill Check, and others. It is commonly used in role-playing games, such as *Dungeons & Dragons*, where a player makes a roll against a stat or target number. Typically, if it is lower than the target, the action succeeds.

Stat Check is frequently used in battle games, like *Axis & Allies*, where each type of unit has a target number that it is trying to meet or exceed to score a hit. *Warhammer* uses a similar system with six-sided dice and rates units as, for example, 2+, 3+, or 4+, if it needs to roll a 2 or higher, 3 or higher, or 4 or higher. The group of minis (or single mini) is then rated for how many dice it gets to roll. One attack may be rolling 8 dice for a 4+ and another might be 5 dice for a 3+. Target numbers may be modified based on characteristics of the defender, such as terrain or special armor, but the rolls are typically not opposed by the defender, as in the High Number Mechanism. The defender may get to respond but as a separate check. For example, in *Warhammer*, defending figures may be able to cancel hits by making a Saving Roll of 3+. Performing a series of Stat Checks not only lengthens the game but also increases tension and can simplify the rules as modifiers and other effects are localized.

Some games keep the target number the same but differentiate units by the type of dice rolled. For example, in the 1986 *Fortress America*, the target number is always a "5" or greater. But some units roll a six-sided die, some an eight-sided die, and others a ten-sided die. This makes it easier for the player to perform combat, as there is only one target number to remember.

In the 2012 reprint, this was simplified further by simply having "hit" or "miss" symbols on the relevant dice, so only two sides of the six-sided die have the Hit symbol, but four sides of the eight-sided die do. While this system was a visual improvement, it was more opaque as to the strengths of the dice. Players would have to examine all sides of the dice and memorize their odds, which was fiddlier than with the target number system.

Some games combine a Stat Check with a High Score system. One example is the miniatures game *Infinity*. The *Infinity* mechanism has each player trying to roll below their stat using a 20-sided die but higher than their opponent. For example, let's say two units are shooting at each other and one has a skill of 17 and the other a skill of 12. First, a player is only eligible to hit if they roll less than or equal to their target. If only one player succeeds on the Stat Check, that player hits their opponent. If both miss, then there is no effect. If both hit, then the player with the higher roll (but still below the target) succeeds and the other fails. Combining systems like this gives a compact and fluid method for a variety of results.

Stat Checks can incorporate modifiers. The same considerations that are discussed in High Number apply here.

Sample Games

Axis & Allies (Harris, Jr., 1981)
Dungeons & Dragons (Arneson and Gygax, 1977)
Europe Engulfed (Evans and Young, 2003)
Fortress America (Uncredited, 1986)
Infinity (Rodriguez, 2005)
Nexus Ops (Cantino and Kimball, 2005)
Titan (McAllister and Trampier, 1980)
Warhammer Age of Sigmar (Uncredited, 2015)

RES-03 Critical Hits and Failures

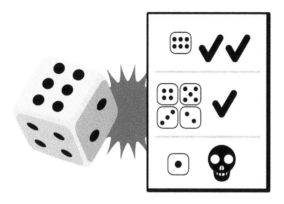

Description

Dice are rolled, and those exceeding a target number generate success. Certain rolls (typically the highest and/or lowest on the die) generate additional success or extreme failure.

Discussion

Critical Hits (and Critical Failures) add variance to a resolution system, in essence lengthening the "tail" of the result distribution. They also add excitement by creating jackpot effects, similar to a slot machine. You have a pretty good idea of what the result range may be, but Critical Hits and Failures, depending on implementation, can give bonuses that make success possible where it normally might not be or add tension to an overwhelming attack.

In its standard implementation, Critical Hits double the damage of an attack or improve the result in other ways. However, there are several novel uses of Critical results.

Uncharted Seas and *Dystopian Wars*, miniatures games from Spartan Games, have an "exploding dice" critical system. In this system, players roll a number of 6-sided dice and get a success on a 4 or higher. On a roll of a 6, however, the player gets 2 successes and also gets to reroll those dice. Additional 6s on the rerolls will yield additional double successes and more rerolls. In this system, it is theoretically possible to get any number of hits on any attack, which can make for dramatic moments as dice are rolled and rerolled, and successes accumulate.

Warmachine/Hordes allows for a critical hit any time at least two dice in an attack show the same result. Normally an attack is made with two dice, but this number may be increased or decreased, naturally changing the frequency of critical hits or removing their possibility (as in the case of a one-die attack) without any additional rules overhead.

Advanced Squad Leader generates extra effects (both positive and negative) on rolls of 2 or 12 on two 6-sided dice. A 2 causes a Heat of Battle effect, which may cause a hero to emerge, a unit to upgrade, or the squad to go berserk and charge the enemy; a 12 may cause weapons to break or other negative results, resolved by rolling on a separate chart (RES-04). These add a lot of variety to combat results and force players to adapt to changing circumstances.

Several games convert special symbols or excess successes (if rolling against a target) into a type of currency that can be spent on various beneficial effects. Sometimes called Surges, these can also give a lot of tools to the player to use tactically, beyond simply resolving the combat. The miniatures game *Malifaux* adapts this by using a card-flipping system to generate random combat strengths but allowing special abilities to trigger if the correct suit flips.

Sample Games

Advanced Squad Leader (Greenwood, 1985)
Dungeons & Dragons (Arneson and Gygax, 1977)
Dystopian Wars (Fawcett, Flack, Glover, Padfield, Sammarco, and Sinclair, 2010)
Malifaux (Caroland, Johns, and Weber, 2009)
Uncharted Seas (Fawcett and Sims, 2008)
Warmachine/Hordes (McVey, Snoddy, and Wilson, 2003)

RES-04 Ratio/Combat Results Table

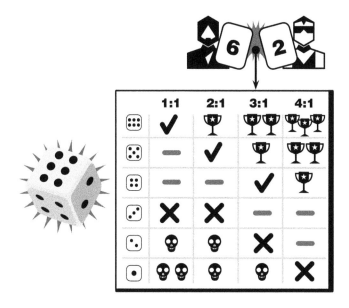

Description

The Attacker and Defender each total their strength. This is then expressed as a ratio and is used to index into a Combat Results Table (CRT). A dice roll then determines the result of the conflict.

Discussion

Pioneered in the earliest war games, the CRT has become a staple of the genre. CRTs are typically indexed by calculating the ratio of the attacker's strength to the defender's. For example, if the attacker has a strength of 8, and the defender has a strength of 4, the 2:1 column would be used, as 8 is 2 times 4. Typically, these are rounded down in favor of the defender, so a 9–4 attack would also be resolved on the 2:1 column (Illustration 4.1).

Once the correct column is determined, a die is rolled to determine the final result. In war games, this is typically some combination of force eliminations, damage, or retreats.

The use of the CRT gives the designer a lot of control over potential results. It is possible to have a tightly grouped range of outcomes from one to six or a wild variation. In addition, the designer has many hooks to apply

COMBAT RESULTS TABLE

DIE ROLL	COMBAT ODDS:						DIE ROLL
	1-1	2-1	3-1	4-1	5-1	6-1	
0	AE	AA	AA	AD	BD	BD	0
1	AA	AA	AD	BD	BD	DD	1
2	AD	AD	BD	BD	DD	DX	2
3	BD	BD	BD	DD	DX	DE	3
4	BD	BD	DD	DX	DE	DE	4
5	DD	DD	DX	DE	DE	DE	5
6	DX	DX	DE	DE	DE	DE	6

Explanation: AE = Attacker Eliminated, AA = Attacker Attrition, AD = Attacker Demoralized, BD = Both Demoralized, DD = Defender Demoralized, DX = Defender Exchange, DE = Defender Eliminated (see Rule 13.4).

Illustration 4.1   Combat Results Table from *The Guns of August*. The modified die roll is cross-indexed with the Combat Odds.

other effects. For example, the attacker or defender strength can be modified, the final die roll can be modified, or the column used can be shifted left or right. This flexibility has led to its continued popularity in the war-gaming community.

Designs have taken the CRT in a wide variety of directions. *Squad Leader* eschews strength ratios and simply has the column chosen by the firepower of the attacker. It also includes a mechanism called Cowering, where if doubles are rolled (two dice are rolled in *Squad Leader*), the column used is shifted one to the left, to a weaker column. Elite troops are typically immune to Cowering. This is a good example of the opportunities CRTs offer to differentiate and apply various effects.

Some games have the column selected by a differential between Attacker and Defender rather than a ratio. This has the benefit of simplicity, as division can be confusing when the strengths get large. Differentials are less realistic, however, as they will treat a 10–8 attack the same as a 3–1 attack. But, if the values are bounded within a reasonable range, differential CRTs can give a lighter feel.

Some games use charts with various conditions as columns to resolve Actions and random events. *Down with the King* has charts that players roll on to determine the result. For example, there are separate charts for Gambling, Seducing, and Carousing. The solitaire game *B-17: Queen of the*

Skies includes charts for damage from German fighters, bombing accuracy, and the result of crew member injuries.

While charts can encapsulate a large amount of information and give a lot of flexibility to the designer, they can be intimidating to players and tedious to use and are considered old-fashioned. However, in the right situations, they can be quite useful.

Sample Games

    B-17: Queen of the Skies (Frank and Shelley, 1981)
    Down with the King (Rahman and Rahman, 1981)
    France 1944: The Allied Crusade in Europe (Herman, 1986)
    The Guns of August (Beyma and Davis, 1981)
    Gettysburg (Roberts, 1958)
    Squad Leader (Hill, 1977)

RES-05 Die Icons

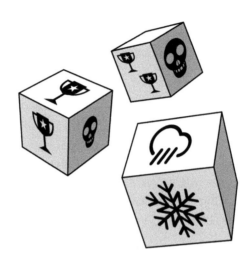

Description

The player rolls dice, and any die showing the target icon is a success.

Discussion

This mechanism is typically a subset of High Number (RES-01) or Stat Check (RES-02), as the number of successes ultimately reduces to one of these. However, we are listing this as a separate mechanism due to some subtleties in the implementation and player interaction.

The use of Die Icons has several advantages over traditional dice with numbers on the sides. First, using an icon makes it simpler for players to interpret the result, if they are properly chosen. Counting icons is inherently simpler from a cognitive perspective than adding numbers or checking to see if numbers on dice exceed certain values. This ease increases as the number of dice rolled increases and is particularly true if the target value may vary depending on the game situation. In this case, icons are easier to parse at a glance, especially if they are thematic.

For example, contrast *Warhammer* with *Memoir '44*. In *Warhammer*, a player may roll 4 dice for an attack, looking for a 5 or higher for a success (a 5+, in the parlance). After rolling, the player needs to look at the dice, remembering the target number. *Memoir '44*, like *Warhammer*, bases the number of dice rolled on the type of the attacking unit. The icon that counts as a hit is based on what is being targeted. When attacking an Infantry, each Infantry symbol counts as a hit. When attacking Armor, each Armor symbol counts as a hit. In addition, the grenade icon always counts as an additional hit. Since there are two infantry icons, one armor icon, and one grenade icon on a die, an attack on infantry is equivalent to a 4+ and an attack on armor a 5+. But the player does not need to have a chart of those numbers or track them in any way. It is intuitively obvious to look for the icons of what you are attacking and just count them up. Advanced players can understand the symbol distribution, but it is not necessary. The die does the heavy lifting.

The distribution of icons also gives the designer fine-grained control over possible combat outcomes and allows for multiple effects to be determined. The *Memoir '44* dice also include a Retreat icon, which applies in conjunction with the removal effects, allowing for a wide variety of outcomes (Illustration 4.2).

Illustration 4.2 The dice from *Memoir '44* are used to resolve battles and are resolved relative to the target. Infantry icons eliminate an infantry, Tank icons eliminate a tank, and the Hand Grenade eliminates either. Flags force a retreat, and the star icons are used for special effects.

A disadvantage of icons is that it is very difficult to deal with modifiers or other ways to modify attacks based on, for example, terrain or different quality forces.

Some games, like *Descent*, deal with this by having dice of different qualities, relating to the power and skill of the character, weapon, armor, or other equipment. The dice can be segregated into types like attack, defense, knockback, special, and others, again allowing the designer fine-grained control over possible outcomes while making it simple for the player to interpret. They just need to see what color dice need to be rolled and then read off the icons to see the results.

Eclipse is a hybrid of this system, with three colors of dice representing different powers—yellow (the weakest), orange, and red. However, *Eclipse* does not use icons on the dice. Standard numeric pips are used but with nonstandard distributions to model the varying power levels.

At the extreme end, *Dragon Dice* has custom dice for every single unit in the game. The same effect can be represented by different icons for different units. For example, Move icons may be boot prints for one creature and hoof prints for another. Although it increases thematic immersion, having so many icons can make it difficult for players to quickly parse results. It can also create production challenges, and indeed, *Quarriors!*, the game that launched the concept of collectible dice games, struggled to find a publisher because of the manufacturing challenge the game presented.

While they are most commonly used on dice, icons can be placed on cards to be flipped for resolution as well. Similar considerations apply, except that it is rare to have draws from multiple different decks the same way games like *Descent: Journeys in the Dark* have players roll different dice.

Sample Games

    Command & Colors (Borg, 2006)
    Descent: Journeys in the Dark (Wilson, 2005)
    Dragon Dice (Smith, 1995)
    Eclipse (Tahkokallio, 2011)
    Memoir '44 (Borg, 2004)
    Quarriors! (Elliott and Lang, 2011)

RES-06 Card Play

Description

Each player simultaneously or sequentially plays one or more cards. These modify the base outcome of a conflict and allow various special abilities to apply.

Discussion

This resolution system places more control in the hands of the players. In its simplest form, the player plays a number card to be added to the base results, as in *Cosmic Encounter*. However, this can be taken in a wide variety of directions to make combat more tactical.

Kemet resolves the conflict by giving players a strength based on the number of units in the battle. The players then each select a single Combat Card that modifies the outcome. It has three values: strength bonus, shield value, and damage caused. The strength bonus is added to the unit strength to determine the victory, while the shield value and damage bonuses determine how many opposing units are killed. Units are only removed based on those values, not winning or losing the battle. Players may know they are most likely to lose and, therefore, choose a Combat Card with little strength bonus but high damage value. This way, they destroy as many units as possible, possibly setting up for a counterattack, or even a Pyrrhic victory, should they succeed in eliminating all the attacking forces. This type of counterplay leads to a lot of Yomi (UNC-01), as players try to outguess their opponent's intent.

Kemet also has players exhaust Combat Cards that they use, plus one additional card, in each battle. When all cards are exhausted, they are recovered, similar to an Action Retrieval system (ACT-03). This gives players more decisions to make and gives savvy players the opportunity to track which Combat Cards may still be in play for their opponents.

A variety of other games allow players to play cards that modify the battle in more extreme ways. *Starship Samurai* allows each player to include one battle card, the effects of which may range from a simple strength addition to the ability to redeploy units into or out of the battle, changing the situation drastically. *Magic: The Gathering* and other collectible card games use card-based Interrupts (TRN-17) to allow for a wide variety of different effects.

Card systems can get quite complex. *We the People* has players draw a hand of tactics cards to resolve battles, the size of which is based on a variety of factors, including strength. Players then alternate playing or matching an opponent play. The first player who is not able to match the opponent loses the battle, so the player with more cards will typically win, but not always, and seizing the ability to lead the card play becomes a critical tactic. In *Starcraft: The Board Game*, players have a small hand of cards with abilities that trigger based on the units involved in the battle. As in *We the People*, players alternate card play to gain an advantage. *Starcraft* allows players to purchase upgraded tech cards to shuffle into their combat decks, but there is no guarantee they will be available, leading to opportunities for bluffing (UNC-01).

The disadvantage of the more sophisticated card-based systems is that they slow down play quite a bit as battles are resolved. In a two-player game, this may not be an issue, but it is a consideration with higher player counts. Nonetheless, these systems can offer enormous design opportunities, and the ability to model a wide range of thematic moments and stratagems, as a play of *War of the Ring* will demonstrate.

Sample Games

Cosmic Encounter (Eberle, Kittredge, Norton, and Olatka, 1977)
Hannibal (Bauza, 2010)
Kemet (Bariot and Montiage, 2012)
Magic: The Gathering (Garfield, 1993)
Starcraft: The Board Game (Konieczka and Petersen, 2007)
Starship Samurai (Vega, 2018)
War of the Ring (Di Meglio, Maggi, and Nepitello, 2004)
We the People (Herman, 1993)

RES-07 Rock, Paper, Scissors

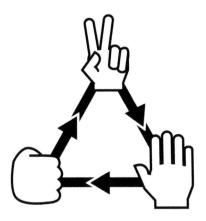

Description

There are three possible options, and they are cyclically superior (A beats B, B beats C, and C beats A).

Discussion

Rock, Paper, Scissors (RPS) is one of the core resolution mechanisms. Unlike High Number or Stat Check, it is *intransitive*. A *transitive* relationship means that if A beats B and B beats C, then A beats C. For example, simply comparing strengths leads to a transitive relationship.

Adding intransitive elements to conflict resolution leads to interesting and novel decisions for the players. For example, many Napoleonic war games treat the relationship between infantry, cavalry, and artillery as intransitive. Infantry beats cavalry (defending in a square), cavalry beats artillery, and artillery beats infantry. Note that "beats" in this context means "has an advantage over." It does not typically mean wins 100% of the time. *Age of Mythology: The Board Game* is an example of this type of system.

There are a variety of ways to implement an RPS-based resolution system. Some games, like *Secret Labyrinth* and *Darkover*, have players secretly select one of three options (literally, RPS in the case of *Secret Labyrinth*), reveal, and compare. Others will give bonuses or penalties to players based on their choices, such as a modifier in a High Number system (RES-01), varying the number of dice to be rolled, or changing or adding target icons.

One system that is infrequently used is Intransitive Dice. In this implementation, there are three different dice with varying values on the faces. These are mathematically designed so that, on average, die A will roll higher than die B, die B higher than die C, and die C higher than die A. Typically, the advantage is around 55–45, so it can be difficult to engineer a dominant advantage, but over the course of many rolls, the player who gets the best matchups will come out ahead.

The RPS mechanism can also arise indirectly from the interaction of player choices. For example, in *Hoity Toity*, players who go to the Auction House may choose to play a Cash card, to buy an artifact; a Thief, to steal a Cash card; or a Detective, to catch a Thief. Similarly, in *Nobody But Us Chickens*, players can play a Chicken for points, a Fox to catch a Chicken, or a Dog to catch a Fox. If there are more than three players, the interactions and choices can get complex for players to decide, while being easy to resolve.

Hoity Toity has the additional wrinkle that if multiple players select Thief, they cancel out, which has shades of the Prisoner's Dilemma (RES-08) and Sealed Bid with Cancellation (AUC-05).

Many games extend a hierarchical system by including a wrap-around with the weakest piece defeating the strongest. For example, in *Stratego*, the Marshall is the strongest piece, but it can be defeated by the Spy, the weakest. Similarly, in *Frank's Zoo*, the Elephant is the strongest card, but it is defeated by the Mouse. This adds a beneficial layer of uncertainty to these games. *Stratego* without the possibility of losing your Marshall would be a much poorer game.

Sample Games

> *Age of Mythology: The Board Game* (Drover, 2003)
> *Darkover* (Eberle, Kittredge, and Olatka, 1979)
> *Frank's Zoo* (Matthäus and Nestel, 1999)
> *Hoity Toity* (Teuber, 1991)
> *Nobody but Us Chickens* (Nunn, 2003)
> *Secret Labyrinth* (Kobbert, 1998)
> *Stratego* (Mogendorff, 1946)

RES-08 Prisoner's Dilemma

Description

Each player has a choice between Cooperating or Defecting. The total payoff is maximized if both players Cooperate, but if one Defects and the other Cooperates, the Defector will score more individual points.

Discussion

The Prisoner's Dilemma (PD) is one of the core Resolution mechanisms. Players choose to either cooperate with each other or defect. A typical payoff chart is shown in the diagram above. Since the payoffs if both defect or cooperate are equivalent for both players, this system only works if there are more than two players, even if only two are involved in the PD. If there are only two players, neither gains ground if they select the same option, so picking Defect is always the correct strategy.

As indicated by the traditional choice names of Cooperate and Defect, the PD brings elements of trust to the forefront and strong elements of Yomi (UNC-01). This can lead to emotional investment by the players, or reaction to being betrayed, particularly in longer games where the outcome can have a significant impact on player position.

An example of this is *Diplomacy*, a 6–8 hour game of conquest in Europe. The players representing Austria and Italy start with two key spaces and armies, Venice and Trieste, adjacent to each other at the start of the game, the only such situation among the seven players. In *Diplomacy*, players write down orders and reveal them simultaneously (TRN-09, for more on Simultaneous Action Selection). After the initial negotiation phase, Italy and Austria need to decide if they will move away from their common border (Cooperate) or invade (Defect). If both Cooperate, it can set them up for a reasonable start and good long-term relationship. If both Defect, no one loses a home supply center, but it will sow distrust and put them behind the other players as their forces will not have moved. And if one Cooperates and the other Defects, a home supply center will be lost, putting one player at a significant disadvantage.

While *Diplomacy* frequently creates high emotional moments like this, the Prisoner's Dilemma does not always need to involve such high stakes. For example, in *Hoity Toity*, players in the Auction House may choose to purchase an item, play a Thief card to steal money, or a Detective card to catch a thief. While this is fundamentally an RPS mechanic (RES-07), if multiple players choose Thief, they cancel out and no thieves gain any benefit. This adds elements of a PD, but in a lighter way as there is no negotiation in *Hoity Toity*, and for players the stakes are much lower.

Another example of this is *Incan Gold*, where each turn players need to decide simultaneously if they are continuing to explore an abandoned temple in search of treasure or will return home. Sometimes earlier treasures and artifacts may be left behind players, to be scooped up by players who leave the cave. In particular, artifacts create a PD, as they are only gained if a single player chooses to leave the temple. If multiple players leave the cave on the same turn, none gain the artifacts. This implementation also tends to be light as there are potential benefits for both staying and leaving, and no negotiation prior to selection.

Cosmic Encounter introduces the PD through Negotiation cards. Conflict is resolved by both attacker and defender selecting a Number card from their hand. The player with the highest Number card plus Force strength wins the battle. Players also have the option to play a Negotiate card, if they have one, instead of a Number card. If both players Negotiate, they are allowed to negotiate a deal, which can be mutually beneficial. However, if only one Negotiates, that player automatically loses, and the player and their allies lose all their involved forces. In an interesting twist, the player who chose a Negotiate card in this situation gains a small compensating benefit but not Allies. Thus, inviting Allies to join you in a battle where you know you will play a Negotiate is its own form of Defection, building a secondary PD into the core mechanism.

Dead Last has two players dividing up four loot cards and adds a third option to the classic PD. In addition to Share and Steal (Cooperate/Defect), players may also choose Grab One, which guarantees exactly one loot card, possibly leaving three for the opponent.

Sample Games

Cosmic Encounter (Eberle, Kittredge, Norton, and Olatka, 1977)
Dead Last (Grosso and Patton, 2016)
Diplomacy (Calhamer, 1959)
Fantasy Business (Boelinger, 2002)
Hoity Toity (Teuber, 1991)
Incan Gold (Faidutti and Moon, 2005)
Zombie in My Pocket (Lee, 2010)

RES-09 Alternate Removal

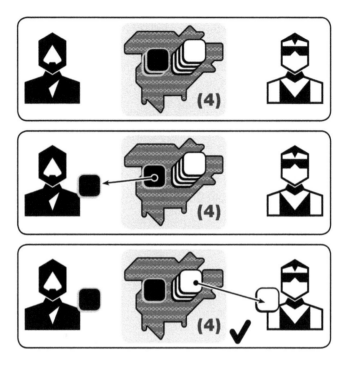

Description

The player with fewer units removes one. Then players alternate removing units until reaching a set number, one player is out of units, or some other stopping mechanism.

Discussion

The system of Alternate Removal was first introduced in the 1980 game *Civilization*. Conflict in *Civilization* only needs to be resolved if the total number of tokens in an area exceeds its carrying capacity (representing the fertility of the particular area), which ranges from one to five. If the total quantity exceeds this, the Alternating Removal process is initiated. Tokens are removed, starting with the player with the fewest until the total number of tokens no longer exceeds the carrying capacity.

If players have equal numbers of tokens, the tied players each remove a token at the same time.

This system has a variety of intriguing features. First, it is strictly deterministic. It is a determinative process with no hidden information. This is rare among conflict resolution mechanisms. Second, coexistence in an area is allowed and common. Many games with conflict or battles for areas only permit a single player to ultimately occupy an area or control it in the case of Area Majority games (ARC-02). This gives more flexibility for players to negotiate and settle borders.

Finally, it gives the design hooks for special abilities later in the game. For example, if only one player in a Conflict has Metal Working, they are always the last to remove a token.

Inis uses a similar removal system, except that players have the option of removing a unit or discarding a card. In addition, players have the option, after taking a casualty, to withdraw from the battle rather than pursuing the conflict. Notably, this doesn't trigger a retreat from the disputed territory.

Sample Games

Civilization (Tresham, 1980)
Inis (Martinez, 2016)

RES-10 Physical Action

Description

A Physical Action needs to be performed by one or more players to determine the outcome of the action.

Discussion

Adding a physical element for resolving player actions makes for an intuitive, tense, and exciting play experience by adding Performance Uncertainty (Chapter 6). Physical Action resolution is somewhat skill-based but also acts as a randomizer. However, its use does give a game a lighter, toyetic feel, as players interact with the game pieces. In a highly strategic game, this can lead to a disconnect, as the strategy is undercut by what can feel like a highly variable resolution mechanism. It also can make players that are poor at performing the activity feel like they are at a disadvantage throughout the game, and it is not something that they can compensate for, leading to a negative experience.

The most common implementation of Physical Action is flicking, which is covered in its own entry, RES-24. Games with balance and stacking elements are also common and are covered in RES-25. While flicking is a popular implementation of a physical resolution mechanism, there are many alternatives. *Flip Ships* has a form of flicking, with a ship being placed on a platform and flipped off of it. *Dungeon Fighter* has players bounce a die off the table surface to land on a target.

Wallenstein introduced the Cube Tower. This is a tower with internal ledges. Players resolve a conflict by taking a specific number of cubes of different colors (the attacking and defending cubes, for example), and throw them into the tower. The cubes that emerge at the bottom determine the outcome. Cubes that get stuck inside are left behind and may emerge in future conflicts. If a player knows he or she has many cubes stuck in the tower, he or she may be more inclined to initiate conflicts, for example.

Other games have objects being removed, like *Ker-Plunk* and *Don't Break the Ice*. There are also games that combine removal with stacking, including *Jenga* and *Villa Paletti*.

Finally, there are a variety of outlier physical mechanics, including throwing darts in *Dart Wars*, distinguishing items by feel in *Space Cadets*, eggremoval in *Gulo Gulo*, the pie launcher of *Pie Face*, finger gymnastics of *Climb!*, and popping balloons in *Kamasutra*. A comprehensive listing of these is beyond the scope of this book.

Another variation on the physical resolution is Speed Matching. Cards are flipped up, and players need to see if two match, and either slap the cards or grab a totem. Games that incorporate this type of system include *Jungle Speed* and *Scan*. The inclusion of physical action can give players an opportunity to feint and induce a mistaken grab by other players, leading to a penalty in some games. *Jungle Speed* incorporates this tactic.

Introducing a physical action gives the designer a chance to add physical handicaps to mix up the challenges and make them harder. It also ups the "zaniness" factor, giving games a lighter feel. *Dungeon Fighter* has players act with their non-dominant hands, eyes closed, and various other physical challenges.

Sample Games

Animal Upon Animal (Miltenberger, 2005)
Ascending Empires (Cooper, 2011)
Bausack (Zoch, 1987)
Catacombs (Amos, Kelsey, and West, 2010)
Climb! (Michaud, 2008)
Dart Wars (Reymond, 2006)
Diskwars (Gelle, Hardy, Jolly, and Petersen, 1999)
Don't Break the Ice (Uncredited, 1965)
Dungeon Fighter (Buonfino, Silva, and Sorrentino, 2011)

Flick 'em Up (Beaujannot and Monpertuis, 2015)
Flip Ships (Klenko, 2017)
Gulo Gulo (Granau, Kramer, and Raggan, 2003)
Jenga (Scott, 1983)
Jungle Speed (Vuarchex and Yakovenko, 1997)
Junk Art (stacking) (Cormier and Lim, 2016)
Kamasutra (Faidutti, 2000)
Ker-Plunk (Goldfarb and Soriano, 1967)
Meeple Circus (Millet, 2017)
Pie Face (Uncredited, 1964)
Scan (Glass, 1970)
Seal Team Flix (Ruth and Thomas, 2018)
Space Cadets (Engelstein, Engelstein, and Engelstein, 2012)
Villa Paletti (Payne, 2001)
Wallenstein (Henn, 2002)

RES-11 Static Capture

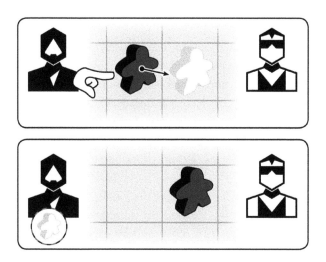

Description

Pieces are captured when another piece occupies or passes over their space.

Discussion

This is one of the oldest conflict resolution mechanisms, going back thousands of years.

Typically combined with a movement system, a token is affected in some way when another enters its space. For example, it may be captured (*Chess*, *Checkers*), be sent back to start (*Parcheesi*, *Trouble*, *Sorry!*, *Backgammon*), or switch sides (*Shogi*).

In order to make capturing challenging and meaningful, the movement of pieces needs to be restricted in some fashion. *Chess* and *Shogi* allow pieces to move to defined squares, while the *Parcheesi* family of games uses a randomizer and the moved piece must, typically, move the full amount. More information about Movement schemes is in Chapter 10, but a few features are worth noting here.

In most cases, the moving piece will make the capture on its final space of movement. This is particularly true of games where movement is controlled by a randomizer, with pieces typically needing to land on an opposing piece by exact count to make a capture. There are exceptions, of course. *Sorry!* has specific areas where a piece may slide through multiple spaces, sending all pieces encountered back to start, and in *Checkers* pieces make jumps to capture and can string together multiple jumps as a single move.

Motion is not a requirement for this mechanism. *Through the Desert* allows players to claim Palm Trees for points by extending a chain of camels across the board. Camels do not move once placed, but players may only add to chains in certain ways. *Expedition* has a similar chain mechanism, as players attempt to "capture" certain cities on the board to earn points.

Tash-Kalar: Arena of Legends has players placing pieces on the board, trying to achieve certain patterns. When those patterns are realized, enemy pieces may be captured.

While not truly Static Capture, there are games that feature pushing as a means to capture, including *Abalone*. In these games, there are typically restrictions on which pieces can move and be captured. In these games, pieces or groups of pieces may push other pieces, typically with the intention of pushing them off the board or into a dead space. Because of the physical nature of pushing, particularly chain pushing, the physical design of the board and pieces usually facilitates the mechanism. *Abalone* has a grooved board that makes it easy to push marbles in the six hexagonal directions.

Sample Games

> *Abalone* (Lalet and Levi, 1987)
> *Backgammon* (Unknown, 3000 BCE)
> *Checkers* (Unknown)
> *Chess* (Unknown, ~1200)
> *Expedition* (Kramer, 1996)
> *Onitama* (Sato, 2014)
> *Parcheesi* (Unknown, 400)
> *Shogi* (Unknown)
> *Sorry!* (Haskell, Jr. and Storey, 1929)
> *Tash-Kalar: Arena of Legends* (Chvátil, 2013)
> *Through The Desert* (Knizia, 1998)
> *Trouble* (Kohner, Kohner, and Kroll, 1965)

RES-12 Enclosure

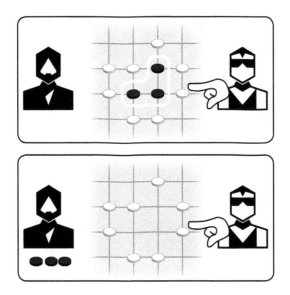

Description

Players try to surround pieces or key areas.

Discussion

Dating back thousands of years, *Go* is one of the most famous examples of this type of conflict resolution. If a group of connected stones has no empty spaces adjacent to it, it is captured. While the stones themselves are static, the evolution of groups gives *Go* a dynamic feel.

Reversi implements Enclosure by allowing players to flip tiles of the opposing color that are between two tiles of their own color.

The nature of Enclosure games makes certain regions of the board more or less desirable. In *Reversi*, the corner and edge spaces are more valuable, as it is harder or impossible to surround pieces located there. Similarly, in *Go*, players typically start near corners, where it is easier to enclose territory and make stones safe, and then extend down the sides and toward the middle (Illustration 4.3).

Elements of Enclosure games can also be seen in games like *Samurai*, where the objective is to surround board elements with tiles. These are both

Illustration 4.3   A game of *Go* in progress. White has surrounded territory on the lower left and upper right.

Enclosure games and a type of Area Majority (ARC-02), where tiles can be placed so that they are adjacent to multiple objectives, contributing strength toward both.

In general, good enclosure games are designed so that pieces are both trying to enclose and at risk of being enclosed themselves, or there are several possible ways they can be used for Enclosure.

Sample Games

Go (Unknown, 2200 BCE)
Reversi (Mollet and Waterman, 1883)
Samurai (Knizia, 1998)
Through the Desert (Knizia, 1998)

RES-13 Minimap

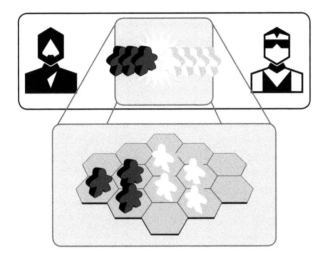

Description

When a conflict is initiated, pieces are moved to a separate board for resolution.

Discussion

This is a meta-mechanic, as it is a way of organizing conflict, and relies on one of the other methods discussed here to actually resolve individual attacks.

One of the earliest examples of the Minimap mechanism is the 1962 game *Bismarck*. In this naval game, players secretly move task forces around a search board. When they discover each other, task forces are moved to the Battle Board, where the conflict is actually resolved (through a Stat Check mechanism in *Bismarck*'s case). It is like "zooming in" on the battle to get more tactical. Video games like *Master of Orion* and *Heroes of Might and Magic* implement a similar system.

The Battle Board was later extended in *Titan*, where players move groups of monsters (Legions) around a master board. When two opposing Legions meet in the same space, they are transferred to a battle board to actually fight the battle. *Titan* is notable in that it has a different battle board for each type of terrain, and the side the defender sets up on depends on the direction from which the attacker entered the space. This makes battles extremely variable and tactical (Illustrations 4.4a and 4.4b).

A variation on this can be seen in *Buck Rogers: Battle for the 25th Century*, which has both a solar system map and separate maps for each planet, co-located on the board. Unlike *Titan*, which has many, many Jungle spaces, all

Illustration 4.4a   When a battle takes place in a Hills space in *Titan*, the battle is conducted on this separate board. Each board has different combinations of terrain. This board features Hill spaces that confer a combat advantage to occupiers and Forest spaces that are impassable. A much simpler version of this mechanism is used in *Axis & Allies*, which uses a Battle Board not to give tactical options to the players, but as a player-aid to help organize and keep track of the strength of units, what they need to roll to hit, and which units are still able to fire. This is more of a graphic design technique than a mechanism. A similar system is seen in many Force Commitment games (ARC-06).

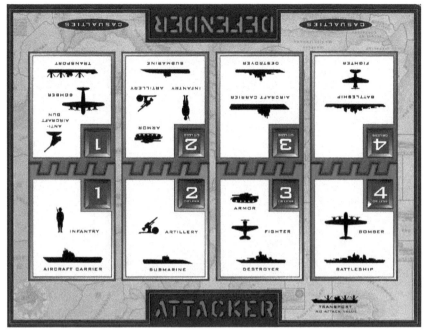

Illustration 4.4b   The battle board in *Axis & Allies: Europe*. The boxes are used to organize units by combat strength and track casualties. It obviates the need for players to memorize the combat strength of all the different units.

of which resolve on the Jungle board, here the planet maps are very specific to the planets in the solar system and act as a place for units on the planet to be located and for ground battles to be resolved.

Sample Games

Axis & Allies (Harris, Jr., 1981)
Bismarck (Roberts and Shaw, 1962)
Buck Rogers: Battle for the 25th Century (Grubb, 1988)
Titan (McAllister and Trampier, 1980)

RES-14 Force Commitment

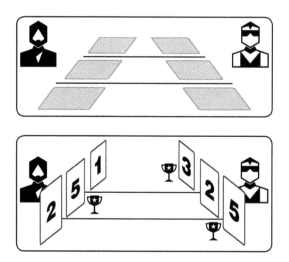

Description

The players select how many of their forces they will commit to the battle to different categories. The players then reveal their assignments and resolve.

Discussion

This is a meta-mechanic that builds on other Resolution means. Typically, players will reveal their strengths in different categories, with the High Number gaining the benefit (RES-01). If the allocation portion of this mechanism is done secretly, it is a Sealed Bid Auction, so considerations noted in that section (AUC-05) apply here.

In one of the earlier implementers of this system, *Dune* and its successor, *Rex: Final Days of an Empire*, have players allocating to just two categories: in the battle or out of the battle. Units that a player commits to a battle will be lost. In addition, all units from the loser are eliminated. This system makes the players evaluate whether to give themselves a higher chance to win by committing larger forces or preserve as much of their force as possible by committing fewer forces.

Dune augments the mechanism by allowing the players to also commit leaders and bonus cards along with forces. This uncertainty is critical for this system to work so that the player with the larger force cannot just bid one more than the size of the smaller (Illustration 4.5).

A modified form of this system has the loser only losing part of its force, not the full force. This makes the decision of Force Commitment for the larger side more challenging, as it introduces more Yomi (UNC-01) by giving a broader possible strength range of the commitment of the smaller force.

Cry Havoc and *Rising Sun* give more options to players for Force allocation. In *Cry Havoc*, players may allocate forces to take control of the area being fought over, cause casualties, or take prisoners. Control and Prisoners are executed by the player with the most forces in that region, while Cause Casualties is executed by all players who have units there. Tactics cards can also be played to affect the battle in various ways.

Rising Sun has a similar system to *Cry Havoc*, except with slightly different assignment options (the ability to sacrifice your own units for victory points, for example). Also, while *Rising Sun* uses the same simultaneous secret assignment of forces, *Cry Havoc* has the Attacker allocate first, followed by the Defender. Secret assignment emphasizes the guessing nature and leads to a lighter, more random feel, while sequential assignment removes luck but

Illustration 4.5   The Combat Wheel in *Dune*. Players select the strength they are committing to the battle and may also add a leader disk and cards. This is held in the hand and then simultaneously revealed.

may give an advantage to the side that places last (the Defender, in the case of *Cry Havoc*).

These types of systems give the players a lot of flexibility in the goals they want to achieve in a battle. Are they trying to hold ground? Cause losses? Earn points? The player can use the options to pursue a variety of strategies.

Sample Games

> *Cry Havoc* (Rodiek, Oracz, and Walczak, 2016)
> *Dune* (Eberle, Kittredge, and Olatka, 1979)
> *Rex: Final Days of an Empire* (Eberle, Goodenoungh, Kitteredge, Konieczka, Olatka, and Petersen, 2012)
> *Rising Sun* (Lang, 2018)
> *Scythe* (Stegmaier, 2016)

RES-15 Voting

Description

Players vote on whether a proposed action will occur or not.

Discussion

The Voting mechanism is often used in games with a political theme, although some, like *Die Regeln Wir Shon*, are more abstract. In some games, each player gets one vote. In others, players may have multiple votes that they can apply.

Voting is in many ways an Area Majority mechanism (ARC-02), except that players are either on the "Yay" or on the "Nay" sides, rather than only able to win something individually. This can lead to shifting coalitions of players on either side of an issue, as interests align and diverge, underscoring the political nature of this resolution means.

The item being voted on can fit at various levels in the game. In *Junta*, players are voting to decide whether the budget proposed by El Presidente passes and the money is distributed to the players. This is an example of a sub-system of the game that links to other key mechanisms. *The Republic of Rome* is similar in that players are voting on which characters should gain offices, how wars are conducted, and even the execution of characters. These decisions then feed into other systems to propel the game forward (Illustration 4.6).

Some games have players vote on actual changes to the rules themselves. *Democrazy* and *Das Regeln Wir Shon* are prime examples of this, as

Illustration 4.6   Two voting cards from *Junta*. Unlike many
voting games, players do not get an equal number of votes.

players play cards that contain possible game rules, and players vote on them. Proposing rules that help several players, including yourself, but yourself a little bit more, is a key skill in the game and can lead to intriguing and exciting game play. These rules changes range from what actions are available to players, how resources can be exchanged, how the game ends, and what contributes toward victory.

Galactic Destiny, which includes a Galactic Senate mechanism, also has players vote on new rules to be added, but these are not the core of the game. They impact what actions players may perform, and what is legal or illegal.

As mentioned earlier, some voting games, like *Das Regeln Wir Shon*, give one vote to each player, and a simple majority wins. However, there are other variations. In *Junta* and *Republic of Rome*, the players represent factions, and so they may have control of various characters or blocks of voters that give them more than one vote. If players are powerful enough, they may even be able to pass anything they want.

Some games vary from simple majority in votes. In *Article 27: The UN Security Council Game*, a unanimous vote is required for a measure to pass. Bribery and other inducements are encouraged to get players to vote your way.

While voting systems can be dynamic and interesting, they also encourage negotiation, which can make this mechanism very time-consuming. This should be carefully considered by the designer when determining if it is appropriate for the player experience desired.

Sample Games

> *Article 27: The UN Security Council Game* (Baden, 2012)
> *Battlestar Galactica: The Board Game* (Konieczka, 2008)
> *Das Regeln Wir Schon* (Schmiel, 1994)
> *Democrazy* (Faidutti, 2000)
> *Galactic Destiny* (Mauro, O'Maoileoin, Pulis, and Pulis, 2007)
> *Hoax* (Eberle, Horn Jr., Kittredge, and Olatka, 1981)
> *Junta* (Goldberg, Grossman, Marsh, Marsh, Tsao, and Vrtis, 1978)
> *The Republic of Rome* (Berthold, Greenwood, and Haines, 1990)
> *The Resistance* (Eskrisdge, 2009)
> *Werewolf* (Davidoff and Plotkin, 1986)

RES-16 Player Judge

Description

One player, the judge, decides the outcome of the Action.

Discussion

The standard use of this resolution mechanism is in games where players are performing a task, and there are no objective criteria as to which is best, so one player acts as Judge to select the winner. For example, in *Apples to Apples*, one player is the Judge, and the other players select one of their noun cards to match an adjective card. The Judge then selects which they think is closest.

Similarly, in *The Big Idea*, players use noun cards to pitch products that fulfill a need, and the Judge selects which they like the most.

In these games, the role of Judge either rotates around the table in a regular fashion or passes to the player who won the last round. The latter is a type of balancing mechanism as the Judge usually cannot score, so it gives other players an opportunity to close the gap (VIC-18).

This Player Judge mechanism allows players to tailor their answers to the Judge's preferences. The best implementations of this system have anonymous responses, as in *Apples to Apples*. In games where it is known which player goes with which answer, the Judge may go against the spirit of the game, and deliberately not select players due to their score, rather than the intrinsic worth of their submission. Personal relationships that are outside of the game may also impinge (like someone giving preferential treatment to a spouse). While this mechanism is typically seen in lighter games, so this may not be that much of an issue, it is still a consideration, particularly when playing with children who may be more emotionally involved.

Some games, like *Say Anything*, sidestep this issue by having the players bet on which answer the Judge will select. This makes it impossible for the Judge to game the system and keeps players more involved in the game.

Sample Games

    Apples to Apples (Kirby and Osterhaus, 1999)
    The Big Idea (Ernest, 2000)
    Cards Against Humanity (Dillon, Dranove, Halpern, Hantoot, Munk, Pinsof, Temkin, and Weinstein, 2009)
    Say Anything (Crapuchettes and Pillalamarri, 2008)

RES-17 Targeted Clues

Description

A player gives clues that he or she wants some, but not all, players to guess.

Discussion

This resolution mechanism is often used in party games or lighter social games. The core idea is that one player gives clues to the group about a word or phrase, and the other players try to guess the answer. However, it is bad for the clue-giver if either no players guess correctly or if all players guess correctly. The player scores the most points when some of the players guess correctly but not all.

For example, in *Barbarossa*, players make small clay sculptures to represent something—a lion, for example. If no one guesses that it is supposed to be a lion or if everyone does, the sculpting player does not score. They need to make a sculpture that is somewhere between obvious and obscure. *Dixit* operates similarly but with pictures.

Decrypto is a variation on this idea. The players are broken up into two teams. One team has a list of four words that all players on the team can see. The clue-giver needs to give a clue that will allow their team to select the right word from the list. The other team can hear those clues but does not see the word list. Over several rounds, players need to give multiple clues for the same word, and if the other team can figure out the word or concept, they can win. Thus, clues need to be given that are straightforward enough for your team to get it, without the opposing team figuring it out.

Sample Games

  Barbarossa (Teuber, 1988)
  Cluzzle (Hamilton, 2004)
  Decrypto (Dagenais-Lesperance, 2018)
  Dixit (Roubira, 2008)

RES-18 Tiebreakers

Description

If a resolution results in a tie, players look to an alternate means to break it.

Discussion

While we include this in Resolution, this is a meta-mechanic that can apply to Victory, Auctions, and many other mechanisms. While there are a wide variety of tie-breaking mechanisms, they typically fall into one of these categories:

- *Resource*: The player with the most or least of a particular resource will break the tie. For example, in *Trade on the Tigris*, if the score is tied at the end of the game, the game is won by the player with the fewest Barbarian tokens. If these are also tied, the win goes to the player with the most Culture tokens. In a two-player game, this resource may take the form of a Priority token, with the player holding the Priority token breaking the tie, and then passing the token to their opponent. This is similar to the Possession arrow in basketball.

- *Positional*: The player in a specific position in the turn order, or on a track, will break the tie. A common tiebreaker is for the player who is closest to the First Player will break the tie. As another example, in *Rising Sun*, the player who is higher on the Honor track wins the tie. In conflict games that use dice to resolve, ties will go to the defender. *Risk* works this way, for example. If the defender rolls a 6, they will win regardless of what the attacker rolls. Most often ties go to the defender, but in some games that want to encourage aggression, ties may go to the attacker.

- *Random*: Players roll off or use some other randomization means to break the tie. This can be exciting but time-consuming. For certain tiebreakers, most notably if players are tied at the end of the game, breaking the tie randomly will be unsatisfying for players.

- *Secondary Values*: Components have a unique secondary value that is used to break ties. For example, in *Libertalia*, the role cards have a number on them that says when in sequence they should be played. For example, the Monkey card is #2 and is executed before the Cabin Boy which is #5. If two players both play a Monkey, they both have #2 on them. However, to resolve the tie, there is a smaller Flag number on each card, which is unique between all players. For example, one player has a 3 Flag on their Monkey card, while another has a 5, so the 3 would go first. The flag numbers are distributed so that on average each player will win the same number of ties. This gives a quick and simple way to break ties.

The procedures described above, as in *Libertalia* and *Rising Sun*, determine which player wins the tie. However, some games award a tie-breaking ability to a specific player, who then decides which player is chosen. For example, in *A Game of Thrones*, the player that wins the auction for the Throne gains the ability to decide who wins all ties. This immediately brings Negotiation elements into the game (ECO-18), as players can lobby the player who resolves ties.

It is also possible to not have a tiebreaker. For in-game resolutions, ties may be resolved as *friendly* or *unfriendly*. A *friendly* resolution means that all tied players gain the benefit of the action. If the leader in a particular category scores ten points, for example, if players are tied, they all score the ten points. In *unfriendly* ties, tied players receive a reduced award or no award at all. Either way, all players are treated equally.

For the final victory, some games do not offer tiebreakers and have the players share in the victory. This may or may not be acceptable to players depending on the likelihood of ties and the length and seriousness of the game. If possible, tiebreakers for final victory should reward the players who have had a harder route to win, for example, by going last in the turn order, by acquiring a harder-to-obtain resource, or by using fewer resources overall.

Sample Games

A Game of Thrones (Petersen and Wilson, 2003)
Libertalia (Mori, 2012)
Rising Sun (Lang, 2018)
Risk (Lamorisse and Levin, 1959)
Trade on the Tigris (Engelstein and Sturm, 2018)

RES-19 Dice Selection

Description

A player rolls multiple dice and selects one based on a rule.

Discussion

The most common implementation of Dice Selection has players roll two dice and select the highest or lowest. *Dungeons & Dragons* uses this system and refers to the two states as "advantaged" and "disadvantaged." An alternative is for players to roll three dice and to choose the median die.

A High/Low selection is a way for designers to skew single die results fairly significantly toward the high or low end. Conversely, a median selection system makes extreme results unlikely.

Result	1 die	2 dice, high (%)	2 dice, low (%)	3 dice, median (%)
1	16	3	31	7
2	16	8	8	19
3	16	14	19	24
4	16	19	14	24
5	16	25	8	19
6	16	31	3	7

The table above shows the chances of rolling different numbers with a standard die roll, rolling two dice and selecting the highest (or lowest), and rolling three dice and selecting the middle value. Rolling 2 dice and selecting the highest almost doubles the chances of a result of 6, and a result of 1 is 80% less likely than with a standard die roll. Selecting the middle out of 3 dice emphasizes results of 3 and 4, while cutting the chances of a 1 or 6 in half compared to a standard roll.

Root presents a related system, where two dice are rolled for battles, with the Attacker taking the higher roll and the defender the lower. This encourages aggression.

Sample Games

13th Age (Heinsoo and Tweet, 2013)
Dungeons & Dragons (Arneson and Gygax, 1977)
Root (Wehrle, 2018)

RES-20 Action Speed

Description

Actions are rated for speed or initiative. Faster actions are executed first.

Discussion

This system is most commonly used in Simultaneous Action systems (TRN-09). In *Critical Mass*, each player selects an action card from their hand and plays it simultaneously. Each is rated for speed, and faster actions go sooner than slower ones.

Critical Mass uses numeric speed ratings. Some games use descriptors, which can be as simple as Fast or Slow, as in *The Ares Project*, or more thematic, like First Strike in *Magic: The Gathering*.

While this often represents the speed of an action, it can also be more abstract. In *Libertalia*, characters have a priority rating and operate in the order of priority from lowest number to highest.

Typically, if actions have the same speed, they are resolved simultaneously, although a tiebreaker may be used (RES-18). Each card in *Libertalia*, for example, has a unique number on it as a secondary tiebreaker.

Speed ratings give players a clear indication of the order of execution of actions, and the designer another resource to use for balance purposes. Faster actions can be weaker, while slower actions can be more powerful, but more likely to not take effect.

Sample Games

    The Ares Project (Engelstein and Engelstein, 2011)
    Critical Mass (Chang, 2018)
    Libertalia (Mori, 2012)
    Magic: The Gathering (Garfield, 1993)
    Titan (McAllister and Trampier, 1980)

RES-21 Rerolling and Locking

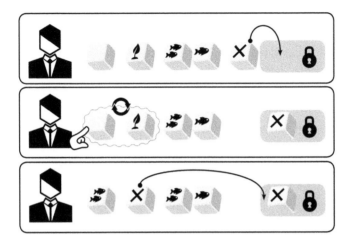

Description

Dice may be rerolled or may be locked, preventing rerolling.

Discussion

Many people are first exposed to the idea of Rerolling through the classic game *Yahtzee*. After rolling, the player may choose to reroll any number of dice and may do this twice, for a total of three throws. *Yahtzee* illustrates some typical characteristics of reroll systems:

- When dice are rerolled you must take the result (you can't go back to the first result)
- You can reroll dice regardless of whether they were rerolled or not

There are variations on this, of course, but this is typical.

From a straightforward perspective, where you are interested only in how high the number rolled is, assuming the player rerolls anything that is less than a "4," the reroll will add, on average, 0.75 to the final number. While it is similar in result to a +1 modifier, rerolls are experienced differently by the player. First, the player is choosing whether to reroll or not. This gives them finer-grained control and gives more tactical nuance to the act of rolling than just gaining a set modifier. Also, rolling dice can be inherently exciting, and rerolls make that happen more frequently. Finally, modifiers (as discussed in RES-02), even +1 modifiers, add to player cognitive load. Just looking at the die result is simpler. However, unlike modifiers, rerolls can result in the final result being worse than the initial roll. Whether this is desirable for the experience is a decision that needs to be determined by the designer.

The opposite mechanism to rerolling is Locking. In a Locking mechanism, certain die faces cannot be rerolled. They are stuck on that face for the remainder of the turn. Having a combination of rerolls and locks brings a Push-Your-Luck mechanism (UNC-02) to the table, as players need to risk improving their results by locking more dice. *Zombie Dice* is one of many games to implement this combination, as shotgun blast results are locked, and getting three shotgun blasts in total ends your turn with a bust.

Escape: The Curse of the Temple uses locked dice in a real-time dice rolling game to force players to interact with each other (to help unlock the dice of other players) and, in general, to disrupt the players' flow and force them to make some tough decisions.

Sample Games

> *Cosmic Wimpout* (Swilling, 1975)
> *Escape: The Curse of the Temple* (Ostby, 2012)
> *King of Tokyo* (Garfield, 2011)
> *Yahtzee* (Lowe, 1956)
> *Zombie Dice* (Jackson, 2010)

RES-22 Kill Steal

Description

Players contribute toward completing a task, but only the player who finally completes it gets a benefit.

Discussion

This Kill Steal mechanism originated in video games, which is where the term came from. In tabletop games, it is most frequently seen in combat games, where the player scoring the last hit to kill a creature gains the experience, treasure, or another reward.

In *Cutthroat Caverns*, players are trying to defeat creatures to reach and defeat the final boss and win the game. If all players are killed, they all lose, but if at least one survives, the player with the most points wins. See Semi-Co-Op (STR-05) for more details about this type of game structure. But while all players collectively battle creatures, only the player that lands the final hit that kills it gains the points. This adds a lot of interesting dynamics as players maneuver to land that final blow.

Similarly, in the purely competitive games *Dungeon Run*, *Wildlands*, and *Space Freaks*, as players attack, if monsters or other players are not defeated, the damage they suffer carries over. Whichever player actually reduces the target's health to zero gains the reward.

This mechanism is easy for players to understand and work with, but it does make things more contentious and raises the stakes, as if you are performing an attack that should defeat an enemy, but you get unlucky and it doesn't, other players can swoop in for the kill and your efforts are for naught. Some conflict games, like *Adrenaline*, avoid Kill Stealing by giving points to all players who contributed to defeating that opponent but at the expense of additional bookkeeping to track who caused what damage.

This mechanism is not limited to combat. It has been used in an economic game like *Valparaiso*, where players construct buildings in districts, but the player who constructs the final house gets a bonus, or in an abstract like *6 Nimmt*, where players place cards into rows based on their number, and the person who plays the sixth card takes the whole row (although taking rows is a bad thing, so perhaps this is better classified as a Reverse Kill Steal).

There are echoes of this mechanism in Gating and Unlocking (ACT-15), as many games have tracks that players advance on, but the first player to reach a certain space gets a one-time bonus.

Sample Games

  6 Nimmt (Kramer, 1994)
  Cutthroat Caverns (Covert, 2007)
  Dungeon Run (Bistro, 2011)
  Space Freaks (Jantunen and Wikström, 2017)
  Valparaiso (Malz and Malz, 2018)
  Wildlands (Wallace, 2018)

RES-23 Hot Potato

Description

Players strive to rid themselves of an item that will incur a massive penalty when it is triggered but can only dispose of the item by passing it to other players.

Discussion

Most gamers are introduced to this mechanism through the namesake childhood game *Hot Potato* or the card game *Old Maid*. *Hot Potato* involves the players sitting in a circle with an object (the "hot potato") being passed around as music plays. When the music stops, the player holding the object is eliminated. In *Old Maid*, players try to avoid being left with the Old Maid card at the end of the game. The Old Maid is the only card without a pair in the deck.

These two games illustrate the two main types of implementation of the mechanism. *Hot Potato* is a Player Elimination game (VIC-08), where the trigger is used to eliminate players one at a time until one remains. *Old Maid* is a Single Loser game (STR-07), where all players except the Old Maid holder win the game. Game loss is not a required feature of this mechanism so long as the penalty is comparatively quite large.

This mechanism gives a very clear focus to the players, although the means of achieving that goal may not necessarily be clear. For example, in *Exploding Kittens*, at the end of each turn, players must draw a card, and if they draw an

Exploding Kitten, they are eliminated unless they hold a Defuse. This gives the players a clear loss condition and basic tactics—try to avoid drawing cards if you can or get a defuse card—but it is vague enough to allow players to determine combos and timing within that framework.

Traditional Hot Potato-style games like *Exploding Kittens* and *Electronic Catch Phrase* focus the action on a single player and perhaps the player after them (see Neighbor Scope, RES-26)—but usually for a brief moment. *Electronic Catch Phrase* (now just "*Catch Phrase*") takes advantage of this feature for an easy-to-play part game. In this game, there is an electronic "puck" that passes around a circle. The player holding it must give clues to their team to guess the phrase shown on the screen. If they guess it correctly, the puck is passed to a player on the other team. The team that is holding the puck when the built-in timer goes off is penalized.

Unlike *Charades* and similar team party games, in *Catch Phrase*, the teams rapidly switch turns as the puck moves around the circle and players avoid being stuck with it. Preserving this sense of momentum and looming disaster is a key feature of the "round the circle" version of this mechanism.

In Old Maid-style implementations of Hot Potato, one of the players has the losing item, but nobody except that player knows who has it. This allows the game to incorporate bluffing and feelings of paranoia as players know when the card moves to other players. *Dread Curse* is a modern game that incorporates this idea, as a player that ends the game with the "black spot" coin cannot win, but stealing from and trading with other players is a key mechanism, which makes stealing have a Push-Your-Luck edge (UNC-02).

This highlights a potential weakness of the Old Maid style, since if the Old Maid is drawn from you, you are traditionally not supposed to show emotion or gloat, as the other players will not draw from that player for fear of gaining that card. This makes it more challenging for children to play but also opens the door for bluffing as players may pretend that the Old Maid was drawn from them when it has not.

Hot Potato can be used as a submechanism. In *Civilization*, there are disaster cards mixed in with trade goods. Players may trade these to other players during the trade phase, who may then trade them on. Whoever is left with the disasters at the end of the trade phase suffers their effect. As in *Old Maid*, most groups adopt an unwritten rule that you keep it secret when you trade a disaster away to another player, so they have the opportunity to pass it on.

A more subtle implementation of Hot Potato is an End Game Elimination condition, where a player is eliminated from contention not because of a specific element they have (like the Black Spot Coin in *Dread Curse*) but due to some characteristic of their position. For example, in *High Society*, players spend money to earn prizes that ultimately determine victory. However, the player with the least money cannot win the game, regardless of the value of their prizes. *Cleopatra and the Society of Architects* does a similar thing with corruption, which players may earn by doing more powerful actions. The state of having the least money or most corruption in these games is a form of Hot Potato in that it is something that may change players and causes the loss of the game.

Sample Games

Catch Phrase! (Williamson, 1994)
Civilization (Tresham, 1980)
Cleopatra and the Society of Architects (Cathala and Maublanc, 2006)
Exploding Kittens (Inman, Lee, Small, 2015)
Falling (Ernest, 1998)
High Society (Knizia, 1995)
Hot Potato (public domain)
Old Maid (unknown, 1874)

RES-24 Flicking

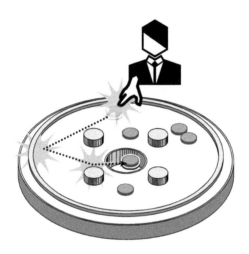

Description

Players use a finger or cue to strike a token and propel it toward a target.

Discussion

Flicking games sit on the line between toys, games, and sports. Flicking is an essential technique with no single or settled definition of what constitutes a flick. *Crokinole* is among the oldest flicking games that remains popular today. It can be played with either fingers or cues, with cues winning out over fingers in high-level play. It is a specific example of RES-10, Physical Action.

Flicking games test a player's accuracy, power, and control in various ways. In *PitchCar*, players flick a round disk representing a race car. Players seek to traverse the course as quickly as possible, which calls for powerful flicks. On the other hand, players must also keep their disks on the board, which requires control. In many instances, players must navigate their disks through small openings, or carom their disk at a specific angle off of a barrier, or even another player, which requires excellent accuracy.

Flicking introduces dynamism to the game that is unusual compared to most board games. In many flicking games, players stand and move around the play surface to find the right angle from which to take their shots. The drama of flicking makes games more suitable to spectators, and the atmosphere of flicking games is more social and celebratory than is typical for tabletop games outside of the party genre.

Because flicking is a learnable skill, there can be a sharp skill gap between players, similar to the skill gap in classic abstract games. When novice players play, flicking introduces randomness in the game's outputs, because players don't typically succeed in flicking as precisely as they intended. However, when experts play, there is very little randomness, and thus, it is near-certain that a skilled player will convincingly defeat beginners.

The most important aspect of flicking design is the physicality of the game. The object being flicked, the method of flicking, and the surface being flicked on must be carefully selected and manufactured. *Ascending Empires*, a 4X game, had players flicking ships across a puzzle-cut board to travel through space. Unfortunately, the production was marred by a warped board. The jigs of the puzzle would sometimes ride up in their pockets and create seams that interfered with the smooth travel of the ships in unintended ways.

Cosmic Kaboom took this lesson and had players flicking across their own tables or any other surface of their choice. *ICECOOL* went in the other direction, creating several nested cardboard boxes that are laid edge-to-edge and clipped together to create a large and consistently smooth surface. *Mars Open: Tabletop Golf* uses a novel approach by creating a folded chipboard component that is flicked into the air. *Flip Ships* has players flicking ships through the air from an elevated platform. Players can create courses on their tables or throughout their homes simply by placing the tee box in one place and the green somewhere else, and letting players navigate their way to the hole. *Sorry Sliders* provides chipboard ramps with plastic rails that create a level surface and help keep players from making invalid flicks.

The characteristics of the flicked object are another opportunity for creativity. ICECOOL's ball-bearing-mounted penguins can be flicked to consistently make them curve and jump, allowing for impressive shots and hilarious goofs. The *Mars Open* folded chipboard golf "ball" can similarly be manipulated to hook or draw shots, as in real golf. In *Flick 'Em Up*, players flick a larger disk to move their cowboys around and a smaller disk to simulate shooting. In *Tumblin' Dice*, players flick the eponymous dice down a tiered set of platforms. The dice bounce in surprising ways as they tumble, making for an unpredictable and thrilling experience.

Some games use flicking for its destructive capacity rather than to traverse a distance accurately. *Crossbows & Catapults* asks players to launch disks to knock over their opponents and their fortifications. Flicking and knocking over opponents as an abstraction of shooting or striking enemies is common to several games including the aforementioned *Flick 'Em Up*, *Catacombs*, and *SEAL Team Flix*.

Sample Games

> *Ascending Empires* (Cooper, 2011)
> *Catacombs* (Amos, Kelsey, West, 2010)
> *Cosmic Kaboom* (Loomis, 2016)
> *Crokinole* (Unknown, 1867)
> *Crossbows & Catapults* (Frigard & Sala, 1983)
> *Flick 'Em Up* (Beaujannot & Monpertuis, 2015)
> *Flip Ships* (Klenko, 2017)
> *Furnace* (Lashin, 2021)
> *ICECOOL* (Gomez, 2016)
> *Mars Open: Tabletop Golf* (Hoyle, 2018)
> *PitchCar* (du Poël, 1995)
> *SEAL Team Flix* (Ruth & Thomas, 2018)
> *Tumblin' Dice* (Grayson, Nash & Soued, 2004)

RES-25 Stacking and Balancing

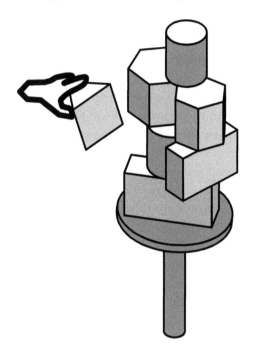

Description

Players must add, remove, or rearrange objects from a stack, a balancing contraption, or a playing surface.

Discussion

Dexterity mechanisms generally test both physical skill and the ability to evaluate the consequences of the physical act. Flicking games (see [flicking reference]) test both the flicking itself and the judgment of accuracy, angles, and ricochets. Stacking and balancing games test the steadiness of a player's hands, as well as their judgment about fulcrums, levers, weights, and densities. Somewhere between balancing and flicking lies pushing and sliding, which we will also discuss in this section. Note that while most games in this section are properly dexterity games (and a subset of RES-10 Physical Action), there are some notable exceptions.

While stacking and balancing games have existed in an oral culture for thousands of years, two of the most well-known modern stacking games are *Jenga* and *Blockhead!* Each is an example of two primary approaches to creating stacking games. *Jenga* uses uniform (though not perfectly identical) pieces, while *Blockhead!* uses pieces in a variety of odd shapes and sizes, with unusual angles and non-level planes.

The advantage of using more uniform pieces is that the tower can typically reach much higher heights than can be achieved with non-uniform pieces. Non-uniform stackers, like *Animal Upon Animal*, offer up interest in how odd shapes, angles, and even curves can support and counterbalance one another. *Catch The Moon* tries to capture the best of both worlds by asking players to stack ladders in a jumble. The ladders are similar but not identical, and players roll a die to determine whether the new ladder must touch one or two ladders or if it must be the highest ladder in the jumble after it is placed. These simple instructions, and the varied opportunities for how ladders can hook and support one another, create structures that are both tall and compelling to behold.

Jenga and its many spiritual successors, like *Rhino Hero*, have players perform both a removal and an addition to the tower. In *Jenga*, players must remove a block from the tower before adding it to the top of the tower. In *Rhino Hero*, the tower is built out of two kinds of cards: folded cards played as walls and flat cards played as roofs. The flat cards show an action that is triggered when the roof is played onto the tower, and one such action requires the next player to remove the eponymous wooden rhino meeple from wherever it is in the tower and to place it on top. The physics of removing this dense, heavy object—relative to the cards themselves, anyway—to place it at the top of a wobbly, swaying structure are tricky, to say the least! *Yura Yura Penguin* takes this concept even further by offering more objects to stack, including ice crystals, penguins of different shapes and sizes, and even a polar bear.

Stacking and balancing typically take center stage in a design, but hybridizing the mechanism is also possible. *Kapitän Wackelpudding* has players stacking wooden shapes onto a small ship, and then pushing it around the board, pick-up-and-deliver-style, to various ports. Goods that fall off of the ship are negative points, and at the end of the game, the player who knocked off the fewest goods wins. *MegaCity Oceania* has players constructing futuristic skyscrapers out of opaque and translucent plastic pieces that are piled on top of cardboard tiles and then sliding the tiles to join the rest of the skyscrapers already on the board. Players build and place skyscrapers to score points based on specifications in building contracts, adjacency to other tiles, and overall building height. If a building loses pieces during its journey to the central area, the player is penalized with a loss of their turn.

In *Tokyo Highway*, players use wooden cylinders and popsicle sticks to create roadways that pivot and loop over and under one another. They then add cars to these roadways—a privilege granted by successfully accomplishing the feat of crossing over another roadway as the highest crosser or crossing under it as the lowest crosser. The winner is the player who places all their cars, but even placing cars is fraught with peril. At any point, knocking over anything will cause a player to take penalties. *Tokyo Highway* differs from most balancing games in that the challenge is less about balance and more about positioning. The wooden roads balance reasonably solidly on the flat sides of the cylinders, and building roadways is not particularly challenging. However, maneuvering your fingers and wooden pieces through the thicket of roadways that quickly springs up and positioning your body to maintain stability in order to place roadways in scoring configurations are quite challenging. In some ways, the game is the inverse of *Jonchets* or its modern successor, *Pick-Up Sticks*, in which players remove narrow wooden sticks from a jumble, without causing any other sticks to move. Both games require intense concentration and fine motor skills but are less about finding balance and equilibrium in a structure.

There is a danger in creating hybrid games. Players may be frustrated by strategizing properly but losing because of failures of dexterity. Or, players may find the physical aspects of the game more compelling and fun than the strategy. In some cases, the dexterity aspects of the game simply may not work well and consistently enough to work as a game, rather than as an activity. *Coaster Park*, a game about assembling cardboard roller coasters and running a steel ball bearing through them, suffered greatly from this. Players assumed that the game was signifying, for example, that the largest starting hill would generate sufficient momentum through gravity alone to climb the next-highest hill or to complete the loop-the-loop but, in fact, it took quite a bit of skill in flicking the marble—to say nothing of carefully assembling and angling the joints between sections—to make the roller coasters work at all. For many players, the difficulty of the physical mechanism made the game as a whole unplayable as intended, but for many players, the issue was not simply the difficulty, but their expectation that the game was not a dexterity challenge at all and that the roller coaster was a novelty and a gimmick, not a gameplay mechanism.

Another hybrid, *Terror in Meeple City* (nee *Rampage*), has players as kaiju monsters who seek to destroy buildings made of meeples that hold up tiers of cardboard tiles. Players can use one of several techniques, including flicking, dropping, and even blowing air from their mouths, to try and dislodge the meeples and destroy the tower. Scoring is relatively complex and includes variable scoring cards that define how sets of different colored meeples score, penalties for allowing meeples to escape the city, and penalties for being struck by other monsters.

While *Terror in Meeple City* is quite ambitious in directly translating a kaiju attack into a dexterity board game, perhaps the most ambitious hybrid dexterity game is *Beasts of Balance*, an app-supported game featuring a virtual world. In *Beasts of Balance*, a central platform, called the Plinth, has an NFC (Near Field Communications) reader that can scan and read the specially shaped, oversized plastic creatures that are stacked atop it. The Plinth also keeps track of the weight of the objects piled on top of it.

When players add a creature to the Plinth, the app displays that creature being added to one of three regions in a virtual world. Adding multiple creatures to a region can lead to the breeding of hybrid creatures, and some creatures prey on others. The dynamic environment and evolving creatures are all virtual, while players interact with that world almost solely through stacking creatures and special objects on the Plinth. When anything comes dislodged from the Plinth, it must be re-stacked within a few moments, as the Plinth recognizes the overall change of weight in the stack. These moments do provide opportunities for rearranging the stack. Note also that *Beasts of Balance* is a cooperative game (though a competitive variant is included in the rules), and we will return to this point later.

Stacking and balancing games are close cousins to Push-Your-Luck games (see UNC-02) in that players are uncertain about the exact impact of their actions on the physical equilibrium of the game. Causing a collapse is similar to busting and, typically, safe moves evaporate as the game progresses.

Auctions are one method designers use to give players control over risk, and a series of very similar games offer several approaches to implementing an auction in this context. In *Bausack*, there are a variety of stacking shapes. The active player chooses one and offers it to another player, who may accept it and add it to their personal structure or discard a bean to avoid it. A player without beans can no longer avoid a block, and players are eliminated when their structures collapse.

In *Bandu*, the core gameplay is the same, but the auction element is even stronger. The active player chooses a block and selects to run a "Use" or "Refuse" auction. The winner of a Use auction or the loser of a refuse auction places the piece. This game offers quite a lot of agency to the players, in selecting the piece up for auction, evaluating whether it is relatively easy or difficult to place for each player, given the current state of their tower, and deciding the auction type to hold. In *Sac Noir*, there are several additional variations on this same gameplay, including building a shared central tower, a set of more difficult shapes, and additional auction types.

Balancing games often include a central contraption whose instability defines the underlying physics of the game. Unlike the level, though small, stage of the Plinth in *Beasts of Balance*, *Topple* features a plastic, tiered platter that looks something like a step pyramid that balances on a long plastic pole, or perhaps the skirt of a ballerina's tutu as they stand on pointe. Players play plastic counters onto the "board" and score points for creating rows and stacks of the same color. When a player causes a topple, all the other players are awarded points. Other interesting central contraptions include the wire hanger structure of *Suspend*, the anthropomorphic and eponymous waiter in *Don't Tip the Waiter*, and the giant wooden pirate ship featured in *Riff Raff*.

Like hybrids mentioned earlier, *Topple* is something like *Connect Four* combined with physics. *Leverage* features a board balanced on a fulcrum, like a teeter-totter. Play is similar to both *Checkers* and *Chinese Checkers* but for two players only. Players move, jump, and capture using pawns of three different weights and sizes. As players advance their pawns, the equilibrium of the board shifts, sometimes causing the board to rest on one player's side. That player must remove one or more special scoring pawns from their back row until the board reaches equilibrium again and is suspended in mid-air again. When a player runs out of scoring pawns to remove, they lose when the board touches down on their side again. A similar, more broadly available game is *Rock Me Archimedes*, which features this same teetering board and central mechanism.

In both *Leverage* and *Rock Me Archimedes*, there is no dexterity element of any kind. Placing and moving pieces is not a challenge of execution, and accidentally toppling pieces lies outside the scope of the rules and is not penalized. The skills being tested, beyond the spatial and tactical skills of maneuvering pawns on the board, are skills of evaluation of weight and equilibrium. These may be the exceptions to the general rule of balancing games as dexterity games. Indeed, in most games, there are specific rules about how the pieces may be handled: with one or two hands, within some time limit, and more. In *Lift It!*, players cannot use their hands at all and instead strap a crane to their heads, using a headband, to build structures together.

Rules like this point to a general concern for accessibility in balancing games. Balancing games are particularly difficult to make accessible to players with various physical limitations, be they limited vision, mobility challenges, or unsteady hands that can accompany normal aging. However, balancing games do provide affordances for managing skill differentials among players, such as playing with an off-hand.

Stacking and balancing games appeal to designers who are designing for younger audiences, precisely because of how easy they are to explain. While most games abstract complex systems, these games leverage simple physical phenomena that can be understood even by the very young. There are some developmental and psychological realities, however, that designers should consider when creating games for families and younger players. For instance, while many stacking games end with a collapse, which can be a cathartic and hilarious moment, this can be a devastating moment for younger children, a moment of deep frustration and even anguish.

Adults are not immune to these feelings, which may explain why cooperative stacking and balancing games have emerged in recent years. *Menara* is a cooperative stacking game in which failures are punished by making players stack to an even higher height to win. This intensification of difficulty is a common trope in cooperative games but is novel in the genre of stacking games. Turning these games into co-ops appears to take some of the stings out of failure and amplifies the aspects of social fun, rather than mastery, in the game.

Creating physical games requires designers to focus sharply on the specifications of the materials of the game pieces. Their weight, shape, the friction of their surfaces, and the ease with which they can be manipulated in hand all play an enormous role in how they work in the game. Manufacturing considerations need to be taken into account quite early in the process, relative to non-physical games. The overall weight and size of these games can be a major limiting factor in terms of the game's marketability and price point (Illustration 4.7).

Illustration 4.7   The stacking in *Junk Art* can be both challenging and aesthetically pleasing.

Finally, we will note that many games of this kind feature multiple modes of play and variants. There are many small and simple twists that can give rise to unique play experiences within the same framework of pieces. *Junk Art*, a highly regarded recent design, features 12 different rules variants on "city cards," representing a kind of world tour that players embark on. The game even contains three blank city cards, inviting players to make up their own variants. This speaks of the essential simplicity and infinite variety of stacking and balancing as a pastime and vehicle for fun.

Sample Games

Animal Upon Animal (Miltenberger, 2005)
Bausack (Zoch, 1987)
Beasts of Balance (Buckenham and Fleetwood, 2016)
Blockhead! (D'Arcey, 1952)
Catch The Moon (Riffaud and Rodriguez, 2017)
Coaster Park (Almes, 2017)
Don't Tip the Waiter (Collicott, 2014)
Jenga (Scott, 1983)
Junk Art (Cormier and Lim, 2016)
Kapitän Wackelpudding (McGuire and McGuire, 1994)
Leverage (Slimp, 1977)
MegaCity Oceania (Draper and Fox, 2019)
Menara (Richtberg, 2018)
Coaster Park (Almes, 2017)
Pick-Up Sticks (Unknown, ~1850)
Rhino Hero (Frisco and Strumpf, 2011)
Riff Raff (Cantzler, 2012)
Rock Me Archimedes (Buchanan, 2012)
Suspend (Uncredited, 2012)
Terror in Meeple City (Bauza and Maublanc, 2013)
Tokyo Highway (Shimamoto and Tomioka, 2016)
Topple (Thibault, 1983)
Yura Penguin (Ryoko, 2019)

RES-26 Neighbor Scope

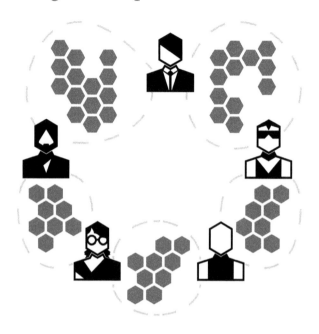

Description

Actions, resources, or resolutions are shared between neighbors.

Discussion

The concept "scope" generally means the range of impact an action has among players. The two most common scopes are global scope—impacting everyone—and personal scope—impacting only yourself.

Neighbor Scope is a specific type of scope that has particular considerations and uses. Before we dive into these details, two game examples will clarify what this term means.

In *7 Wonders*, there are two Neighbor Scope systems. When placing cards, players may use a resource that their neighbor produces by giving them two coins. And when the military is resolved, each player compares their strength only to their immediate neighbor to see if they take a victory or defeat token.

In *Between Two Cities*, each player builds two cities—one to their left and the other to their right. Their cities are shared by the neighbors on either side. Each round, players draft tiles and place them into their shared cities. At the end of the game, each city is scored, and each player scores points equal to their lowest-scoring city (a form of Highest-Lowest scoring—see VIC-20). Players work with their neighbors to make each city as good as possible but are incentivized to emphasize improving their lower-scoring city.

Neighbor scope has a number of positive features. The most important is that by restricting the interactions a player needs to worry about, it is easier to scale the game to higher player counts. This is evident in *7 Wonders*, which comfortably goes to seven players. If you could potentially get resources from any other player or attack them, it would slow the game down quite a lot as players have more options to consider. Limiting the scope limits the number of possibilities that need to be considered and presents a smaller decision space to players.

Similarly, the neighbor scope of *Between Two Cities* allows for negotiation and player discussion but in a controlled way. This makes it more comfortable for players who don't like open negotiation games and also reduces the time required for negotiations—always a potential issue with these types of games (see ECO-18 Negotiation).

The downside of this mechanism is that, particularly at larger player counts, players often do not need to interact, even socially, with players other than neighbors, particularly players that are across the table from them, the farthest players from them positionally. Players may go an entire game and not know how those players are doing, what their strategies are, or good or bad players they are making. Since they are only interacting with their immediate neighbors, that is who they are focusing on. Then, when the game ends, they find out how other people did, which often comes as a surprise.

Players at far distances impact them only indirectly, if at all. While this may make sense from a simulation standpoint or from allowing the game to scale smoothly, it does make for a certain type of social experience that is more fragmented and doesn't create a group "story" per se.

There are many other expressions of neighbor scope. One is the standard card draft (CAR-06 Card Drafting), where players select a card from their hand and pass the rest to their left. You most immediately impact your "downstream" neighbor as, depending on the game, you may be able to judge what people are collecting and potentially block them from gaining a set or combo.

A unique implementation can be found in *Crude: The Oil Game*. Each player builds facilities on a 6×6 grid. At the start of a player's turn, they roll two dice, and one activates a row in the grid and the other a column.

Any facilities found in these produce resources. However, the row die also activates the same row in the right-hand neighbor's grid, and the column die activates the matching column in the left-hand neighbor (Illustration 4.8).

Another is in party games. The classic game "telephone," where players whisper a message down a chain of people, is an example. Another is *Telestrations*, where players alternately draw or describe a picture based on what they are given by their neighbor. Both examples underscore how this allows games to scale to a large group while keeping the action understandable and focused.

The concept of scope can be applied in other ways as well. Some multiplayer games will extend neighbor scope by including effects that impact the player directly across from you, or a player two to your left or right. Again, the objective is to restrict the decision space.

To a certain extent, the Destiny system in *Cosmic Encounter* also applies a scope limitation. At the start of each turn, a player draws a card or disk

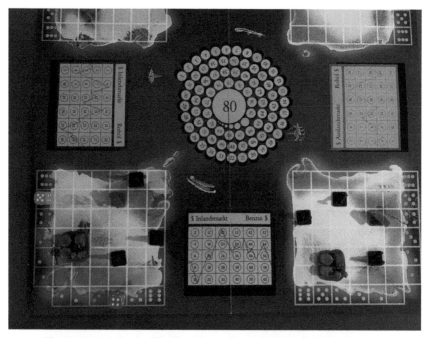

Illustration 4.8   In *Crude*, the active player rolls two dice and activates buildings in that row and column. The dice also activate the buildings of the active player's neighbors. In this example, the red die in the lower left would activate the red "5" row in the right-hand neighbor's grid.

(depending on game version) from a pile, and it directs which player they must attack. The targets aren't limited to neighbors, of course, but the system does limit the interaction to two players only.

Thoughtful consideration of action scope allows the designer to control complexity, decision space, and player interaction.

Sample Games

    7 Wonders (Bauza, 2010)
    Between Two Cities (O'Malley, Pedersen, Rosset, 2015)
    Between Two Castles of Mad King Ludwig (O'Malley and Rosset 2018)
    Crude: The Oil Game (St. Laurent, 1974)
    Kodama Forest (Iglesias and Riley, 2020)
    Telephone (Unknown)
    Telestrations (Uncredited, 2009) [Published version of public domain Eat Poop You Cat]

5

Game End and Victory

Two characteristics that separate games from other activities are having a goal and a defined end-game point. Even in a role-playing game (RPG), which may not have a formal end-game point, a campaign or narrative arc reaches a climax, and though the characters may continue on to the next adventure, goals still exist. Achieving goals, or achieving them better than other players, defines who wins the game. Goals and end-game points are frequently intertwined in games, so we are exploring them together in this chapter. The first section primarily features ways of determining the winner, and the second section contains triggers for ending the game. We conclude this chapter by looking at several ancillary considerations for these topics.

The first few mechanisms detail different aspects of *Victory Points* (VPs). Giving points to players is a straightforward way to determine who wins a game. Indeed, any victory system can be expressed as VPs. For example, *Snakes & Ladders*, which is a Race game (VIC-07), could be treated as having points. Rather than reaching square 100, players have points based on the square they are on. The first player to get 100 points (exactly) is the winner and ends the game. This is a trivial example, but designers should be on the lookout for other ways to define victory that better meet the theme of the game. For example, in many business or economic games, the victory goes to the player with the most money or the one who surpasses a monetary threshold.

Many games allow players to collect points from several different activities. Thousands of years ago, *Go* allowed the players to score points by both surrounding territories and capturing enemy stones. Having multiple ways to gain points gives players multiple strategic approaches and allows players to judge the relative values of actions.

VIC-01 Victory Points from Game State

Description

An event causes the Game State to be evaluated relative to some scoring condition. Players earn points based on how that state matches the condition.

Discussion

In most points-based games, players manipulate the Game State and then gain points based on that State. In some games, such as *7 Wonders* or *Agricola*, points are only tallied at the end of the game. However, there are a variety of ways with which scoring can be triggered, which can be grouped broadly into three categories: Scheduled, Player Action, and Random systems.

In Scheduled systems, there are predefined intervals for when scoring will happen, and players know when they are approaching. For example, in *El Grande*, scoring happens three times during the game, after a set number of rounds. Regardless of which actions the players take, scoring will happen at exactly those intervals. In *Galaxy Trucker*, players score at the end of each run, when a fixed number of hazards are encountered.

In a Player Action system, players are the ones who trigger scoring. Sometimes this is completely at the discretion of the players, and sometimes the precise timing falls within a band of possible values. For example, in *Twilight Struggle*, players who have dealt a Region Scoring card must play it sometime during that hand. However, the exact timing is dependent on a Player Action. *The Expanse Board Game* is more open-ended, as players can draft a Scoring card any time one is available. They do not have to do it within a certain time frame.

In a Random system, there are Scoring cards or tokens that are mixed in with other items. When these are drawn, scoring occurs. In *Airlines*, Scoring cards are shuffled into the deck. As each is drawn, scoring happens. The drawing of the last card also ends the game (VIC-12). In practice, truly random scoring systems are rare. Frequently, Scoring cards are shuffled into the bottom third of the deck or some similar range. Other random triggers involve seeing two or even three more of the same type of card, as in *Incan Gold*, where the second hazard of the same type drawn ends the round, or *Ethnos*, where the third dragon drawn ends the age. These systems are random, but their likely outcomes fall within a predictable range.

Games that score just one time, at game end, can fall into any of these categories depending on how the end of the game is triggered.

Many systems are a blend between these categories. *Twilight Struggle* has elements of all three, as Scoring is under player control (somewhat), must occur by a definite point in the game (Scheduled), but it is also Random in that it is not known in which round the Region Scoring cards will be in play. Rather than seeing these differences as categorical, we can say that scoring systems have some or all of these characteristics.

Area Majority (ARC-02) and Economic games (Chapter 7) in particular tend to use the VP from the Game State mechanism. Area Majority games are very concerned about board state, and their core concept is maneuvering your resources to be able to obtain the most majorities when scoring is triggered. Similarly, in Economic Games, where money is often a proxy for VPs, businesses can pay out based on the state of the boards and markets. *Power Grid*, for example, pays out money based on connected cities at the end of each turn.

A Scheduled trigger is best suited for more strategic games, as it allows for long-term planning. Random triggers are excellent at creating tension but can reward players who simply happened to be in a superior position when scoring occurs. Player Action triggers can be highly strategic or quite tactical, depending on implementation. Players can plan and trigger scoring when it is most beneficial to them, leading to interesting choices. It can also add tension as other players try to take advantage of another player triggering scoring, particularly in games where the possibility of a scoring option is hidden (as in *Twilight Struggle*).

While Scheduled trigger systems are more strategic, they can also lead to bad edge effects. An "edge effect" is a distortion of gameplay when it approaches a boundary. If players know exactly when scoring will occur, the final actions leading up to scoring can be subject to over-analysis and game-lengthening delays as players attempt to optimize their scores, particularly if there are no hidden elements. Depending on the nature of the game, this can impact players' enjoyment.

Some Schedule-based systems put scoring at the end of each player's turn, like *Small World* and *Through the Ages: A Story of Civilization*. Because of the proximity of the player's actions to when scoring occurs, this blurs with Victory Points from Player Actions (VIC-02). It is worth noting that sometimes these systems award points at the start of a player's turn, not the end; *King of Tokyo* is an example. This means that players need to maintain their state as the other players take their turns and can lead to interesting interactions.

Sample Games

   7 Wonders (Bauza, 2010)
   Agricola (Rosenberg, 2007)
   Airlines (Moon, 1990)
   Azul (Kiesling, 2017)
   El Grande (Kramer and Ulrich, 1995)
   Ethnos (Mori, 2017)
   The Expanse Board Game (Engelstein, 2017)
   Galaxy Trucker (Chvátil, 2007)
   Go (Unknown, 2200 BCE)
   Incan Gold (Faidutti and Moon, 2005)
   King of Tokyo (Garfield, 2011)
   Power Grid (Friese, 2004)
   Primordial Soup (Matthäus and Nestel, 1997)
   Small World (Keyaerts, 2009)
   Through the Ages: A Story of Civilization (Chvátil, 2006)
   Twilight Struggle (Gupta and Matthews, 2005)

VIC-02 Victory Points from Player Actions

Description

Players earn points by performing actions.

Discussion

In contrast with Victory Points from Game State, this mechanism gives players points based on discrete actions which may be very local. An example would be capturing stones in *Go*, where each stone is worth one point. Surrounding territory in *Go*, the other way of scoring points, is only evaluated at the end of the game and until that point can be invaded, shrunk, or expanded.

Eclipse and *Kemet* offer VPs for winning battles. Many games, like *Lords of Waterdeep*, *Nexus Ops*, or *Splendor*, have players take actions to complete or claim private or public goal cards (VIC-11), which are worth points.

The relationship between the Action that you perform to gain VPs and how that affects your position and the game state has an important impact on the flow of the game. In some, like *Lords of Waterdeep*, completing quest cards is the main point of the game and doesn't aid or hinder your ability to perform other actions in the future.

However, in games like *Dominion* and *Splendor*, taking Victory cards can hinder your ability to gain more Victory cards. In *Dominion*, the point cards become part of your deck, but they have no purpose if drawn. They simply clog things up. In *Splendor*, purchasing high-value cards does not give you as much of a "bang for your buck" for getting gem bonuses as purchasing lower-cost cards. In these games, the players need to choose between building up their engine or economy and cashing in on it. It creates what we call a "pivot," where players need to transition between building and scoring. This can be an interesting puzzle for players to work through.

Sample Games

> *Carcassonne* (Wrede, 2000)
> *Codenames* (Chvátil, 2015)
> *Dominion* (Vaccarino, 2008)
> *Eclipse* (Tahkokallio, 2011)
> *Go* (Unknown, 2200 BCE)
> *Kemet* (Bariot and Montiage, 2012)
> *Lords of Waterdeep* (Lee and Thompson, 2012)
> *Nexus Ops* (Cantino and Kimball, 2005)
> *Splendor* (André, 2014)

VIC-03 Temporary and Permanent Victory Points

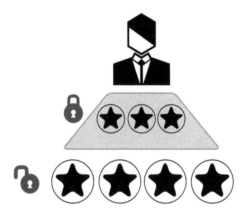

Description

Some Victory Points (VPs) are never lost. Others depend on the game state and may be lost if that state changes.

Discussion

This mechanism is typically used in games where the ending condition is a player reaching a certain number of VPs. For example, in *Catan*, the game ends when a player reaches 10 points. In *Kemet*, it ends when a player reaches 8 points.

Gaining permanent VPs is important to help drive the game to a conclusion. If all points are temporary, it encourages players to try to take down the leader and pull them further away from winning, which can lengthen the game. *Munchkin*, where player level is a proxy for VPs, has this issue, as do *Dune* and *Cosmic Encounter*, which require players to hold a certain number of spaces.

Having a mix of temporary and permanent points is a good way of dealing with this issue, as it both drives the game toward a conclusion and offers opportunities for players to make a sudden grab for victory or move their opponents away from victory if they have a lot of temporary points (Illustration 5.1).

Kemet is a good example of this technique. Permanent VPs are gained through winning battles, controlling temples, certain Power cards, and other

Illustration 5.1   *Kemet* has permanent Victory Points (square tokens) and temporary Victory Points (round tokens). The image on the tokens indicates the source of the points, which is of particular help in remembering when the temporary points are lost.

means. Temporary points are gained by holding special regions on the board. So, if a player has a bank of VPs but is a few points shy of victory, he or she can launch attacks on spaces to try to gain those last few points and win. This can lead to dramatic moments in the game and can also incentivize players to overextend themselves and take a chance, which increases the tension.

Sample Games

   Catan (Teuber, 1995)
   Kemet (Bariot and Montiage, 2012)

VIC-04 Victory Points as a Resource

Description

Victory Points (VPs) may be spent as a currency to impact the game state.

Discussion

Economic games, where money represents victory, are the primary examples of this mechanism. Having players spend and invest money to make more money is at the core of the business and finds representation in many business games. This forces players to think about valuation and Return on Investment as key drivers in their decisions. What is the expected payback on the available options?

This mechanism is used outside of economic games as well. *Small World* is a great example, where players must spend VPs to skip over certain options on a Draft Track, creating an auction-like mechanic for valuing the races available (AUC-08).

Typically, players will be more cautious about spending VPs when they are not themed as money. In the context of an Economic game, players may not even really think about money as a "Victory Point" currency. We are so used to using it in our everyday lives that we inherently understand the concept of investing for future payout. However, when they are represented as VPs, Honor, or other thematic elements, they take on a different connotation, and players tend to be more emotionally attached to them.

Understanding this underlying psychology gives the designer another tool for shaping the player experience.

Sample Games

1830 (Tresham, 1986)
Age of Steam (Wallace, 2002)

Empire Builder (Bromley and Fawcett, 1982)
The Expanse Board Game (Engelstein, 2017)
Power Grid (Friese, 2004)
Small World (Keyaerts, 2009)

VIC-05 Hidden and Exposed Victory Points

Description

Victory Points (VPs) may be public or private information.

Discussion

The decision of whether to have the number of VPs each player has as public or private information can have a big impact on the play experience. It is particularly dependent on the method for ending the game and the overall amount of hidden and public information.

If a game has a set number of turns, so that players know exactly when the end is coming, and most information is public, including VPs, it can lead to over-analysis during the last turn, as players try to optimize that last play. Alternatively, there can be situations where the last turn is meaningless because the leading player cannot be unseated (in which case consider VIC-15 Short Circuits). Typically, this is considered undesirable by players, although certain types of games and players can support this. If the points are hidden or if players are not sure what other players can do, through hidden information, this tendency is alleviated.

As an example, the 1999 game, *Vinci*, had players controlling civilizations that would rise and fall across Europe. Scores were open, and the number of turns was fixed. *Vinci* was, in general, positively regarded; however, many reviewers found the final turn very unsatisfying. Players scored points at the end of their turn, and turns were deterministic. Players could calculate exactly how to maximize their score and often spent quite a bit of time doing so to squeeze out one more point. Years later, the game was reworked and re-released as *Small World*. The main structural change was the introduction of hidden scores and a minor random element. These changes were sufficient to alleviate the last turn issue and give the game a much lighter feel, turning it into one of the staples of the hobby gaming market.

Conversely, having too many hidden bonus points at the end of the game can lead to an unsatisfying play experience. See VIC-06 for a full discussion.

Sample Games

> *Azul* (Kiesling, 2017)
> *Small World* (Keyaerts, 2009)
> *Suburbia* (Alspach, 2012)
> *Tigris & Euphrates* (Knizia, 1997)
> *Vinci* (Keyaerts, 1999)

VIC-06 End-Game Bonuses

Description

Players earn bonus VPs at the end of the game.

Discussion

This is a popular technique for giving players strategic direction. Giving players a specific goal to earn points early in the game gives new players an idea of what they should be doing.

End-Game Bonuses can be either Personal or Public. Points from Personal goals can only be earned by the owner, while Public goals may be pursued by multiple players. In some games, goals are non-exclusive and can be scored by multiple players, while in others, only the player who achieves the goal "the best" receives the points.

Public goals provide a natural interaction point for players and can be used where there is not as much player interaction through the other mechanisms. In their simplest form, public goals are a method for turning any puzzle into a competitive game. In *Dimension*, for example, players use the same set of spheres to build a pyramid that satisfies as many of the six public goals as possible.

Private goals help differentiate players and can give a strong direction to their play. For example, in *Ticket to Ride*, the tickets tell players which cities to connect to, but points are awarded (or lost) only at the end of the game. This gives players a literal roadmap of their goals.

There are a number of benefits of keeping personal goals hidden, like making it impossible to precisely determine who is winning and adding an element of deduction as players attempt to block each other. *Ticket to Ride* with exposed goals would be a very different, and more frustrating, experience.

Another design consideration is when and how goals are assigned. Sometimes they are random, and sometimes players must construct or choose their goals. A concern for designers is that if goals are assigned randomly, later in the game, players may luck into points by being randomly dealt a goal that they have already achieved. This is one reason that earlier assignment of bonuses is generally preferred unless countered by a penalty for not achieving them (as in *Ticket to Ride*). Games such as *Race for the Galaxy* may give players access to a random selection of possible End-Game Bonuses, but players may choose to build them or not. *Concordia* allows players to draft cards which will give bonus points in specific categories. Having more cards in a given category increases the point value.

Terraforming Mars has an interesting approach to assigning end-game goals. Players may use an action and spend money to unlock specific public End-Game Bonuses. The amount of money required increases each time a new goal is unlocked, so waiting until you are certain about what you want to unlock means spending more resources. Only three goals at most can be unlocked, putting more pressure on players to decide which goals they think they can win at.

Designers should also consider the ratio between points earned during the game and points earned at the end. If the ratio is very large and bonuses are complex or hidden, it can be very difficult for players to know where they stand. This increases the skill and experience required to play the game well.

For example, in *Concordia*, all points are earned from End-Game Bonuses. To offset that issue, the game includes an optional intermediate scoring step which is basically a practice scoring so that players can make sure they understand the available bonuses, as well as get a better feel for their relative position.

Sample Games

Concordia (Gerdts, 2013)
Dimension (Luchau, 2014)
Race for the Galaxy (Lehmann, 2007)
Suburbia (Alspach, 2012)
Terraforming Mars (Fryxelius, 2016)
Ticket to Ride (Moon, 2004)

VIC-07 Race

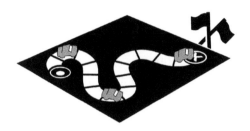

Description

The winner is the first player to reach the end of a track.

Discussion

This mechanism is both a way of determining when the game ends and determining a victor. Both typically occur at the same time as one or more players cross a finish line or reach a goal.

Some of the oldest games in human history are Race games, including *Senet*, *Backgammon*, *Snakes & Ladders*, and *Parcheesi*. They are intuitive about the goal and it is clear who is in the lead at any point.

There are a variety of games that are mechanically Race games but don't have the trappings of a physical race. Any game that has players trying to reach a certain target quantity of VPs is, in essence, a race game. *Catan* is a race to get to ten points. *Empire Builder* is a race to get to $250,000,000.

Conversely, there are games that appear to be a Race but that are actually not. Typically, these involve betting on the outcome of a race, as in *Royal Turf*, *Downforce*, and *Long Shot*. These are actually equivalent to VIC-01 Victory Points from Game State, where the situation on the board feeds into a point total.

More discussion on actual Race mechanisms is included in Chapter 10, "Movement."

Sample Games

Ave Caesar (Riedesser, 1989)
Backgammon (Unknown, 3000 BCE)

Catan (Teuber, 1995)
Empire Builder (Bromley and Fawcett, 1982)
Formula De (Lavauer and Randall, 1991)
Hare & Tortoise (Parlett, 1973)
Kemet (Bariot and Montiage, 2012)
Lord of the Rings (Knizia, 2000)
Mush! Mush!: Snow Tails 2 (Lamont and Lamont, 2013)
Parcheesi (Unknown, 400)
Senet (Unknown)
Sky Runner (Glimne, Karlsson and Sevelin, 1999)
Snakes & Ladders (Unknown, ~200 BCE)
Sorry! (Haskell, Jr. and Storey, 1929)

VIC-08 Player Elimination

Description

The winner is the only player remaining in the game.

Discussion

Player Elimination is typically considered an anti-pattern, a mechanism to be avoided. From a purely practical standpoint, elimination may result in a player not being able to participate with the group for an hour or more, leading to awkward social situations.

However, it can be effectively used in shorter and lighter games that may be played multiple times in rapid succession. If being eliminated means that you are out of the game for 5 or 10 minutes, as in *Love Letter* or *Liar's Dice*, that is very different than being eliminated early from a game of *Risk* or *Monopoly*.

Player Elimination can also be effective if it fits into the narrative and theme of the game. For example, winning in *Nuclear War* requires all players but one to be eliminated. However, when a player is eliminated, they are given a special Final Retaliation turn where they can launch all the missiles that remain in their hands at the players of their choice. This is both satisfying and thematically consonant and results in many plays having no winner at all.

A different social dynamic arises in team-based games with elimination, like *Werewolf*. After being eliminated, players can still participate vicariously, as they may still be part of the winning team. *Werewolf* also benefits from being interesting for non-participants to watch.

BANG! extends this two-team concept by adding a third side that switches allegiance. The two main teams are the Lawmen (led by the Sheriff) and the Outlaws. The Outlaws win if the Sheriff is killed. The Lawmen win if the Outlaws and the Renegade are killed. The Renegade wins if all the Lawmen and Outlaws are killed. The Renegade's strategy is to initially help protect the Sheriff and then turn on the Lawmen once the Outlaws are eliminated. Since roles are hidden, this makes for a very exciting dynamic, even for players who have been eliminated, as their team may still win.

Another variation on Player Elimination is *End-Game Elimination*. Based on certain criteria, one or more players may be eliminated from the possibility of winning the game. For example, in *High Society*, players spend money to gain objects that are worth VPs. The player with the most VPs wins, except that the player with the least money remaining cannot win, so players need to track what other players are doing and avoid over-spending. Similarly, in *Cleopatra and the Society of Architects*, players may take more powerful actions by taking Corruption tokens. At the end of the game, the hidden Corruption totals are revealed, and the player with the most Corruption cannot win.

While these examples are deterministic, End-Game Elimination can also be applied randomly. For example, in *The Hunger Games: District 12 Strategy Game*, during the game, players may choose to, or be forced to, place tokens into the Tribute pool. At the end of the game, one Tribute token is drawn at random, and the player it belongs to is eliminated from a chance at victory. This system gives players a chance to do risk-reward analysis and is highly thematic with the source material. However, in general, it is not received as favorably as a deterministic End-Game Elimination mechanism as players may have many fewer tokens in the pool and still get chosen, making them feel they lost due to an unlucky break rather than mistakes they made.

Sample Games

BANG! (Sciarra, 2002)
Cleopatra and the Society of Architects (Cathala and Maublanc, 2006)
Coup (Tahta, 2012)
High Society (Knizia, 1995)
The Hunger Games: District 12 Strategy Game (Guild, Kinsella, and Parks, 2012)

Liar's Dice (Unknown, 1800)
Love Letter (Kanai, 2012)
Monopoly (Darrow and Magie, 1933)
Nuclear War (Malewicki, 1965)
Risk (Lamorisse and Levin, 1959)
Werewolf (Davidoff and Plotkin, 1986)

VIC-09 Fixed Number of Rounds

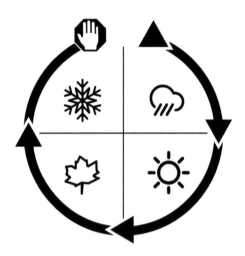

Description

The game ends after a set number of rounds.

Discussion

This is a basic approach to determine when the game will end. However, there are still some considerations for the designer.

First, players must track the current round, often with a marker on a track. It's not a big burden on the players, but it does require them to remember to advance the token at the end of each round.

If possible, a more natural way of tracking the current round is advised. An elegant approach is to have items used in the game come off of the round tracker, instead of pushing a maker along it. In *Castles of Burgundy*, the new building tiles that populate the board each round are divided into stacks and placed on the round tracker. Those tiles are placed on the board each turn, which is a step that players are unlikely to forget, and players can glance at the round tracker and see, based on how many stacks remain, how many rounds are left in the game.

Similar techniques can be used for an end-game trigger. *The Speicherstadt* has a deck with a fixed number of cards. When the cards run out, the game is over. This eliminates the need for players to act to advance a marker. The depletion of the cards happens naturally over the course of the game. The number of turns and rounds is the same every game—but the players do not directly track them.

For example, in *Modern Art*, the end of each round features the valuation of paintings, with players placing markers for the most valuable paintings for that round. However, there are only three slots for these markers, corresponding to the rounds in the game. The valuation step will not be missed by players, so this does not increase the rules' burden on the players.

The other consideration is end-game edge effects. If the players know that this is the final round, it may change their behavior, which may be undesirable. One aspect of this is discussed in Hidden and Exposed Victory Points (VIC-05).

Sample Games

Castles of Burgundy (Feld, 2011)
Die Macher (Schmiel, 1986)
Guilds of London (Boydell, 2016)
Modern Art (Knizia, 1992)
Small World (Keyaerts, 2009)
The Speicherstadt (Feld, 2010)
Twilight Struggle (Gupta and Matthews, 2005)

VIC-10 Exhausting Resources

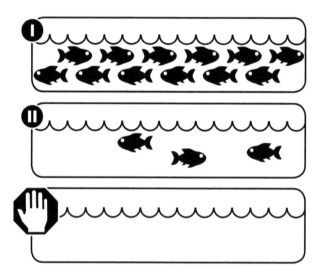

Description

The game end is triggered by a resource being exhausted. Players can affect the length of the game by how these resources are used.

Discussion

The Exhausting Resources mechanism is a nice balance between driving the game toward a conclusion and giving the players some control over the pacing.

In the *18xx* series of games, the game end is triggered by all money being taken out of the bank. In *Through the Ages: A Story of Civilization*, when the final Age III cards are drawn, the game ends, giving players the option to draw a lot or a few of the cards to manage the pace. *Race for the Galaxy* has a pool of VP tokens, which end the game when exhausted, and *Dominion* concludes when three stacks are exhausted.

While these examples all have a shared resource pool, some games end when an individual pool is exhausted. *Ticket to Ride* ends when one player has 0–2 trains left. In *Light Speed*, the game moves on to final scoring after one player has placed all of their ships on the table.

This technique is frequently used as a loss condition for cooperative games. For example, in *Pandemic*, having to place a disease cube but having none available in the pool will end the game in a loss, as will placing all the ghosts in *Ghost Fightin' Treasure Hunters*.

Sample Games

1830 (Tresham, 1986)
Dominion (Vaccarino, 2008)
Ghost Fightin' Treasure Hunters (Yu, 2013)
Light Speed (Ernest and Jolly, 2003)
Pandemic (Leacock, 2008)
Race for the Galaxy (Lehmann, 2007)
Through the Ages: A Story of Civilization (Chvátil, 1986)
Ticket to Ride (Moon, 2004)

VIC-11 Completing Targets

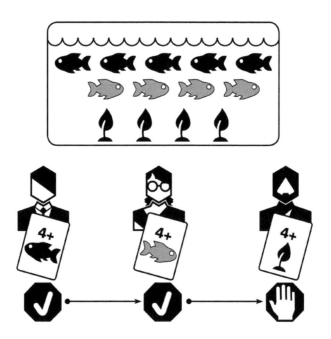

Description

The game ends after a set number of targets or goals are completed.

Discussion

In one sense, the Completing Target mechanism is related to Exhausting Resources (VIC-10), as meeting X targets could be represented by removing "mission accomplished" markers from a pool and having the game end when those markers are exhausted. The difference in player experience is substantial, though, and gaining accomplishments is thematically more coherent in most cases than exhausting "mission accomplished" tokens.

Completing Targets is also similar to Race end-game conditions, where the game ends when players hit (typically) a victory point goal. However, the goals can be more than just the accumulation of points, such as curing all diseases in *Pandemic*, taking enough keeps in *Dune*, or destroying the One Ring in *War of the Ring*.

In all of these examples, the game is won by the player(s) triggering the event that ends the game. However, this is not necessarily the case. For example, in *Race for the Galaxy*, the game can end several ways, one of which is by a player getting seven cards into their tableau. But the player who does this does not necessarily win. Winning is determined by other means than the game ending.

As there is no reason to end the game if you're not going to win, this type of trigger can lead to over-analysis. For this reason, designs that can be triggered by a player's action often include hidden points or bonuses that can make it difficult to judge who is leading. Another design technique that can be considered is giving a bonus for triggering the end of the game, to incentivize players to take that action. This mechanism can be found in *Concordia* and *Azul* and is often a factor used to balance issues like players getting an equal number of turns, but some players knowing that the game will end when they take their final turn and others now knowing it. See our discussion of End-Game Bonuses (VIC-06).

Sample Games

Azul (Kiesling, 2017)
Concordia (Gerdts, 2013)
Dune (Eberle, Kittredge, and Olatka, 1979)
Pandemic (Leacock, 2008)
Race for the Galaxy (Lehmann, 2007)
War of the Ring (Di Meglio, Maggi, and Nepitello, 2004)

VIC-12 Fixed Number of Events

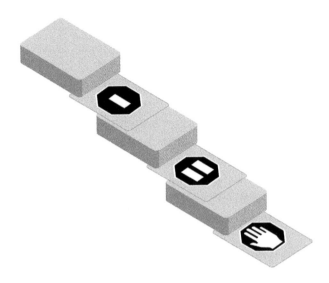

Description

The game ends after an event occurs a specified number of times.

Discussion

The Fixed Number of Events mechanism is most closely associated with card decks. A number of special trigger cards are shuffled into the deck. When the last of these is turned up, the game will end.

Airlines implements this system by mixing five into the stock deck. Each time a Scorecard is turned up, an intermediate scoring will occur. The last Scorecard initiates Final Scoring and the end of the game.

A similar system is used in *High Society* but is not directly tied to scoring. Instead, four special Red cards are inserted into the Auction deck, along with 11 Yellow cards. When the fourth Red card is turned up, the game ends.

This system can add a lot of variability and tension to a game, as players know approximately when it will end, but not exactly. A possible downside of this system is that the special cards may all happen very early in the game or very late, which creates long stretches with no scoring. It is possible in *High Society* for the four Red cards to be the first four cards turned over!

To combat this, many games that incorporate this mechanism use an initial deck construction method to ensure that the special cards are reasonably well distributed. *The Expanse*, for example, has the players divide the deck up into three piles, and shuffle two Scoring cards into each section. This ensures somewhat even distribution, without the players knowing exactly when Scoring cards will be turned up.

Get the Goods controls the distribution by shuffling ten Scoring cards into the deck, with scoring happening when the 4th, 7th, and 10th cards are turned up. This allows tension to build as Scoring cards are turned up, while still giving a high probability of a reasonable spread of Scoring cards throughout the deck.

This mechanism does not require card decks. In *Pandemic*, players lose if there are a certain number of Outbreaks. Players track these on a chart on the board.

Sample Games

Airlines (Moon, 1990)
The Expanse Board Game (Engelstein, 2017)
Get the Goods (Ado and Moon, 1996)
High Society (Knizia, 1995)
Pandemic (Leacock, 2008)

VIC-13 Elapsed Real Time

Description

The game ends after a set amount of actual time has elapsed.

Discussion

Games with the Elapsed Real-Time mechanism have an overall timer that is independent of the actions the players are taking. The key advantage is, of course, that players know exactly how long the game will take, which helps them schedule and plan. Also, having a timer naturally adds an element of tension to the game.

The exact implementation of the timer varies. While some older games, like *Escape from Colditz*, had players set any timer they had around the house, or simply check a clock, most modern implementations use some electronic means. *The Omega Virus* has the timer built into the taunting computer in the center of the board, which gleefully tells the players as time runs out. *Break the Safe* has a digital countdown timer, evoking many heist films. *Atmosfear* had players play a videotape to time the game. *Escape: The Curse of the Temple* and *Space Alert* have an external soundtrack that is played, which provides ambient sound effects as well as advising the countdown.

Electronic voices and soundtracks also have the advantage of being able to incorporate mid-game instructions for players.

Escape Room games, like the *Exit: The Game* series, also rely on elapsed time, typically tracked by a smartphone.

This mechanism needs extra attention when used in competitive games. The possibility that players may stall when winning, to run out the clock, needs to be addressed. This was a weakness in *Escape from Colditz*, a one-vs.-many game (see "STR-03, Team-Based Games" in Chapter 1), where one player controlled the German guards trying to prevent the Prisoner Of War (POW) players from escaping. In the original version of the game, the German players had a strong incentive to stall and take as long as possible to make their moves.

The Omega Virus tackles this issue by having an "everyone loses" condition if time runs out, turning it into a semi-co-op (STR-05). Another option is to have a simultaneous play, which disincentivizes players from stalling.

Sample Games

Atmosfear (Tanner, 1991)
Break the Safe (Uncredited, 2003)
Escape from Colditz (Brechin, Degas, and Reid, 1973)
Escape: The Curse of the Temple (Ostby, 2012)
Exit: The Game (Brand and Brand, 2016)
FUSE (Klenko, 2015)
The Omega Virus (Gray, 1992)
Space Alert (Chvátil, 2008)

VIC-14 Connections

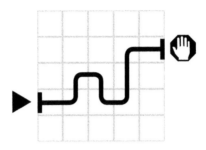

Description

The game ends when a specified number of connections are made on the board.

Discussion

The Connections mechanism can be both an end-game trigger and a means of victory. It is related to the Race mechanism (VIC-07).

In basic Connection games, like *Twixt*, it serves as the measure of victory. The first player to connect opposite sides of the board ends the game and determines the victor. In *TransAmerica*, the round is won by the first player to connect all of their cities into a single network (Illustration 5.2).

There are many games, however, that end based on connections but in which connections don't ensure victory. The most prominent example is the *Crayon Rails* series, which started with *Empire Builder*. In *Empire Builder*, players build rail networks. The game ends when a single player connects a certain number of major cities together in their network, as well as passes a certain threshold of cash. Both conditions are required for game end and victory.

Connection can also be used as a sub-game. In *Android*, players try to create connections between different groups, which gives in-game benefits. In the *18xx* and *Age of Steam* series, players place hexagonal tiles that have tracks printed on them onto the board in different configurations. *Cable Car* does the same with square tiles. Placing those tiles enables players to create routes between stations allowing for delivery of goods and earning money. Typically, these routes are shared by all players.

Connection games need to deal with several topology issues. Can players cross the paths of other players? Games that do not permit it, like

Illustration 5.2 Nearing the end of a game of *TransAmerica*. The first player to connect all five of their cities (one of each color) wins the round.

Twixt, often become static and have an optimal strategy. It is more typical to allow players to cross or even parallel other players' connections by paying a penalty or increasing resource cost to do so, and/or by requiring a special tile.

Sample Games

18xx (Tresham, 1974)
Age of Steam (Wallace, 2002)
Android (Clark and Wilson, 2008)
Cable Car (Henn, 2009)
Empire Builder (Bromley and Fawcett, 1982)
Santa Fe (Moon, 1992)
TransAmerica (Delonge, 2001)
Twixt (Randolph, 1962)

VIC-15 Circuit Breaker/Sudden Death

Description

The game has a fixed and known victory condition and a special variable condition that ends the game prematurely.

Discussion

Sudden Death conditions can be used for two purposes. First, they can help end a game once one player is far in front, out of the reach of the other players. This is referred to as a *Circuit Breaker* and is commonly seen in war games. For example, in *Rise and Decline of the Third Reich* and *The Russian Campaign*, if one player controls a certain number of key locations, they win immediately. In *Twilight Struggle*, if one player reaches 20 VPs on the tug-of-war style Victory Point track (VIC-19), then the game immediately ends.

The Circuit Breaker is good for ending a lopsided game, leading to a more positive play experience (or at least a shorter one!) for the losing side. Playing out an obviously lost game is typically not a fun experience.

This mechanism can also be used to add an alternate way for players to pursue victory. In *Liberté*, the game normally ends after all faction blocks have been placed. However, there are two special conditions that players can try to meet (Radical Landslide and Counter-revolution) to win immediately. *Space Base* includes a card that says "You Win." If a player manages to complete the task shown on the card, the game ends immediately and they win. This technique can be used to open different strategic options for players or to give players that are behind the chance for a Hail Mary attempt to win the game. When they happen, they can be exciting and memorable victories.

Most of the loss conditions for Cooperative Games are also Sudden Death. This adds to the puzzle that the players need to solve to reach a successful conclusion.

Somewhat related, *Hearts* has an alternate condition that adds a fun twist. Players normally gain 1 point for each heart they take, and 13 points for the queen of spades (points being bad). But if a player takes all the hearts and the queen of spades, they force each opponent to take 26 points. This mechanism works especially well, as it turns what is normally bad into something great. Looking out for someone trying to "shoot the moon," as it is called, adds a lot of interest to *Hearts*.

Sample Games

    7 Wonders Duel (Bauza and Cathala, 2015)
    The Fog of War (Engelstein, 2016)
    Hearts (Unknown, 1850)
    Liberté (Wallace, 2001)
    Rise and Decline of the Third Reich (Greenwood and Prados, 1974)
    The Russian Campaign (Edwards, 1974)
    Space Base (Clair, 2018)
    Twilight Struggle (Gupta and Matthews, 2005)

VIC-16 Finale

Description

When the main game ends, a special mini-game is played to determine the victor.

Discussion

This Finale mechanism adds a coda to a game, as it transitions to an alternate play mode at the end.

In *Monsters Menace America*, players spend the bulk of the game moving their monsters around the US, stomping on cities, battling the military, gaining upgrades, and becoming more powerful.

When the endgame is triggered, the players begin a monster demolition derby of sorts. The board is ignored, and the monsters simply battle against each other to determine the final victor. While the player that did the best during the first part of the game has the best chance to win, it could still be anyone.

Cable Car is a connection game. But when players complete their connections they do not simply win. Instead, they need to begin running their cable car from one end of their track to the other, moving a few spaces per turn. The remaining players continue taking their turns, and anyone who completes their track can start moving their car. The player who gets their car to the end of their track first is the winner.

This final contest rewards efficiency in both building the track as well as maximizing the speed of the car. If you complete a very circuitous route first, you may still lose to a player who was better able to manage their tiles better and build an efficient route.

Killer Bunnies and the Quest for the Magic Carrot is another example. Players can earn a numbered Magic Carrot during the course of the game. When they are all claimed, the game ends, and the winner is determined via lottery. The players draw one carrot at a time from a second carrot deck. The carrots drawn are losing carrots. Whoever has the final carrot remaining in the deck is the winner.

This mechanism makes it clear to players what they need to do during the game to win and adds an exciting end-game element. However, it can also cheapen the meaning of the first part of the game, as a player may dominate the main game, earning ten tickets while the other players each get only one and still lose. As such, this is best suited for quicker and lighter games.

The Finale mechanism is infrequently used as it often requires players to learn a whole different set of mechanisms to be used for the ending.

Sample Games

Cable Car (Henn, 2009)
Killer Bunnies and the Quest for the Magic Carrot (Bellinger, 2002)
Monsters Menace America (Connors and Knight, 2005)

VIC-17 King of the Hill

Description

Players earn points by occupying a special position on the board.

Discussion

King of the Hill (KotH) brings several positive attributes to a game. First, it is simple for players to understand what they need to do to achieve victory. Gaining points or other benefits by controlling the key location makes the objective clear to first-time players. In *King of Tokyo*, players earn points by remaining in the center of the board throughout the turn, giving the board state great clarity.

Second, it forces players into conflict. Staying in your own corner of the board ("turtling") will not move you closer to victory.

Finally, it gives players a safe space to rebuild and lick their wounds if they are weaker. If a player is in a bad position, they can simply stay out of the line of fire until ready. This can push battle games to a more casual place, as the strong either cannot or are not incentivized to pick on the weak. It also leads naturally to a Catch the Leader mechanism (VIC-18), as everyone will gang up on the player earning points in the center.

Because of all these items, pure KotH can make a game feel lighter. Players will try to knock each other out of the center, but conflict does not extend beyond that (Illustration 5.3).

Illustration 5.3 Controlling the center Monolith in *Nexus Ops* allows players to draw special cards. Photo by Board Game Geek user Mijjy.

Some games have a reward other than Victory Points associated with holding the center. For example, in *Nexus Ops*, the player controlling the center Monolith may draw special Energy cards that aid in various ways. This encourages players to head for the center and the bonuses there but also allows for alternate paths to victory.

Sample Games

The Ares Project (Engelstein and Engelstein, 2011)
King of Tokyo (Garfield, 2011)
Nexus Ops (Cantino and Kimball, 2005)

VIC-18 Catch the Leader

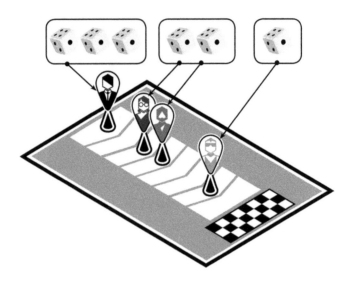

Description

The game systems advantage players that are behind or disadvantage players that are ahead.

Discussion

This is a meta-mechanism that can be implemented in a variety of ways. For example, *Power Grid* changes turn order based on who is leading. The player in last always takes the most advantageous position. *Age of Steam* forces players to reduce their Victory Points (VPs) based on how many they have. Players who have more points must lose more. Other games may give special tokens or abilities to players that are lagging.

While these are all overt, some Catch the Leader mechanisms are more subtle. A King of the Hill mechanism (VIC-17) typically exposes the leader to attack, and not other players—or players that are further behind are less attractive targets. This will naturally incentivize players to try to pull back the leader.

The designer should consider the severity of the Catch the Leader mechanism. If it is too strong, it can be advantageous for players to sandbag and try to stay back to make a strong late move rather than be penalized earlier.

Depending on the theme and nature of the game, this may or may not be desirable.

Designers should also look out for the opposite of a Catch the Leader mechanism ("snowballs"), where the game mechanisms make it easier for players in the lead to get further ahead. Economic games are susceptible to this, as the measure of victory (money) is also the resource that helps growth and power. *Monopoly* is an example. Splitting the victory currency from cash can alleviate this issue. For example, players may need to use cash to buy antiques, which actually give VPs. This forces players to decide when to turn their working resource into a victory resource. See Victory Points as a Resource for more details (VIC-04).

Sample Games

Age of Steam (Wallace, 2002)
The Expanse Board Game (Engelstein, 2017)
Monopoly (Darrow and Magie, 1933)
Power Grid (Friese, 2004)

VIC-19 Tug of War

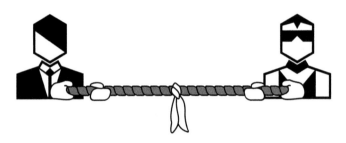

Description

A marker is moved up and back on a track toward or away from a neutral position.

Discussion

Tug of War can be both a scoring mechanism and an end-game trigger.

In its simplest form, two players will move a marker back and forth along a track, with each of them owning one end of the track. If the marker reaches the end of a track it typically triggers an event, such as ending the game, as in *Twilight Struggle*. In this case, it also triggers victory for the player who moves the marker to their end (Illustration 5.4).

It may also trigger a scoring event, as in *Guardians*, where each location has a short tug-of-war track. If the marker reaches the end of a track, the

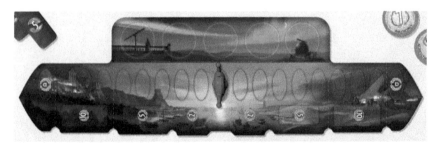

Illustration 5.4   The Military track in *7 Wonders Duel*. If either player reaches their end, they score a military victory. In addition, they gain bonus tokens the first time they reach certain spaces on their side.

player owning that end scores points for the location, and it is removed from the game and replaced.

Tug of War is not limited to two players. When there are three or more sides represented, each has a branch leading from a central neutral point. *Churchill* is a three-player game, with players debating over issues around World War II. Each issue starts in the center of the track. When a player influences an issue, it moves toward their track, or, if it is on another player's track, first toward the neutral point and then up their track. *Churchill* also has a special trigger if an issue reaches the end of one of the tracks. In that case, the issue is locked for that player, and it can no longer be influenced up and down the tracks. The game also features multiple issues on the tug-of-war track at the same time, allowing the designer to introduce more complexity and player options by allowing multiple issues to be influenced with one action or special bonuses for certain types of issues.

Another example of multiple players influencing multiple items is *Starship Samurai*, where players are trying to sway factions to their side. Each player has a track on the alliance board, and if a faction is on another player's track, in order to sway them to your side, you first move the faction token down toward a neutral zone off of that player's track and then up your track.

The location of the marker can also award points or abilities at certain times. In *Twilight Struggle*, for example, if no Sudden Death conditions are triggered (VIC-15) and the game ends by concluding the final turn, the winner is decided by the location of the marker on the track. The location of the markers at Conference end in *Churchill* at the end of the debate phase determines who gets to decide on the outcome of the issue. *Starship Samurai* awards Victory Points or resources based on the location of each faction at the end of the round.

This mechanism is very clean and easy for players to understand, particularly in the two-player version. It is easy for players to see where they stand and what actions influence the track. When used for an end-game condition, it is typically used as a Sudden Death condition, as requiring that the marker reach the end means that there need to be some means to drive the game toward a conclusion. It also means that as one player moves closer to victory, the other moves further away. This can reduce tension as compared to a Completing Targets system (VIC-11), where all players may be close to victory at the same time.

Sample Games

7 Wonders Duel (Bauza and Cathala, 2015)
Churchill (Herman, 2015)
Guardians (Flores, 2018)
Starship Samurai (Vega, 2018)
Twilight Struggle (Gupta and Matthews, 2005)

VIC-20 Highest Lowest

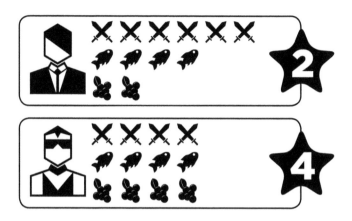

Description

Each player's score is equal to the lowest value of several categories. Whoever has the highest lowest value is the winner.

Discussion

As the title of this Highest Lowest mechanism may be a bit unclear, here is a more lengthy explanation using the diagram above. Let's say players are collecting the four icons in the image above—swords, fish, leaves, and grapes. Player A has 10 swords, 5 fish, 7 leaves, and 2 grapes. Their final score will be the lowest of those four—in this case, the 2 grapes, so 2 points.

First used in Knizia's *Tigris & Euphrates*, this scoring mechanism forces players to pursue multiple paths equally. Specializing in gaining red, for example, will not be a winning strategy. This forces players to generalize and typically encourages player interaction as they compete in the same areas.

Tigris & Euphrates has players collecting cubes of different colors to determine the final score. When using cubes, this system is the same as collecting sets of one of each color. Later implementations like *Ingenious* and *Wendake* use tracks, which can make it easier to visualize the current score, as it is just the lowest track marker.

Ingenious adds an additional twist, as while final scoring is based on the lowest color value, during the game, bonuses are awarded for getting a high value of a particular color. So, tension is introduced between staying balanced and specializing.

Wendake has two separate pairs of tracks, and the value of each pair is equal to the lowest of the two. Then, the scores for each pair are added together to determine the final score. Adding this additional level of detail groups certain aspects together and opens up more strategic design space.

Sample Games

Between Two Cities (O'Malley, Pedersen, and Rosset, 2015)
Ingenious (Knizia, 2004)
Tigris & Euphrates (Knizia, 1997)
Welcome to Centerville (Jensen, 2017)
Wendake (Sabia, 2017)

VIC-21 Ordering

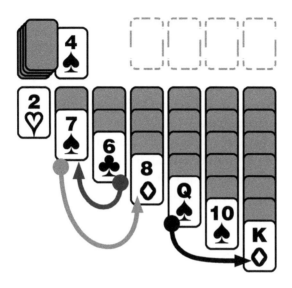

Definition

The objective of the game is to rearrange a group of game elements from a disordered to an ordered state.

Description

For many of us, our earliest exposure to this mechanism is *Patience Solitaire* (called *Klondike* or just *Solitaire* in the US and Canada). A deck of cards is dealt out into seven columns, and the objective is to convert the random shuffle into four stacks, each of a single suit ordered from ace to king.

The strength of the Ordering mechanism is the clarity of the goal. In addition, it takes advantage of a combinatorial explosion to create a huge number of potential starting positions. However, depending on the rules, it may be impossible to achieve the goal, and the game may be lost before a single move is played. People seem to be more accepting of this in solitaire games. In *Klondike Solitaire*, for example, about 20% of deals are impossible to win— and that is assuming that the player knows where each of the 52 cards is in the deck. However, this has not diminished the popularity of the game.

Ordering has a puzzle-like feel, making it a good fit for cooperative games. The different elements can be randomly distributed to the different players, who need to follow rules to reach the winning configuration. Two examples that use numeric sequences, like *Patience Solitaire*, are *Hanabi* and *The Mind*. The main component in *The Mind* is a deck of cards numbered from 1 to 100. Players are randomly dealt a hand, and they need to collectively play them in ascending order to a pile in the center of the table. In *Hanabi*, there are five color suits with values from one to five, and players need to play cards of each suit in numeric order.

Both these games work because of Communication Limits (UNC-06). *The Mind* prohibits all direct communication, forcing players to rely on interpreting pauses and the occasional raised eyebrow. *Hanabi* has players place their cards outwards, so their partners know what they have but not themselves, and restricts players to ask specifically defined questions to determine what to play.

In both cases, the simplicity of the goal gives the designer more space to explore the communication restrictions and how those manifest.

In the competitive space, the popular game *Rack-O* uses this mechanism. *Rack-O* has a deck of cards numbered from 1 to 60, and 10 are dealt randomly to each player. Players must put them into their rack in the order they were received. Each turn, players draw from the deck or discard and replace a card in their rack. A player wins when they have an ascending sequence.

Like *Rack-O*, most competitive games that use Ordering are Race games (VIC-07). Players win by being the first to achieve the ordered state.

While all the examples so far have been numeric, this is not required. Some notable examples are the *10 Days* series, *Space Sheep*, and *Rail Pass*. *10 Days* is similar to *Rack-O*, except that instead of numbers, the cards have geographic areas (states in *10 Days in the USA* and countries in *10 Days in Europe*, for example) or means of transportation (airplanes and cars in *10 Days in the USA*). The goal is to put together a series of cards that represents a valid "trip" where you can get from one card to the next in order. In the *10 Days in the USA* version, you can travel by foot between states that share a border, by airplane between two states of the same color, and by car between two states that are separated by a third state. The general play follows the same rules as *Rack-O*—draw a card and replace an existing card in your rack.

Space Sheep is a cooperative game that has planets, sheep, and shepherds of different colors. At the start of the game, the positions are randomized and the goal is to move the sheep and shepherds to their matching planets. Each planet has a different instruction about how pieces may be moved away. *Space Sheep* emphasizes the puzzle nature of the Ordering mechanism, as players endeavor to figure out how to untangle the situation.

Like *Space Sheep*, *Rail Pass* also uses color ordering. Each player represents one or two colors, and cubes of those colors are randomly distributed. Players must use trains, following various rules, to shuttle the cubes between each other in an attempt to deliver the right colors to the right locations.

Both *Space Sheep* and *Rail Pass* use a real-time mechanism (TRN-07) to prevent players from being able to exhaustively analyze the situation to determine the best moves. This serves a similar purpose as the communication limits in *Hanabi* and *The Mind*.

Sample Games

10 Days in the USA (Moon, Weissblum, 2003)
Hanabi (Bauza, 2010)
Klondike Solitaire (Unknown, c. 1780)
The Mind (Warsch, 2018)
Rack-O (Uncredited, 1956)
Rail Pass (Green, 2019)
Space Sheep (Rubbo, 2013)

6

Uncertainty

Games, like life, are full of uncertainty: the roll of the dice, the turn of a card, and the cube tumbling through the cube tower. But even in games of perfect information, such as *Chess*, our opponents' choices make our knowledge of how the game will unfold imperfect.

The source of uncertainty and how uncertainty is perceived contribute much to the shape of the overall player experience. Uncertainty that comes from a truly random process, like a die roll, creates a lighter and more chaotic feeling for players—even if the design calls for throwing enough dice enough times to smooth out the worst ends of the distribution curve. Players participating in a rock-paper-scissors contest, however, will feel a greater sense of agency and will harbor a belief, right or wrong, that the outcome of the contest is not random.

Uncertainty lurks in many unexpected places. Can you rely on your memory? Did the King of Hearts already go out? Did you properly deduce where Jack the Ripper moved to? What is your partner signaling to you with that drawing? Who is the werewolf? Can you balance Rhino Hero on the next card up the tower?

Uncertainty can create chaos, but players can also manage uncertainty using different tools. Betting, bluffing, and even deck-building all help manage card-draw randomness. Letting players see the result of a random process before needing to make a decision about it, such that the random result is an input in their decision-making—*input randomness*—makes randomness something players respond to, rather than rely on. On the other hand, forcing players to make a high-stakes decision contingent on a random outcome—*output randomness*—creates enormous drama and tension.

Because uncertainty can have a powerful impact on the game experience, designers often seek to control its influence in a variety of ways. In some

DOI: 10.1201/9781003179184-6   261

cases, this is baked into the design itself, through the distribution of cards in a deck or the number of dice that must be rolled, and similar systemic design elements. In many cases though, the power to mitigate uncertainty is given to players. Dice manipulation powers, card- and deck-manipulation powers, and other kinds of special abilities do give players greater agency.

While there is a loud contingent of players who disdain randomness and luck in games, a word to the wise: the most successful commercial games typically have far more luck in them than the most highly regarded hobby games. Games with more uncertainty and randomness tend to be accessible to more players and facilitate enjoyment even when there are large skill differences between players at the same table. Having a clear focus on the intended market for your game will serve as a crucial guide in determining how to handle uncertainty.

Designers have a broad palette of colors to paint with when it comes to the sources of uncertainty, its framing, and how players experience it. Managing uncertainty properly is key to the art of game design.

UNC-01 Betting and Bluffing

Description

Players commit a stake of currency or resources to purchase a chance of winning everyone's stake, based on some random outcome like being dealt a superior set of cards or rolling a higher number. Players typically have partial information about the overall game state and may "bluff" by representing through their in-game actions that they hold a stronger position than they do. Conversely, players may "fold" or quit the contest and limit their losses to whatever they had already staked.

Discussion

Some of the oldest games in human memory are betting games, often involving dice, and rather than trying to recapitulate every type of betting game and mechanism, we'll restrict ourselves to how the mechanism is used in the modern board-gaming context. Nevertheless, a field trip to your local casino is highly recommended for extended study of these topics.

One common group of games that feature betting is trick-taking games, like *Tichu*, where players place a "bet" by predicting the number of tricks they will take. The role of betting in these designs is to allow players to self-balance the outcomes of a random card deal. Players will bet more aggressively with a stronger hand. Racing games like *Camel Up* offer wagering to allow players to wager for the same reason. One might pedantically note that the game doesn't actually simulate or model camel racing as much as it models wagering on camel races. Nevertheless, this is a very popular way for designers to make games about racing, while sidestepping many of the challenges of modeling an actual race.

The games above have wagering, without any real bluffing elements. Conversely, there are games like *Coup* which feature bluffing but not any wagering. In *Coup*, players hold role cards that enable certain actions. These cards are held in hand, as secret information, and a player can declare that they possess any card and take any connected action. As long as no player challenges, the action occurs, but if a challenge is issued, the active player must show the card they claimed and force the challenger to discard a role card, or the player must discard one of their own role cards if they do not hold the role card they claimed. Players who discard their last role cards are eliminated from the game. This dynamic is present in many social deduction games, which we discuss in a dedicated section (see "UNC-04" in this chapter).

Other games that are only about bluffing include *Skull and Roses*, *Liar's Dice*, *Cockroach Poker*, and the classic game *Cheat* (which our saltier readers may know by its more bovine name). What these games share in common is that they have no currency to wager and that when a player makes a challenge, uncertainty exists only based upon player actions.

A key design element for including bluffing is not only hidden information, of course, but also some form of information transmission. In poker, the information is in the form of betting patterns, and the community cards visible on the table. In *Coup*, the character a player chooses gives them special abilities. The actions a player may perform based on the role give context to the choice and the possibility of the bluff. It is better if the hidden information doesn't change too frequently, to give a history to the choices a player makes. If the hidden information constantly changes, it reduces the opportunities for players to try to see through a bluff, leaving players with a random guessing game.

Bluffing is common in the party game space, but *Wits & Wagers* introduced betting into the trivia genre. Players answer numbers-based questions and arrange their numerical answers on a betting line in order from lowest to highest. Players may then make two bets on which answer is closest to the actual answer printed on the card. By cleverly allowing players to make two wagers, the game expands from being only about how much confidence players have in their own knowledge to a richer set of choices. Players must consider whether their wagers are revealing too much to their opponents, while also looking to how other players bet to try and suss out likely answers based on those betting patterns. If you're playing with a doctor, for example, you might follow their bets on biology and medical topics—until they catch on to your strategy and lay a trap for you!

One of the most interesting places to find bluffing and wagering is in modern resolution mechanisms for combat, some of which are discussed in Chapter 4. In various games, players put forward some combination of known strength, and some hidden amount of strength, and simultaneously reveal and then resolve abilities to determine a winner. The hidden strength may be represented by a number on a die, as in *Tiny Epic Kingdoms*, a leader card, as in *Dune*, or a battle card, as in *Kemet*. Combat is entirely deterministic, and all possible combat modifications are also known, such that in many combats, players know which player will win if they spend their maximal strength. The game is in out-thinking or out-guessing your opponent as to how much strength he or she will spend. These combat systems are what we might call all-pay, in that the committed resources are discarded. This is a key distinction between auctions and wagers more generally: in auctions only the winner pays, but in a wager, the losers pay.

The ability to read and out-guess your opponents, to know their minds, is described by the Japanese word "Yomi." Yomi is especially prominent in games with a simultaneous reveal mechanism like 1v1 fighting games. However, role-selection games (ACT-02) like *Race for the Galaxy* have this flavor too: assessing which roles your opponents will select, and thus, which you should select is the Yomi experience. In *The Mind*, that same notion is pushed to the limit, but in a co-op game. In *The Mind*, players must, without communicating, somehow play hands of cards in ascending numerical order. There are no turns, and not all cards are dealt from the deck, so players must simply play based on their instincts and their ability to sense what their partners might hold.

Sample Games

Camel Up (Bogen, 2014)
Cheat (Unknown)

Cockroach Poker (Zeimet, 2004)

Coup (Tahta, 2012)

Dune (Eberle, Kittredge, and Olatka, 1979)

Kemet (Bariot and Montiage, 2012)

Liar's Dice (Unknown, ~1800)

Manila (Delonge, 2005)

The Mind (Warsch, 2018)

Race for the Galaxy (Lehmann, 2007)

Skull and Roses (Marly, 2011)

Tichu (Hostettler, 1991)

Tiny Epic Kingdoms (Almes, 2014)

Wits & Wagers (Crapuchettes, 2003)

UNC-02 Push-Your-Luck

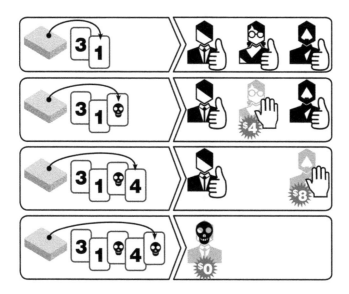

Description

Players must decide between settling for existing gains and risking them all for further rewards. Push-Your-Luck is also known as press-your-luck.

Discussion

A good example of a game whose central mechanism is Push-Your-Luck is Sid Sackson's *Can't Stop*. In *Can't Stop*, the active player rolls 4 dice and advances up to 2 pawns in tracks numbered from 2 to 12, based on matching the sum of any 2 dice to the numbers on the tracks. The player may choose at any point to stop rolling, and lock in their progress along the tracks, or reroll to attempt to advance again. However, if after rolling, the player cannot match the sum of the dice to any of the three active tracks the player is advancing on, the player "busts," and all progress from that turn is lost. Push-Your-Luck is a type of wager in which players have less control over the ante or the stakes than in most casino games.

An important dynamic in push-your-luck games is how changes to the stakes can alter player behavior. In *Can't Stop*, when a player reaches the top of any numbered track, the track is closed, and nobody else can score it. The first player to reach the top of three tracks is the winner. Players may be more timid at the start, but when one player is close to reaching the top of a track, competitors also racing up that track usually become much more aggressive and risk-tolerant, as they attempt to close the track themselves. This is doubly so when a player is close to winning the game, and the other players try to win it all themselves in one epic turn. When there's nothing to lose, why not press-your-luck?

Some of the behaviors and emotions that Sackson evokes in *Can't Stop* stems from behavior that echoes the sunk-cost fallacy, in which investing additional resources into some goal is based not on the chances for succeeding, or the expected return on the investment, but on an emotional connection to what has already been invested in the past. In addition, Sackson is also depending on the difficulty in computing probabilities in *Can't Stop*. Avid gamers, whether raised on *Backgammon* or *Catan*, are adept at calculating probabilities featuring 2d6, but calculating the probabilities of successfully rolling at least one of two or three different numbers on 4d6 is the kind of thing that few players can do in their heads. This obfuscation is critical since games in which expected values can always be calculated exactly can feel stale and boring.

Can't Stop is unforgiving. A single miss, a single roll of the dice that fails to advance a runner on a track, leads to a bust. In *Yahtzee*, players roll five dice and may choose to keep any number and reroll the rest before being forced to score the results. However, players are limited to a total of three rolls. In *Favor of the Pharaoh*, there is an additional restriction that players must keep, or lock, at least one die result before rerolling the remaining dice. In *Tiny Epic Galaxies*, players may spend a specific resource to purchase additional rerolls.

Alternatively, instead of focusing on the die roll, Push-Your-Luck can be implemented in the chase for rewards. In *Roll Through the Ages: The Iron Age*, players race to build monuments, but the first player to complete the monument will get a larger reward than all subsequent players. Players must choose between participating in the race for monument completion and devoting their resources to a different pursuit. Similarly, in *Incan Gold* (also known by its original name, *Diamant*, which remains its European title), players simultaneously choose whether to explore more deeply into a temple in hopes of turning up more gems on the next turn of a card from the expedition deck or to leave. At first, there is no risk attached to staying in, but after the first of a type of hazard card is revealed, the danger is that a matching hazard will be revealed and all gems discovered will be lost. Players who leave early get to retain all their gems gained so far, while players who remain will be splitting new treasure with fewer players, making staying in the cave more rewarding as well as riskier.

Formula De ties a player's movement to gears represented by dice. Higher gears allow players to roll dice with more sides, up to a D30 for top gear—but curves offer a speed limit past which cars take damage. Take too much damage and you're out of the race!

Dice are a common means of implementing a press-your-luck mechanism, but they are far from the only one, as per the aforementioned *Incan Gold*. In *Oh My Goods!*, cards representing resources are played face-up into a market row until two cards showing a half-sun icon are revealed. Players must assign their workers after seeing one market row revealed, and can assign workers to tasks that require more goods to be completed than are currently showing in the market row. A second market row is then revealed, which may provide sufficient resources for players to complete their work ... or not! Notably, the game allows players to assign workers to work in a way that will yield the maximum reward, which requires all resources are available, or to work for a lesser reward, in which case, a resource can be missing. This allows players to choose the stakes and probabilities of their wager while retaining the "bust" outcome that characterizes these games.

Press-your-luck can be the central mechanism in a game, but it appears just as frequently as a part of a larger game. In *Ra*, players draw tiles from a bag to create an auction lot. Prior to each draw, the active player may call an auction, but auctions are more often triggered when a *Ra* tile is drawn out of the bag. There are multiple dimensions of luck-pressing baked into play: tiles are worth different amounts to players based on a set-collection mechanism (see Chapter 12 "Set Collection"), some tiles will impact players negatively, while other tiles are highly desirable to all players. Drawing another tile instead of calling the auction can radically change the overall value of the lots, and change them differently for each player. Toward the end of the round, when only one player remains, that player continues drawing tiles until he or she wishes to stop and purchase the lot. However, if a *Ra* tile is drawn at this point, the round ends immediately and the player loses his or her opportunity to buy. It is not uncommon to hear chants of "Ra! Ra! Ra!" during this phase of a game, demonstrating how meaningful the stakes feel in this masterpiece.

Ra's Push-Your-Luck mechanism permeates the whole game, yet it is clearly in service to the auction-and-set-collection core. In many games, the Push-Your-Luck element is a layer of flair rather than a core of the experience. In *Mystic Vale*, a kind of deck-building game (see "CAR-05" in Chapter 13) players flop cards to establish their mana pool for the turn, until three spoils symbols are showing on the cards. Players may choose to risk flopping an additional card to expand their mana pool, but if another spoils symbol shows, the player busts and loses his or her turn. This mechanism is entirely optional and additive, and players can play and win without ever engaging in it, but it can be wisely leveraged to accelerate a deck's construction too.

Push-Your-Luck as a mechanism is straightforward to understand, even if the risks can be difficult to calculate, and it easily creates drama, tension, and excitement. It should be considered an essential part of every designer's toolkit.

Sample Games

Backgammon (Unknown, 3000 BCE)
Can't Stop (Sackson, 1980)
Favor of the Pharaoh (Lehmann, 2015)
Formula De (Lavauer and Randall, 1991)
Incan Gold (Faidutti and Moon, 2005)
Mystic Vale (Clair, 2016)
Oh My Goods! (Pfister, 2015)
Ra (Knizia, 1999)
Roll Through the Ages: The Iron Age (Lehmann, 2014)
Tiny Epic Galaxies (Almes, 2015)
Yahtzee (Lowe, 1956)

UNC-03 Memory

Description

Hidden, trackable information whose tracking gives players an advantage.

Discussion

Memory can be a game mechanism or a capability a player draws upon when engaging with one or more mechanisms. It's an important design ingredient, a lever whose setting will have a substantial impact on a game's weight, intended audience, and general reception. Our discussion will focus on games where memory is at the center of the game design, rather than where memory is an ancillary skill that the game tests.

Memory games can be seen on a spectrum. At one end, are games like the classic game *Memory* and the modern game *The Magic Labyrinth*, in which the only skill the core game mechanism tests is whether players can remember things. In *Memory*, it's the specific location of various items in the face-down grid of tiles. In *The Magic Labyrinth*, players need to remember the correct path through the maze, because the walls of the maze are invisible, and the game uses magnets on the underside of the board to define that path. *Memoarrr!* borrows a bit from both of these games, with cards that feature two elements that must be remembered, and then arranged spatially.

Further down this spectrum are games where memory is crucial to the core gameplay in patent and obvious ways. *Stratego* and *Lord of the Rings: The Confrontation* features player pieces on standees or blocks. These pieces have unit information on only one side, such that players can't see the identities of opposing pieces before they encounter them. In an encounter, players reveal the pieces, then flip them back, leaving the players to use their memories to track the location and identity of the revealed pieces. These games have fairly small and stripped-down rulesets that put the spotlight squarely on memory, but block-style war games like *Sekigahara: The Unification of Japan* use this same mechanism to add fog of war—the uncertainty of the disposition of enemy forces that is typical in war.

This type of memory mechanism, sometimes called "Hidden Trackable Information" (HTI), for short, challenges players to remember information that was once revealed to them. We've discussed positional examples so far, but those examples are perhaps the least polarizing. In *Small World*, players must announce how many coins (i.e., victory points or VPs) they have collected at the end of their turn but not their total. It would be trivial to track this information with a paper and pencil, but in the context of a fast-moving game of territory control, it's easy for players to lose track of who is ahead. This is intentional on the part of the game designer! *Small World* is the successor to *Vinci*, a Roman-themed game that is mechanically almost identical. One key change between the two games was making the victory points hidden, trackable information. This helped to prevent dynamics which plagued *Vinci:* bash-the-leader behavior and the extent to which players optimized their play on the last turn. This change, along with cute art and a light-hearted feeling, turned *Small World* into an evergreen success in the casual games space.

Another example of HTI is found in *El Grande*. In addition to placing cubes onto the board, players may choose to place them into the Castillo, a tall tower. Players cannot look in the Castillo; they need to remember how many cubes are there. At the end of the round, each player secretly selects a province in which to place his or her Castillo cubes. Remembering how many cubes of each player are in the tower can be challenging—even remembering how many of your own are in there can be difficult for players. But this lends a fun, swingy punctuation to what otherwise is a very calculable game.

HTI can be especially controversial when it exists in more complex games, but it is nonetheless common in *18xx* games and other heavy economic or auction games (see Chapter 7 "Economics" and Chapter 8 "Auctions", respectively), where a player or corporate cash holdings are hidden. To some extent, this thematically reflects the ways in which corporations are secretive about their finances. Mechanically, pricing an auction or predicting an opponent's actions is much simpler when the total money in the system is known and is even easier when the allocation of that money is known.

Memory and HTI sharply reduce accessibility and inclusion. To help players who have trouble remembering, many games provide tracking components, like *Clue*'s guessing pad. Other games provide some aid to memory, like *Hunt for the Ring*, where the Nazgul players have a handful of tokens with different markings that they can use as they wish. In *Hanabi*, the rules explicitly encourage players to find a limit on communications that maximized the fun for the group. This leaves open an enormous range of possibilities, from playing *Hanabi* as a strict memory game where each individual must keep track of his or her own hand, to one with almost no memory component since players are free to remind one another what each of them has been clued to in his or her own hands previously. Even under such rules, however, players must remember when they were clued about the state of their hands, and which new cards they have drawn since then.

Many games rely heavily on memory, even though they're not explicitly memory games, and players with better memory (or card-counting systems) will have a substantial advantage. Trick-taking games and classic card games in general fall into this category, since players who can remember which cards have already been played can make better decisions about what to play next, and the relative values of cards still in their hands. Another common dynamic is games in which remembering the types of sets your opponent is collecting allows you to interfere with them effectively, as in *Animals on Board*. In these games, cards or tiles collected by players are hidden away after collection. These are important design considerations, but they relate to memory as a player skill rather than as a game mechanism. Admittedly, the line between these two is fuzzy, but we will wrap our discussion of memory mechanisms here.

Sample Games

Animals on Board (Sentker and zur Linde, 2016)
Clue (Pratt, 1949)
El Grande (Kramer and Ulrich, 1995)
Hanabi (Bauza, 2010)

Hunt for the Ring (Maggi, Mari, and Nepitello, 2017)

Lord of the Rings: The Confrontation (Knizia, 2002)

The Magic Labyrinth (Baumann, 2009)

Memoarrr! (Bortolini, 2017)

Memory (Unknown, 1959)

Sekigahara: The Unification of Japan (Clakins, 2011)

Small World (Keyaerts, 2009)

Stratego (Mogendorff, 1946)

Vinci (Keyaerts, 1999)

UNC-04 Hidden Roles

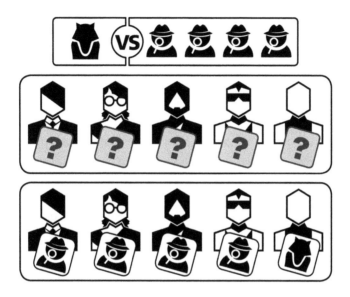

Description

One or more players are assigned differing roles that are not publicly revealed at the start of the game.

Discussion

While uncertainty lurks in many games, in Hidden Roles games, uncertainty is at the very heart of the gameplay. We can broadly talk about three types of Hidden Roles games: social deduction games, traitor games, and competing roles games. We touched on this topic earlier in the chapter about game structure (see Chapter 1). Social deduction games are team games in which the object of gameplay is to deduce the team allegiances of the players, as in the classic open-source game *Mafia* (which, ten years after its invention, was recast as *Werewolf*).

It's worth noting that in these games, usually, only one team faces uncertainty. The werewolves know who all the villagers are, and as such, the werewolves are playing a role-playing game whose win condition is to successfully deceive the villagers for long enough to devour them. The villagers are playing a deduction game where the evidence is mostly in the social interactions at the table rather than the almost non-existent mechanical interactions. In this section, we'll generically refer to the "villagers" to represent the team, typically positioned as the thematic protagonists, that has less knowledge of the game state, and "werewolves" to describe their opponents, who know the identities of most or all players.

Shadow Hunters, *Two Rooms and a Boom*, and *BANG!* are exceptions to this general rule. In these games, the players do not know the identities of any of the other players (except for the Sheriff in *BANG!*, who is known to all). This gives these games a different feel, as there is less paranoia, as all players are on an equal footing, and an early part of the game is players trying to determine who is on their team without tipping their hand.

Traitor games, as distinct from social deduction games, have some other win condition for the "villager" side besides revealing the traitors. In *Battlestar Galactica: The Board Game*, players try to reach Korhol (or some other destination), and the game operates as a cooperative game (see "STR-02" in Chapter 1). However, a traitor may lurk among the players, secretly sabotaging them. In traitor games, the traitor, upon discovery or self-revelation, often shifts into a different role with a new win condition, new actions, and different player powers.

Traitor games need to use hidden resolution systems so that players can cause trouble while maintaining anonymity. In *Battlestar*, players play cards face-down during the crisis phase, trying to sum up to a value of cards of a certain color. Because the cards are played face-down, the traitor can sabotage the crisis resolution effort without revealing himself or herself; although, through deduction, the other players may start to uncover their identity. *Dark Moon* has players roll dice behind a screen. Each player must select one die to use to resolve the action. Traitors may use their worst rolls so as not to benefit the team, but showing a bad roll does not guarantee a traitor, as a loyal player may just have a bad roll and have no good dice to choose from.

In our final category, competing roles games, players are not on fixed teams and have hidden identities, but revealing those identities is not directly tied to winning or losing. *Ravenous River* and *Coup* are examples of competing roles games. In *Ravenous River*, each player is secretly assigned one of seven animal identities. Animals eat one other type of animal and are in turn eaten by one other type. Players use cards to manipulate the positions of any animals, not just their animal, seeking to end the round in the same region as their prey and not their predator. Deducing the identities of the other players can help in executing a strategy but isn't worth any points toward victory.

The uncertainty in all of these types of games is not the operational uncertainty of attempting an outcome without knowing whether it will succeed, but it still is a kind of output randomness that injects noise between a player's intention and the results of his or her action. In *Mascarade*, player roles can move around from player to player, such that a player may not know what role he or she has at any given time, which creates a lot of uncertainty. Like in *Coup*, players can claim the actions associated with any role, but unlike in *Coup*, roles can get shuffled and players may not look at their own role cards freely; they must spend their turn doing so.

An important source of uncertainty in social deduction games in particular is in the unstructured conversation during which players discuss potential targets and coordinate for the upcoming resolution phase, typically a vote. The conversation phase offers players the opportunities to lie, obfuscate, bluff, posture, or hide in a shroud of silence. Experientially, this phase is crucial, and whether players enjoy this genre of the game rests largely on how much they enjoy this part of the game.

Some games attempt to enforce some structure in the discussion phase, by creating mechanisms with in-game consequences that players must grapple with. In *Salem 1692*, players play action cards on one another that impact status and abilities, including accusation cards that operate in place of the voting phase of other social deduction games. In *Shadow Hunters*, players give cards with yes/no questions to other players, which they must answer. In *Ravenous River*, as mentioned above, a player may have the opportunity to manipulate the positions of a few animals, including animals other than themselves. These actions, and their potential point-scoring consequences, provide evidence of the player's secret identity. This is related to hidden endgame goals (VIC-06).

We've touched briefly on *Werewolf* in its most basic form. However, its most popular commercial iterations, such as *Ultimate Werewolf* and *The Resistance: Avalon*, feature a dizzying array of additional roles, each of which changes the dimensions and possibilities of gameplay. Some roles offer players additional private information about other players and their roles or team identities. Others can protect players from being eliminated, which injects performative uncertainty into the elimination action. Some roles provide an elimination power, which can be helpful to the "villager" side but might actually cloud the situation and make it more difficult to assess who the "werewolves" are because players don't know which team eliminated which players.

There's much more to be said about the various types of roles possible in these kinds of games, which is beyond the scope of this work. However, one role is critical to consider: the role of the moderator. In many social deduction games, the need to hide substantial aspects of the game state from a shifting set of audiences makes these games inherently fragile and subject to inadvertent revealing of information or even tolerance for some mild cheating. Because these games also have unstructured conversation phases, driving the game toward a conclusion can sometimes be difficult. That's why many of these games call for a moderator who does not play the game, at least in the sense that the moderator can neither win nor lose, but simply administrates the game, and especially enforces time limits, whether formal and agreed upon or informal and socially accepted.

Since the moderator is the only person who knows the complete game state, playing as the moderator can be quite appealing to players who enjoy spectating and people-watching. The moderator role can also be performed with theatricality and has an element of role-playing that sits in its own layer of game-engagement that is separate from the core game engine. And of course, like any refereeing role, the moderator can have both unintentional and intentional impacts on the course of the game through their manipulation of soft power, like when to call a discussion to a close and insist on a vote.

Perhaps for these reasons, the moderator role has been eliminated in many modern designs. In *One Night Ultimate Werewolf*, a prerecorded voice, run by an app, takes players through the paces of each round, such that a moderator is not required. In *Dracula's Feast*, both the moderator and the idea of player elimination are removed, and players have asymmetric win conditions, some of which are not tied to discovering other players but to being accused of inhabiting certain roles. These differences put the game firmly into the competing roles category rather than the social deduction category. In order to get around the problem of sharing information secretly, players each have a "Yes" and "No" card that they can show to the one player asking them a question. These games can often have multiple players winning by fulfilling different conditions. *Two Rooms and a Boom* is particularly instructive in this area.

Voting-based player elimination is very common in social deduction games, and that mechanism can create negative social consequences. From the perspective of a cultural critic, these games are intended to recreate uncomfortable social and political realities like mob justice, betrayal, and schoolyard cliques. Some games lean into these dynamics, like *Secret Hitler*, which not only requires that players step into a magic circle where they may have to self-identify as a Nazi, or as Hitler himself, but must also participate in a morally gray universe in which even non-Fascists might pass Fascist policies. Designers need to take care that players understand the nature of the magic circle that they're stepping into, and what might be expected of them in their suspension of real-world rules during play.

Sample Games

BANG! (Sciarra, 2002)
Battlestar Galactica: The Board Game (Konieczka, 2008)
Coup (Tahta, 2012)
Dark Moon (Derrick, 2011)
Dracula's Feast (Hayward, 2017)
Mascarade (Faidutti, 2013)
One Night Ultimate Werewolf (Alspach and Okui, 2014)
Ravenous River (Shalev, 2016)
The Resistance: Avalon (Eskrisge, 2012)
Salem 1692 (Hancock, 2015)
Secret Hitler (Boxleiter, Maranges, and Temkin, 2016)
Shadow Hunters (Ikeda, 2005)
Two Rooms and a Boom (Gerding and McCoy, 2013)
Ultimate Werewolf (Alspach, 2010)
Werewolf (Davidoff and Plotkin, 1986)

UNC-05 Roles with Asymmetric Information

Description

One or more players are secretly assigned roles at the start of the game which has different win conditions and receives different starting information about the game state.

Discussion

In Hidden Roles (UNC-04), we speak of games where the "werewolves" have complete or nearly complete knowledge of the identities of the other players. The opposite dynamic is also possible, where the "werewolf" may know the identities of the other players, but is missing some other critical information that all the other players share. Generally, the goal for the "werewolf" is to figure out that secret, and the goal for the "villagers" is to both keep that secret safe and to guess the identity of the "werewolf." In some games, one or the other is sufficient to secure the victory for the "villagers" and in others, both are required.

In *Spyfall*, for example, players are told that they are at one of many potential locations. One player, the spy, doesn't know the location, but their identity as the spy is hidden from the other players. The spy attempts to deduce the location all the players are at, while the other players attempt to figure out who the spy is, through asking and answering questions related in some way to the location. Non-spy players must be careful to ask and answer in a way that signals only to other players that they know the location, without giving it away to the spy. The spy must ask and answer questions in a manner that doesn't draw suspicion, even though they don't know where they are!

Another example that introduces a third role with Asymmetric Information is *A Fake Artist Goes to New York*. In this game, the moderator is a player and also wins or loses. The moderator chooses both a category and the secret word within the category and chooses who the fake artist will be by revealing only the category to them but not the secret word. The other players then each begin play, adding one line to a shared drawing on their turn, attempting to signal to other players that they know what the secret word is.

Similar to *Spyfall*, the players don't want to give away what they're draw-ing, since the fake artist wins if they can guess the secret word. The modera-tor is aligned with the fake artist and is thus incentivized to choose a category and word that will make it easy for the fake artist to correctly guess the word. The moderator is the only player at the table with complete knowledge of the game state.

There is a genre of games which leverages this same type of informational asymmetry, but with less emphasis on player roles. For example, games in which cards or tiles are held facing out, like *Hanabi* and *Abracada... What?*, don't put players into different roles, but each player is denied knowledge of only their own hand. Each of these is subtly different: *Abracada ... What?* is closest to *Spyfall* in that each player faces the tension of acting despite igno-rance, but there is no doubt as to the player's identity or goals in the game from the perspective of the other players. *Hanabi* is cooperative, and the dramatic irony that the inactive players feel because they can see the active player's hand as they agonize over the right play is part of what makes that game special.

The mass-market game *Headbanz*, in which one player tries to guess at a word on a card that all the other players can see, leverages this type of hid-den information that isolates a single player, whether for the whole game or just for their turn, through sharp informational asymmetry. So does the absurdist *Win, Lose, or Banana*, where the player who draws the "Win" card tries to guess which player holds the Banana card but is the only player who doesn't know the disposition of all the cards. What's notable about these games is that the social dynamic of being the only person not in the know creates enormous pressure, tension, and the possibility for humor—often at one player's expense.

This technique does not have to be used only in competitive games. Cooperative games may put communication restrictions on one or more players, and challenge them to convey information to other players (STR-02). *Mysterium* places one player in the role of a ghost, who needs to get the other players to correctly identify the elements of a mystery (location, person, and weapon), but can only communicate by playing one or more elaborately illustrated cards to the players as a "dream."

Though hidden information not generated by player actions is everywhere, little of it exists in classic European-style games. Though we often draw the line between these styles based on whether they employ input randomness or output randomness, the element of having only public information also aligns closely with the European design school.

Sample Games

> *Abracada … What?* (Kim, 2014)
> *A Fake Artist Goes to New York* (Sasaki, 2012)
> *Hanabi* (Bauza, 2010)
> *Headbanz* (Glimne and Strandberg, 1991)
> *Insider* (Kwaji, Okano, Shinma, and Itoh, 2016)
> *Mysterium* (Nevskiy and Sidorenko, 2015)
> *Nyctophobia* (Stippell, 2018)
> *Spyfall* (Ushan, 2014)
> *Werewords* (Alspach, 2017)
> *Win, Lose, or Banana* (Cieslik, 2009)

UNC-06 Communication Limits

Description

Games may limit players from communicating with one another openly. These restrictions can be absolute as they relate to certain specific pieces of information, or they may restrict certain types of communication, such as speaking.

Discussion

Communication limits are most common in cooperative games, but they exist in other kinds of games as well. Many games limit players from revealing privately held cards. In *Cosmic Encounter*, players may openly discuss which cards they intend to play, but the actual cards cannot be shown in order to preserve the possibility of a double cross. In traitor games, identity cards are an obvious example of communication limits.

In cooperative games or games with intra-team cooperation, communication limits operate to make the game more difficult. Party games like *Charades*, *Pictionary*, and *Show & Tile* all ask players to communicate non-verbally, with pantomime, drawing, or building with tangrams, respectively. These games are all games of inductive reasoning (UNC-13), where the clues provided suggest an answer. *Hanabi* is particularly notable in that the more players come to the game with agreed-upon principles and conventions for how to play, the more the game shifts from being about inductive reasoning to deductive reasoning. Games with deduction mechanisms, in which players gain information by asking specific types of questions—like *Clue* or hidden movement games like *Specter Ops*—are another example of communication limits as a mechanism to manage uncertainty, preserving enough of it for interesting play.

Team3 is a three-player cooperative game where the team is attempting to recreate a blueprint showing how blocks are to be arranged. Each player has a different restriction on information or communication. One player can see the blueprint but cannot speak, only gesture. The second player can watch the first player and describe to the third player, who has their eyes closed, how the blocks should be arranged. Only the third player may touch the blocks. This combination of different communication restrictions leads to varied and entertaining gameplay.

Returning to *Hanabi*, players are restricted not only in the type of information they are allowed to provide or the modality by which it may be provided but also by the frequency with which they may communicate. Players have a limited number of clues, and if no clues are available, players may not communicate at all. *Mysterium* takes a similar approach, except that communication is only limited between certain player roles. The ghost and the mediums may only swap information through cards, but the mediums may freely converse with one another. In *Witness*, players may only communicate their information once, which leaves players unable to confirm what they've heard or to clarify anything they might have missed.

In the absence of specific rules of what information can be shared, playgroups are left to manage themselves. In *The Game*, the rules indicate that players may not share the specific values of cards in their hands but may say "don't play on that pile" or "don't make a large jump on this pile." In practice, this can often lead to results very similar to players playing with open hands, especially when players at the table have different ideas about what should and should not be allowed. This dynamic is on full display in *The Mind*, where the rules bar all communication, yet the gameplay is all about reading the slightest and most subconscious of cues. Once again, each group will have very different mores and norms by which they play.

Sample Games

    Charades (Unknown, early 19th c.)
    Cosmic Encounter (Eberle, Kittredge, Norton, and Olatka, 1977)
    Crazy Karts (Perret, 2016)
    The Game (Benndorf, 2015)

Hanabi (Bauza, 2010)
The Mind (Warsch, 2018)
Mysterium (Nevskiy and Sidorenko, 2015)
Pictionary (Angel, 1985)
Show & Tile (Loomis and Shalev, 2018)
Specter Ops (Matsuuchi, 2015)
Team3 (Cutler and Fantastic, 2019)
Witness (Bodin, 2014)

UNC-07 Unknown Information

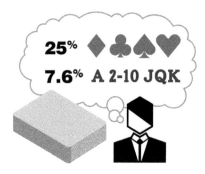

Description

Aspects of the game state are unknown to all players but lie within a known range.

Discussion

There are three categories of hidden-yet-knowable information: information known to no players, information known to one or more players, and information known to all but one player.

Unknown Information creates uncertainty during any given play of a game and creates variety in repeated plays. Event decks are a good example of this kind of uncertainty. Players know the range of possible results, and often the cadence by which information will be revealed, but they don't know the specifics, and the specifics can substantially impact strategy. In an initial play, players may not even know the true range of possibilities, and indeed, some game instructions encourage players to look through the deck to familiarize themselves with the possibilities or provide a card manifest or similar catalog of possibilities. *Pandemic*'s infection deck generates enormous tension precisely because the uppermost cards, formerly the discard pile, are known to the players.

How unknown information will impact players on reveal can vary mechanically too. When modeling exploration, like the face-down sector tiles of *Eclipse*, explored tiles are revealed to all players. In *Karuba*, a new path tile is revealed each turn but each player may use the tile differently, either adding it to their personal board or discarding it for movement. Cards that enter a market, like the ability cards in *King of Tokyo*, can be seen by all players, but an acquisition mechanism limits and determines who can take advantage of them. In tile-laying games like *Carcassonne*, where players don't have a hand, the new tile drawn is known to all players, but only one player has agency over its placement.

Sample Games

Carcassonne (Wrede, 2000)
Eclipse (Tahkokallio, 2011)
Karuba (Dorn, 2013)
King of Tokyo (Garfield, 2011)
Pandemic (Leacock, 2008)

UNC-08 Hidden Information

Description

Aspects of the game state are hidden from all but one or a few players.

Discussion

Information can be known to one or more players but not to all players. This includes information we've covered elsewhere, like Hidden Roles (UNC-04), or private hands of cards. However, in this context, we refer less to those sets of information which are permanent elements of a player's role in a game, like their hand of cards. Instead, we're considering things like the strength of the monsters that all players can battle for victory points in *Champions of Midgard*. The types of information that may be hidden in this manner typically fall into a few categories: secret player abilities, secret goals, the strength of enemies, and the location of specific items or resources. Players might spend actions or resources to gain this knowledge, or not. Another type of information of this sort is specific knowledge of another player's hand based on deduction. If you hold the Princess in *Love Letter*, you can be certain that nobody else does, but no other player can be certain about whether the Princess is in your hand, any other player's hand, or the draw deck.

Designers employ a variety of mechanisms and components to manage hiding and revealing this kind of information. Cards are especially common, as in

Clue, where players respond to an accusation by showing a disproving card only to the accusing player. Other options include face-down cards, player screens, tokens with common backs but different fronts, and figures with information on the bottom of their bases. More exotically, in *Pikoko*, a competitive trick-taking game, players hold their hands facing out, so each player can see every card in hand, except those held in their own hand. *Careers* begins with players selecting their own victory conditions as a mixture of Fame, Happiness, and Money, and recording it on their personal play sheet.

These techniques can help add new layers of strategy for advanced players. Once players understand what the range of the hidden information is, they can try to deduce what it is from players who know it. This also offers an opportunity for bluffing. For example, paying attention to what elements players include in a guess in *Clue* may give astute players knowledge of what cards other players have been shown. But knowing that players may be looking out for that may cause advanced players to continue to include elements in their guesses that they think will lead their opponents to draw erroneous conclusions.

Sample Games

> *Careers* (Brown, 1955)
> *Champions of Midgard* (Steiness, 2015)
> *Clue* (Pratt, 1949)
> *Kingsburg* (Chiarvesio and Iennaco, 2007)
> *Love Letter* (Kanai, 2012)
> *Pikoko* (Porter, 2018)

UNC-09 Probability Management

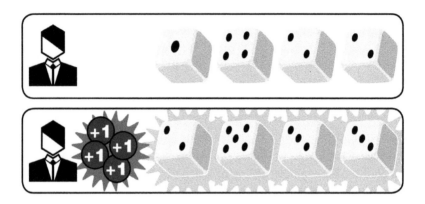

Description

A mechanism which allows players to influence the probabilities of certain outcomes but not directly determine them.

Discussion

Probability Management is intrinsic to all dice and card games. At its most direct, players can gain dice modifier tokens that allow them to add or subtract from the value of a die, as in *Kingsburg* or *Sagrada*. More obliquely, in *Backgammon*, players can move their blots (the name given to the checkers) into positions that minimize the probabilities of good rolls for their opponents and maximize those probabilities themselves.

Betting games allow players to assign stakes to probabilistic events like dice rolls or card deals. However, the type of Probability Management we'll cover here is exemplified by deck-building games. In a deck-building game, such as the progenitor of the genre, *Dominion*, players draw a hand of cards from a private deck each turn and play those cards to acquire other, more powerful cards, usually from a central market. Players try to acquire more powerful cards, and cards that synergize together. By keeping the deck tuned so that draws consistently surface those cards, players seek to increase the average output of their deck, in whatever terms—currency at the start of a game, and victory point later is a typical framework. We'll discuss Deck-Building in depth in its own section (CAR-05) (Illustration 6.1).

Some games offer probability manipulation at rarified skill levels. In *Twilight Struggle*, some cards leave the game after being played for their events. High-level players are careful not to trigger cards showing their own events, and to trigger, in as safe a manner as possible, their opponent's events. Over time, the weight of the deck shifts and forces the opponent into many difficult hand-management situations where they must trigger highly damaging events. In *Alhambra*, players can draw currency into their hands, either by taking a single card, or any number of cards adding up to no more than five. Players gain a bonus action when purchasing tiles with exact change, and a great deal of the skill in this game lies in managing a hand that can match many values. Failure to realize this aspect of gameplay results in a substantial loss of player agency.

Illustration 6.1   In *Kingsbridge*, players can earn +2 tokens, which allow them to modify future dice rolls. Here, a +2 token is used to place the 6/3 dice into the "11" space, where normally they would have to go in the "9" space.

Sample Games

Alhambra (Henn, 2003)
Backgammon (Unknown, 3000 BCE)
Dominion (Vaccarino, 2008)
Kingsburg (Chiarvesio and Iennaco, 2007)
Orleans (Stockhausen, 2014)
Puzzle Strike (Sirlin, 2010)
Sagrada (Andrews, 2017)
Twilight Struggle (Gupta and Matthews, 2005)

UNC-10 Variable Setup

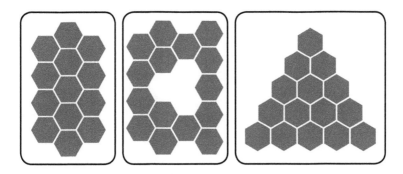

Description

The starting game state varies from game to game, through changes to shared game components like the map, and/or changes to starting player setups, resources, objectives, etc.

Discussion

Variable Setup is sometimes equated with replayability and can certainly contribute to it, though they are not the same thing. The line between setup and gameplay isn't always that clear either. But setup can have an outsize effect on uncertainty and overall game outcomes. *Catan's* rules recommend new players play with a specific board layout and provide rules for board construction that ensure that no one spot is over-powered relative to others. Players often ignore this rule, and this imbalanced setup can easily advantage one player over the other. Similarly, the randomly dealt alien powers in *Cosmic Encounter* define the game almost entirely and shape its dynamics even more dramatically than *Catan's* setup. *Dominion's* selection of ten kingdom cards is similarly impactful—those cards can be considered the last page of the rules (Illustration 6.2).

In many cases, variable setups don't impact uncertainty once the setup is complete, because nothing that happens in the game is probabilistically dependent on setup. After faction board tops and bottoms are selected in *Scythe*, for example, there is no further uncertainty. This is as distinguished from *Battlestar Galactica: The Board Game*, where more interactions are

Illustration 6.2   A sample setup at the start of a *Dominion*
game. The 10 card types played with can be chosen
randomly or specifically selected, at the players' option.

available with the loyalty deck and the makeup of that deck can change prior
to the next loyalty phase.

Some variable setups incorporate hidden or unknown information. In
Specter Ops, the runner who is trying to evade the hunters gets to secretly
select a few equipment cards out of the available pool. In theory, hunters
can know the complete set of equipment cards and how they work, though
whether that's true in practice—whether players do in fact look in the rulebook to read about all the equipment—is questionable. Designers should
provide player aids summarizing this type of information if it's important
that players know all the possibilities.

Designers need to be careful that randomized setups don't create balance issues. This is particularly true in longer games. Often, having limitations on the randomization (like redoing a setup if a certain number of the
same type of tile are placed in a row) or giving players a pregame chance
to respond to the random setup is required. An example of the latter is
found in *Catan*, where there is a snake draft for placement of player's initial settlements. This allows players to moderate the vagaries of the initial
chance board setup.

Sample Games

Battlestar Galactica: The Board Game (Konieczka, 2008)
Catan (Teuber, 1995)
Cosmic Encounter (Eberle, Kittredge, Norton, and Olatka, 1977)
Dominion (Vaccarino, 2008)
Scythe (Stegmaier, 2016)
Specter Ops (Matsuuchi, 2015)

UNC-11 Hidden Control

Description

Players have hidden influence on locations or characters, which they reveal to perform actions.

Discussion

In a game of this kind, play is divided up between assigning influence and either declaring or spending that influence to trigger the effects of the character or location in question. In *Mythology*, players secretly assign control points to heroes (or monsters, events, etc.) in one phase. In a later phase in the round, any player may attempt to activate these heroes by announcing that they are taking control. If nobody challenges that control, the action succeeds. If another player challenges, the players engage in an auction-like process of declaring an amount of control points that they had previously assigned. Players may choose to reveal none, some, or all of the control points they have assigned in an effort to take control of the hero, and the player who reveals the most influence is awarded control.

In *Kremlin*, players influence politicians in the Soviet party, each of whom can trigger certain actions based on their altitude in the party hierarchy. Players write down the influence they assign to politicians on a secret log sheet and then reveal some or all of the claimed influence to control these politicians. Revealed politicians are targets for exile, or, in some versions of the game, execution by the KGB, so players must balance the risks and rewards of revealing control.

This mechanism can also be used as part of a traditional public influence system. In *Colossal Arena*, players bet on battling creatures. The player who has placed the highest value of bets on a creature may use its special ability. However, at the start of the game, each player may place a secret bet on a single creature. Timing when to reveal your secret bet to seize control of a creature is a key tactic in the game.

This kind of revealed influence is an uncommon mechanism, perhaps because it requires a log sheet or some other form of tracking, which can be cumbersome. It is also fragile to player deception that is hard to discover. But, used judiciously or with proper physical techniques, it can be compelling. This is perhaps an area that will be explored more in digital hybrid games.

Sample Games

    Colossal Arena (Knizia, 1997)
    Conspiracy (Solomon, 1973)
    Kremlin (Hostettler, 1986)
    Mythology (Peek, 1980)
    Nothing Personal (Avery and Vasel, 2013)

UNC-12 Deduction

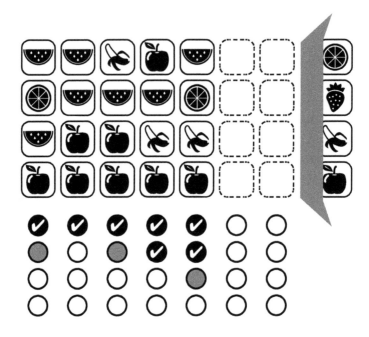

Description

Reasoning by process of elimination to discover a crucial piece of information.

Discussion

Deduction is a familiar mechanism from mass-market classics like *Clue* and *Guess Who?*, as well as informal games like *20 Questions*, *Jotto*, and *Bulls and Cows*. In these games, deduction is nearly the whole of the gameplay. Players are racing to solve the puzzle either before their opponents or before their time and resources run out.

Deduction games typically fall into one of a few structures. Most deduction games have a central mystery that all players are trying to solve. A few games feature a puzzlemaster, a player who knows the solution, and one or more players who are trying to solve the puzzle. The role of the puzzlemaster may be oppositional, supportive, or neutral. In another approach, each player may be solving their own personal puzzle, and sometimes players are both puzzlemasters trying to prevent others from solving a puzzle they're charged with defending, while simultaneously racing to solve another puzzle.

A hallmark of deduction games, and a key consideration in their design, is in the choice of affordances that are provided to the players to track their deduction process. Paper pads are a common approach, as in *Sleuth* and the aforementioned *Clue*. *Mastermind*'s board and pegs system is perhaps the most famous method of tracking guesses. It may therefore come as no surprise that the game was initially published by Invicta Plastics, a plastic toy company that took a chance on Mordecai Meirowitz's unusual design.

While deducing the identity of a murderer or the value of a specific card is common, some games employ a spatial approach. In *Tobago*, players close in on the location of a treasure located somewhere on an island. Rules cards specify, for example, that the treasure must be on a particular terrain, like the mountains, or in the largest region of type of terrain, or within a few spaces of a feature like an idol. With each rules card played, the possible locations of the treasure shrink. When only a single valid location exists, the treasure may be recovered. *Tobago* uses deductive reasoning, but because players decide which rules cards to play, they are not deducing where the treasure might be. Rather, they are determining, based on their card choice, where the treasure will be found.

Tobago's approach is quite fun and refreshing, but a later game, *Cryptid*, uses a very similar engine to drive a more traditional deduction game. In *Cryptid*, each player holds clues about the location of the eponymous creature. These clues are structured like *Tobago*'s rules cards. With each turn, a player asks another about a specific board location, and that player responds by placing a disc on the board if they cannot rule that location out, or a cube if they can.

The key distinction between the two games is that in *Tobago*, the location of the treasure is not fixed prior to play. Rather, the rules cards eventually force the treasure to resolve its location to a single valid space. In *Cryptid*, the monster is in a specific place, and each play of the game is chosen from a very large set of puzzles, with the corresponding deck of clues distributed to players to match. From a design perspective, *Cryptid* requires creating many puzzles, while *Tobago* is, in a sense, a means of generating those puzzles.

Word-association and image-association games like *Mysterium*, *French Toast*, and *Codenames* share a lot in common with deduction. Players use evidence to narrow their choices, but the evidence is far less definitive than pure logical deduction should provide. Social deduction games, which we cover under their own heading, also introduce uncertainty into the deduction process. Just as adding randomness into a game will tend to lower its weight and increase the chances that a less-skilled player will win, attenuating the effectiveness of pure reasoning will make a game lighter and less competitively balanced.

Many games call for deductive reasoning, though they may not be classified as deduction games. Hidden movement games, e.g., *Hunt for the Ring*, rely heavily on deduction, as do games with pawns that have hidden values, like *Lord of the Rings: The Confrontation*. Cooperative and team games with communication limits, like *Decrypto*, *Trapwords*, and *Hanabi* also call for players to use deductive reasoning skills. And just about every numbers-on-cards game, from trick-takers to rummy-style games to poker-style games calls for card-counting and deduction to be played at a high level. While we don't see these as specifically using a deduction mechanism, they share many features.

Sample Games

Clue (Pratt, 1949)
Codenames (Chvátil, 2015)l
Cryptic (Duncan and Veevers, 2018)
Decrypto (Dagenais-Lespérance, 2018)
French Toast (Hayward, 2021)
Guess Who? (Coster and Coster, 1979)
Hanabi (Bauza, 2010)
Hunt for the Ring (Maggi, Mari and Nepitello, 2017)
Lord of the Rings: The Confrontation (Knizia, Lang and Peterson, 2005)
Mastermind (Meirowitz, 1971)
Mysterium (Nevskiy and Sidorenko, 2015)
Sleuth (Sackson, 1971)
Tobago (Allen, 2009)
Trapwords (Chvátil, 2018)

UNC-13 Induction

Description

Players attempt to determine the rules governing a situation. Typically, a game master creates a hidden rule. Players then create a pattern or play a game element and are told by the game master whether that matches the rule.

Discussion

Induction is a similar mechanism to Deduction but with distinct differences.

The textbook definition of the concepts of "deductive" versus "inductive" reasoning is that deductive starts with facts (or theories) to draw a conclusion. Inductive reasoning starts with observations and then tries to come up with an explanation that ties together those observations. There is a lot of overlap between these approaches, which leads to confusion in their everyday usage.

"Induction" as a game mechanism is best understood through an example. *Eleusis* is played with a standard set of playing cards. The dealer secretly comes up with a rule and lays out a starter card on the table. The other players in turn then play a card and are told whether it fits the rule and can be added to the line of cards on the table (beginning with the starter card) or not. If the card does not fit the rule, it is played next to the main line so players can have a history of both what did and did not work.

Examples of simple rules in *Eleusis* include black and red cards have to alternate, or the value of the card cannot be more than three away from the last card. A more complex rule might be that cards must alternate red and black, but that face cards can only be played after cards that are a perfect square (1, 4, 9).

If a player thinks they know the rule, they can declare that they are "the prophet." They take over the roles of declaring whether any card played is right or wrong. So long as they are correct, they continue in this role. If the dealer says they are incorrect, they are no longer the prophet and are penalized.

Scoring rules for *Eleusis* are fairly complex, as they want to reward the dealer for coming up with a complex rule but not so complex that no one figures it out. This is reminiscent of Targeted Clues (RES-17), where a player wants some, but not all, of the other players to guess something.

Zendo is another classic example of an induction game. It is based on *Eleusis* but uses pyramidal blocks of various shapes and colors. The "Master" devises a secret rule. Players then construct a "Koan" from the stackable pyramid pieces on the table and the master marks with a white stone if it meets the rule, or a black stone if it doesn't (Illustration 6.3).

For purposes of games, the distinguishing characteristics of induction games are:

- Open-ended rule
- Players make guesses. They are only told if they fit or don't fit the rule.

Illustration 6.3   Two sample guesses, or "Koans," in *Zendo*. The first meets the rule, and the second does not, as indicated by the stone color. The rule might be that there is a yellow piece, but it does not touch the table. Photo by W. Eric Martin.

This seems similar to deduction games like *Clue*. There, players make guesses and are told whether they are right or wrong. But the difference comes from the open-ended nature of the possible answer to the puzzle. In *Clue*, players know that the solution contains exactly one Suspect, Room, and Weapon. In *Eleusis*, there is no bounded list of possibilities.

Another distinction between induction and deduction games is that in deduction games you are almost always given some information when making a failed guess—being shown a card disproving the accusation in *Clue*, for example. In Induction, you are merely told "right" or "wrong" and need to come up with your own "experiment" to try to figure out why you were right or wrong, so you can limit the possible rule space.

The crux of induction games is the creation of the rule. First-time players are often stymied for ideas on rules, and players also tend to dramatically underestimate the complexity of their rules. There is a small sweet spot of a satisfying rule that players are gradually able to zero in on versus an obscure rule that only leads to a long, frustrating play experience.

To help with this, some games come with "starter rules" or some other way to generate rules. However, this undercuts the strength of Induction, as once players know what the possible rules are, it reverts to a deduction game.

The public domain game *Mao* is a metagame activity, where experienced players, who know the rules, play with novices, who do not. When a card is played, the novices are told whether it is a legal play or not. At the end of the game, the winner secretly adds a new rule for the next game. The secret rules usually go beyond the expected mechanisms of a card game. They may be tied to what players are wearing, what they might say, which hands they use, or anything else. The knowledge imbalance between the novices and the experienced players encourages the development of a ruleset based on in-jokes and private group dynamics.

A commercial version of *Mao*, called *Quao* (pronounced "cow"), jump-starts this organic rules-growth, by including a small deck of starter rules. One player selects some of these, at random, to start each game. Reviews of the game have noted that if these rule cards have all been seen and begin to be reused, the game loses much of its charm. A vast potential playspace is an important component of Induction games.

In addition to how rules are created, the designer also needs to consider how guesses are made. They can be bounded, as in *Eleusis*, where a player must play a card from their hand as a guess, or unbounded, as in *Zendo*, where players can arrange their pyramids as they see fit. This makes *Zendo* more challenging than *Eleusis*.

Unbounded guesses do not automatically translate to complexity, however. The classic guessing game *20 Questions* is also a form of Induction. One player thinks of (typically) a noun, and the other players need to ask yes or no questions to determine what that player is thinking of. The flexibility of language helps the players narrow things down the category fairly quickly (e.g., Is it an animal? Is it larger than a toaster?).

Another example of a game with bounded guesses is *Visitor in Blackwood Grove*. One player is an alien who crashes into a forest and creates a forcefield around the ship. The alien player creates a rule about what objects may pass through the forcefield (e.g., objects containing metal will pass). The "kid" player is working to get objects to the alien player before the government agents figure out the rule.

The use of object cards cleverly opens up a large body of "world" knowledge to possible rules that do not exist in *Eleusis* or *Zendo*. *Visitor* also shows that Induction games can be thematic, unlike almost all Induction games published to date.

Sample Games

   20 Questions (Unknown)
   Eleusis (Abbott, 1956)
   Mao (Unknown)
   Quao (Rivaldi and Rivaldi, 2007)
   Visitor in Blackwood Grove (Flanagan and Seidman, 2018)
   Zendo (Heath and Looney, 2001)

UNC-14 Questions and Answers

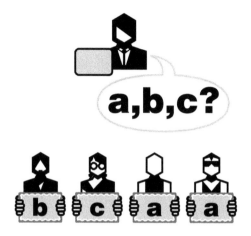

Description

Players ask and answer questions in a manner constrained by rules.

Discussion

Questions and answers appear in many different game genres. Broadly, we can group these games into a few functional categories. Games can use questions to obtain information and resources useful to winning the game, questions can directly be worth points, and questions can be prompts to encourage player-generated content.

Questions for information are broadly covered in Deduction (UNC-12) and Induction (UNC-13). This mechanism can also appear in games, which otherwise do not feature deduction, in the form of special power or ability that allows players to look at another player's hand or to inquire about a particular piece of hidden information or even future action. These games almost always require closed-ended questions with very clear directions about how questions may be structured and how they must be answered. Ideally, no ambiguity should exist in whether a question can be asked, and what the answer must be. In practice, the more complex or abstract a deduction game becomes, the more players are likely to be confused or to make mistakes about how to answer a question properly. Because it is often impossible for players to ask clarifying questions without spoiling the game, the onus is on the designer to make sure the rules are crystal clear and definitive.

Some information games feature questions as both information and demands for resources. In *Go Fish*, players must answer honestly if they hold cards of some given rank, but they must also surrender them. Along similar lines, trades can be seen through the lens of questions and answers too but are probably better described as negotiation.

Trivia games offer points or earned progress for answering questions. Sometimes a question is reserved for one player or team, sometimes players race to "buzz in" and answer the questions, and yet other times, all players answer the question simultaneously and reveal their answers. In *Wits & Wagers*, players reveal their answers and then bet on which answer is closest to the correct answer—a conceit that depends on all questions being answered in numerical form.

Party games show how player-generated content can be inspired by questions. Common variations on the theme call for players to answer unusual questions as in *Loaded Questions* or to take a set of answers and apply them to existing questions like in *Bed, Wed, Dead: A Game of Dirty Decisions* (which is based on the public domain game sometimes known as *Kiss, Marry, Kill*). A similar approach can be seen in *Who in the Room*, which asks players who in the room would survive some situation, or be most likely to perform some act, and similar questions.

Just as designers need to structure questions and answers carefully in deduction and hidden information games, they should take great caution with this mechanism in the party game space as well. The dangers here are less from ambiguity and more from potentially creating uncomfortable or dangerous environments. The rules, packaging, and accompanying material should clearly signal to players the types of questions and content they are likely to encounter, and ensure that players consent to playing a game of this kind.

Sample Games

Bed, Wed, Dead: A Game of Dirty Decisions (Murray, 2016)
Go Fish (Unknown)
Loaded Questions (Poses, 1997)
Who in the Room (Uncredited, 2018)
Wits & Wagers (Crapuchettes, 2005)

7

Economics

In one sense, games are about gaining and using assets to achieve victory. Maximizing efficiency, utilization, and value are all important as players strive to win.

Many things can be considered "assets" in a game. They can be obvious, like money in *Monopoly* and goods like bricks or grain in *Catan*. Or they can be capital assets, like properties or buildings that generate other resources, or intangible, like turn order, board position, network efficiency, or hand size. In this text, we will use the generic term "asset" to represent any of these. The term "resource" will refer to money and goods and not structures or intangibles.

Economics is the study of the allocation of scarce resources. It is not surprising that many aspects of business and economics are adapted into board game mechanisms. In this chapter, we examine a variety of mechanisms that derive from manipulating resources and other sources of value.

ECO-01 Exchanging

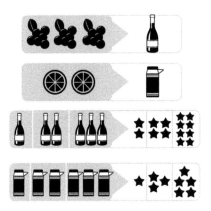

Description

Players Exchange a set of assets for a different set with the bank.

Discussion

While traditionally this mechanism is thought of as Exchanging similar types of resources, for example, Exchanging two sheep for a wood at a sheep port in *Catan*, under the expansive definition of assets, it also covers purchasing as a mechanism. For example, in *Monopoly*, players exchange the asset *money* for the asset *property*. Similar considerations apply, so they are both covered here.

Often there are fixed formulas for exchanges. Again using *Catan* as an example, a Road costs a Brick and a Grain, and a Town costs a Brick, Grain, Wool, and Wood. These types of requirements can be used to give relative value to different paths, or add an arc, as different resources may be required in different ways under different strategies or at varying points of the game. What was valuable early may become less so later on.

Some systems feature a hierarchical organization of resources. For example, in *Roads and Boats*, Wood is used to make Boards, Boards make Fuel, Fuel and Gold make Coins, and Coins and Paper make Stock Certificates. As is typical in this style of game, each of these transformations is a one-way trip.

Another example of hierarchical resources is *Century: Spice Road*. In this game, yellow turmeric cubes are the least valuable, followed by red saffron cubes, green cardamom cubes, and then the most valuable brown cinnamon cubes. In this case, exchanges are possible (and common) between all levels.

Certain cards allow the conversion of a brown cube back into several yellow and red cubes.

Hierarchical systems give players a clear sense of value. However, if this value is too clear, other mechanisms need to be introduced to obstruct players from getting used out of that value. Otherwise, the resources are basically fungible like coins of different denominations. For example, in *Century: Spice Road*, players may exchange cubes for the Victory Card resource. The point value of those cards is strictly equal to the value of the cubes, from one point for yellow cubes, up to four points for brown cubes. Although not explicitly stated, this 1–4 valuation of colors helps players quickly determine the relative value of the converter cards. One that turns a green (value 3) into a brown and yellow (value 4 + 1 = 5) gives a net gain of +2. A card that turns a red into a green has a value of +1. While the value of the cards is known, the players need to collect cards that enable them to perform exchanges as efficiently as possible to get the specific set of cubes required by the victory card. Thus, time becomes another resource that players must consider when determining the value of exchanges.

Non-hierarchical systems allow players to transform resources in different directions, laterally. The sheep port in *Catan* that was mentioned earlier is an example. At that port, any other commodity may be obtained by turning in two sheep. Permitting lateral exchange of resources gives a system more flexibility and allows players to specialize, as focusing on just a few resources will not limit them from getting others they may require.

Sample Games

 Castle Dice (Peterschmidt, 2013)
 Catan (Teuber, 1995)
 Century: Spice Road (Matsuuchi, 2017)
 Concordia (Gerdts, 2013)
 Factory Fun (van Moorsel, 2006)
 Gizmos (Walker-Harding, 2018)
 Glass Road (Rosenberg, 2013)
 Monopoly (Darrow and Magie, 1933)
 Roads and Boats (Doumen and Wiersinga, 1999)
 Sidereal Confluence (Deichmann, 2017)

ECO-02 Trading

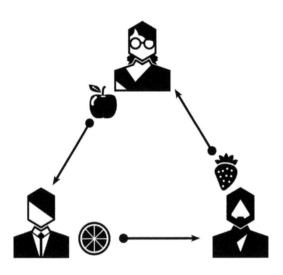

Description

Players may Trade assets with each other.

Discussion

This is a form of Exchanging (ECO-01), except that players determine the terms of the exchange. In order for Trading to work, the resources being traded need to have different values to different players. This is often accomplished through the use of Sets. See Chapter 12 for full details on the supporting mechanisms. The value also needs to be difficult to precisely determine. Again, sets are often used to accomplish this, as players may not know exactly which cards their opponent has. Future value can also be obfuscated, usually based on random future events.

Games typically limit what can be traded. For example, *Civilization* gives players commodity cards, and only those may be traded. In *Sidereal Confluence*, on the other hand, where a variety of types of resources may be combined in different deals. Sometimes games will strictly require like-for-like trades (e.g., two cards for two cards).

The actual mechanism of Trading can be conducted in several ways. Most common is a defined open Trading session, where players shout out deals and proposals, as in *Civilization, Trade on the Tigris, Sidereal Confluence,* and many other games. Open Trading is fun and chaotic but has several downsides. First, trade phases tend to be time-consuming, as players haggle. It can also leave out players who don't have many things to trade or are otherwise uninvolved. Also, players who are less assertive may suffer a handicap. For these reasons, Trade Phases often are timed, and players may only make deals within those windows. If players can make a trade at any point during the game, it may lengthen the game noticeably and also lead to odd timing effects—what if the players can trade between a combat resolution and removal of casualties? Questions that are not covered by the rules are likely to arise and outright exploits may lurk beneath the surface.

However, there are games that allow Trading at any time. *Monopoly* is a good example.

Another consideration in trades is the truthfulness factor. Most games require some level of truth on the part of the players. In *Civilization*, players must tell the truth about two cards out of the minimum of three they are required to include in a trade. They may say whatever they would like about the others. In *Trade on the Tigris*, each trade card has a top and bottom half with different resources. Players must tell the truth about the top but may say anything about the bottom. Introducing deception elements into the trade mechanism can add some spice and excitement, but some players will feel uncomfortable about it, and others will simply not have a poker face.

Regardless, however, when Trading resources, the deal typically must be performed as defined. Because of this, most games ban future promises as part of a trade, as it is difficult to police and requires rules for what happens if an agreement cannot be fulfilled. This is in contrast with Negotiations, where players often do not do what they promise (ECO-18). It is also worth mentioning that introducing Trading gives players a tool to self-balance a game. If one player is in the lead, others may refuse to trade with them, or force them to accept less favorable trade. This is a soft Catch-the-Leader mechanism (VIC-18).

Sample Games

Catan (Teuber, 1995)
Chinatown (Hartwig, 1999)
Civilization (Tresham, 1980)
Monopoly (Darrow and Magie, 1933)
Pit (Cayce, Gavitt, and Parker, 1903)
Sidereal Confluence (Deichmann, 2017)
Trade on the Tigris (Engelstein and Sturm, 2018)

ECO-03 Market

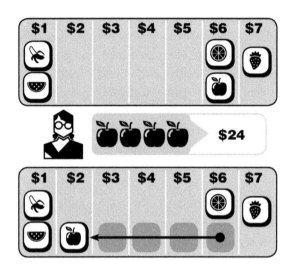

Description

Players may buy from or sell resources to Markets, where prices and quantities can vary.

Discussion

Markets are a specialized form of Exchanging (ECO-01), as players are typically exchanging stocks or commodities for money, all of which are resources. However, there are some specific considerations for this implementation, particularly around changing prices. Note that we are defining a Market mechanism as one where prices change. Mechanisms like that, found in *Concordia*, where you can buy or sell for a fixed value throughout the game would fall under Exchange, even though it is called a Market.

One mechanism for varying prices is using a track as in *Supremacy*, where there is a price track for each commodity, with a marker indicating the current buy/sell price. If a player sells that commodity the price is reduced, and if they buy it, the price increases. If a player buys or sells multiple units, all units can either be sold at the same price prior to adjustment (as in *Supremacy*) or can drop one space with each good sold (as in *Crude*). While the latter makes it more difficult for players to exploit the system, it makes the calculations a bit more complex.

Price tracks can be 2-dimensional grids, as in the *18xx* series. In those games, selling shares makes prices move down within a pricing column, while issuing dividends moves it to another column with a different price scale. This gives more fine-grained control to the design, and there can be special effects when the price hits the top or bottom of a row or column.

Rather than have a marker record the current price, the actual commodity tokens can do so. This is done by placing one commodity per space on the pricing track. The price of the commodity is based on the farthest space up the track covered by the commodity, or sometimes the farthest visible space. As commodities are bought, higher price spaces are revealed, and as they are sold, the higher price spaces are covered so the price drops. Visually, the former method usually calls for numbers to be printed above or below the track spaces, which takes up more room, while the latter allows the numbers to be printed on the track spaces themselves.

This elegant track system is used in *Crude*, *Power Grid*, and others. When players take a resource off the track, they simultaneously are adjusting the pricing for that resource, without having to remember to do anything else. *Wealth of Nations* adds a twist in that the buy and sell prices are not the same in each space. There is a delta that creates friction in the market system (Illustration 7.1).

Markets can sometimes be one-way ratchets. In *Acquire*, players may only buy shares from the market, not sell them. And as the hotel chains they represent expand, the price of the shares goes up and can never go down. In other cases, like *Rococo*, prices for thread and fabric go down throughout the course of the turn, decreasing as each player makes purchases. This ostensibly models the decline of prices in a bazaar as closing time approaches and is also helpful for balancing first-player turn-order advantage.

Market systems create a lot of player interaction, as players may attempt to manipulate the price to their advantage or deprive their opponent of the

Illustration 7.1   The market in *Power Grid*. Coal (the brown cubes) cost 6, oil (black) 5, and trash (yellow) 7. If two coals are purchased, the next would cost 7.

ability to gain needed resources. They also help to self-balance resource production. If one resource is being over-produced or under-used by the players, the price will be driven downward, and players will adjust accordingly. In a system where the physical resource tokens are placed on the market track, they may even become completely unavailable if players are hoarding them.

Sample Games

1830 (Tresham, 1986)
Acquire (Sackson, 1964)
Chicago Express (Wu, 2007)
Concordia (Gerdts, 2013)
Crude: The Oil Game (St. Laurent, 1974)
Greed Incorporated (Doumen and Wiersinga, 2009)
Power Grid (Friese, 2004)
Rococo (Cramer, Malz, and Malz, 2013)
Shark (Vanaise, 1987)
Stockpile (Sobol and Orden, 2015)
Supremacy (Simpson, 1984)
Wealth of Nations (Carroll, 2008)

ECO-04 Delayed Purchase

Description

Items that are purchased do not enter play right away but arrive on a future turn.

Discussion

In most games, when you purchase an item, it is immediately available to use. However, in the real world, it can take time to produce something, or get something delivered.

Several games use this Delayed Purchase mechanic to force players to plan ahead. A simple implementation is to place purchased items directly on a turn track, and they become available when the turn marker moves into that space. This can also be done with a specialized production or training track, where units are advanced one box each turn. This was used in *Time War*, where Teams are trained by advancing them through a schematic of a training facility. Each turn, they move one box through the facility, and when they reached the exit, they are fully trained. However, players can remove teams early, but then they are only partially trained and less effective. In *Star Wars: Rebellion*, ship construction is managed this way too. But various special cards can move ships down the track, accelerating production.

Strategic war games use this production track mechanism but have wanted, for realism purposes, to have different durations to produce different units. For example, an infantry unit might take a month, while an aircraft carrier might take a year. Because of the number of units being built, moving tokens from box to box is unwieldy, so designers created the Production Spiral. When units are being built, the tokens are placed by following the spiral arm out from the current month until the matching unit type is found. The tokens are then placed in the section of the arm. When the Month marker is moved, all tokens in that wedge become available to the player. *World in Flames* is a good example (Illustration 7.2).

Another way to implement this is to place purchased items into a discard area, as is common in deck-building games like *Dominion*. Here the delay before the purchases are available is randomized, since the discards are shuffled before creating the draw deck. This can create an issue with games

Illustration 7.2   The build queue in *Star Wars: Rebellion*.
Each unit takes a certain number of turns to construct and is placed in the appropriately numbered box when built.
Each turn units slide down one box. When they move out of the "1" box they are placed on the map.

with a fixed number of turns, as items that are acquired late in the game may never see play. This can be avoided by making late game purchases just worth Victory Points, or by having a special shuffle toward the end of the game. *Core Worlds* uses that latter technique, as the discards may be shuffled in before the final turn, regardless of whether the draw deck is depleted or not. While not guaranteeing that cards purchased at the end will be drawn, it does increase the chances.

Sample Games

> *Core Worlds* (Parks, 2011)
> *Dominion* (Vaccarino, 2008)
> *Star Wars: Rebellion* (Konieczka, 2016)
> *Time War* (Peek, 1979)
> *World In Flames* (Pinder and Rowland, 1985)

ECO-05 Income

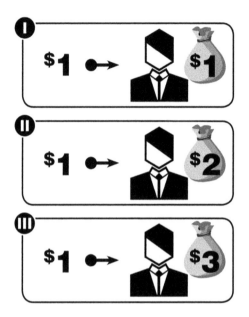

Description

Players gain resources at defined times.

Discussion

To foster a sense of growth and forward progress, most games with economic elements have some form of Income, where players receive additional resources. This is a large topic, and several specific mechanisms discussed in this chapter fall into this category. See "Automatic Resource Growth" (ECO-06), "Loans" (ECO-07), "Exchanging" (ECO-01), "Market" (ECO-03), and "Random Production" (ECO-12). However, there are some broad generalizations that can be discussed.

First, the designer needs to consider the timing of when Income is received. It can be scheduled, player-controlled, or random. *Brass* and *Eclipse* are examples of games with scheduled Income phases. They come at a definite point in the sequence of play, and players can plan around that.

Player-controlled systems rely on players to take actions that result in Income. Typically, it is self-controlled: a player makes a decision to take a

Production action that generates resources (as in *Global Mogul*) or sells something via a Market (ECO-03). However, in some systems, part of a player's Income may rely on the actions of other players. For example, in *Le Havre* and *Caylus*, a player gains Income if other players use their buildings (ECO-14).

This increases player interaction and rewards players that consider their opponents' positions. However, this is typically implemented as only a portion of a player's Income and not a significant one.

There are games where all, or close to all, of a player's Income is dependent on other players. In *Container*, players produce and ship containers. But other than taking loans, you may only gain money by enticing another player into purchasing one of your containers. As can be expected, this makes these games a lot less forgiving and subject to social pressures. *Container* in particular has this reputation.

Income can also be random. Roll and Move games like *Monopoly* typically incorporate this. Players rely on others either landing on their property spaces or passing Go to collect money. But, there are other more sophisticated systems for randomly allocating resources. See Random Production (ECO-12) for details.

Games can also be Open Economies or Closed Economies. In an Open Economy, there is a bank that pumps more resources into the game system. In contrast, in a Closed Economy, all the resources that exist are already in the player's hands, and they just move between players during the course of the game. The vast majority of games are Open Economies. This helps foster a sense of progress and is easier for designers to balance. An example of a Closed Economy game is *Dream Factory*, which is discussed in detail in the (appropriately named) Closed Economy mechanism in Chapter 8, "Auctions."

Sample Games

> *Brass* (Wallace, 2007)
> *Catan* (Teuber, 1995)
> *Caylus* (Attia, 2005)
> *Container* (Delonge and Ewert, 2007)
> *Dream Factory* (Knizia, 2000)
> *Eclipse* (Tahkokallio, 2011)
> *Global Mogul* (Crenshaw, 2013)
> *Le Havre* (Rosenberg, 2008)
> *Monopoly* (Darrow and Magie, 1933)
> *Nippon* (Sentieiro and Soledade, 2015)

ECO-06 Automatic Resource Growth

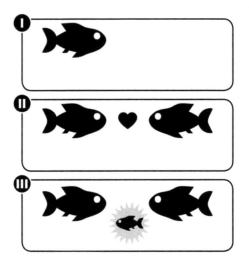

Description

Resources held by a player will automatically grow over time.

Discussion

In the purest form of this mechanism, one or more resources increases by a set amount (usually one) each turn. This allows the designer to gradually ramp up player power in a simple and intuitive manner.

A popular example of this is in the digital card game *Hearthstone*. The resource Mana is used to play cards. The Mana available at each turn begins the game at one and is increased by one at each turn until it reaches a maximum of ten. This gives the game an arc, as the options are much more restricted at low Mana values, and complexity and combos are gradually introduced. It also encourages players to balance their decks. If they only select cards with high Mana values, they will not be able to play for several turns. But if they only select low Mana cards, they may run out of cards quickly as they play multiple cards per turn later in the game (Illustration 7.3).

A variant on this system has unused resources grow. Thematically, this can be expressed as bank interest or as breeding animals. *Agricola* uses the latter option. If a player has two or more of the same type of animal, they gain an

Illustration 7.3 *Agricola* player board. If there are two or more of a given type of animal, one more is added. So in this example, one more sheep (white) and cow (brown) will be added. The lone pig (black) does not create an additional pig.

additional one. This encourages efficiency and can force players into deciding the value of using resources now, versus having more for later.

Civilization uses a similar system for population growth. At the start of each turn, each area that has a single token gains one more, and those that have two or more tokens gain two more. Setting up to properly manage this population growth is an important part of Civilization strategy.

Sample Games

Agricola (Rosenberg, 2007)
Civilization (Treshem, 1980)
Hearthstone (Donais and Sakomoto, 2014)

ECO-07 Loans

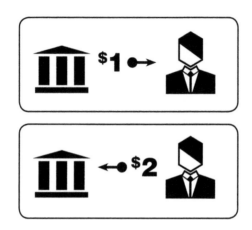

Description

Players may take a Loan from the bank to get more money.

Discussion

Many games with money allow players to borrow. These can serve several purposes for the design. First, they can be punishments for players who do not manage their money properly and exist to keep those players in the game. But they can also provide a means to victory, giving players the resources required to jump-start their engine or complete a big project. In fact, some games, like *Railroad Tycoon: The Board Game*, essentially require taking Loans to be a part of a winning strategy. Designers need to be careful to frame the concept of Loans in their game to incentivize players in the appropriate way.

There are several varieties of Loan mechanisms in games, around the way they are paid back, and other effects they have on the game. In some games, Loans are never paid back during the game. They simply count against a player's final money totals or victory points.

In other games, such as *Railways of the World*, players pay interest each turn based on bonds they have issued (another way of representing Loans). Whenever a player wishes, they may take a bond certificate and $5,000. Each turn they must pay $1,000 per bond, and bonds may never be repaid. Players lose one victory point (VP) for each bond they have at the end of the game.

In *Brass*, players may use an action to take a loan of $30. This never has to be repaid but immediately reduces ongoing income.

Wealth of Nations adds a few wrinkles to this system. Each Loan gives cash in declining increments ($20 for the first, $19 for the second, and so on) but can be repaid for $25. Any Loans held at the end of the game reduce the score by three VPs.

In *Monopoly*, players may take Loans but need to disable one of their properties to do so. Flipping a property allows the player to take the mortgage value from the bank. While it is flipped, the player may not collect rent if someone lands on the property. To unmortgage a property, a player must pay the mortgage value plus 10% interest. Other than the loss of the use of the property, there is no penalty for having a property mortgaged through the entire game. By rule, players must mortgage properties when faced with a cost that they cannot pay. This mechanism takes choices away from players, while needlessly extending a trailing player's long, slow, death spiral. Designers should avoid this type of mechanism.

Sample Games

Age of Steam (Wallace, 2002)
Brass (Wallace, 2007)
Container (Delonge and Ewert, 2007)
Monopoly (Darrow and Magie, 1933)
Railroad Tycoon: The Boardgame (Drover and Wallace, 2005)
Railways of the World (Drover and Wallace, 2005)
Wealth of Nations (Carroll, 2008)

ECO-08 Always Available Purchases

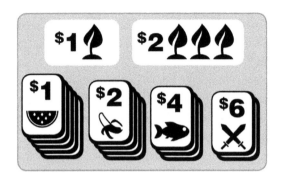

Description

Certain resources are Always Available to Purchase, while others may not or may be limited in quantity.

Discussion

This mechanism has traditionally been used in Deck-Building games (CAR-05). In *Ascension: Deckbuilding Game*, for example, there are two basic actions for players: purchasing an available card or attacking a card. In addition to a rotating queue of cards in the center, there are three cards that are always available: Heavy Infantry and Mystics are always available for purchase, and Cultists are always available to be attacked.

Having these cards gives a safety valve for players who face a board filled with high-level cards that they cannot afford, or early in the game when their hands may be weak. These cards are weaker than standard cards but are a reasonable consolation prize in case players get stuck with a low-value draw or allow them to use excess purchasing or attack power.

Dominion does not have random cards in the center, so the cost range of the cards is more constrained, and there is almost always something affordable. However, this mechanism is still used in the form of coin cards. Having these standard cards helps players develop a sense of value and gives them a target to know what they need to do to gain the highest-scoring Province cards.

Sample Games

Ascension: Deckbuilding Game (Fiorillo and Gary, 2010)
Dominion (Vaccarino, 2008)
Star Realms (Dougherty and Kastle, 2014)

ECO-09 I Cut, You Choose

Description

One player divides a set of resources into different groups. Other players have the first choice of which group to select.

Discussion

This I Cut, You Choose mechanism is based on a technique that parents often use with two children who are, for example, dividing up a bar of candy. One child breaks it into two pieces, and then the other selects which one they want. This ensures that the one doing the dividing is incentivized to make it as equitable as possible, because they know the other will take the larger piece.

In general, when this mechanism is used, it is between two players. For example, in *San Marco*, players are paired up each turn, and one is designated to divide drawn cards into two stacks. Then the other player selects which stack they want to keep.

This mechanism forces players to consider a wide variety of factors, both present and future, to put together offers that will entice the choosing player to pick the desired stack while giving them as little as possible.

Some games, like *New York Slice*, extend this mechanism beyond two players. In *New York Slice*, one player divides a stack of pizza ingredients into several stacks equal to the player count. Then, going clockwise, each player selects one stack, with the dividing player getting the last one remaining. In this multiplayer variation, it is next to impossible for four or more divisions to have even roughly equivalent value, so it is customary for each player to have equal turns being the divider.

For this mechanism to be interesting, the value of each division can't be obvious. True value for each player must be hidden or obscured. The most common way to do this is by integrating a variety of Set Collection mechanisms, which is the go-to method for having the same thing be worth different things to different players. See Chapter 12 for full details.

Sample Games

New York Slice (Allers, 2017)
Piece O' Cake (Allers, 2008)
San Marco (Moon and Weissblum, 2001)
Sundae Split (Bivins, 2017)

ECO-10 Discounts

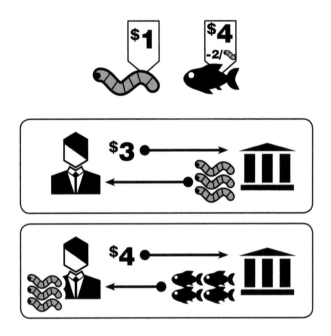

Description

A player can obtain an asset at a reduced cost.

Discussion

In the typical implementation of this mechanism, players accumulate Discounts that make future purchases less expensive, these Discounts persist, and they stack (build on each other). These characteristics make this mechanism well suited to create an engine-building effect, where players are able to achieve more as the game continues.

In *Splendor*, for example, cards are obtained by cashing in gems (ECO-01). Many of these cards Discount all future purchases by one or more gems. As the game progresses, it becomes easier for players to obtain more expensive cards, as they need fewer gems once they take the discounts into effect.

7 Wonders takes Discounts to an extreme by allowing players to acquire a card at no cost if they have the prerequisite building. This is distinct from an Upgrade mechanism (ECO-11), as the original card is retained. It is not converted into a new building—it merely allows for its acquisition at no cost. However, these Discounts are not fungible. They only apply to the single building specified on the card.

One of the earliest examples of Discounting is *Civilization*. Technology advances (called Civilization cards) gives players Discounts toward a specific category of Civilization card, usually the same category as the card itself. For example, Music, which costs 20 and is in the Art category, gives a 10 Discount toward any future purchases in Art for the rest of the game. This encourages players to specialize in certain areas. It also helps to create a Technology Tree (ACT-16) without actually defining any prerequisites, by having the most advanced cards be so expensive that they realistically can only be obtained through Discounts.

Sample Games

7 Wonders (Bauza, 2010)
Civilization (Tresham, 1980)
Splendor (André, 2014)

ECO-11 Upgrades

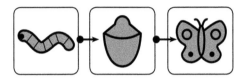

Description

Assets may be Upgraded to improved versions.

Discussion

Upgrades share many characteristics with Discounts (ECO-10) but with some distinctions. Typically, they are implemented by first representing the action or ability with a card or tile and then replacing it with a better version or adding another card or element to it to show its improved status.

Implementing Upgrades can nudge players to specialize, particularly if it is much more expensive or even impossible to go directly to the upgraded resource without the lower-level resource. As such, this can also be used to implement a Tech Tree (ACT-16).

A specialized form of upgrade is seen in train games such as *1830* and other *18xx* games. Early in the game, players place yellow tiles, which have simple single-track sections. Later, they may place more complex green or brown tiles that include overpasses and junctions. However, when upgrading a tile all existing tracks must be preserved. This limits the types of upgrade tiles that can be used and creates competition and bottlenecks for certain limited key tiles.

Some games force upgrades through obsolescence. At certain points, the game advances to a new stage (ACT-15), and some items may become obsolete and be discarded. The *18xx* games use this mechanism by having trains go obsolete, constantly forcing players to reevaluate their board position and future growth.

The physicality of the upgrade is typically done by replacing a card or tile; however, sometimes it is done by rotating or flipping. *Maiden's Quest* and *Flip City* make full use of this option by having players rotate or flip cards within a deck to increase (or reduce) their strength. While this gives designers a lot of flexibility in a small space, it places a burden on players to shuffle properly and maintain orientation. Other means for upgrading include adding a new card or card portion. *Mystic Vale* does this with clear plastic cards, each of which is populated in its top, middle, or bottom third. Layering the cards together enables all three sections to be seen at the same time. Cards are not the only elements that can be upgraded, nor the only way to show upgrades. In *Monopoly*, a property can be improved by adding houses and, eventually, hotels to it. In *Catan*, settlements can be upgraded to cities, each represented by a different token.

Upgrades are a common mechanism outside of the specific economic lens taken in this chapter. From promoting pawns in *Chess* to leveling up characters in a dungeon crawl to adding a fortification to a territory or hex, Upgrades represent a means of investment that increase player power, contribute to the narrative, and help players create connections to elements in the game.

Sample Games

1830 (Tresham, 1986)
Attika (Merkle, 2003)
Brass (Wallace, 2007)
Catan (Teuber, 1995)
Chess (Unknown, ~1200)
Flip City (Chen, 2014)
Maiden's Quest (Shannon, 2018)
Monopoly (Darrow and Magie, 1933)
Mystic Vale (Clair, 2016)
Through the Ages: A Story of Civilization (Chvátil, 2006)

ECO-12 Random Production

Description

Resources are generated from a random process and distributed to qualifying players.

Discussion

The Random Production mechanism was introduced in *Crude* but was popularized in *Catan*. In both of these games, players begin their turn by rolling two dice. In *Catan*, the die result determines which tiles activate, and any players with settlements or cities touching that tile receive resources. In *Crude*, the dice activate both the related row and column for the active players, and either the related column or row for their neighbor (Illustration 7.4).

This mechanism keeps all players involved in other players' turns, by offering the possibility of gaining resources. Players must remain flexible in their planning since they can't guarantee resource production or the specific mix of resources they'll get. There's also a slot machine effect, as players may hit a small "jackpot" if they hit a needed number.

This system was extended by *Machi Koro* by defining special abilities that only trigger on a player's turn or that only trigger on other players' turns.

This was further refined in *Space Base*, where each ability card has two sides. The blue side has an ability that triggers on your turn. If the card is

Illustration 7.4 Each turn in *Crude* the active player rolls two dice, which activates a row and column in their grid of facilities, allowing production or transformation of resources. In addition, the blue die also triggers the matching column in the player to the left, while the red die triggers the row of the player to the right.

replaced, it rotates to its red side and now triggers when an opponent rolls that number. Since, in games with more than two players, there are more opponent turns than your turns, getting cards to their red side is an important strategy.

A weakness of these systems is that they can be susceptible to player perception of streaky dice rolls. In actuality, given the number of dice rolls in a typical game of *Catan*, it is inevitable that some numbers will be rolled more than average, which means that some will be rolled less. This introduces a level of randomness that may or may not match the design intent and player expectation. Designers also need to realize that players are poor judges of what is a normal "streak" in a game like this and will perceive their frequency as worse than average even when they are exactly as expected. The *Catan* Event Cards expansion introduces a deck of 36 cards featuring each of the different possible outcomes of a roll of 2d6. A reshuffle card sits five cards from the bottom, indicating when the deck is to be reshuffled. Whether this is an improvement or not is largely in the eyes of the beholder and the designer.

Sample Games

Catan (Teuber, 1995)
Crude: The Oil Game (St. Laurent, 1974)
Machi Koro (Suganuma, 2012)
Space Base (Clair, 2018)

ECO-13 Investment

Description

Players own a share of an entity.

Discussion

Typically, this Investment mechanism represents ownership in the form of stock. Players may buy shares of stock and accrue benefits based on the amount of stock owned.

The benefits take two basic forms. In the simplest, players earn a dividend based on the number of shares owned. This may occur periodically, or at specific trigger points. Other systems give benefits to the player who owns the most shares, or to the top shareholders. This is very similar to an Area Majority system (ARC-02), so the considerations there apply.

Often it is a combination of these two. In *Acquire*, for example, players buy shares in hotel chains, which grow during the game, and merge if they touch. When a chain merges, each share pays a set amount, with the top two shareholders earning special bonuses.

In *Airlines*, scoring happens at variable intervals based on Card Draw (CAR-04). Each airline awards points based on the number of flight paths it has claimed on the board. The player with the most gains one VP per flight path, and the player with the second-most gains half of that.

The parallels with Area Majority are clear, as having one more share than your opponent is just as good as owning 100% of the shares. The number of shares that are available is usually limited. In *Airlines*, it varies by company, so players can lock in a guaranteed majority by having, for example, 4 shares in a 7-share company. This is distinct from the typical Area Majority game, where players can put as many resources as they like into a single entity. This distinctive mechanism is sometimes referred to as Area Control.

Another instructive example in *Airlines* is the way values change for different airlines. Each has a different number of markers that can be placed on the map to claim more routes. Airlines with more shares have more markers. This makes them potentially more valuable, but players must do more to gain and have the most shares. See Connections (VIC-14) and Network Building (SET-04) for further discussion (Illustration 7.5).

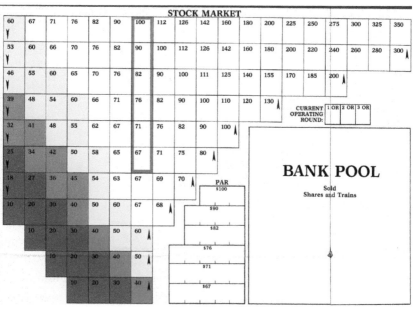

Illustration 7.5   The stock market track in *1830*. A marker on this track indicates the current value of a stock share for each corporation. Buying stock moves the marker up and selling moves it down. Issuing dividends moves it to the right while withholding them shifts it to the left.

An analogous but different form of Investment is Contribution. Players who contribute to a particular effort are entitled to a share of the spoils. For example, in *Tobago*, players contribute clues to narrow down the location of a treasure. When it is located, players who contributed clues to the correct location earn a reward. In *Dragon's Gold*, players cooperate to slay a dragon, and players who participate (no matter to what degree) are entitled to participate in the negotiations to divide the treasure.

Sample Games

Acquire (Sackson, 1964)
Airlines (Moon, 1990)
Chicago Express (Wu, 2007)
Dragon's Gold (Faidutti, 2001)
Get the Goods (Ado and Moon, 1996)
Shark (Vanaise, 1987)
Tobago (Allen, 2009)
Wheedle (Knizia, 2002)

ECO-14 Ownership

Description

Players own entities and perform actions for those entities or collect benefits if others use them.

Discussion

In *Le Havre* and *Caylus*, players may build buildings, which become new action spaces that all workers can use (see "Worker Placement" in Chapter 9 for more details). Typically, the owner can use the space free of charge, but when other players use the space, they must pay a fee to the owner.

This type of Ownership mechanism introduces a lot of different value calculations for the player. If I invest in this building, is it attractive enough that other players will use it and I will recoup my investment? If I take advantage of a building owned by another player, will it benefit my opponent more than me? As such, this mechanism can create a lot of player interaction.

In many rail games, including *Empire Builder*, *Railway Rivals*, and *Rail Baron*, players may use tracks built by other players for a fixed cost. This leads to decisions about how often a player may need to take a certain route in the future and rent-vs.-buy calculations (Illustration 7.6).

A more advanced form of Ownership is featured in *1830*, *18xx* games more generally, *Imperial*, and more. In these games, players purchase shares in companies (or countries in the case of *Imperial*), and the player with the most shares is the executive owner and has the ability to take actions on behalf of that entity. In *1830*, players can build tracks and stations, buy

Illustration 7.6 In *Lords of Waterdeep*, players may
construct buildings which they then own. This is indicated
by the color chip placed in the lower right. They gain a
benefit if other players visit them, as shown in the bottom
"OWNER" section of the building.

trains, and decide whether or not to issue dividends. In *Imperial*, players may
build armies or navies, declare war on other countries, or build up their economy. Typically, the money and assets of the company belong to the company.
Players have their own money and assets, and these are strictly separate. There
are specific means by which players can profit from running the company,
not all of which are to the benefit of the company or the other shareholders.
Like in real-world business, there are many strategies for enrichment, and
these games offer a high level of complexity and steeper learning curves.

If a player obtains more shares than the current owner, they take over
Ownership. This can lead to major shifts in board state. While owners usually don't like to lose their position, it can sometimes be an important tactic,
particularly in the *18xx* series of games. In those, the corporations, which
represent railroad companies, must have trains. When trains become obsolete, they are discarded, and new ones must be purchased. If the railroad does

not have enough money, the owner must pay for new trains out of pocket. An important tactic is for the owner to drain money out of the company treasury and then dump their shares to stick the almost-bankrupt company with another player.

Greed Incorporated is also based around this idea, as the key strategy in this game is getting Ownership of a company, getting it pay you bonuses, and bailing out before it goes under.

Ownership of this type makes a game multilevel. Players need to consider the individual player positions within companies, the companies' positions on the board, and the relative strengths and cash positions of all.

Sample Games

1830 (Tresham, 1986)
Acquire (Sackson, 1964)
Belfort (Cormier and Lim, 2011)
Caylus (Attia, 2005)
Empire Builder (Bromley and Fawcett, 1982)
Greed Incorporated (Doumen and Wiersinga, 2009)
Imperial (Gerdts, 2006)
Le Havre (Rosenberg, 2008)
Lords of Waterdeep (Lee and Thompson, 2012)
Rail Baron (Erickson and Erickson, 1977)
Railway Rivals (Watts, 1984)

ECO-15 Contracts

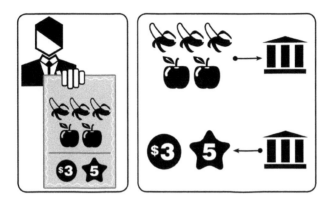

Description

Players fulfill Contracts to earn rewards.

Discussion

Typically, to complete a Contract, players turn in a specific combination of goods and earn a reward, which is usually money or VPs.

Contracts can either be *public* or be *private*. Public Contracts are face-up and shared by all players who race to fulfill it first. Often the Contract is discarded, but sometimes, other players can fulfill the Contract later for a lesser reward. *Century: Spice Road* is an example game with Public Contracts.

Private Contracts, by contrast, may only be fulfilled by the player that has them. They may be known to all or kept hidden until fulfilled. In *Empire Builder*, players have three Contract cards to deliver a specific good to a specific city. These are face-up so all players can see them, but only the owner may complete the delivery (Illustration 7.7).

There are a variety of ways that players may obtain Contracts. They may be obtained via random draw (as in *Empire Builder* or *Century: Spice Road*), by selecting from a tableau, by drawing several and selecting which to keep and which to discard, by draft, or even by auction (as in *Mow Money*).

Contracts give players immediate direction and goals, which can be particularly important for new players. Public Contracts increase player interaction but also may lead to "feel-bad" moments if a player is really close to

Illustration 7.7   Two sample contract cards from *Century: Spice Road*. Paying the cubes shown on the bottom yields the victory points shown just above them.

completing a Contract but is scooped by an opponent at the last second— particularly if the second place rewards aren't available. In these cases, it is helpful if whatever is used to fulfill the Contract is generally useful so that the effort to acquire that specific set of resources, or bring them to a specific location, is not completely wasted.

Sample Games

Century: Spice Road (Matsuuchi, 2017)
Empire Builder (Bromley and Fawcett, 1982)
Goa (Dorn, 2004)
Mow Money (Saunders, 2016)
Ora et Labora (Rosenberg, 2011)
Schoko & Co. (Hirschfield and Monnet, 1987)
Undermining (Tolman, 2011)

ECO-16 Bribery

Description

Players offer bribes to other players to get them to perform specific actions.

Discussion

Bribery is a subset of the Trading mechanism (ECO-02); however, it is typically more structured and given a different thematic basis. In a Bribery mechanism, a player needs to make a decision, and the other players then make monetary offers to entice the active player to make a particular choice.

Santiago uses this mechanism to great effect. Players are constructing irrigation canals around fields. Each turn, one player is the overseer and needs to decide where they will be constructed. The other players may influence the decision by laying a stick of their color in the direction they prefer, along with some coins. If the overseer decides to build in a way that contains another player's bribe, they take it. However, they are free to build in a completely different direction than any of the bribers would like. Bribes that are not taken are returned to the players.

This system rewards players that are able to judge where the overseer may want to build anyway and also gives the overseer opportunity for bluff, convincing the other players that the overseer wants to build in a different direction than they truly do, to entice other players to place bribes where they were planning to go anyway. The overseer also needs to value the benefit of a particular build to their opponent, as opposed to the bribe that they would receive.

While Bribery usually involves one active player and many potential bribers, *Tonga Bonga* implements a multiplayer simultaneous bribe system. Players have sailor tokens, but they cannot staff their own ships. Their sailors must be sent to other players' ships. At the start of each round, players place bribes on different positions around those ships. Then, in sequence, each player places a sailor on an available space, potentially gaining the bribe there. Sailors have different ratings, and a higher-rated sailor can kick out a lower-rated sailor from a position—a kind of Auction or Area Majority mechanism (ARC-02). After all the sailors have been placed, players gain coins on their spaces.

Players need to balance gaining coins, versus sending their best sailors to help their opponents move their ship, which ultimately is the way to win the game. Money is only a means toward an end and does not yield direct victory points.

Sheriff of Nottingham uses Bribery as a one-on-one mechanism. Players are trying to bring goods into the city and need to declare what they are bringing in to the Sheriff, who is played by a different player each round. Players place the cards they wish to get into the city in a sealed pouch and must declare the contents to the Sheriff, truthfully or not. The Sheriff has to decide whether to inspect the bag or not. If the player was lying, the Sheriff gains, if not, the player gains. Before the Sheriff decides to inspect or not, the player may offer a bribe for them to not inspect, which can lead to interesting negotiations and Yomi (UNC-01).

Sample Games

> *Intrigue* (Dorra, 1994)
> *Santiago* (Heley and Pelek, 2003)
> *Sheriff of Nottingham* (Halaban and Zatz, 2014)
> *Tonga Bonga* (Dorra, 1998)
> *Traders of Genoa* (Dorn, 2001)

ECO-17 Increase Value of Unchosen Resources

Description

If players do not select certain Actions or Resources, then they increase in value.

Discussion

Puerto Rico is one of the earliest examples of this mechanism. Each player selects one role during a round, but there are more available roles than players. The roles that are not chosen gain a coin at the end of each round. In the future, when players select that role they also gain the coins on it. This mechanism is a specific type of Dutch Auction (AUC-08).

Small World and *Century: Spice Road* also implements this system in a different guise. When players select a new faction in *Small World*, they select it from a queue. They may take any available faction in the queue but must place a coin on each one that they skip over (Illustration 7.8).

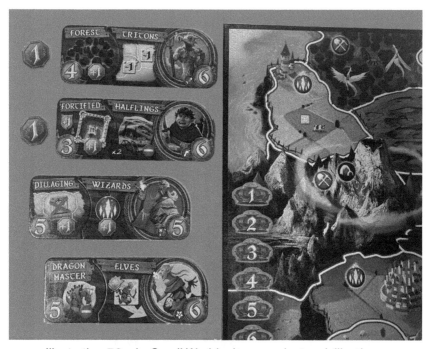

Illustration 7.8   In *Small World*, players select a civilization they want to play from a queue and must pay a coin to skip over earlier civilizations. In this example, the player wishes to take the Pillaging Wizards and so must place a coin on the Forest Tritons and Fortified Halflings. Those coins are earned by players that take those civilizations. If another player goes and also skips the Forest Tritons, another coin would be placed there, and the person to take them would take both coins.

In *Agricola*, a worker placement game (Chapter 9), some spaces are stocked with additional resources each turn. If those spaces are not selected, they will accumulate more and more resources until a player claims them and takes all the resources on the space.

These systems all have in common that they allow the players to value the choices. The value of unselected options gradually increases, until the value reaches a point that entices a player to choose it. While this doesn't eliminate the need for the designer to balance options, it gives some flexibility to price options that have values that may change over the course of the game or are random combinations that vary in power (as in *Small World*).

Sample Games

Agricola (Rosenberg, 2007)
Century: Spice Road (Matsuuchi, 2017)
Puerto Rico (Seyfarth, 2002)
Small World (Keyaerts, 2009)
Vinci (Keyaerts, 1999)

ECO-18 Negotiation

Description

Players make agreements about courses of action.

Discussion

Negotiation as a mechanism is very similar to Trading (ECO-02). We are drawing a distinction here between the exchange of resources, which defines Trading, and the influencing of actions that people take, usually in exchange for a promised action by the negotiating player. Bribery (ECO-16) combines these, exchanging resources for an action. The dividing line here is certainly fuzzy but useful.

Negotiation games often include deals that are non-binding. *Diplomacy* is a classic example. Players can discuss and coordinate moves, but nothing in the game binds players to follow through when they secretly write their orders.

Designers may include rules that mandate binding Negotiations. Typically, these require that the terms of the deal be resolved immediately and not extend to future turns or actions. This is a practical matter, as it becomes difficult to remember what the negotiated deal terms were and eliminates the need to include rules for what happens if the agreed-upon action physically cannot be performed.

Non-binding deals raise the emotional stakes for many players because they raise questions of honesty and loyalty, which are social rather than economic norms. Negotiations can also dramatically lengthen games, and so negotiation periods may need to be time-limited.

While any game is potentially subject to players negotiating, there are a few techniques for designers to add it as a specific feature. One is to have a dedicated Negotiation or discussion phase, as is done in *Diplomacy* or *The Resistance*. The rules should contain some structure around the length of Negotiations and what is or is not binding.

Negotiation can also be encouraged through Voting (RES-15), Hidden Roles (UNC-04), and Simultaneous Action Selection (TRN-09). These mechanisms introduce discussion and negotiation naturally, although it is recommended that the legality of negotiation (and again, the scope), be referenced in the rules.

Finally, negotiation can be supported thematically. Games that are modeling deals or politics (like *I'm the Boss* or *Republic of Rome*) will naturally lead to player negotiation.

Sample Games

Cosmic Encounter (Eberle, Kittredge, Norton, and Olatka, 1977)
Diplomacy (Calhamer, 1959)
A Game of Thrones (Petersen and Wilson, 2003)
I'm the Boss (Sackson, 1994)
Intrigue (Dorra, 1994)
Republic of Rome (Berthold, Greenwood, and Haines, 1990)
The Resistance (Eskrisge, 2009)
Werewolf (Davidoff and Plotkin, 1986)

ECO-19 Alliances

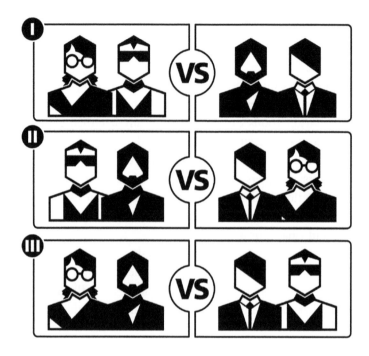

Description

Players have formal relationships that may change over the course of the game.

Discussion

In pure Negotiation games (ECO-18), agreements to cooperate are informal and can be made or broken at will. This mechanism differs in that there is a formal step to enter into and leave an Alliance, and the game rules specify how the Alliance operates.

For example, in Dune, each turn, cards are revealed from the Spice deck. If one of them is a Worm card, the players are allowed to make and break alliances. These alliances are in force until the next Worm card is revealed. Players that are allied may not attack each other, combine their score for winning purposes, win together, and may cooperate in other ways. When the next Worm is revealed, players may decide if they want to continue the alliance, ally with another player, or go it alone. *Empires in Arms*, a detailed simulation of the Napoleonic Wars, has a robust and complex alliance system, with a variety of possible formal relationships between players.

In *Struggle of Empires*, each Round begins with players bidding for the right to divide the players into two teams of their choosing. Like *Dune*, players who are allied fight together and may not attack each other. However, players still win or lose individually, which creates interesting dynamics.

Cosmic Encounter has players trying to conquer planets from their opponents. Each time this occurs, there is a formal alliance step, where players may choose to ally with the attacker, defender, or stay out of it, and there are defined benefits and penalties if their side wins or loses. So this is a similar system, although it is much shorter in duration, lasting one turn.

There are a variety of other takes on this system. *Through the Ages* has Treaty cards that players can offer to their opponents to gain mutual (sometimes asymmetrical) benefits. The Trick-Taking card game (CAR-01) *Mu* has partners assigned for the hand based on a bidding phase. Hidden Role games (UNC-04) secretly put players on different teams.

Sample Games

    Cosmic Encounter (Eberle, Kittredge, Norton, and Olatka, 1977)
    Dune (Eberle, Kittredge, and Olatka, 1979)
    Empires in Arms (Pinder and Rowland, 1983)
    Mu (Matthäus and Nestel, 1995)
    The Resistance (Eskrisge, 2009)
    Struggle of Empires (Wallace, 2004)
    Through the Ages: A Story of Civilization (Chvátil, 1986)
    Werewolf (Davidoff and Plotkin, 1986)

ECO-20 Resource Queue

Description

Resources are in an ordered queue and can only be pulled from one end or, rarely, both ends but not the middle.

Discussion

A pure expression of this mechanism can be found in *Walk the Dogs*. During the setup, players lay out a long line of dog figures of different breeds. Players play cards that allow them to pull a certain number of dogs from the head or tail of the line, with the objective of forming sets (SET-01 Set Valuation) (Illustration 7.9).

Marracash uses multiple resource queues. Players are merchants inside the city and can purchase stalls of different colors. Customer pawns with these same colors are randomly placed in a line outside the city gates (one line per gate), and players may bring a few into the city each turn but must bring the pawns at the head of the line.

Illustration 7.9   The line of dogs in *Walk the Dogs* is a
Resource Queue. If the card shown is played, the player will
take the two dogs at the head of the line.

This mechanism restricts player's abilities to act while giving them great visibility into future possibilities. All of the customer pawns are placed at the start of the game, so players have complete knowledge of the sequence at the start of the game and can plan accordingly. This is a great example of Input Randomness, where players must react to initial randomization rather than have randomness result from dice or some other randomizer to determine the outcome of an action.

This mechanism is distinguished from Action Queue (ACT-06), Shared Action Queue (ACT-07), and Programmed Movement (MOV-10) in a variety of ways. First, in Resource Queue you typically only deal with the head or tail, while in the action queues you execute the entire queue each turn. Also, action queues are most often laid out, resolved, and pulled back in full each turn, rather than being laid out at the start of the game.

Patchwork has a circular Resource Queue with a pawn defining the "head" of the queue. Players may take one of the next three pieces ahead of the pawn. Again, the entire circle is randomly laid out at the start of the game, so players have full visibility over everything from the start.

In some games, the resource queue is constructed or manipulated by the players. In the darkly satirical Guillotine, at the start of each round nobles are laid out in a line. On their turn, each player will chop the head off the noble at the start of the line and earn their points. Players have cards that allow them to manipulate the line to try to arrange for the least popular (and most valuable) nobles to be at the head of the line on their turn. Similarly, in *Retreat to Darkmoor*, players try to maneuver their minions so that they are not last in the queue, where they may be slain by the marauding hero. Minions at the head of the line will escape to the havens in *Darkmoor*, where they will score for their owners.

In another example, *Kolejka* is set in Communist-era Poland, and you send family members to different stores to wait in line to purchase goods. Players both construct the queues by sending pawns to different queues, as well as have action cards that allow them to manipulate those queues.

The game *Bohnanza* is built around this concept of queues. Each player has a hand of bean cards and must play the leftmost card each round into their gardens. Since you are trying to plant sets of the same bean, you may not want to play the leftmost card. Trading (ECO-02) with other players allows you to pull cards from the normal queue and keep your sets intact.

A card-based queue system can also be found in *Aeon's End*. In this deck-building game (CAR-05), at the end of the turn players place all their discarded cards on top of their discard pile in any order. When the draw deck is exhausted, instead of reshuffling the discard pile, it is simply flipped over to form the new draw deck. Players have complete knowledge of the state of their deck (although admittedly with a memory element).

In a looser interpretation of Resource Queue, players are not just restricted to certain elements at the head or tail but may dig deeper by paying more of a resource. This mechanism becomes a Dutch Auction (AUC-08) under these conditions and is discussed more fully in that section.

Sample Games

Aeon's End (Riley, 2016)
Bohnanza (Rosenberg, 1997)
Guillotine (Peterson, 1998)
Kolejka (Madaj, 2011)
Marracash (Dorra, 1996)
Patchwork (Rosenberg, 2014)
Retreat to Darkmoor (Loomis and Shalev, 2016)
Walk the Dogs (Moon, Weissblum 2005)

8

Auctions

A common concern in game design is how to allocate resources fairly among players. One of the most versatile solutions is an auction. Auctions provide for player agency, drama, interaction, strategy, and calculation. They are engaging and skill-testing, while providing players the opportunity to acquire whatever they wish, as long as they are able to pay.

The branch of mathematics called Game Theory studies auctions extensively, and game designers can draw on a rich trove of auction types with widely varying dynamics. Auctions can help keep a game in balance because players can dynamically adjust their pricing in response to fluctuations in the value of goods in a game.

For a time, auction mechanisms were wildly popular, and Reiner Knizia, the master of the auction, dominated the tabletop industry and the awards circuit with a dizzying array of clever and innovative auction games. Other genres, like *18xx*, also incorporated auctions, especially on setup. Yet, over time, the auction has waned in popularity, as Worker Placement (Chapter 9) and Drafting Mechanisms (CAR-06) presented alternative methods for allocating actions and resources in games.

Why did this shift occur? To some extent, gamer tastes change, like fashion, but designers should be aware of some of the drawbacks of the auction mechanism that contributed to its decline. Auctions depend on players being able to make accurate valuations of the lots up for auction. As players gain experience with a game, these assessments are easier to make, but for many players, the first few plays can be very frustrating. Auctions are also fragile to players who make bidding mistakes, like over-spending early. In many auction games, one bad judgment can cripple a player for the rest of the game.

A challenging counterpoint to players being able to accurately judge value is that they should not be able to judge it *too* accurately. As an example, consider

DOI: 10.1201/9781003179184-8

how much you would bid for a $10 bill. Any bid other than $10 doesn't make sense: bid more and you'll overpay. Bid less, and you'll be. There needs to be some obscuring of the precise value of the lot up for bid. Some ways to do that include hidden goals, having the values depend on what lots may be available in the future, or a mechanism like set collection (Chapter 12), which makes the same good have different values to different players.

Auctions can also slow a game down quite a bit. While this isn't a problem when auctions are the central mechanism of the game, it can present problems for pacing and playtime when they are a subsystem in a bigger game. Fortunately, there are many auction mechanics that are specifically designed to address this challenge, and we discuss them in this chapter. Multiple-lot auctions, simultaneous or single-bid auctions, and auctions with substantial constraints on bidding amounts all help make auctions work better in the context of tabletop games.

As you read this section, you may find that many other mechanisms can be described as a kind of auction or are isomorphic to an auction. We'll point to examples throughout this section that may be surprising or eye-opening. Keep in mind, however, that the math underlying an auction, or any mechanism, is only one piece of the puzzle. How players experience a mechanism, how it's presented, and the way it supports the game's theme and setting are as much a part of the mechanism as the underlying math. Nonetheless, auctions are like the skeletal system of games, even games with no explicitly named auction mechanisms. In many cases, it is their mathematical dynamics and structure that support the rest of the game.

AUC-01 Open Auction

Description

Players shout out bids as they will, with no turn order. While an Open Auction will typically end when a certain amount of time with no increases occurs or it becomes clear that no one wishes to raise the current bid, a true Open Auction allows a seller to accept any bid at any time and close the Auction. Though the usual outcome is that the high bidder is the winner, no rule requires this outcome.

Discussion

An Open Auction is quite unusual in that it has no auctioneer and no rules—not even the rule that the highest price must win. In a sense, an Open Auction is more like an out-loud simultaneous negotiation. The reality is that very few auctions, in the real world or in board games, are truly open. That is because Open Auctions are pretty messy! Multiple bidders often want to bid the same amount, and the bidding increments can be all over the place. Some bidders may not hear all the bids, and confusion is all too common. Without an auctioneer, these auctions can be difficult to govern fairly. In the board game context, it is worth pointing out that they also tend to be really noisy and frenetic. The only game we could find that uses anything like an Open Auctions is *Monopoly*. In perhaps the most-overlooked rule in the game, when a player decides not to buy a property from the bank, the property is sold to any player (including the one who chose not to buy it from the bank initially) at any price. *Monopoly* does specify that the Banker auctions the property and must sell to the highest bidder but no other rules on how to govern the auction are provided.

Despite their weaknesses, Open Auctions do have some important features. First, iterative bidding provides a lot of information as players reveal their preferences and for the goods up for auction. The auction integrates a means for allocating resources with a way for players to trade opinions about how valuable they are.

Another important feature of the Open Auction is that the dominant strategy for any bidder is to stay in the auction until their value for the auctioned goods is reached. This means that absent external issues, like very large disparities in player wealth, or a bidder risking bidding up the price past their valuation, the winner will pay a price close to the actual value for the item—or, to be precise, they will pay, at most, one dollar (or other bidding increment) more than the price at which the second-highest bidder valued the item.

In general, Open Auctions are more theoretical than practical. There are many small tweaks to the basic structure that create much more suitable dynamics for use in tabletop games. We include the mechanism of Open Auctions here as a foundation on which to build.

Sample Games

Monopoly (Darrow and Magie, 1933)

AUC-02 English Auction

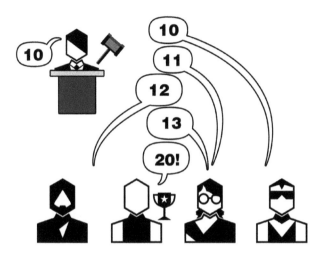

Description

An auctioneer asks for bids of a certain amount and players indicate their willingness to bid at that amount, usually by holding up a hand or paddle, or by calling out. Players are permitted to adjust the increment of the bid, usually by shouting out their actual bid, though this is done infrequently, and usually either to indicate a smaller increment than the auctioneer requests or a much larger one. When a certain amount of time elapses with no increases, or it is clear that no one wishes to raise the current bid, the auctioneer declares that the high bidder is the winner.

Discussion

The English Auction is probably what most people think of when they hear the word "auction." The auctioneer, at the front of the room, speaking in a too-fast-to-follow cadence while various bidders use paddles to signal their intent to bid in ever-increasing amounts until, at last, the "going, going, gone!" is sounded and the winning bid is declared.

The primary differences between an English and an Open Auction are in their governance. An English Auction employs an auctioneer to recognize bidders, to determine which bids are valid, who the current winning bid is, and what is the appropriate bid increment to maximize the settlement price of the auction, while also bringing the auction to a swift conclusion. The compensation of auctioneers in the real world suggests that these skills are non-trivial and that better auctioneers execute better auctions, which produce higher prices for sellers.

For designers, the need for an auctioneer can make English Auctions less appealing, even though the benefits they provide in terms of certainty, fairness, and speed are substantial. Fortunately, designers can turn to a variety of similar auctions that capture those benefits without requiring mediation— including auctions in which the auctioneer may bid. We'll look at those in the next sections.

An overlooked feature of English Auctions is that the price of the auction moves against the preferences of the bidders—that is, it goes up. While that's what most of us think of when we think of auctions, there are auctions in which the price moves the other way, starting at some high number and then moving down. See Dutch Auction (AUC-08) as an example.

English Auctions are dynamic and dramatic, but they share the core of the Open Auction in that they reveal a lot of information to the bidders about one another, and they have a weakly dominant strategy of simply staying in the bidding until your value is reached.

There are some other strategies that bidders employ though, whose effects are primarily psychological. Players might make a large jump in bid increment to intimidate other bidders, or they might leave their paddle in the air (aka "lighthouse bidding") to show they're in for the long haul. Bidding quickly and crisply is another way to demonstrate an intention to stay in the bidding for a while. These strategies may have the desired effect of driving other players off, but they can also inadvertently raise prices beyond what was necessary to win the auction. Finally, a player may make a bid that is larger than her own value for the lot in order to inflate the final settlement price of the auction. This move can backfire, however, if no other bidder raises the bid further.

An important aspect of English Auctions, and auctions with auctioneers more generally, is to whom the closing price is paid. In some auctions, rather than paying the bank, the player who chooses the item up for bid receives payment, unless they are the winner of the item, in which case payment is made to the bank. In practice, the result of this mechanism, which is featured in *Modern Art*, is that the auctioneer player, the one who put the item up for bid, very rarely purchases it, because effectively, they pay double: the cost of the item and the forgone gains from letting someone else win it and collecting the payment. Thus, effectively, the player who puts the item up for bid plays as the auctioneer, rather than an active bidder, for the duration of that auction.

The dynamic and engaging nature of English Auctions is exciting, but designers will typically have to turn to another mechanism for implementation at the table in games where the auction is not the centerpiece.

Sample Games

Chicago Express (Wu, 2007)
Modern Art (Knizia, 1992)

AUC-03 Turn Order Until Pass Auction

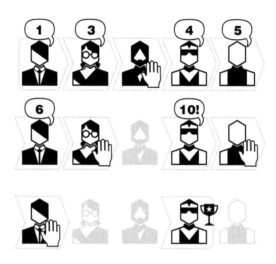

Description

Starting with one player and going in turn order, players may raise the current bid or pass. When all players but one have passed, the player remaining in the auction is the winner.

Normally, players that pass may not re-enter the auction. However, allowing re-entry is a variation that is not uncommon.

Discussion

The benefits of this Turn Order Until Pass mechanism are in its simplicity and how it aligns with players' expectations. Players are rarely confused by how to run this kind of auction, so it doesn't require an auctioneer. Popular games, like *Power Grid* and *Through the Ages: A New Story of Civilization*, feature this type of auction, and in a board game-adjacent space, auctions in fantasy sports are typically of this kind, perhaps adding to the popularity and familiarity of the mechanism.

From a game theory perspective, the dominant strategy for bidders is the same as in an Open Auction, namely to stay in the bidding until their value for the item for bid is reached. This can help prevent any player from receiving an unearned windfall simply because of the mechanics of the bidding.

Turn Order Until Pass provides a structure to govern the uncertainties that normally exist in Open and English Auctions. A player may only bid on his or her turn and must exceed or, in some cases, at least match the previous high bid. This ordered and clear structure makes it an excellent choice for board games.

Turn Order Until Pass does have some drawbacks. For one, it's not as dynamic as Open Auctions, as the ordered process of bidding removes some of the energy from the auction process.

The imposition of a turn order on bidding also creates a bit of inequity. If the current bid is $10, and it's not my turn, I can't bid $11. If $11 is the most I'm willing to pay, but the active player goes ahead and bids $11, there's nothing I can do. If nobody else bids, that player will win the auction at $11 even though more than one bidder was willing to pay that amount. In an English Auction, a skilled auctioneer will recognize when more than one bidder is stuck on the same bid and will cajole one or the other to raise their bid. Failing that, the auctioneer will recognize the bid of whomever bid first—which may not be perfectly fair either but at least provides all bidders with the theoretical opportunity to bid any number they wish. In a Turn Order Until Pass Auction, by contrast, some players will simply not have the opportunity to bid certain values.

Another issue introduced when there is no auctioneer is that an auction can drag if players don't increment their bids reasonably. In games where players hold a lot of money, players incrementing their bids $1 at a time can be painful. However, incrementing by $1 at a time is theoretically the dominant strategy to avoid overpaying, so it's tough to put the blame on the players for doing so. It's the designer's responsibility to incentivize behavior that leads to a better experience!

Turn Order Until Pass remains one of the easiest types of auctions to implement, run, and participate in. The mechanism exists in many different games as a relatively quick way to allocate resources or benefits. However, games that place a central focus on the auction mechanism usually introduce some additional twists. In recent years, Drafting (CAR-06) has overtaken simple bidding as the preferred method for quick allocation of resources— not least because auctions require more precise valuation by players, which can be challenging, especially for new players. This issue is not unique to this specific kind of auction and has been discussed at greater length in the introduction to this section.

Re-entry after passing is a variant that allows players to pass but re-enter the bidding when their turn comes around again. Passing is risky, in the sense that if all but one player passes, the auction will close. However, re-entering after passing does create some interesting drama but at a high cost in terms of playtime. When players pass, an auction speeds along since it has fewer participants. When re-entry is allowed, the number of participants in the auction never decreases. Perhaps the main advantage of allowing re-entry is preventing accidental windfalls by allowing a previously passed player to raise the bid on a lot that should sell for more but whose value is languishing for whatever reason.

Sample Games

> *Power Grid* (Friese, 2004)
> *Raccoon Tycoon* (Drover, 2018)
> *Through the Ages: A Story of Civilization* (Chvátil, 2006)

AUC-04 Sealed-Bid Auction

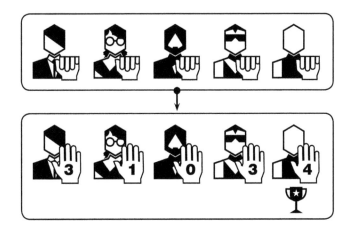

Description

Players secretly make a bid. All bids are revealed simultaneously, and the high bidder wins.

Discussion

Sealed-Bid Auctions, also called Blind-Bid Auctions, compress all the excitement of an auction into one tense bidding decision, followed by a big reveal. Designers favor them for these features and for their speed. In games in which an auction is one subsystem in a larger game, or in which there are many sequential auctions, a single sealed-bid system is perfect for moving the game along. A good example of this is the *Game of Thrones* board game, in which players run a gauntlet of three auctions in a row every few rounds. The consecutive auctions allocate special abilities among the players and thus must be quick and decisive, as the rest of the game involves intricate and time-consuming planning, negotiations, and troop movements.

Sealed-Bid Auctions sacrifice some of the informational value of other iterative bid systems. Players who assess correctly that they will not be the winners of an auction will often bid nothing, or perhaps a token amount, to deny other players knowledge of their true valuation. This may be a feature or a bug, depending on the intent of the designer and the needs of the design, but is worth keeping in mind when employing this mechanism.

Sealed-bid systems typically require some type of tiebreaker, since nothing stops players from bidding the same amount. Various tie-breaking methods exist. In the aforementioned *A Game of Thrones*, one of the abilities that players bid on is tie-breaking—an ability one of the player factions starts the game with. Other common tiebreakers include turn order or reverse order of the current score (a kind of catch-up mechanism). Some games feature rebidding by the tied players, like *Spartacus: A Game of Blood and Treachery* and *Container*. *Fist of Dragonstones* breaks ties through a rebid with a special currency that is only used for that purpose. This approach is decisive, but it lengthens the bidding process that sealed bidding is meant to curtail.

An ergonomic consideration for sealed bidding is the componentry used for currency. The easiest way to do sealed bidding is by placing currency in a closed fist. Designers should carefully consider the size and material for the currency to ensure that bids fit comfortably in most hands, that tokens are easy to stack and pick up, and that they are at least somewhat resistant to the palm-sweat these auctions engender. Other approaches to sealed bids include using a dial to set a value, as in *Dune*, setting a die to a value, as in *Tiny Epic Kingdoms*, or placing bids behind a screen, as in *Modern Art*.

Sealed-Bid Auctions are often used for combat resolution. In both *Dune* and *Tiny Epic Kingdoms*, players bid military strength, which might be further modified by other effects, to determine the victor of a military encounter. *Scythe* offers a similar auction, but players bid a resource to power their mechs rather than bidding actual troops.

Sealed bidding, more than any other type of bidding, may require losers to pay their bids (sometimes referred to as an "all-pay" auction). This has stronger thematic consonance when the bids represent a battle, rather than the purchase of goods. The lost bids make sense when they represent battle losses, but they make less sense when the bids are surrendered but no goods are acquired in return. All-pay auctions are used in game theory to model, among other things, elections and political contests, which perhaps makes them more fitting for use in the *Game of Thrones* board game. There is a lot of design space available in all-pay auctions, though players often express strongly negative reactions to these auctions, so proceed with care. Note that variants like loser-pays-half, as in *For Sale* (which is a turn-order auction, not a blind bid), can help remove some of the stings, while incentivizing higher bids, ironically.

Sealed bids are also used in unlimited bidding, which is an unusual mechanism that allows players to bid any amount they wish. For example, in *QE*, players can write in a bid of any amount, so long as it fits on their bidding placard. Players do not have a store of money of any kind, since they represent sovereign nations that can print any amount of money. *Magic Money* takes a similar approach, with players in the roles of wizards, who can conjure however much money they desire. In both games, the player who spends the most money, in total, over the course of the game, is eliminated, regardless of how many points they may have earned from winning the lots up for auction throughout the game.

The best-known unlimited bidding games use modified sealed bids. In both *QE* and *Magic Money*, the opening bid is revealed to all players, but only the auctioneer sees the remaining bids. In *Magic Money*, that player reveals the winning amount to everyone, but in *QE*, the auctioneer only reveals the winning bidder, but not the value of their bid.

The mix of hidden information and elimination of the player who spent the most money leads unlimited bidding games to feel less like an auction and more like a bluffing game. Auctions generally call for tightly evaluating values and costs, but unlimited auctions reward players who correctly assess when they have won enough lots that they can break off and not pursue an ever-rising spiral of bid prices.

Unlimited bidding games appear to be mechanically fragile, and they operate as a social experiment as much as they do as a competitive game. While it is easy to be enamored of their central conceit of unlimited bidding, it may be that the more durable and useful innovation is in dispensing with the final revelation of all the bids. Auctions are excellent at price discovery, but uneven distribution of bidding information is an interesting way to limit that price discovery so that future auctions retain more tension and mystery.

Sample Games

   Container (Delonge and Ewert, 2007)
   Dune (Eberle, Kittredge, and Olatka, 1979)
   Fiji (Friese, 2006)
   Fist of Dragonstones (Faidutti and Schacht, 2002)
   For Sale (Dorra, 1997)
   A Game of Thrones (Petersen and Wilson, 2003)
   Magic Money (Hiwiller, 2020)
   Modern Art (Knizia, 1992)
   QE (Birnbaum, 2019)
   Scythe (Stegmaier, 2016)
   Spartacus: A Game of Blood and Treachery (Dill, Kovaleski, and Sweigart, 2012)
   Tiny Epic Kingdoms (Almes, 2014)

AUC-05 Sealed Bid with Cancellation

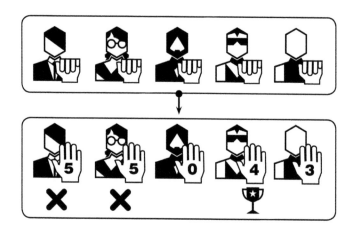

Description

Players secretly make a bid. All bids are revealed simultaneously and the high bidder wins unless there are ties for the high bidder. Tied bids cancel each other out and are treated as the lowest bids.

Discussion

The purpose of ties canceling out is in some sense a response to the challenge of running auctions without an auctioneer. A skilled auctioneer can help sort out two tied bidders and create some separation between them. Cancellation acts as a kind of heavy-handed auctioneer who refuses to acknowledge tied bids.

Mechanically, this type of auction works best when coupled with constrained bids that increase the chances of ties. When players are working from a defined and limited set of bid markers, they may have a much better idea about what their opponents could bid. The bidding game begins to resemble a bluffing or betting game more than a regular auction, as players know that bidding big can't guarantee their victory. If players are good at tracking which markers players have already used to bid, they can deduce which low bids might actually win the auction and which high bids are more susceptible to cancellation. This interaction does echo real-world dynamics in which the two strongest competitors can impede each other sufficiently to allow a weaker competitor to emerge from the fray with the prize.

This counter-intuitive mechanism hasn't proven especially popular over the years. The non-thematic notion that a seller would ignore a higher bid simply because more than one bidder made it flies in the face of economic rationalism. As such, this is a mechanism that can feel "gamey," or anti-thematic.

Another drawback to this mechanism is that bidders can find it quite punishing while also feeling random. When players reveal their bids and discover they both valued the lot really highly but neither gets it, and that can be very frustrating.

However, this same feature can lead to fun and dramatic moments and increases the element of Yomi (UNC-01) for the players. As such, it works best in lighter games with more chaos. Players looking for a highly strategic experience will not be attracted to this mechanism.

Sample Games

Hol's Der Geier (Raj) (Randolph, 1988)
Sky Runner (Glimne, Karlsson and Sevelin, 1999)

AUC-06 Constrained Bidding

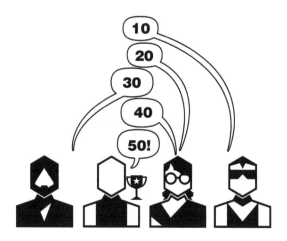

Description

This is a meta-mechanism that can modify other auction techniques. Players may not bid any number that they wish. They may only bid based on increments and/or combinations of certain resources.

Discussion

The greatest drawback of auctions as a game design mechanism is their length. The second-biggest defect is that it is difficult for players to make small distinctions in the value of the lots up for bid. Is some collection of goods worth 13? 14? 15? At small increments, it can be very challenging to make a determination.

Constrained Bidding offers a cure to both of these defects. Since there are fewer valid bids, and the increment required to raise the bid is higher, auctions come to a close more quickly. Players are rarely faced with the decision to increase their bid by one or two units, and the larger required increments make it easier for players to value the lots up for bid.

One of the effects of Constrained Bidding is a reduction in the uncertainty of auction outcomes. It is easier for players to predict which other players might be interested in a lot and how they'll bid. Some games will have bidding tokens be hidden information to retain some of the tension in the auction (Illustration 8.1).

Illustration 8.1   In *Ra*, players have a subset of these bidding tokens, either three or four depending on player count. Any bid they make must be a single bidding token. Photo by Board Game Geek user kevintlee.

Constrained Bidding is a favorite for designer Reiner Knizia, appearing in *Ra*, *Amun-Re*, and *High Society*. Yet it hasn't caught on as a generally popular auction mechanism, and designers should be aware of some substantial drawbacks to it.

For one, Constrained Bidding, aside from the basic constraint of some minimum bid increment, is an especially artificial device. The need to raise a bid by a specific amount or to bid only the amounts on the bidding tokens you hold does not typically have any thematic justification. It is hard to imagine a real-world auction that would use this kind of mechanism.

Constrained Bidding also introduces a challenge in redistributing the used bidding tokens. In most auction games, the money system is either closed or based on some economy that enables you to buy and sell the goods up for auction. But in a fixed token system, all the advantages those fixed increments grant to speed of auction come at the cost of their non-liquidity. Put simply, you can't make change! Designers need to carefully consider both the balance of initial apportionment of bid tokens and how they come back to their owners after use.

One area in which there is still considerable design space is multiuse bidding counters. Will you use a powerful card as currency to bid in an auction?

Or will you save its power for use in another aspect of the game? One might see *Twilight Struggle* (and many other area majority games) as a series of simultaneous auctions, with the multiuse cards representing a kind of fixed bid. Admittedly, in *Twilight Struggle*, the cards, when used as action points, are more liquid than a true Constrained Bid Auction, but it is in the same family.

Indeed, there is an entire category of games that are based on bidding cards with multiple uses, often with players having duplicate decks. *Libertalia* and *Eggs & Empire* come to mind immediately. The cards can be seen as a kind of Constrained Bidding token, and players typically have to use each card once before being allowed to pick up the discards. What distinguishes these games from true auctions is twofold. First, the games do not always have an actual lot up for bid. The revealed cards may interact with a pot of gold, for example, but they do not represent contingent offers to purchase some lot as in most auctions. Second, even when a lot or lots do exist, like in *Eggs & Empire*, winning the auction does not necessarily lead to winning the lot. More generically, the player with the highest bid does not necessarily win the auction. Typically, in these games, in addition to the currency value on the card, there are some additional effects and interactions that can impact the auction's outcomes dramatically. Nevertheless, these games merit a mention here as they are a means of using the Constrained Bid structure in an engaging and more thematically resonant way.

Sample Games

> *Amun-Re* (Knizia, 2003)
> *Cyclades* (Cathala and Maublanc, 2009)
> *Eggs & Empire* (Pinchback and Riddle, 2014)
> *High Society* (Knizia, 1995)
> *Libertalia* (Mori, 2012)
> *Ra* (Knizia, 1999)
> *Stockpile* (Sobol and Orden, 2015)
> *Twilight Struggle* (Gupta and Matthews, 2005)

AUC-07 Once-Around Auction

Description

The players each have one opportunity to bid, either passing or raising the prior bidder. The order of bids is determined by one of the Turn Order structures. After the last player has the opportunity to bid, the high bidder wins.

Discussion

The Once-Around Auction structure takes a straightforward approach to shortening auctions by simply collapsing the whole auction into one round. This works very well for speeding the auction, but it does have disparate impacts on players depending on their position in the turn order. The first player is faced with the substantial challenge of making a bid without any other information. Their bid will set the market and is vulnerable to being outbid by any player, who can bid as little as one dollar more. By contrast, the last player in turn order has perfect information. They know exactly how much to bid to win the lot. Often, the player in the next-to-last place is faced with a lot that is relatively inexpensive, but which they do not want. However, they feel like they must police the auction and raise the bid to prevent the last player from getting a windfall and, in doing so, take the risk of having to purchase a lot they did not want at a relatively high price.

Whether the strong left-right binding (the term used to describe games that are strongly impacted by turn order and, specifically, the players seated to the right and left of a given player) of this mechanism is positive or negative is largely a matter of perspective, but it is something to design around.

For example, turn order can itself be priced in such a manner that the advantage provided by going last in the auction is accounted for. Alternatively, going first in other aspects of the game may be quite powerful, to help balance the disadvantage of going first in the auction.

Another approach is to use constrained bids that require bidders to raise the current winning bid by a more substantial increment, or to provide the first bidder with the right to match the final bid and take the lot.

Once-Around Auctions aren't that common in modern designs, having been superseded by Sealed-Bid Auction (AUC-04) that are agnostic to turn order or by drafting mechanisms that eliminate the role of currency entirely. Generally, they should be used when tight coupling to turn order is desirable and turn order is central to the design.

Sample Games

Medici (Knizia, 1995)
Modern Art (Knizia, 1992)
New Amsterdam (Allers, 2012)
Tin Goose (Clakins, 2016)

AUC-08 Dutch Auction

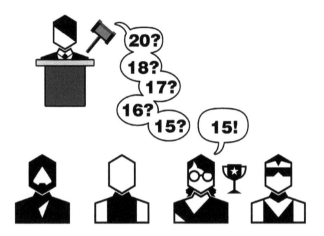

Description

A simultaneous single-bid system in which the lot starts at a very high price and then is gradually decreased by the auctioneer or other controlling mechanism until someone agrees to claim the item at its current price, ending the auction. The first bidder to accept the current price is the winner, such that there are no ties. A Dutch Auction is sometimes also called a one-bid auction because of this feature that the first bid made is also the only bid in the auction.

Discussion

The Dutch Auction has a storied history, having been invented in the seventeenth century in Holland to manage the sale and trade of tulip bulbs that arrived in Holland via the Ottoman Empire. A Dutch Auction maximizes the price at which a good is sold and incentivizes buyers to act quickly since once a bid is made, there is no opportunity to counter the bid; the auction is over!

Dutch Auctions only work well when there is a single item up for bid or a single lot. All bidders must receive information of the offer price dropping simultaneously and must be able to respond immediately. Any bidder with an informational time lag is highly disadvantaged in this kind of auction, whether that time lag is on hearing the newly announced price or in submitting a bid (Illustration 8.2).

One way to execute a Dutch Auction is with an actual clock that counts down prices, as in *Merchants of Amsterdam*, but the componentry alone makes this an unusual approach.

Dutch Auctions spread over multiple turns are very common in board games and are often implemented as a row or river of cards. Each position in the row is tied to a price and players may purchase a card from any position. When a card is purchased, more expensive cards slide down and become cheaper. In many games, the last card is free, and in others, the cheapest card will disappear from the market every turn and a new card will enter at the pricey side. Examples of this market row include *Suburbia*, *Pax Pamir Second Edition*, and *Through the Ages*. A common variant can be seen in *Small World*, in which players can purchase the first card in the row for free or pay one coin per card they want to bypass until they reach the card they wish to purchase. The trick here is that a player acquires any coins on a card they purchase, which means it's not necessary to have a card-clearing mechanism in the market. Eventually, the first option will be worth taking for the coins piled on it.

This implementation isn't strictly a traditional Dutch Auction, since more than one good is up for auction at the same time. It's also typically mediated

Illustration 8.2   The Dutch Auction clock from *Merchants of Amsterdam*. The dial rotates automatically via a spring mechanism. The first player to slap the center button stops the clock and pays the currently indicated price.

by turn order: you can only make a purchase on your turn. Because of different mechanisms for adjusting the market each turn, every player does not have an equal opportunity to pay any price they wish for a given good. In some cases, like *Through the Ages*, calculating at what cost a card will become available to you and manipulating that price by purchasing cards that are cheaper and forcing cards to slide down multiple positions is a key strategy.

Despite some of these issues, the market row has become a staple of game design and a favorite method for reasonably fair resource allocation. The logic of this mechanism can sometimes find its way into worker placement games. For example, in *Agricola*, some buildings will accumulate resources if nobody places a worker there. Eventually, the rewards available are so rich that someone claims them. Through the lens of the Dutch Auction, we'd say that the price per share kept going down until a buyer was willing to purchase the whole lot. This isn't quite a Dutch Auction, it's really an auction with a fixed price (one worker, though it could be a monetary price in a different context) but in which the rewards increase. However, note that unlike traditional auctions, this auction shares a primary feature with Dutch Auctions, which is that the value moves in favor of the buyer. Dutch Auctions use price to effectuate this, rather than the size of return, but they are conceptually quite similar.

Dutch Auctions as implemented through market rows are quite a robust and durable solution for game designers. They typically don't take up too much board space, they're ergonomic, decisive, quick, and make for interesting decisions. In some games, like *Morels*, or *Majesty: For the Realm*, they can be a bit tedious when it comes to constantly sliding down cards. *Vikings* uses an ingenious wheel mechanism to address this situation elegantly by placing the prices on the wheel and rotating it to adjust the prices of the tiles laid around its perimeter.

Designers will frequently turn to this river-of-lots mechanism when using some non-monetary currency for resource acquisition. The aforementioned *Through the Ages* uses an Action Point currency (ACT-01) for card acquisition. Though *Small World* themes the cost as monetary, money is worth an equal number of victory points, so the actual cost to acquire a lot is victory points. This mechanism is also quite amenable to variations involving allowing players to reserve a card in the market for purchase later at a lower price or claiming a card so that its eventual acquisition cost is paid directly to the player.

Sample Games

Agricola (Rosenberg, 2007)
Majesty: For the Realm (Andre, 2017)
Merchants of Amsterdam (Knizia, 2000)
Morels (Povis, 2012)
Pax Pamir Second Edition (Wehrle, 2019)
Small World (Keyaerts, 2009)
Suburbia (Alspach, 2012)
Through the Ages: A Story of Civilization (Chvátil, 2006)
Vikings (Kiesling, 2007)

AUC-09 Second-Bid Auction

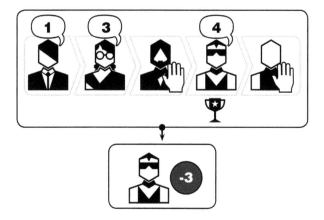

Description

This mechanism modifies other auctions, such as Turn Order Until Pass or Sealed Bid. The amount paid by the Highest Bidder is equal to the second-highest bid.

Discussion

In game theory, Second-Bid auctions, also called Second-Price auctions or Vickrey Auctions, are well-studied in relation to the question of how will the choice of auction type impact the price of a good? If I have a car that I want to sell, for example, which auction type will fetch me the best price? One way to ensure the highest possible price for the seller is to use an auction mechanism that encourages bidders to make mistakes in their bidding strategies. A Dutch Auction (AUC-08) is a great example. The added pressure of the clock and the possibility of someone else making a bid that can't be countered leads to somewhat higher settlement prices than a traditional English Auction.

In many cases, there is a desire to create a fast and fair auction, in which the best strategy for all bidders is to simply bid the highest price they are willing to pay. In a traditional auction, the correct strategy is to bid $1 more than the previous bid until your reserve point is met. You don't increase your bid by more than $1 over the previous bid because maybe nobody will outbid you and you'll win the auction at a lower price than the amount you were willing to pay. This makes for slow going at times.

A second-highest auction is the solution to the question of how to make auctions fast and fair for buyers and sellers. In essence, your bid in a Second-Price auction is not an offer to pay that amount but to pay anything up to that amount. Your bid of $1,000 is really a bid of $999, such that anyone who wants to buy the item must pay $1,000 or more. The dominant strategy in a Second-Price auction is to bid your true value for the lot. If all other players value the lot at a lower price, you'll pay their valuation, not your higher price. If other players value the lot higher than you, you won't win, but they'll never pay less than your true value.

Vickrey Auctions are extremely rare in board games. The only example we were able to turn up was Reiner Knizia's *Das letzte Paradies* (*The Last Paradise*), a largely forgotten title. In part, this is because Vickrey Auctions aren't that different from other auction types when it comes to board games. In any non-blind auction method, a Vickrey settlement method will yield a final price that is roughly the same as the non-Vickrey, or perhaps one-bid increment smaller. That's a lot of rules overhead for such a small change in price. In blind bidding systems, the Vickrey does impact actual prices more substantially, but in many cases, the game design capitalizes on that inefficiency in the auction. Put another way, the returns to bidding skill are higher in Non-Vickrey Auctions, whereas Vickrey Auctions provide a clear dominant strategy to the bidders. In a sense, the efficiency of Vickrey Auctions may make them less interesting for gameplay.

Perhaps another important reason Vickrey Auctions aren't used is that their game-theoretical impact isn't patently obvious to players. If you explain the way the auction works, most players don't intuitively understand that their best bet is to bid their true value. A game that uses Vickrey to try and make auctions more fair and less chaotic may find that players are simply confused by it.

Where Vickrey Auctions really shine is in a situation that doesn't come up in board games very often, which is in allocating a large lot of identical goods. Want to sell 100 tons of cinnamon? A Vickrey Auction is a great way to find the settlement price at which all 100 tons will sell. Once that price is found, even bidders who offered more for some portion of the lot are charged the market-clearing price, not their higher bid. In essence, the buyer is trading away the highest possible returns for speed and the certainty of selling out their whole inventory. An echo of this idea can be found in *Harbour*, where a player must sell their entire lot of goods when they choose the sell action, but this sale is to the bank. One might imagine that this transaction is the end result of a Vickrey Auction that happened off-screen, so to speak. Vickrey Auctions, though important for the study and for understanding auction strategies, have relatively few practical applications in board games, at least so far.

As board games have moved into digital arenas, Vickrey Auctions may find new applications, especially in asynchronous game modes. When games are player asynchronously, multiple-round bidding structures can slow the game down enormously. In the case of *Through the Ages: A New Story of Civilization*, players can bid military strength to claim colonies. Colony auctions occur during the Events phase of each player's turn, should a colony be drawn from the Events deck. The Events phase is the first part of a player's turn, and until the auction is fully resolved, the player is frozen and cannot proceed to the main phase of their turn. Instead, a Turn Order Until Pass Auction (AUC-03) to determine the high bidder. The colony is then awarded, the winner spends the necessary military strength, and the active player can then complete their turn.

When adapting *Through the Ages* for digital play, the designer offered a modification to this system to prevent games from stalling for hours or even days at each auction. Players simply enter one bid, which represents the maximum that they are willing to bid. Once all bids are in, the highest bidder wins and pays one more than the amount bid by the second-highest bidder.

In practice, the difference between this auction and the turn-order auction is mainly that, in case of ties, the winner is the player closest to the active player in turn order, and the winner pays the amount of the tied bid, rather than one more. In a turn-order bidding system, ties are not possible.

As we've noted above, these types of auctions are uncommon in analog games. One reason may be that it is hard to conceal the highest price the top bidder was willing to bid. In a Vickrey Auction, the winner pays the amount bid by the second-highest bidder. The amount that the winner bid is not typically revealed. This information can be quite consequential, especially in a game like *Through the Ages*, where players may have hidden resources that they can optionally apply. Revealing a bid that is high enough to require using hidden resources effectively reveals that a player has those resources. In a digital format, the game's internal logic can determine and declare the winner without revealing the total bid amount. It may not be possible to achieve that same outcome in an unmoderated analog format.

Sample Games

Das letzte Paradies (Knizia, 1993)
Harbour (Almes, 2015)
Through the Ages: A New Story of Civilization (Digital) (Chvátil, 2006)

AUC-10 Selection Order Bid

Description

Selection Order Bid is a form of multiple-lot auction in which players are not directly bidding on the lots themselves but the order in which they'll draft the lots. As the bid increases, players may pass and accept a later place in the order. In some cases, players must pay their entire current bid (an all-pay mechanism), and in others, they may recover some of their bid.

Discussion

There are many systems for auctioning off multiple lots, but Selection Order Bid may be the most elegant. In *For Sale*, players bid to draft first from a collection of property cards. The cards range in value substantially, and a given flop of cards can either cluster closely, with the lowest being separated from the highest by only a few dollars, or be spaced quite widely apart. Players bid in turn order for the right to draft first. A player may choose to pass and collect the lowest-value card remaining. When passing, they pay half their previous bid. The last player to remain in the auction receives the most valuable card but must also pay his or her full bid.

Another way to think of the pay-half-when-pass variant is that it's actually a simultaneous bid on two lots: a full-price bid on the most valuable card and a half-price bid on the least valuable card. Considered in this fashion, Selection Order Bid is a type of constrained bidding system or even a sort of ante. If you want to bid $10 on the high-value card at the open of the auction, you're essentially agreeing to pay $5 for the lowest-value card, which you could have had for free, had you chosen to pass. This is somewhat analogous to a penny auction, where players must pay a fee for each bid they make, even if it is not the winning bid. The halved value of the bid that is forfeit whether or not the player wins the auction can be seen as the bid fee, rather than a bid itself.

In certain games, this type of auction also forces players to estimate the value of lots to other players. For example, if players are collecting different symbols or colors, the lots will have different values for different players. If a certain lot is only good for one player, that player can take a chance and bid low assuming that the lot will be remaining when the player's selection opportunity comes.

Sample Games

   Age of Steam (Wallace, 2002)
   Eggs & Empire (Pinchback and Riddle, 2014)
   For Sale (Dorra, 1997)

AUC-11 Multiple-Lot Auction

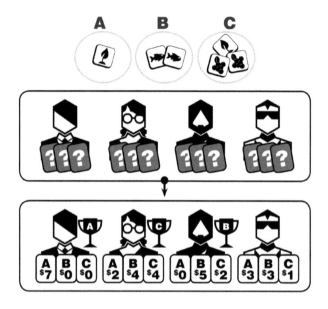

Description

An auction in which players simultaneously bid on Multiple Lots in parallel, instead of bidding for one lot at a time, serially.

Discussion

Multiple-Lot Auctions are very common in tabletop board games because they compress the time it takes to allocate lots among the players. The physical affordances of board games, like tableaus and player-colored tokens, all lend themselves to organizing and displaying information needed to run these types of auctions clearly.

Multiple-Lot Auctions ask players to manage two different axes of decision-making at the same time: which lots to bid on and how to divide the money between those lots. In a serial auction, a player's valuation of a later lot might change dramatically based on winning or losing a previous lot. In an extreme case, like *Fresh Fish*, once a player has won a fish market stall, they do not bid at all for a second fish market stall. Simultaneous auctions don't have this kind of rebalancing of player valuations (Illustration 8.3).

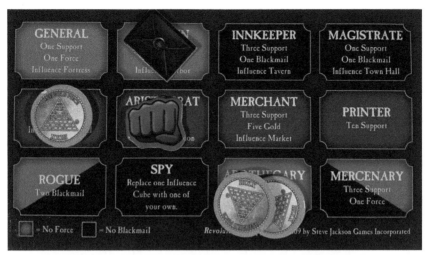

Illustration 8.3   The bidding board from *Revolution*. Each player has one of these boards and allocates different currencies (gold, force, and blackmail) to the different spaces, behind a screen. When all players have allocated their currencies as desired, the screens are revealed, and each space is reviewed to determine the auction winner.

Another interesting characteristic of Multiple-Lot Auctions is that the lots themselves may be of entirely different types. A classic Gamemaster game, originally called *Shogun* (and later *Samurai Swords* and *Ikusa*) features a Multiple-Lot Bid in which players secretly allocate money to a mix of auctions and market purchases. Players can assign money to bid for turn order and for the services of the ninja. The rest of their money can be allocated to build fortifications, hire ronin, and levy additional units. Upon revealing their secret allocations, the auctions for turn order and ninja are resolved, and players can then use the other allocated funds to purchase their fortifications, ronin, and other units. Not only are the benefits of turn order and the ninja quite different from purchasing units or defensive structures but also the auctions themselves operate by somewhat different rules. Any players bidding on turn order will receive priority over non-bidders in choosing their preferred ordering—their bid grants them some benefit, even if they are not the highest bidder. However, the ninja auction is an all-pay auction, but only the highest bidder receives the services of the ninja. If the top bidders are tied, they will pay, but none of them get to use the ninja!

Multiple-Lot Auctions bear a very close resemblance to another game mechanism: Area Majority (ARC-02). Though area majority games often model military conflicts, as in *El Grande*, they are mathematically similar to Multiple-Lot Auctions. The troops, or influence cubes, etc. can be abstracted to bidding tokens, and the player with the highest bids wins the lot. Area majority games typically offer rewards to more than only the highest bidder. This is a nested Multiple-Lot Auction. Each different area that players seek to influence houses its own set of lots, worth different amounts of victory points to bidders.

Multiple-Lot Auctions are compatible with many other auction mechanisms like Fixed-Placement Auction (AUC-15), Sealed-Bid Auction (AUC-04), and Dutch Priority Auction (AUC-16). Their resolution can be all-pay, winner-pay, cancellation, and others. In some Multiple-Lot Auctions, players are limited in how many lots or how many types of lots they can win too. This mechanism is among the most common and most flexible in the auction family.

Sample Games

El Grande (Kramer and Ulrich, 1995)
Fresh Fish (Friese, 2014)
Revolution! (duBarry, 2009)
Shogun/Samurai Swords/Ikusa (Gray, 1986)

AUC-12 Closed-Economy Auction

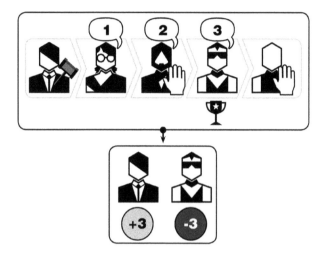

Description

Closed-Economy is a meta-mechanism that can modify any auction type. In a Closed-Economy Auction, all the money spent in the auction is paid out to the auction participants themselves. The total amount of money in the system never changes.

Discussion

While many auctions feature the winning bid being paid to one of the players at the table, as in *MarraCash* and *Modern Art*, a true Closed-Economy is relatively rare. There's typically some way to earn more money or inject money into the system. However, Closed-Economy systems do exist and are perhaps more common in constrained bidding systems that feature unique bidding markers, like *Ra*.

True Closed Economies create a zero-sum game where each player's loss is one or more players' gain. The auction mechanism provides players with opportunities to convert their paper wealth, their opportunity capital, into actual wealth in the form of in-game resources or benefits. The core dynamic for players is timing the game properly and being wealthy at the right time and poor at the right time.

In some implementations, like *Dream Factory*, money paid is split among all the players. In this case, the "remainder" issue needs to be dealt with for sums of money that don't divide evenly among the players. Typically, this is handled by leaving the remainder in the center of the table, where it is added to the next winning bid before being distributed.

Sample Games

Dream Factory (Knizia, 2000)
Modern Art (Knizia, 1992)
No Thanks! (Gimmler, 2004)
Ra (Knizia, 1999)

AUC-13 Reverse Auction

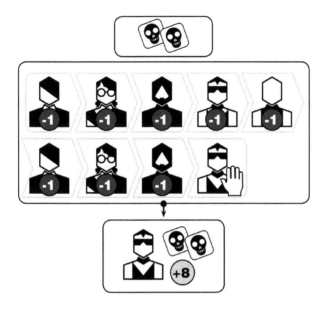

Description

Players bid to avoid taking the lot up for bid because it has some negative effects. Common effects include a negative victory point value, or a requirement to discard something of value such as a resource or special ability. Typically, in a Reverse Auction all players, except the claimant of the lot, pay their bids. Sometimes, the lot claimant will receive those payments.

Discussion

No Thanks! is a classic example of Reverse Auctions. The structure of the auction is Turn Order Until Pass, with a constrained bid of one victory point per bid. Each lot is worth some number of points, but the winner of the game is the player with the fewest points. Bidding tokens cancel out one of these "bad" points, so they're helpful toward winning the game. When a player passes, they take both the card and all the bidding tokens placed on the card. The key mechanism in the game is that each sequence of consecutive cards is worth bad points equal to the lowest card in the sequence. Thus, a "9" card is worth 9 bad points to all players, except for the player who already has the "10." For that player, the "9" is actually worth a good point, because the "10" card will no longer count against them, and instead they'll get only 9 bad points. This twist, which leads to players having sharply different values for a given lot, creates a fascinating auction dynamic.

In the world of classic card games, *Hearts* stands out as the Reverse-Auction variant of the familiar trick-taking genre. In *Hearts*, players play with straightforward trick-taking rules but seek to avoid winning any hearts in the tricks they collect. Hearts are worth bad points … unless a player collects all of them (and the Queen of Spades) to "shoot the moon." In that case, all the other players collect the bad points for that hand. While trick taking is its own mechanism, and indeed a genre of games unto itself, it has a close relationship with auctions, which is a topic we'll explore in greater depth in Trick-Taking Games (CAR-01) in Chapter 13. Suffice it to say that trick taking is almost like a Once-Around Bidding Auction with multiple currencies. In most games, the tricks are inherently valuable, but in H*earts*, they are only meaningful based on whether they contain hearts or the queen of spades.

In *High Society*, players bid for valuable possessions and title cards via traditional auctions but have Reverse Auctions for Misfortune cards. The claimant of the Misfortune card recovers any money cards they previously bid to avoid taking the lot, but all other players must discard the money cards they bid. In this implementation, the lot up for bid defines the auction procedure.

By contrast, *Eggs & Empire*, a simultaneous-bid multi-lot auction game, provides auctions that have both positive and negative lots mixed into the same auction. The player bidding the lowest will be forced to accept the negatively valued lot. One can think of this auction as a Reverse Auction in which bidders who avoid the negative lot receive an extra reward, or as a traditional all-pay auction in which the lowest bidder receives a penalty. Another similar hybrid auction can be seen in the *Game of Thrones* board game. Players make simultaneous sealed bids of Power tokens to defeat the Wildlings. If the sum of the Power bid by the players is equal to or greater than the Wildlings' strength, the Wildlings are defeated, and the highest bidder receives the benefit of reclaiming a discarded leader back into their hand. If, however, the sum of Power bid is less than the strength of the Wildlings, all players must remove two points worth of military units from the board. The lowest bidder must remove four points worth of units.

As these examples demonstrate, a Reverse Auction is usually implemented within some more complex auction environment. In part, this may be because Reverse Auctions are inherently negative in experience. The "winner" receives a negative effect, and the "losers" all pay money. Everyone's a loser! Because of this negative experience, designers use Reverse Auctions as a seasoning, a way to flavor a game, rather than as its central mechanism. *No Thanks!* remains the seminal example of a Reverse Auction as the central mechanism of play.

Sample Games

Eggs & Empire (Pinchback and Riddle, 2014)
A Game of Thrones (Petersen and Wilson, 2003)
Hearts (Unknown, 1850)
High Society (Knizia, 1995)
No Thanks! (Gimmler, 2004)

AUC-14 Dexterity Auction

Description

A Dexterity Auction requires the performance of some act of dexterity to submit a valid bid. Typically, this would involve the bid marker itself being placed into some valid bidding area, but other methods for implementing this may be used.

Discussion

Going, Going, GONE! by Dr. Scott Nicholson is the design that most readily comes to mind because of its explicit auction theming. In the game, multiple items are up for bid simultaneously, and players bid in real time by dropping their bid tokens into cups corresponding to each lot. Only tokens that land in the cups count, and the time available for bidding can be fast enough that placing a bid is not assured.

While *Going, Going, GONE!* is squarely a Dexterity Auction, one could perhaps view games like *Crokinole* and *Shuffleboard* as being Dexterity Auctions.

Consider *Crokinole*, where players flick their bid markers, attempting to acquire points by occupying board areas. Each side only scores when more of its markers are in a scoring zone than the other side's markers. The main difference between this and an auction is that in *Crokinole*, if you land two more markers than your opponent in a scoring zone, you score points for each marker. That would be like bidding on a diamond and winning one diamond for each dollar by which you outbid your opponent.

One can readily imagine a mechanism which awards to the player with the most darts, or stones or markers in some area a singular benefit. This would be a Dexterity Auction where player skill in landing the bid would be more important than player intent to bid some amount.

Dexterity Auctions have been implemented in video games that are board game-like in nature, most notably *M.U.L.E.* and *Sumer*. In these games, players move on-screen avatars against the clock, representing offers to buy or sell. This allows players to "fake" a bid by moving far ahead and then pulling just behind their opponents as time runs out, to force them into winning an item at a higher price than they might have intended.

It's worth noting that dexterity is one of those mechanisms, like memory, that can be deeply polarizing and potentially inaccessible to those with physical disabilities. It can be especially dissonant when it is one component in a multi-mechanism game. A game that otherwise emphasizes planning and calculation may frustrate players when their plans are ruined by an errant toss.

Sample Games

Crokinole (unknown, before 1876)
Going, Going, GONE! (Nicholson, 2013)
M.U.L.E. (Berry, 1983)
Sumer (Favorov, Gunnarrson, Raab, and Suthers, 2017)

AUC-15 Fixed-Placement Auction

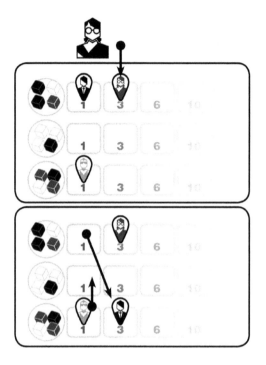

Description

Fixed Placement is a meta-mechanism that modifies a multiple-lot auction by creating rules about which lots players may bid on and representing bids visually on a board or cards. It is often combined with constrained-value bids. A Fixed-Placement auction ends when every player passes and/or no player has the right to bid further. The highest bidder for each lot wins the lot.

Discussion

Multiple-Lot Auctions are fairly common in board games. These auctions introduce a new wrinkle into bidding by forcing players to evaluate several lots at once. Depending on bid timing rules, there may also be strategic elements to sequencing your bids or forcing an auction to close early.

Multiple-Lot Auctions present some challenges to tracking. How should the top bid be represented for each lot? What rules should govern bid order?

How can the game prevent multiple-lot bidding from devolving into a series of one-lot auctions, in which players ignore all but one lot up for bid at a time?

Fixed Placement can help solve all of these problems. Visually, Fixed-Placement Auctions provide a track on which players can mark the value of their bid using a player pawn. The right to bid can be governed by turn order. In some games, like *Amun-Re*, turn order is interrupted whenever a player is outbid. That player becomes the active player, who takes the bid marker representing the bid that was just surpassed and makes another valid bid with it, on another lot. The entire auction ends when each player is the top bidder for some lot. In *Cyclades*, there are more lots than there are players, but each player has only a single bidding token, so each player will win exactly one auction and some lots will go unpurchased each turn.

Critically, in both of these games, a player may not immediately rebid on the lot for which they were just outbid. This rule encourages players to bid close to their actual value for a lot, since if they bid lower, they may not have an opportunity to return to rebid on that lot. In theory, this should speed these auctions, though, in practice, new players may evaluate this dynamic incorrectly, leading to frustration and overlong analysis. Both of these games also feature triangular increases in valid bid increments, which prevents the tit-for-tat, raise-by-one bidding that can grind an auction to a near-halt (Illustration 8.4).

In *Vegas Showdown*, bids are submitted strictly in turn order. Bidding too low has multiple consequences: not only will a player be outbid but they will have to wait until the next turn to bid. In the meantime, other players will get to place bids, potentially raising the costs of lots the passed player was interested in purchasing. *Vegas Showdown* does allow immediately rebidding on the same lot, though the value of the next valid bid increases in a delayed triangular pattern (each interval is repeated three times before increasing).

Perhaps the greatest strength of Fixed Placement is that it offers an opportunity to integrate bidding with other game actions. Since there is a visible record of current bids, a design can invite players to take unrelated actions, instead of restricting bidding to its own phase. While *Vegas Showdown* takes advantage of this feature, there remains a lot of design space here.

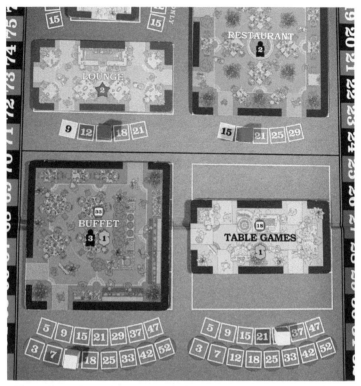

Illustration 8.4   The auction tracks from *Vegas Showdown*. Each player places a token on the track to indicate their bid on that lot. If a token is overbid, it is returned to the owner to be placed again.

Sample Games

Amun-Re (Knizia, 2003)
Cyclades (Cathala and Maublanc, 2009)
Vegas Showdown (Stern, 2005)

AUC-16 Dutch Priority Auction

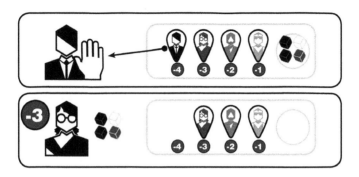

Description

A Dutch Priority Auction, a term of our own invention, is a multiple-lot auction in which prices for the lots are determined based on the number of bids placed on the lots up for bid. The winning bidder is the first player, in bid priority, who chooses to pay the current price for a lot, which is equal to the number of bidding tokens there. Priority may be determined by a variety of factors, including global turn order or turn order for each lot based on the order of bid placement. Players may typically pass on the purchase when they are the priority bidder by removing their bidding token. This has the effect of reducing the price for the lot by one.

Discussion

A Dutch Priority Auction has features of a Dutch, or descending-bid auction, coupled with an ordered, turn-based bidding system to help direct traffic and coordinate the sale of multiple lots simultaneously. In this system, prices will initially move toward the seller (i.e., they'll rise) as bids are added and then move back toward the buyers as prices descend when bidders decline to buy at a given price.

Unlike a traditional Dutch auction, in which any player may accept the going price and end the auction by calling out, a Dutch Priority Auction determines an active player, the priority player, who may choose to accept the going price or pass. In *Die Speicherstadt* (available in the US as *Jórvík*, with a Viking theme and some minor balance tweaks), this priority is determined in an initial round of bid-marker placement. Earlier placement provides earlier priority in the auction resolution phase (Illustration 8.5).

Illustration 8.5   The board in *Die Speicherstadt*. In the position shown, Blue would have the first option to purchase the Counting Office, for four coins. If they choose not to, White would have the next option, at two coins (since is no reason for them to pay for their first meeple). If White declines, Purple may purchase it for one coin.

The priority player may choose to pass. In most cases, passing means removing a bid marker and thus lowering the asking price by one. Usually, passing in this kind of auction simply means not acting at this time. If the passing player has another bid marker at a lower priority, should the auction continue until that marker comes up, the player will be allowed to purchase the lot at that time.

Spyrium adds another element to this core, which is that a player, when passing, receives money equal to the bid markers remaining on the lot. The choice is between a current purchase at a higher price and receiving an equal amount of money but passing on the purchase. In some cases, an early pass can fund a later purchase of the same lot!

The effect of this style of auction is to require players to declare the lots they're interested in, somewhat separately from the price. Players may not have enough bid markers to claim the right to bid on every lot they like and must restrict themselves to only those lots that are most meaningful to them. However, bid markers must do double-duty. They can not only be used to stake out lots that a player desires but must also be used to raise prices on other players. There is no other way to raise the price for a lot except to place a bid marker on it. Bid markers placed late in the first phase may have no other function since they are late in the priority order for auction resolution too.

Sample Games

Die Speicherstadt (Feld, 2010)
Jórvík (Feld, 2016)
Spyrium (Attia, 2013)

AUC-17 Bids as Wagers

Description

Players bid that they can achieve some outcome in the ensuing gameplay phase. Scoring is based on whether and how well players achieve their bids.

Discussion

This style of auction is common among classic trick-taking and ladder-climbing games. Many of these are team games, with each team trying to capture a majority of the tricks. In a standard 52-card deck, there are 13 tricks, so bidding is declared as the number of tricks over 6. A bid of one, for example, is a bid of seven total tricks. The auction itself is almost invariably a bid-until-pass auction (AUC-03). The team that wins the auction must now try to win the number of tricks specified by the winning bid, which is sometimes called the contract. Usually, teams can score more points by making a contract than by preventing the other team from making a contract.

In free-for-all games, players may make only a single bid. Often, as in *Wizard*, the last player is not permitted to make a bid of the number of tricks that would make the sum of all bids equal to the number of tricks in the game. This is to ensure that at least one player is unable to make their bid at the end of the round. All players have a contract in this setting, in contrast to the team games discussed above.

Games may vary in how they treat over-tricking or collecting more tricks than declared. In some games, over-tricking is rewarded with bonus points. In others, it is penalized, either immediately or after some threshold number of over-tricks are taken. One devilish game, *Skull King*, requires players to bid simultaneously on how many tricks they'll take and only awards points for winning exactly that number of tricks.

One reason to use bidding like this is to give players agency to respond to the random cards dealt with their hands. Some deals will strongly favor one player or one team. Bidding tricks offer a means for handicapping these uneven deals. Trump suits offer another leveling opportunity. Players bidding for tricks also declare the trump suit if their bid wins and winning the bidding round usually grants the winner the lead in the first trick.

Auctions are information-rich environments, and trick auctions are no different. Players each begin with a hand of cards representing one-quarter of the cards in play. With each bid, players reveal more about their hands. Games with trump bidding as well as trick bidding have especially rich auctions. In Western countries, the game of bridge is the grand doyenne of trick-taking bidding games. Because these are team games with communication restrictions, bidding is especially important. Players abide by conventions, or standard rules, about what a bid means about their hand in terms of the highest cards they hold and the overall distribution of cards among suits. Unusually for modern games, conventions in bridge must be agreed upon explicitly by partners prior to play and must be disclosed in full, with all their implications, to the opposing team, too!

Modern games differ from traditional trick-taking games in that they typically simplify the auction and reduce the overall number of tricks in the game. Predictive bidding is a complex, high-skill mechanism that is very demanding of players in terms of memory, deduction and induction, and experience with the dynamics of cardplay. This depth and complexity are suitable for a lifestyle game like bridge, which players can play for decades. Modern games seek to distill the essence of the mechanism, while lowering its skill threshold for greater accessibility.

This mechanism is not limited to trick taking. In *25 Words or Less*, players are broken up into two teams. One player on each team is the clue giver, who receives a list of five words that they need their to team guess. The clue givers then bid for the number of words that they are allowed to use to get their team to guess all five target words. Bids start at 25 words and go down. The clue giver with the lowest bid must get his team to guess all the target words using only as many clues as they bid. This is reminiscent of the game show *Name That Tune*, where players bid for naming a tune in the fewest notes.

Sample Games

25 Words or Less (Sterten, 1996)
Bridge (Unknown, ca. 1800s)
Skull King (Beck, 2013)
Sluff Off (Dorra, 2003)
Wizard (Fisher, 1984)

AUC-18 Auction Compensation

Description

Losing bidders in an auction receive a lesser award in place of the lot they bid on.

Discussion

This is a meta-mechanism that can be overlaid on other mechanisms that determine the structure of bidding. It is most commonly found in all-pay auctions, in which all bidders pay their bids but only the bidder receives a prize.

Designers turn to all-pay, single-bid, and multi-lot auctions because they are fast, but these auctions can lead to negative experiences or even game-threatening imbalances. In serial auctions, the market rebalances with each auction's resolution, which makes it easier for players to adjust their plans and predict what they will and will not be able to win. Multiple-lot auctions and the like are faster to resolve but are more likely to yield odd outcomes, like players winning no auctions, or winning mismatched lots of goods. Compensation is a tool that can help account for these potentially imbalanced outcomes.

In *The Artemis Project*, players bid on fixed pools of resources using dice. The number on the die corresponds to the number of resources they will receive, but dice are resolved in ascending order and not in order of placement. Thus, the total resource pool can be exhausted after paying out the smaller bids leaving nothing for the larger bids. Any player who receives nothing for their bid gets a consolation prize. *The Artemis Project* offers a "relief track" that shows the consolation prize. Each time the player is diverted to the relief track, they move up one space on the track. Later spaces on the track feature more valuable rewards, so players who are repeatedly left out of the auction payouts get better relief track rewards.

Games with more exotic auctions are amenable to consideration through this lens. For example, *Spyrium* features players placing workers next to cards in a grid, such that each worker is adjacent to two cards. Following the placement phase, players may purchase a card adjacent to their worker for the base cost listed on the card, plus one pound more for every worker adjacent to the card. Alternatively, they may remove their worker without claiming a card and collect one pound for each worker adjacent to the card. The front half of this auction is akin to a Dutch or declining price auction, with the overall price of the card dropping until a player is willing to pay it. However, the twist of gaining money for removing a worker and reducing the price of the card can be considered compensation for losing the auction.

In *Furnace*, players bid on cards to add to their tableaus. Each card has a permanent ability that can be triggered from its owner's tableau and an action or resource that is provided to losing bidders just once, at the conclusion of the auction. The auction mechanism is constrained bids, using a set of bid markers valued 1–4. The highest bidder receives the card, while the lower bidders receive the compensation action or resource. The amount of compensation received is equal to the number on their bid marker. At first glance, this may appear straightforward, but in a turn-based auction, the puzzle begins to emerge: when a player bids a "2," for example, are they bidding on the card or on the compensation? And once a player has bid "4" on a card, the lot is not closed and all other players are welcome to bid any smaller number afterward to collect the compensation.

Auction compensation can also be implemented indirectly. In *Power Grid*, each player must purchase exactly one power plant per round. Once a player purchases a plant, they cannot bid on subsequent auctions in the same round. When all players but one have purchased plants, the last player may purchase any remaining power plant of their choice for the minimum cost of that plant. They do not have to pay any auction premium, and this can be thought of as a kind of compensation for having lost the previous auctions.

Turn order auction can be seen in this light, with the second-place bidder choosing when to act in the turn order second, and so forth. There is not a lot of conceptual daylight between auction compensation, on one hand, and auctions that order players based on their bids and provide a lesser reward to each bidder in descending order, on the other hand. For example, in *A Game of Thrones: The Board Game*, the highest bidder on the King's Court track will be allowed to use three of the superior, starred order tokens. The next-highest bidder will get only two starred orders, then one, then none. The key distinction between these for designers is that auction compensation mechanisms can be more dynamic and flexible than a fixed declining rewards system. The flexibility comes at a price, though, because players must evaluate compensation values afresh each time.

Sample Games

The Artemis Project (Chow and Rocchi, 2019)
Furnace (Lashin, 2021)
A Game of Thrones: The Board Game (Petersen and Wilson, 2003)
Power Grid (Friese, 2004)
Spyrium (Attia, 2013)

9

Worker Placement

Worker Placement, a type of Action Drafting (ACT-02), is often credited to designer Richard Breese and his game, *Keydom*, in 1998. Nonetheless, it was *Caylus*, by William Attia, that popularized the mechanism and inspired its name.

Mechanically, Worker Placement is isomorphic to action drafting. Players select actions in turn order by placing one of their pawns, or workers, into the action space, or building. This is the core mechanical concept and thematic conceit, and the mechanism has proven so durable because of that tight theme-mechanism correspondence. It's easy to understand why placing the worker in the sawmill will generate wood.

Worker Placement can be described as action drafting, or even as a highly specialized type of auction, but while resource allocation mechanisms may share mathematical similarities and incentivize similar player behavior, the experience of these mechanisms can vary a great deal based on how they're presented. Their intelligibility to the player will also vary a great deal based on the setting, theme, and logical coherence of the mechanism. *For Sale*'s auction is readily understood by players, as it is squarely in context. An auction for property is a familiar concept, even if most players haven't ever bought a house at an auction. The thematic scaffolding, provided by *Dungeon Petz*, on the other hand, falls short in terms of making its mechanism intelligible. Why is it that the largest group of workers secretly assigned to an action get to take the action first? There's no strong connection to a real-world dynamic that helps players remember and understand the rule. The Worker Placement metaphor of placing a worker in a production building to generate a good helps players understand the structure and incentives of the underlying game system, which is one reason why it is such a popular core mechanism.

DOI: 10.1201/9781003179184-9

In this chapter, we'll talk about other implications and expectations of the mechanism, including blocking, gaining workers, adding buildings, and more, as we delve deeper into this touchstone of modern design.

The term "Worker Placement" has lost some of its cohesion, and today, it is often used as a synonym for a Euro-style game, irrespective of the presence of workers or action drafting. Thus, it would not be out-of-place for *Terraforming Mars* or *Roll for the Galaxy* to be described as "Worker Placement." We will restrict our analysis to games which use action drafting, recognize some form of blocking, and conceive thematically of some kind of worker. This narrower definition also excludes quite a few games which employ the worker metaphor but not its underlying mechanism. For example, we exclude cooperative games like *Charterstone* and *Robinson Crusoe: Adventures on the Cursed Island*, because these games lack a true drafting or blocking element. Games with workers placed onto private tableaus like *Orleans* and *Through the Ages: A Story of Civilization* or games in which workers represent a currency or bid marker rather than a draft marker, as in *Jórvík*, *Spyrium*, and *Keyflower*, are also outside the scope of our definition. However, our definition is intended only to limit the scope of our analysis and not to stake a claim on how the term should be used by anybody else. Whatever words we use, we believe these elements of drafting, blocking, and thematic coherence are important distinguishers that deserve a term by which to refer to them.

WPL-01 Standard Worker Placement

Description

Players select actions, in turn order, by placing a worker from their supply on a building associated with a specific action and then execute that action immediately. The round ends when all workers have been placed, at which point they return to their owners' pools and a new round begins.

Discussion

This familiar structure, typified by games like *Lords of Waterdeep* and *Agricola*, is an improvement over the ur-game, *Caylus*, in which buildings resolved after all Worker Placements were complete. The immediate resolution makes for faster play and obviates the need for players to remember which resources they will receive when making their next placement. Later games, like *The Manhattan Project* and *Tzolk'in: The Mayan Calendar*, have workers returning only when their owners recall them. In the former, players get the building's reward on placement, while in the latter, the reward is tied to the moment of recall, since the reward escalates the longer the worker is left out on the board. With each passing turn in *Tzolk'in*, workers rotate over on the ingenious gear system to a higher tier of rewards that will be distributed when the worker is recalled.

Most Worker Placement games employ the mechanism for all actions in the game. Turn order is typically set by placing a worker on a building that grants turn order priority. Increasing the number of actions that may be taken in a turn is themed as getting new workers, which is an action tied to a building. Maintenance costs are represented as feeding or paying for your workers.

Increasingly, there are games that incorporate some Worker Placement elements in the context of a broader game. Examples include *Copycat*, *Rococo*, and *Belfort*.

Sample Games

Agricola (Rosenberg, 2007)
Belfort (Cormier and Lim, 2011)
Caylus (Attia, 2005)
Charterstone (Stegmaier, 2017)
Copycat (Friese, 2012)
For Sale (Dorra, 1997)
Jórvík (Feld, 2016)
Lords of Waterdeep (Lee and Thompson, 2012)
The Manhattan Project (Tibbetts, 2012)
Mint Works (Blaske, 2017)
Orleans (Stockhausen, 2014)
Robinson Crusoe: Adventures on the Cursed Island (Trzewiczek, 2012)
Rococo (Cramer, Malz, and Malz, 2013)
Roll for the Galaxy (Huang and Lehmann, 2014)
Spyrium (Attia, 2013)
Terraforming Mars (Fryxelius, 2016)
Through the Ages: A Story of Civilization (Chvátil, 1986)
Tribune: Primus Inter Pares (Schmiel, 2007)
Tzolk'in: The Mayan Calendar (Luciani and Tascini, 2012)

WPL-02 Workers of Differing Types

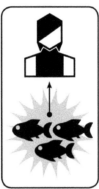

Description

Workers can differ in abilities, or can be upgraded and downgraded, or are valid for placement in different areas and buildings.

Discussion

Improved workers are a common variation on standard worker placement. Improved workers can count as more than one basic worker as in *Belfort*, or they may allow you to break standard placement rules, as in *Leonardo Da Vinci*. *Tzolk'in* puts a different spin on this idea by having the rewards for a space improve the longer that a worker is allowed to stay out on that space. Thematically, this can be understood as a worker spending more time working. Another take on this idea is the notion that workers can improve. In both *Praetor* and *Euphoria: Build a Better Dystopia*, workers, represented as dice, are more capable and provide better returns when they show higher numbers. Players can take actions to increase the values of these worker dice. In *Village*, workers can age and gain experience, which improves their effectiveness (Illustration 9.1).

Some games have workers who participate in different placement contests or have buildings that can only be accessed by certain types of workers. *Pillars of the Earth* has workers who can collect resources and master builders, who are placed during the second round of placement and who can access other actions besides resource collection. *The Manhattan Project* similarly features specialists, like scientists and engineers, and certain buildings require those

Illustration 9.1   Three different workers from *Manhattan Project*—Engineer, Scientist, and Laborer. Some placement spaces only allow specific types of workers to be placed there.

specialists to operate. *Glenn Drover's Empires: Galactic Rebellion* (previously known as *Age of Empires III: The Age of Discovery*) and *Viticulture* feature as many as eight different kinds of workers who might participate in majority contests and even battles in addition to taking actions.

Sample Games

> *Age of Empires III: The Age of Discovery* (Drover, 2007)
> *Belfort* (Cormier and Lim, 2011)
> *Euphoria: Build A Better Dystopia* (Stegmaier and Stone, 2013)
> *Glenn Drover's Empires: Galactic Rebellion* (Drover, 2016)
> *Leonardo Da Vinci* (Acchittocca, Brasini, Gigli, Luperto, and Tinto, 2006)
> *The Manhattan Project* (Tibbetts, 2012)
> *Pillars of the Earth* (Rieneck and Stadler, 2006)
> *Praetor* (Novac, 2014)
> *Tzolk'in: The Mayan Calendar* (Luciani and Tascini, 2012)
> *Village* (Brand and Brand, 2011)
> *Viticulture* (Stegmaier and Stone, 2013)

WPL-03 Acquiring and Losing Workers

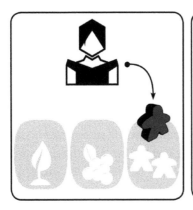

Description

Workers beyond the original complement may be acquired in some manner, either temporarily or permanently. Workers may also be lost as the game progresses.

Discussion

Rather than improving existing workers, many games allow the acquisition of new workers. These new workers represent substantial growth in a player's overall action budget, and as such, acquiring more workers is often a dominant strategy. In *Stone Age*, the reproduction hut is typically chosen first or second in every round. Because of the power of adding workers, designers have taken to metering worker growth. In *Lords of Waterdeep*, all players receive a new worker on a fixed turn in the middle of the game. *Caverna* requires that players build housing for new workers to acquire them—an investment of resources up front that the new worker's productivity will pay for in the future. Any kind of purchase price on a worker has to be considered in light of the number of actions that the worker will be able to take and the returns those actions will provide. Usually, buying workers early has a higher payout than buying them late for this reason.

In *Last Will*, the number of workers a player may deploy varies each turn based on the place in turn order that they choose. More workers mean going later in the turn order, thus reducing the expected value of those additional workers, since the best spots will be taken by the time those extra workers are up for placement. *Euphoria* sets a hard cap on the total value of pips that can be showing in a player's pool of available worker dice, which sharply limits a player's incentive to collect more workers.

Temporary additional workers are featured in *Snowdonia*, *Russian Railroads*, and *Power Grid: Factory Manager*. These workers will return to the general pool after use and must be hired or acquired again for reuse. A similar way to throttle player appetites for more workers is through a feeding or worker upkeep cost for permanent workers. *Agricola* is famous for the unforgiving tightness of its feeding mechanism and the substantial penalties incurred for failing to feed your family, while *Stone Age*'s toothless approach makes a starvation strategy quite viable.

Worker attrition is the flipside of this dynamic of gaining workers. *Euphoria*'s workers may get too smart and, as a group, have too high a pip value, at which point one escapes (or perhaps, is sent for re-education …). The aging workers of *Village* eventually pass on, and the workers in *Praetor* retire. Other games actively encourage sacrificing workers for a benefit. *Asgard* is a visceral example, but discarding a die in *Alien Frontiers*, themed as landing a spaceship (the die) on a planet to establish a colony, is mechanically identical.

Sample Games

> *Agricola* (Rosenberg, 2007)
> *Asgard* (Zizzi, 2012)
> *Caverna: The Cave Farmers* (Rosenberg, 2013)
> *Euphoria: Build a Better Dystopia* (Stegmaier and Stone, 2013)
> *Last Will* (Suchy, 2011)
> *Lords of Waterdeep* (Lee and Thompson, 2012)
> *Power Grid: Factory Manager* (Friese, 2009)
> *Praetor* (Novac, 2014)
> *Russian Railroads* (Ohley and Orgler, 2013)
> *Snowdonia* (Boydell, 2012)
> *Stone Age* (Brunnhofer, 2008)
> *Village* (Brand and Brand, 2011)

WPL-04 Workers-As-Dice

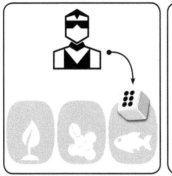

Description

Workers are represented by dice whose pip values impact play.

Discussion

Workers-As-Dice is a broad genre, and it is frequently accompanied by the mechanism of playing a combination of workers in a building. In *Alien Frontiers*, players allocate all of their dice on their turns to buildings that take a different combination of dice and values and have different requirements for placement. This approach leads to some analysis paralysis because of the large number of combinations that are possible with as many as six dice. Other titles, like *Kingsburg*, limit the dice pools to three dice. Each roll presents a substantially smaller set of placement permutations for players to consider, not only because of the smaller number of dice but because there are fewer valid buildings for any given combination.

Workers-As-Dice can also function to determine the effectiveness of workers. In *The Artemis Project*, worker dice collect a number of resources equal to their pip value—as long as resources remain available in the supply. However, the higher pip value dice are awarded resources last, which may leave the placing player out of luck if the resources run out before they can collect the reward.

Champions of Midgard features warrior dice whose faces represent attack strength. The dice are assigned to overcome monsters and are rolled together, summed, and compared to the monster's strength. For some players, this is an unacceptable level, and type, of randomness in a worker placement game.

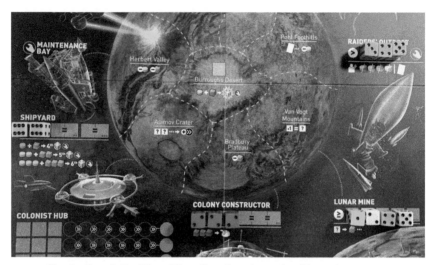

Illustration 9.2   The *Alien Frontiers* board, with various spaces occupied by dice. The Shipyard requires matching pairs of dice. All dice in the Colony Constructor must be the same value, while the Raider's Outpost requires a "run" of increasing values. Finally, dice placed in the Lunar Mine must be increasing but do not need to be consecutive.

Whatever your position on the matter, it is representative of the ongoing hybridization of game styles and game mechanisms (Illustration 9.2).

The manner in which the dice change values over the course of the game can vary. In some games, the dice are rolled each turn, giving a random distribution that players need to work with. *Alien Frontiers* works in this way. In other games, the players obtain the dice on a certain side or have to expend resources to change them to other, perhaps more powerful, sides.

Sample Games

> *Alien Frontiers* (Niemann, 2010)
> *The Artemis Project* (Chow and Rocchi, 2019)
> *Champions of Midgard* (Steiness, 2015)
> *Kingsburg* (Chiarvesio and Iennaco, 2007)

WPL-05 Adding and Blocking Buildings

Description

Buildings, and their corresponding actions, may be added to the pool of actions players may select from. Buildings may also be occupied to prevent or hinder players from accessing those actions.

Discussion

Buildings define available actions in a worker placement game, and how designers manage the availability of actions is critical to the overall flow of the game. Some games retain a static set of actions throughout the game, like *Stone Age*. Other games introduce new actions in a set pattern. *Agricola* features new actions that reveal themselves each round, but the actions are drawn from a very small subset, guaranteeing, for example, that the "Family Expansion" action will reveal itself in one of three consecutive rounds.

Many games allow players to add buildings and to claim ownership for them. As early as *Caylus*, players could add a building and receive victory points when another player occupied it. *Lords of Waterdeep* has variable owner rewards for building usage by others. Some games break the core notion of action drafting by introducing private actions. *Russian Railroads* themed these as engineers, rather than buildings, but private buildings, themed as buildings, exist in *The Manhattan Project*. On the opposite end of the spectrum are public actions that are always available to all players, like the resource-gather actions in *Stone Age*, which are in a public area, or the brewery actions in *Brew Crafters*, which are depicted on each player's board. The section on Ownership (ECO-14) has more details on this concept.

Underlying the difference between these actions is the concept of blocking. Worker placement is a kind of action drafting, and drafting denotes a dwindling set of possible choices. Worker placement depicts claimed actions as a building staffed by a worker, so a building that cannot take an additional worker is considered blocked. The typical worker placement game allows each building to be used by one player each round and is blocked when one worker is in it. Modest exceptions allow for two or three players to use a building—an easy way to scale the actions available in a game as the player count increases.

Some games eschew "hard" blocking in favor of "soft" blocking. In *Coal Baron*, players don't block buildings by occupying them, but they simply increase the costs of other players accessing them. *Carson City*, a Western-themed game, has workers in the same space duel to see who claims its reward. Bumping, another kind of soft blocking, allows an occupied building to be reused, but the worker currently occupying the building is removed, and the owner gains some kind of bonus. In *Euphoria*, a game which otherwise requires players to spend a turn recalling workers, simply the act of being bumped is beneficial to the player being bumped—an especially elegant combination of mechanisms.

Blocking is a player-driven placement restriction, but the game itself may impose placement restrictions as well. Some games require multiple workers to be played in order to activate a space, as in *Russian Railroads* or *Francis Drake*. This is especially common among Worker-As-Dice games. Sometimes, players must exceed a particular pip value with one or more dice. Other times, a building calls for a sequential run of dice or a pair or larger set of values, as in *Alien Frontiers*. Both *Egizia* and *Francis Drake* establish a linear relationship between buildings, such that once you skip over a closer building to activate one further down the river or road, you can never go back. A more prosaic placement restriction is a cost, like in the case of a resource-conversion or building action, which requires inputting resources to build some finished product or obtain some advanced resource. *Kingdom of Solomon* offers players bonus action buildings that are substantially more powerful than the standard spaces, but which require assigning all remaining workers. This can be viewed as a declining price auction (AUC-08) for these bonus actions, with the price expressed in terms of workers, that is folded into the larger worker placement structure.

Sample Games

Agricola (Rosenberg, 2007)
Alien Frontiers (Niemann, 2010)
Brew Crafters (Rosset, 2013)
Carson City (Georges, 2009)
Caylus (Attia, 2005)
Coal Baron (Kiesling and Kramer, 2013)
Egizia (Achittocca, Brasini, Gigli, Luperto, and Tinto, 2009)
Euphoria: Build a Better Dystopia (Stegmaier and Stone, 2013)
Francis Drake (Hawes, 2013)
Kingdom of Solomon (duBarry, 2012)
Lords of Waterdeep (Lee and Thompson, 2012)
The Manhattan Project (Tibbets, 2012)
Russian Railroads (Ohley and Orgler, 2013)
Stone Age (Brunnhofer, 2008)

WPL-06 Single Workers

Description

Players control only a Single primary Worker and cannot acquire more workers.

Discussion

On the far end of the worker placement spectrum are the Single-Worker games, which we include in our definition only when they retain a blocking element—otherwise, we characterize these as Action Point games (ACT-01) when players can't interfere with or block each other at all, and Action Drafting games (ACT-02) when players can block each other absolutely.

In the intermediate space between these lies a game like *Kanban*. Players block and influence each other's placements along at least three different axes: (1) players cannot take an action space occupied by another player, (2) they cannot take an action space in the same department they occupied the last turn, and (3) they must consider the role Sandra, the neutral boss, will play. In Easy mode, Sandra's presence in a department may encourage players to work in that department in order to win her approval. In Hard mode, they may choose to avoid Sandra's critical eye and the penalties that accompany it.

Another Vital Lacerda game, *The Gallerist*, takes an opposite approach to Single-Worker blocking. Players have a primary worker and can acquire several assistants. When players move their primary workers to a new space, they may choose to leave an assistant behind. If that assistant gets bumped by another player, the assistant will be able to take an action as compensation. In a sense, the game records a kind of history of where each player has been and enforces consequences for collisions, snake-like, between the head of one player and the tail of another. It is arguable whether this actually qualifies for our definition of worker placement, though, since no cost is imposed on the placing player in a manner that could be construed as blocking. Instead, a benefit is given to the player whose assistant is being bumped. *Istanbul* implements this trail concept more fully and is perhaps the game that most successfully implements substantial movement and spatial relationships within a worker placement framework. Here, blocking is more fully realized, as the placing player must pay the blocker to use the space.

Single-Worker games are quite similar not only to role-selection games, as mentioned above, but also to Rondel Games (ACT-10) and Time-Track Games (TRN-13). The worker metaphor and the use of meeples and similar tokens have as much to do with how we categorize the games as the underlying action selection method itself.

Sample Games

Fabled Fruit (Friese, 2016)
The Gallerist (Lacerda, 2015)
Istanbul (Dorn, 2014)
Kanban (Lacerda, 2014)

WPL-07 Building Actions and Rewards

Description

Buildings can offer varying rewards to different players, based on ownership and turn order, or they may be upgraded to increase their rewards to all players.

Discussion

Buildings may offer a greater reward for the first player to claim the building and lesser rewards for players following. This is quite similar to selection bonuses in a role-selection game, a flavor of Action Drafting (ACT-02). Other versions of reward choice allow for the player to choose among one of two or more rewards, as in *Caylus*, where players may sometimes take two of one resource or one of another. *Yedo* offers an extreme version of this mechanism: players place workers in districts, rather than specific buildings, and may choose from a variety of possible resolutions, including collecting resources, purchasing weapons, or completing a mission specific to that district.

One way buildings can vary in rewards is through improvements of different kinds. In *Wisdom of Solomon* (originally released as *Kingdom of Solomon*), players can build roads between different spaces, creating resource regions that yield the cumulative benefit of all the connected spaces when activated by a worker. In *Agricola* and other Uwe Rosenberg designs, some spaces will accumulate an additional resource from turn to turn, growing richer and richer until a player finally selects them. Various games offer cards or special abilities that improve the conversion rate of some building or set of buildings that have a cost or offer some exchange. Conversely, buildings may become deactivated or workers may be hindered from doing their work, as with the Provost in *Caylus* or the City Watch in *Yedo*. A radical approach to varying buildings can be seen in *Fabled Fruit*, in which buildings can be replaced entirely with others in mid-play.

Sample Games

Agricola (Rosenberg, 2007)
Caylus (Attia, 2005)
Fabled Fruit (Friese, 2016)
Wisdom of Solomon (duBarry, 2018)
Yedo (Ginste and Plancke, 2012)

WPL-08 Turn Order and Resolution Order

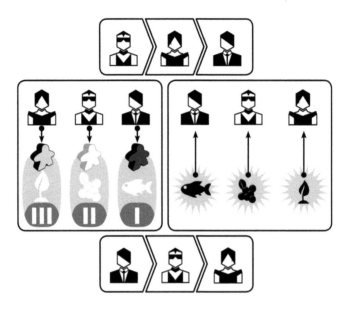

Description

Worker placement is ultimately a drafting mechanism, and the order by which actions are selected and resolved is an opportunity for design variations.

Discussion

Allocation of resources is a foundational concern of nearly every game, and allocation by draft means that Turn Order is crucial. While some worker placement games simply rotate Turn Order clockwise, like *Stone Age*, most fold Turn Order into the worker placement engine itself. The simplest approach is a building that grants Turn Order priority, as in *Lords of Waterdeep*. While this is a simple approach, it has a substantial drawback in that it's a choice with strong left–right binding. In other words, the impacts on the players adjacent to the new starting player are large: the player to the left gains an unearned windfall because they get to go second, and the player to the right, through no fault of their own, is pushed to the end of the line. One design answer is to allow for multiple players to play into the Turn Order building, with the player playing earliest getting the most favorable placement. More discussions of this topic are in Claim Turn Order Action (TRN-05).

As discussed in Acquiring and Losing Workers (WPL-03), *Last Will* has players draft a combination of Turn Order, workers available, and assistant actions in one. Earlier positions in Turn Order have fewer workers and abilities, while later positions have more.

An especially unusual mechanism for Turn Order is the master builder token-pull system in *Pillars of the Earth*. Each player's master builders are placed in a bag and pulled at random, one at a time. The player whose builder is pulled may choose to pay the current price in gold to take the action or may pass and accept a much later position in Turn Order. The price of the action is then decreased by one gold. If this sounds familiar, it's because it's another variation on the Vickrey auction (AUC-08, Dutch Auction). See also Random Turn Order (TRN-11).

The randomness of this mechanism drew widespread critique, but it did have a spiritual successor. In *Lords of Waterdeep*, up to three players can visit Waterdeep Harbor to play an Intrigue card. In addition, once all players have exhausted their available workers, the workers assigned to Waterdeep Harbor can be reassigned to any available actions space. The similarity to the mechanism in *Pillars of the Earth* is that placing a worker in Waterdeep Harbor offers the reward of playing an Intrigue card, at the cost of having to wait for the remaining workers to be placed before getting another choice at an action with that worker. This implied cost goes down with every succeeding turn, just as the explicit cost of the master builder goes down with each player's turn. The random aspect of *Pillars of the Earth* was not reproduced, but the core notion of variable price for placement priority was retained.

Returning to variations on Turn Order, *Francis Drake* has Turn Order for the following phase set by the previous phase. The player who takes the fewest actions in the first phase goes first in the next phase. *Belfort* allows players to spend a worker to exchange Turn Order position with another player during the placement phase. However, the game features a strong polarity in the benefits of Turn Order. In the worker placement phase, going early is best, but in the building phase, which features an area majority contest, going last is most advantageous.

This phase difference brings up another point of design distinction, which is when worker actions get placed versus when they get resolved. The simplest placement rule is that each player places one worker on their turn (*Agricola*), which encourages good pace in play. Increasing the complexity, players may be allowed to claim a building, even if it requires more than one worker (*Francis Drake*), or may be allowed to play either one worker or assign all their remaining workers to a group of public action (*Belfort*). Sometimes, each player places all their workers on their turn (*Alien Frontiers*).

Placement is not synonymous with a resolution, however. *Caylus* resolved placements and distributed rewards only at the end of the placement phase, when all workers are out. This delay in resolution creates space for the provost mechanism, which may cause buildings too far down the road to fail to activate, even though they are staffed by workers. It also allows players to set up combos, where resources gained earlier along the road can be used by workers further down the road, regardless of the order that those workers were placed in. Similarly, the *Tzolk'in* escalating rewards case requires resolution to occur when workers are recalled, rather than placed. However, in *Tzolk'in*, the decision is to either place a worker or return all workers from one building, rather than recalling the whole class of workers from across the board. *Belfort* workers don't collect their goods until all players have completed placement, because the player with the most workers gathering in each building will gain a bonus resource.

When workers return home is another element of the worker placement mechanism that designers have experimented with. In *The Manhattan Project*, players resolve their actions on worker placement but must spend a turn retrieving workers. This tends to create a strong blocking dynamic, since players receive benefits up front, and their workers continue to block other players until they are retrieved. Timing your retrievals relative to other players is critical for effective play. In *Istanbul*, workers can be retrieved for free by moving back through the spaces they were left on or by spending a valuable action recalling all workers to the fountain in the center of the bazaar. Through careful planning, players can plot efficient courses, recover workers for free, and gain an action advantage over their opponents.

Sample Games

> *Agricola* (Rosenberg, 2007)
> *Alien Frontiers* (Niemann, 2010)
> *Belfort* (Cormier and Lim, 2011)
> *Caylus* (Attia, 2005)
> *Francis Drake* (Hawes, 2013)
> *Istanbul* (Dorn, 2014)

Last Will (Suchy, 2011)
Lords of Waterdeep (Lee and Thompson, 2012)
The Manhattan Project (Tibbetts, 2012)
Pillars of the Earth (Rieneck and Stadler, 2006)
Stone Age (Brunnhofer, 2008)
Tzolk'in: The Mayan Calendar (Luciani and Tascini, 2012)

10

Movement

Perhaps the most common dynamic in games is movement. In large part, this is because movement is inherent in what games model, whether it's an armed conflict, a journey, or a race. Movement is an incredibly effective and powerful tool in the designer's arsenal because of how dense movement can be in terms of information. Moving a single piece changes its relationship to every other piece on the board. And yet, signaling that change, communicating that it has occurred, is as simple as picking up a piece and placing it down again.

The most ancient board games we know of, like the Egyptian games *Mehen* and *Senet*, have pieces moving around a board. *Chess, Checkers, Shogi, Parcheesi, Backgammon, Monopoly*, and *Candyland* all feature movement as a key mechanism. Some of these games feature movement in a single direction, along a fixed path, while others offer greater choice, or even free play within a two-dimensional space. In some games, the pieces on the board are all identical, while in others the power to move is encoded in the pieces themselves. Some games have specific spaces that are more valuable to occupy, while in others, the positional value of any space can change as the board develops

Movement is a way of creating dynamic and evolving situations that can force players to change their plans and react to their opponents. Done well, movement rules are easily understood, yet lead to emergent gameplay. But movement rules are hard to get right. Dealing with questions like blocking, line of sight, terrain types, movement along a diagonal, and more can turn what seems like an elegant and simple concept into a tangle of conflicting and confusing rules. Among the innovations of the European design school was an increasing abstraction of movement rules or even total abandonment of movement.

DOI: 10.1201/9781003179184-10   429

Despite the challenges, the movement remains a durable feature of many board games. Movement is fun, and it lends itself well to many different kinds of games in a huge variety of implementations and specific mechanisms, while being conceptually familiar and intuitive, no matter what the context.

MOV-01 Tessellation

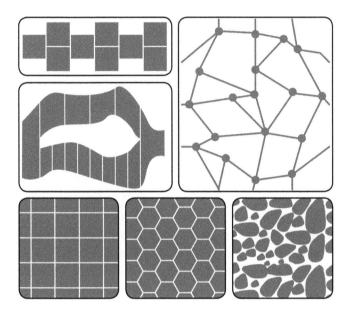

Description

The playing field is divided into spaces to regulate movement.

Discussion

There are several ways to subdivide boards, all of which are covered in this section.

The most basic is a one-dimensional division. This is often called a *track*, and it is commonly used in Race games, Roll-and-Move games, and others. There are several variations on the standard track.

First, there may be alternate paths that branch off of the main path. These can be a shortcut that reduces the distance needed to travel or a path that gives bonuses or other information, as in *Careers*, where each potential career choice has its own path.

Second, certain spaces, or collections of spaces, may be divided into subspaces in the width of the track. This is typically used in racing games to create lanes, allowing multiple players to occupy the same space, and to create "inside" and "outside" lanes. The number of lane spaces can be reduced, sometimes even down to one, to create bottlenecks that create challenges for players. This is used to great effect in *Ave Caesar* and *Downforce*, where vehicles move a set number of spaces based on cards. Forcing players to waste a good card because they cannot get through a bottleneck is a key strategy.

Boards can also be laid out in two dimensions, either with a regular pattern or with irregular shapes. The most common regular patterns are squares (as in *Chess*) and hexagons, used in many war games, such as *PanzerBlitz*. Triangles may also be used but are uncommon as they limit options for adjacency and tend to look busy.

If squares are used, the designer needs to decide if pieces may move diagonally. From a distance standpoint, a diagonal move is approximately 50% further than an orthogonal move, which needs to be compensated for in games striving for realism. Hexagonal Tessellations do not have this issue, and all natural moves are the same distance. This is why they are commonly used for war games and others require realistic movement. Note that a square grid with each row shifted 50%, making a brick pattern, is isomorphic to a hex grid (and easier to prototype, particularly when creating tiles—even rectangular cards can be used for this purpose).

Some games need to model three-dimensional space, typically those that take place in space, in the air, or under the sea. A common approach is a dashboard or log sheet for each vehicle that tracks the altitude. This system is used in *Richtofen's War* and *Air Force*. Some, like *Attack Vector: Tactical*, have tokens placed next to or beneath pieces to indicate height above or below the playing surface. Others, like *Chopper Strike* and *Sub Search*, physically create multiple levels of the play area by vertically stacking boards, separated by supports. These are physically striking and easy for players to interpret but need to limit the number of levels due to cost, the physical size of the board, and ease of reaching in between levels to reach pieces.

Irregular patterns are called Area Maps. *Diplomacy* is an example. There are several design considerations for Area Maps. First, if they regulate movement, the areas should be approximately the same size, or at least "movement equivalent." For example, a mountainous region may be divided into smaller, more numerous spaces so it takes more moves to traverse.

If possible, regions should not touch at a corner, and they should only touch along an edge.

Area maps are isomorphic to point-to-point movement, where boxes or circles are connected by lines. Sometimes point-to-point maps can be preferable, as they clearly show connections, and connection information (like rivers or borders) may be more evident. Point-to-point maps are also common in space games, where the connection between stars is shown.

Some maps are a combination of two-dimensional point-to-point and one-dimensional tracks. For example, *Trains and Stations* has tracks in between cities that players must build along.

If a region contains important information, like terrain type or resources, the graphics should be visible and distinct even if pieces are present.

Sample Games

Tracks

Ave Caeser (Riedesser, 1989)
Careers (Brown, 1955)
Downforce (Daviau, Jacobson, and Kramer, 2017)
Monopoly (Darrow and Magie, 1933)
Snakes & Ladders (Unknown, ~200 BCE)
Sorry! (Haskell, Jr. and Storey, 1929)

Squares

Chess (Unknown, ~1200)
Checkers (Unknown)
Go (Unknown, 2200 BCE)

Hexagons

Blitzkrieg (Pinsky and Shaw, 1965)
PanzerBlitz (Dunnigan, 1970)
Squad Leader (Hill, 1977)
Lords of Creation (Wallace, 1993)

Three-Dimensional

Air Force (Taylor, 1976)
Attack Vector: Tactical (Burnside, Finley, and Valle, 2004)
Chopper Strike (Uncredited, 1976)
Richtofen's War (Reed, 1972)
Sub Search (Uncredited, 1973)

Area

Diplomacy (Calhamer, 1959)
El Grande (Kramer and Ulrich, 1995)
Risk (Lamorisse and Levin, 1959)

Point-to-Point

A House Divided (Chadwick and Emrich, 1981)
Pirate and Traveller (Sanderson, 1908)
Twilight Struggle (Gupta and Matthews, 2005)

Combination

Master of the Galaxy (Bokarev and Seleznev, 2018)
Trains and Stations (Lang, 2013)
World in Flames (Pinder and Rowland, 1985)

MOV-02 Roll and Move

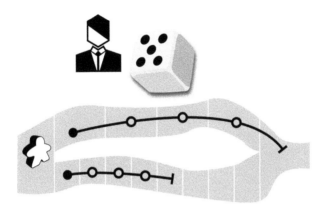

Description

A randomizer is used to determine how far to move a piece. The space landed on determines the action(s) a player can take.

Discussion

Roll-and-Move games are emblematic of many of the earliest games people are exposed to. This Roll-and-Move mechanism has also been used in some of the oldest known games, including *Senet* and *Backgammon*.

Because Roll and Move has been used in so many simplistic children's games, it has the reputation as an anti-pattern. Players do not feel in control of their actions and are at the mercy of the randomizer, which could be dice (*Monopoly*), a spinner (*Chutes and Ladders*), or cards (*Candyland*).

To mitigate this, the designer should extend the mechanism to allow for more player choice. One way is to give the players more ways to apply the results of the randomizer, as in *Backgammon*, where the player can use the dice in a variety of ways. Other options are to have mechanisms that allow the players to modify, use a subset of the number, or choose a direction, as in *Talisman*, wager on movement as in *Long Shot* and *Camel Up*, or wrap it in a Push-Your-Luck mechanism like *Nur Peanuts!*. Other options are discussed in sections Different Dice (MOV-07) and Probability Management (UNC-09).

Sample Games

Backgammon (Unknown, 3000 BCE)
Camel Up (Bogen, 2014)
Long Shot (Handy, 2009)
Monopoly (Darrow and Magie, 1933)
Nur Peanuts! (Meister, 2001)
Parcheesi (Unknown, 400)
Senet (Unknown)
Snakes & Ladders (Unknown, ~200 BCE)
Talisman (Harris, 1983)

MOV-03 Pattern Movement

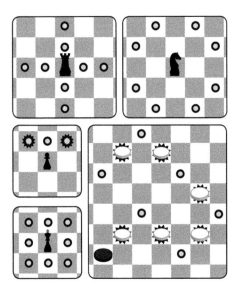

Description

Pieces move in a specific pattern relative to the board grid.

Discussion

This Pattern Movement mechanism gives pieces specific ways that they can move relative to a grid. There are three basic styles:

1 *Fixed Target Spaces*: This is similar to the way that knights move in *Chess*. There are a few specified target squares, and the piece may be moved to any of them. They may or may not be able to jump over spaces that are blocked by friendly or enemy pieces. These moves do not need to be reversible. While a *Chess* knight may return to the square it came from, a pawn may not move backward. In *Shogi* the Gold, for example, may move diagonally forward but not diagonally backward (although it may move straight backward).

2 *Any Distance in a Direction*: The Queen in *Chess* would be an example of this movement style. Pieces may move any number of spaces in a given direction until blocked by another piece. Sometimes, the

directions are fixed relative to the board, so pieces cannot return to where they came from. The Lance in *Shogi*, for example, may move any distance forward but may never move backward until it is promoted.

3 *Jumping*: Jumping over pieces may be a requirement for moving or may be used to capture. Sometimes jumps can be chained, as in *Draughts* (*Checkers*) and *Chinese Checkers*, which can lead to dynamic and dramatic play.

Games with Pattern Movement often have a Promotion mechanism, where pieces that reach the end of the board (or close to the end, as in *Shogi*) are converted into a more powerful version of the piece.

Navia Dratp has pieces that promote by spending a currency to upgrade them. It is earned by moving and capturing, and different pieces cost different amounts to upgrade, which gives a great tool for balancing.

A different take on Promotion is shown by *The Duke*, where pieces are tiles with different movement patterns on either side. When a piece is moved, it is flipped over to its other side (Illustration 10.1).

Illustration 10.1 Pieces in *The Duke* have their movement pattern printed on them. After moving, they are flipped over to show a different pattern. Photo by Dan Thurot.

Movement Patterns can be difficult to learn if there is a different pattern for each piece and it is not part of the piece, as in *Chess* or *Shogi*. However, some modern games, such as the aforementioned *Navia Dratp* and *The Duke*, print the movement pattern directly onto the piece, which makes it much smoother for newer players to learn and allows for even more different styles of pieces. Nevertheless, games like *The Duke* do present players with the challenge of remembering the movement pattern on the reverse side of each piece. Player references can help alleviate these issues.

Sample Games

Checkers (Unknown)
Chess (Unknown, ~1200)
Chinese Checkers (Monks, 1892)
The Duke (Holcomb and Mclaughlin, 2013)
Navia Dratp (Yamazaki, 2004)
Shogi (Unknown)

MOV-04 Movement Points

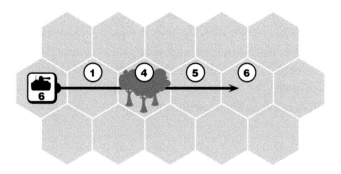

Description

A piece is given a number of points to spend on movement.

Discussion

This Movement Points mechanism allows the designer to differentiate units as well as movement conditions. It is commonly used in war games, as in *Rise and Decline of the Third Reich*, for example, where infantry units have three movement points, and armor units have six. However, it is also used in train games like *Empire Builder* and racing games like *Formula De* to control movement. Normally, each space takes one Movement Point, but certain obstacles and terrain, like mountains or swamps, may take more. In more tactical games, rivers and roads may slow or accelerate movement by controlling how many Movement Points are used. Movement Points may be further generalized as Action Points (ACT-01), where movement is just one of the actions that points may be spent on, as in *Tikal*.

Another extension is to allow normal Movement Points to be increased by incurring some limitation or penalty. For example, many war games allow for units to "double-time" or "redeploy" at the expense of not being able to conduct an attack or come within a certain distance of an opposing unit. Others allow units to take on a status of "exhausted" by moving farther than normal but having their other skills degraded until a "rest" turn is taken.

Sample Games

BattleTech (Brown, Leeper, and Weisman, 1985)
Empire Builder (Bromley and Fawcett, 1982)
Formula De (Lavauer and Randall, 1991)
Melee/Wizard (Jackson, 1977)
Rise and Decline of the Third Reich (Greenwood and Prados, 1974)
Tikal (Kiesling and Kramer, 1999)

MOV-05 Resource to Move

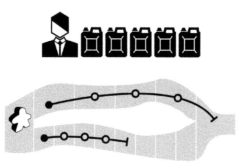

Description

Players expend a Resource to Move.

Discussion

Games where players are moving a limited number of pieces (typically one) may give them a resource that needs to be expended to move. This can take the form of a card with a numeric value, as in *Ave Caesar* or *Ben Hur*, or it can be a currency such as fuel or something more abstract. In *Hare & Tortoise*, players need to spend carrots to move and can acquire them through various actions (Illustration 10.2).

The resource may also have to be expended to change velocity. This is most commonly seen in space games, such as *Attack Vector: Tactical*, where fuel modifies velocities. However, it can also apply to traditional racing games, like *Mississippi Queen*, where players are racing steamships on the Mississippi River. In *Mississippi Queen*, players may normally increase or decrease their speed by one. If they wish to accelerate or decelerate at a higher rate, they must expend coal, which is a limited resource.

Scotland Yard gives players a limited number of tickets of different types—Subway or Bus, for example—one of which must be used each turn depending on the type of transportation taken. If the detectives exhaust their tickets before catching Mr. X, they lose the game.

Giving players a resource that they need to manage is one way to mitigate the common issues with random Roll-and-Move games (MOV-02), as it increases player choice.

Squares moved	Cost in carrots	Squares moved	Cost in carrots	Squares moved	Cost in carrots
1	1	9	45	17	153
2	3	10	55	18	171
3	6	11	66	19	190
4	10	12	78	20	210
5	15	13	91	21	231
6	21	14	105	22	253
7	28	15	120	23	276
8	36	16	136	24	300

(See relevant section in rules regarding moving more than 24 squares.)

Illustration 10.2 The movement chart in *Hare and Tortoise*, which uses a triangular cost system. Moving 4 spaces costs 10 carrots, while moving 8 spaces costs 36 carrots.

Sample Games

Attack Vector: Tactical (Burnside, Finley, and Valle, 2004)

Ave Caesar (Riedesser, 1989)

Ben Hur (du Poel, 1987)

Elfenland (Moon, 1998)

Hare & Tortoise (Parlett, 1973)

Mississippi Queen (Hodel, 1997)

Mush (Moon, 1994)

Scotland Yard (Burggraf, Garrels, Hoermann, Ifland, Scheerer, and Schlegel, 1983)

MOV-06 Measurement

Description

Pieces may be moved up to a certain distance, measured by a ruler.

Discussion

In this Measurement system, there is no grid or other tessellation breaking up the map. Pieces are free to move any amount up to their movement limit, expressed in inches, centimeters, or using a game-supply ruler. This system is typically seen in miniatures games, which are played directly on a tabletop.

Because of the analog nature of Measurement, these systems have several unique issues they need to deal with. First, attack, like movement, is also expressed in the Measurement units. The designer needs to decide whether to allow for Measurement at any time to determine the range or only after attacks or moves have been declared. Not allowing premeasurement gives an edge to players that are better at estimating ranges but tends to make for a lighter experience as sophisticated plans and strategies may fall apart because a charge falls a fraction of a centimeter short. Most modern games allow for premeasurement, although this does slow things down (Illustration 10.3).

This is compounded by the second issue, that there is always some imprecision in moving and Measurement. These systems require players to communicate about the intent of moves and to act in a reasonable fashion.

Finally, unlike Movement Points systems (MOV-04), the measuring can be challenging with different terrain types. Does movement in difficult terrain count as moving "farther" than in other terrains? How are those

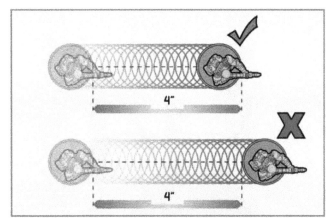

Illustration 10.3   The measurement diagram from the *Infinity* rules. They specify that movement measurements are made from the front of the unit base at the start to the front at the destination.

Measurements handled? These considerations make games more complex. These downsides are offset by games that feel more cinematic and realistic due to the open-ended nature of the scenery, movement, and combat.

Sample Games

Dropzone Commander (Lewis, 2012)
Infinity (Rodriguez, 2005)
Warhammer Age of Sigmar (Uncredited, 2015)

MOV-07 Different Dice

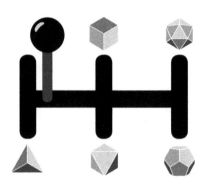

Description

Different Dice are used to move depending on unit or game state.

Discussion

As an alternative to giving fixed Movement Points to units (MOV-04), this mechanism assigns a particular die or dice that are rolled to determine how far a unit may move. This introduces some randomness in movement rates but allows the player (and designer) to control the range.

In *Formula De*, each gear is represented by a different die. Players roll the specific gear die to see how far they will move. These are special dice that have a specific min and max value—the D20 fifth gear die, for example, goes from 21 to 30.

Battleball assigns a different die to each unit—D6s for the slow linesman and D20s for the speedy wide receivers. In this case, however, the dice are standard and go from 1 to 6 or 1 to 20 in these particular cases. This makes the wide receivers much more variable.

In the dog-sled racing game *Mush*, dogs are represented by different dice depending on the type of weather they prefer.

One of the advantages of this system is that there are very few rules overhead. Once the die is selected, you roll it to generate that number of Movement Points.

Sample Games

Battleball (Baker, 2003)
Formula De (Lavauer and Randall, 1991)
Mush (Moon, 1994)

MOV-08 Drift

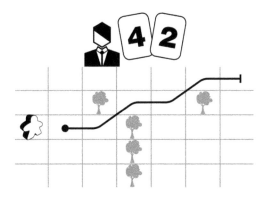

Description

Two movement cards are played to move. The sum represents the distance forward moved; the difference represents the sideways movement (Drift).

Discussion

First introduced in the dog-sled racing game, *Snow Tails*, this Drift system is both thematic and gives players options for clever play. Each of the two dogs pulling the sled has a number card placed on it. The sled is moved forward by the sum of the numbers, and it must change lanes equal to the difference, in the direction of the dog that was assigned the higher number.

Since players may only play one card per turn (with the card on the other dog remaining the same), careful management of the resource, and how you Drift through the course, is essential for winning play.

While this system has not been used outside of *Snow Tails* and its successor *Mush! Mush!: Snow Tails 2*, we feel that it is worth including here because it shows how different movement mechanisms can be thematic, clever, and straightforward. It may well be that the close consonance between theme and mechanism is precisely why this hasn't been reused.

Sample Games

Mush! Mush!: Snow Tails 2 (Lamont and Lamont, 2013)
Snow Tails (Lamont and Lamont, 2008)

MOV-09 Impulse

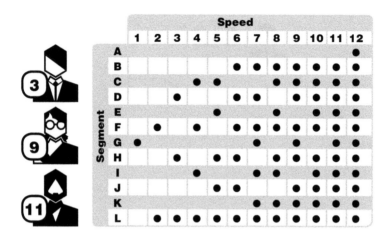

Segment	Speed 1	2	3	4	5	6	7	8	9	10	11	12
A												•
B						•	•	•	•	•	•	•
C				•	•		•	•	•	•	•	•
D			•			•	•		•	•	•	•
E					•			•		•	•	•
F		•		•		•	•	•	•	•	•	•
G	•						•		•		•	•
H			•		•	•		•	•	•	•	•
I				•			•	•		•	•	•
J					•	•			•	•	•	•
K						•	•		•	•	•	•
L	•	•	•	•	•	•	•	•	•	•	•	•

Description

A turn is broken up into a series of small Impulses. Depending on their speed, units will be able to move in specific Impulses.

Discussion

Originally pioneered in *Star Fleet Battles*, this system simulates the simultaneous movement of player pieces. Rather than one player moving their full distance, and then the next, moves are interleaved. There is a chart that shows which Impulses a ship will move in for different speeds. When a ship becomes active, it moves a single hex.

As an example, in *Star Fleet Battles*, ships may have speeds from 0 to 16, so there are 16 Impulses. A ship that is moving at speed 4 will move every fourth Impulse. A ship that is moving at speed 6 will move in Impulses 3, 6, 8, 11, 14, and 16.

This system increases realism by having ships gradually approach each other, rather than jump to a new location and fire from there. However, it does so at an increase in complexity and bookkeeping that requires one of the players to keep track of the progress of the turn and alert players to when particular ships need to move.

Sample Games

Attack Vector: Tactical (Burnside, Finley, and Valle, 2004)
Car Wars (Irby and Jackson, 1981)
Star Fleet Battles (Cole, 1979)

MOV-10 Programmed Movement

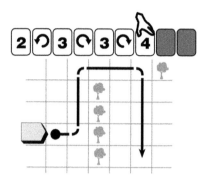

Description

Players simultaneously program their movement and then reveal and execute it.

Discussion

This is a subset of Action Queues (ACT-06), so the considerations there apply. However, there are some specifics relating to movement to cover here.

First is the Right-Left issue. Programmed Movement games often have turning as one of the orders. *Robo Rally* is an example. This can often be difficult for players to visualize and can result in turning the wrong way. It can be beneficial to have the turn cards labeled as Clockwise and Counterclockwise, rather than Right or Left, as these may be simpler for players to visualize, but the issue remains.

To avoid this, some Programmed Movement games either have a generic Turn action, allowing the players to choose facing at that time, or allow free rotations. *The Dragon & Flagon* is an example (Illustration 10.4).

Another is how challenging the spatial puzzle will be and how that fits into the game theme. *Robo Rally* creates a complex space for players to navigate by constraining them in two ways. First, players draw a hand of nine cards and must select five to be programmed. It is frequent that players do not have the exact cards they need to get where they would like to go, so that forces them to evaluate a variety of alternatives. In addition, there are features on the board like conveyor belts, pits, and pushers that, although deterministic, make it even more challenging to picture the

Illustration 10.4   A sample queue in *Robo Rally*. The cards are executed in sequence from left to right, relying on the player to be able to visualize the action.

result of a sequence of cards. There is also bumping—if players move into the same space as another robot, they push it out of the square, which can have a huge effect on where that robot ends up. Then, if robots take damage, they may have cards "locked" into place, making coming up with a plan even more challenging. All of these elements foster a feeling of chaos, which is the goal of *Robo Rally*, which players tend to either love or hate.

Space Cadets uses a similar system, with cards being drawn and placed in sequence to plot movement. But it gives a little more control to players, as there are fewer obstacles on the board, and ships pass through each other or may occupy the same space. Players also have more control, as they can slow down, reducing the number of cards played or allocating more of the Energy resource to Helm, allowing for more cards to be drawn.

Another lever for the designer is the number of cards to be placed in the queue. This materially impacts the complexity of planning. While *Robo Rally* has players plot five cards, *duck! duck! Go* only has them plot one, befitting its intended younger audience. *Volt: Robot Battle Arena* has players place a die on a chart indicating the direction they want to move, with the die face indicating the distance. There is no facing—robots can move or shoot in any direction chosen. This puts the emphasis in *Volt: Robot Battle Arena* on guessing what the opponents will do, rather than on how to control your own robot.

Programmed Movement can also be used as part of a Hidden Movement game (MOV-24).

Sample Games

The Dragon & Flagon (Engelstein, Engelstein, and Engelstein, 2016)
duck! duck! Go! (Nunn, 2008)
Robo Rally (Garfield, 1994)
Space Cadets (Engelstein, Engelstein, and Engelstein, 2012)
Twin Tin Bots (Keyaerts, 2013)
Volt: Robot Battle Arena (Matsuuchi, 2014)

MOV-11 Relative Position

Description

The precise location of units is not tracked. Only their Relative Position is important.

Discussion

The standard use case for this mechanism is in racing games that track relative order but not specific position. For example, in *Formula Motor Racing*, the cars for the players are simply in sequence from first place to last. Players take actions to try to move further up toward the front of the line and be in the first place when the game ends. The distance between first and second place is always the same. There is no further representation of distance or gaps between cars.

Similarly, in *Get Bit!*, players are swimmers trying to escape from a shark and only their relative position is tracked. The shark attacks the player last in line (Illustration 10.5).

This system has the benefit of simplicity and focuses on specific aspects of racing. It also eliminates the need for a board, track, or lanes, and the rules and space overhead that go with that. It also keeps the games competitive, as it is literally impossible for a car to get too far into the lead to catch or drop too far behind the leader. Everything is constrained.

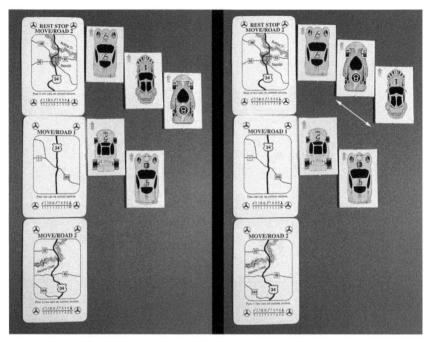

Illustration 10.5   In *Roadkill*, players move along a track formed of cards. On each card, players are placed in relative order. In the image on the left, Car #8 is in last place on the top card. If it passes Car #1, it moves up in order, as shown in the right.

Roadkill is a hybrid version of this system, which has a series of location cards that players race through. Not all players need to be on the same location card but those that are placed in a ranked line.

The air combat game *Ace of Aces* uses an innovative book system, where each page shows the view out of the player's cockpit. The positions are determined by a relative movement system, as players select moves secretly and simultaneously, and the planes are shifted relative to each other, with each player remaining the center of their own play space.

Another type of Relative system is used in *Up Front*. This card-based tactical combat game has squads that move toward or away from other squads. Their location is represented by an abstract concept called Relative Range, which goes from 1 (far away) to 5 (right on top of each other). Abstracting movement in this way allows *Up Front* to focus on other tactical elements of the battle.

Racing or movement does not need to be the central metaphor for use of this mechanism. In *Guillotine*, players manipulate a line of people, with the character at the head of the line needing to put their head on the chopping block.

Sample Games

Ace of Aces: Handy Rotary Series (Leonardi, 1980)
Formula Motor Racing (Knizia, 1995)
Galaxy Trucker (Chvátil, 2007)
Get Bit! (Chalker, 2007)
Guillotine (Peterson, 1998)
Roadkill (Greenwood and Verssen, 1993)
Up Front (Allen, 1983)

MOV-12 Mancala

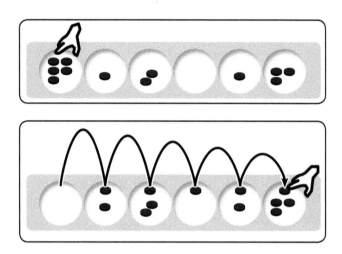

Description

Movement is based on the number of units at the starting location.

Discussion

This system arises from a family of games from Africa, most notably *Mancala*. In *Mancala*, the board is a series of pits organized essentially in a ring. Various numbers of playing pieces are in each pit. On their turn, a player selects a pit and removes all the pieces in that pit and places one in each successive pit in a single direction. If there are three pieces in a pit, for example, one each will be placed in each of the next three pits going around the ring.

A common variation on this mechanism is that only one piece moves, but the distance it gets to move is exactly equal to the number of pieces in the space it starts in. In *Finca*, this system is used to move around a Rondel for action selection (ACT-10), and all pieces, regardless of owner, count toward the distance moved. *Finca* also has the twist that the strength of the action is based on the number of tokens in the destination space. In *Downfall of Pompeii*, players begin the game by placing their pawns into buildings in the city. After the first eruption, players can add pawns to a building equal to the number of pawns already in the building, and finally, after the second eruption, players move pawns a number of spaces equal to the number of pawns on the originating space.

In *Theseus: The Dark Orbit*, players move their pieces around a space station, again based on the number of pieces located in the starting area. However, they have the choice of going clockwise or counterclockwise.

These systems have a lot of opportunity for clever play and are highly interactive as pieces from all players are commingled and directly impact the options available to each.

Sample Games

Downfall of Pompeii (Wrede, 2004)
Finca (Sentker and zur Linde, 2009)
Mancala (Unknown, 700)
Theseus: The Dark Orbit (Oracz, 2013)

MOV-13 Chaining

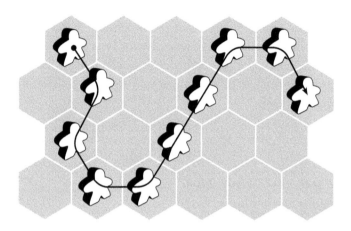

Description

Pieces are stationary but are built out in chains.

Discussion

While the pieces in these games are stationary, building them in chains gives a dynamic feel of movement. In fact, most of these games are typically about taking journeys and traveling.

In *Expedition* and *Lazer Ryderz*, players place a chain of arrow tokens or templates to show the path they are taking. They are considered to be at the tip of the chain. In both cases, if the chains cross, something special happens, which is the rationale for leaving the chain.

In *Through the Desert* and *Quartermaster General*, players do not have to play from the tip of the chain. They may extend from anywhere. This is more in keeping with the themes of establishing caravans or supply lines (Illustration 10.6).

Using chains, rather than just a single unit, creates opportunities to blockade other players, forcing them to cross your path, or topologically isolate them. The static nature of the placements makes these games simple to teach but can open up tactical options for deeper play.

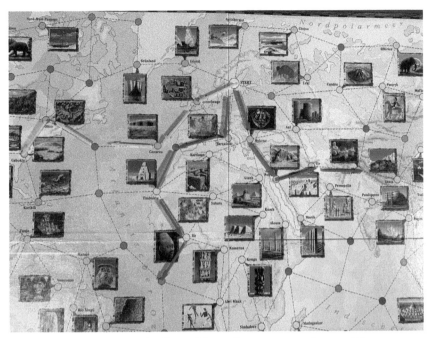

Illustration 10.6   In *Expedition*, players expand one of three shared expeditions (red, blue, and yellow) by adding an additional arrow token to the tip. Players are attempting to steer the expeditions to cross spaces they secretly control.

Sample Games

Blue Lagoon (Knizia, 2018)
Expedition (Kramer, 1996)
Lazer Ryderz (Amato and Kline, 2017)
Quartermaster General (Brody, 2014)
Through the Desert (Knizia, 1998)

MOV-14 Bias

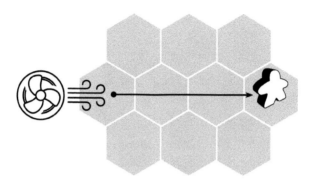

Description

Pieces automatically move in a certain direction, or it is easier to move in a certain direction.

Discussion

The Bias mechanism is typically used to simulate wind, currents, conveyor belts, and other physical systems. There are typically two types: Automatic and Influencers. Automatic Bias mechanisms move pieces in a set direction, typically at the end of each turn. An example is the conveyor belts in *Robo Rally*, which automatically move all robots on them, as well as possibly rotating them. Others are the rivers in *Niagara* and *The Adventurers: The Temple of Chac*, which slide all pieces on the river toward the falls, or the magnets or fans in *Darter*. This is also commonly seen as gravity in space games, such as *Demon's Run*, which move players that go too close to black holes (Illustration 10.7).

These effects are often indicated to the player by arrows on the board showing the effect on pieces. If movable elements are causing the effect, the iconography on the piece is often used.

Influencer mechanisms make it easier to move in certain directions. This is very common in sailing games, but it can also be seen in other themes, like mountain climbing. In *Yacht Race*, the distance a ship can move is directly related to the wind direction.

This mechanism can give texture to an otherwise featureless map, as in a sailing or space game. When players have some control over the element in

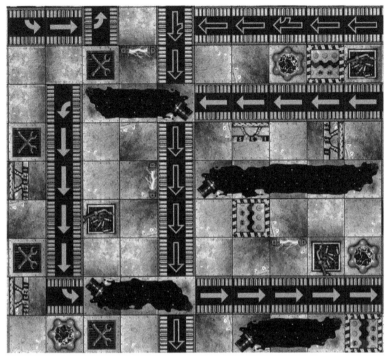

Illustration 10.7   A sample board from *Robo Rally* showing
the two types of conveyor belts. A robot moving onto a red
conveyor is moved one space in the direction of the arrows;
a blue conveyor moves it two spaces. Some conveyor
spaces also rotate robots, as shown by the turned arrows.

question (moving magnets in *Darter*, or changing wind direction in *Yacht
Race*), it can present the players with really interesting tactical possibilities.
For example, in *Niagara* players can influence how fast the river flows each
turn.

These mechanisms need to be used with some care, particularly with automatic biases when positioning is critical. If the system gets complicated, it
can be difficult for players to picture where they will be at the end of their
turn, particularly if this is combined with Programmed Movement (MOV-
10), as in *Robo Rally*.

There are more complex variations on the mechanism. One is *Gravwell:
Escape from the 9th Dimension*, where the Bias point depends on player location. Players move relative to the closest ship to them, whether ahead or behind.

A related mechanism is used in *Tutankhamen*. Players move along a track
and may only move in one direction. They may move as far as they want but

only get to use the ability of a piece they land on. This one-way nature of the board gives the players challenging decisions of whether to race ahead for a desirable space further along the track or to move slowly and get more actions but have to use only those spaces skipped by other players.

Sample Games

The Adventurers: The Temple of Chac (Blossier and Henry, 2009)
Darter (Byrne and Conkey, 2004)
Demon's Run (Matheny, 1981)
Gravwell: Escape from the 9th Dimension (Young, 2013)
Niagara (Liesching, 2004)
Primordial Soup (Matthäus and Nestel, 1997)
Robo Rally (Garfield, 1994)
Tutankhamen (Knizia, 1993)
Yacht Race (Uncredited, 1960)

MOV-15 Moving Multiple Units

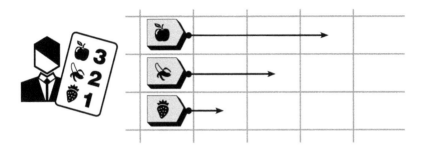

Description

Actions may Move one or Multiple Units.

Discussion

This is a subset of Command Cards (ACT-05). The considerations there apply.

This mechanism is used in its Command Card form by *Thunder Alley*, where players control a number of cars, and the cards are used to move a subset of them.

There are also games where players play cards that move Multiple pieces that may or may not belong to them. The Wolfgang Kramer card system, which includes *Daytona 500* and *Downforce*, gives players a hand of cards, each of which moves cars that may belong to them or to opponents. The key to the game is playing cards at a time when the cars you want to move a long way forward are relatively clear and can use the full movement, whereas cars you are not interested in are blocked in and waste some or all of the movement (Illustration 10.8).

This type of system is frequently associated with Betting (UNC-01), allowing player interests to overlap or conflict at different points.

Another example is *Panamax*. In this game, ships move through the Panama Canal, and certain sections are too narrow for ships to pass each other. So, if you wish to move your ship in that section, it pushes ships ahead of them, giving them free movement.

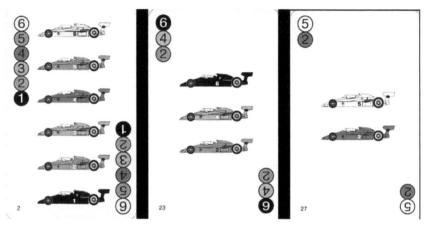

Illustration 10.8   Sample cards from *Detroit-Cleveland Grand Prix*. Cars of all the colors shown must be moved for the distance shown, but the player playing the card can choose the order of movement. This can greatly impact the distance the cars are actually moved.

Sample Games

Daytona 500 (Kramer, 1990)
Detroit-Cleveland Grand Prix (Kramer, 1996)
Downforce (Daviau, Jacobson, and Kramer, 2017)
Long Shot (Handy, 2009)
Panamax (d'Orey, Sentieiro, and Soledade, 2014)
The Really Nasty Horse Racing Game (Knock, 1987)
Thunder Alley (Horger and Horger, 2014)

MOV-16 Map Addition

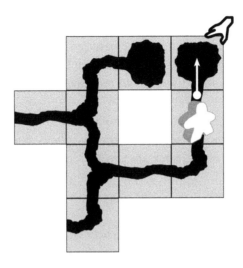

Description

The map is added to as it is explored.

Discussion

This Map Addition mechanism is commonly used in exploration games, as players expose new areas of the map. There are two broad types of games in this category: *Constrained*, where the shape of the board is known and players must explore within those bounds, and *Unconstrained*, where players are free to explore as they wish (sometimes with some rules). There are also games where the map shape is defined by the scenario or mission but is hidden by the game mechanics, as in *The 7th Continent*, or known to only one player, as in *Descent: Journeys in the Dark*.

This mechanism is often implemented with tiles and so is a subset of Tile Laying. Much of that discussion applies here. But there are some specific points for map building.

If players can build in any direction, it may keep them somewhat separated as each explores their own area. If more interaction is desired, some incentive to move to the center needs to be included. The cooperative real-time game *Escape: The Curse of the Temple* implements this rather bluntly, by requiring players to gather on a single tile periodically. In the stress and hurry of a real-time game, it can be challenging to avoid getting spread out.

If using tiles, edges can be used to gate movement. For example, in *Eclipse*, tiles may be marked with a gate or be blank. If two gates match up on adjacent tiles, players may move between them. Later, a technology may be developed that permits movement even if only one gate is between two tiles. This allows for structure and movement restrictions even in the openness of space.

The Map Addition mechanism can also be used to introduce uncertainty into an essentially linear track. In *Mississippi Queen* and *The Mushroom Eaters*, new portions of the track are revealed as they are moved onto. In *Mississippi Queen*, this acts as a type of Catch-The-Leader mechanism (VIC-18), as the leader may be out of position to take advantage of the newly revealed tile.

Exploration can also be procedurally generated. In *Source of the Nile*, when exploring an empty hex, players roll on a series of tables to determine the base terrain type, rivers, and other features. The system cleverly incorporates adjacent spaces to make it more likely, for example, for a block of adjacent jungle spaces to emerge rather than a series of isolated jungle spaces.

Sample Games

     The 7th Continent (Roudy and Sautter, 2017)
     Descent: Journeys in the Dark (Wilson, 2005)
     Dragon Island (Fitzgerald, 2017)
     Eclipse (Tahkokallio, 2011)
     Escape: The Curse of the Temple (Ostby, 2012)
     Mississippi Queen (Hodel, 1997)
     The Mushroom Eaters (Hayden, 2013)
     Source of the Nile (Maker and Wesley, 1978)
     Xia: Legends of a Drift System (Miller, 2014)

MOV-17 Map Reduction

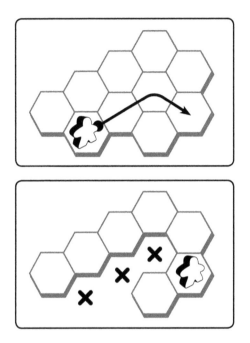

Description

Over the course of the game, the map shrinks.

Discussion

Removing parts of the map can be psychologically interesting for the players, as they feel more constricted both in space and in options. We are exposed to this Map Reduction mechanism first as children through the game *Musical Chairs*.

Isolation and *Hey, That's My Fish!* are classic representatives of this mechanism. In both, players take a move and then remove a tile. In *Isolation*, it may be any tile on the board. In contrast, in *Hey, That's My Fish!*, it must be the tile that the player began their turn on.

In *Sinking of the Titanic*, the board is shrunk in a fixed fashion, rather than under player control, as the ship rotates beneath the water board and the board gradually becomes reduced more and more.

In some games, the board closing is something that happens toward the end of the game. In *The Omega Virus*, sectors of the board may suddenly be closed to the players completely as the game nears its timed conclusion.

Also worth mentioning are the *Survive: Escape from Atlantis* series of games, where the board as a whole does not shrink, but safe tiles (land tiles in this case) are slowly removed, forcing players into shark-infested waters.

Many other games don't shrink the physical board; they simply reduce the options available to the players. *Ticket to Ride* and many other rails games naturally reduce the options available to players as more and more routes get claimed. To a substantial extent, the question of whether the board gets smaller or the options on it become fewer is mostly a matter of thematic consonance and what is practical given the physical components involved.

Sample Games

Hey, That's My Fish! (Cornett and Jakeliunas, 2003)
Isolation (Kienitz, 1972)
The Omega Virus (Gray, 1992)
Sinking of the Titanic (Uncredited, 1975)
Survive: Escape from Atlantis (Courtland-Smith, 1982)
Ticket to Ride (Moon, 2004)

MOV-18 Map Deformation

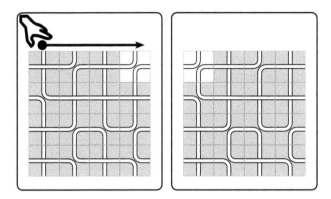

Description

The map is modified during the course of the game through rotation or shifts.

Discussion

In this Map Deformation mechanism, the map is traditionally composed of a series of (typically square) tiles, composed of smaller spaces. Player tokens are located on these tiles. When the tiles are rotated or relocated, the player tokens are moved along with them.

Because this can often radically change the game situation, this mechanism introduces a large dose of chaos into the proceedings. It can also make it difficult for certain players who may have spatial relation issues to visualize the result of the deformation. This is particularly true as tiles with more spaces on them are used.

This mechanism can be implemented through means other than tiles. In *Stay Alive* players move sliders around the edge of the board to control where holes are located, possibly dropping marbles out of the game. In both *Dune* and *Yedo*, an entire section of the board is blocked each turn by the sandstorm and watchman, respectively.

Because of the impact of Map Deformation, it is typically the centerpiece of the game and not a secondary mechanism.

Sample Games

Dune (Eberle, Kittredge, and Olatka, 1979)
Dungeon Twister (Boelinger, 2004)
Stay Alive (Barlow, 1965)
Wiz-War (Jolly, 1983)
Yedo (Ginste and Plancke, 2012)

MOV-19 Move Through Deck

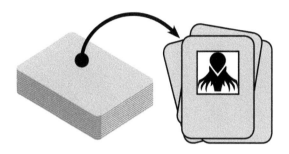

Description

Players Move Through a Deck of cards.

Discussion

This mechanism gives players the feeling of movement by forcing them to work through a deck to get to the bottom or some goal card. In *Chainsaw Warrior*, for example, the deck thematically represents the house players are exploring, with cards representing rooms or encounters, and players take "move" actions to delve deeper.

This mechanism is also used in *Incan Gold*, where players flip cards to move deeper into the temple.

Adopting this metaphor allows designers to give players a sense of forward momentum while keeping the game compact, eliminating the need for a board or large map. It also makes it easier to randomize. The Gating and Unlocking mechanism (ACT-15) is good to use here to tier difficulty.

Sample Games

Chainsaw Warrior (Hand, 1987)
Incan Gold (Faidutti and Moon, 2005)
Maiden's Quest (Shannon, 2018)
One Deck Dungeon (Cieslik, 2016)

MOV-20 Movement Template

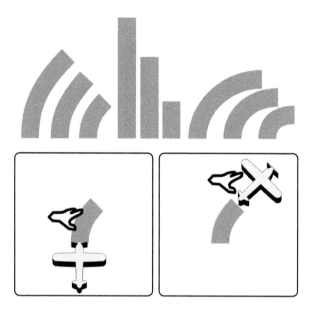

Description

A defined Movement Template is used to determine where a piece moves to.

Discussion

First pioneered in *Wings of War*, this system has been widely used since, most notably in the *Star Wars: X-Wing Miniatures Game*. Each turn, players simultaneously select which Movement Template will be used by each of their units. For example, it may be a Short Straight, a Gradual Left, or a Sharp Right. Moves are revealed, and the templates are used to determine where each piece will end.

Because of the use of the templates, this mechanism is best thematically integrated with pieces that need to keep moving, such as airplanes (Illustration 10.9a).

These games are similar to Programmed Movement (MOV-10), except that only one move is programmed, as opposed to the 3–5 that are common in traditional Programmed Movement games. These systems also typically

Illustration 10.9a   A movement template in *X-Wing*. There is an indent on the side of the plastic base that allows the template to be placed accurately. The rear of the unit is then moved to the end of the template.

do not have a board or spaces to regulate movement but are played directly on a tabletop. While this introduces some of the analog issues discussed in Measurement, the use of the templates keeps things better constrained. However, rules for collisions also need to be developed.

The use of templates also allows for unit differentiation by defining which templates may be available to them.

Lazer Ryderz introduces a variation on the system by incorporating an Action Retrieval system (ACT-03) for when players are allowed to reuse certain templates (Illustration 10.9b).

A related system, included here for brevity, is *Diskwars*, where the units are discs. They are moved by flipping a certain number of times. The diameter of the disc and the number of times it may be flipped define the speed. In essence, the discs themselves are serving as the Movement Templates.

Sample Games

Diskwars (Gelle, Hardy, Jolly, and Petersen, 1999)
Lazer Ryderz (Amato and Kline, 2017)
Star Wars: X-Wing Miniatures Game (Little, 2012)
Wings of War (Angiolini and Paglia, 2004)

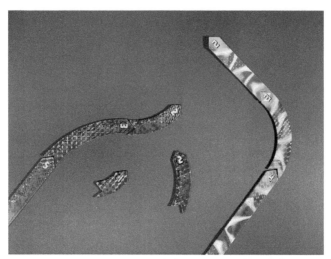

Illustration 10.9b   In *Lazer Ryderz*, players move by placing templates but older templates stay on the table for a few turns. This both limits where a player can move, as certain templates may be unavailable, and also creates obstacles on the table as templates cannot be crossed. Two separate templates are shown for a better sense of scale.

MOV-21 Pieces as Map

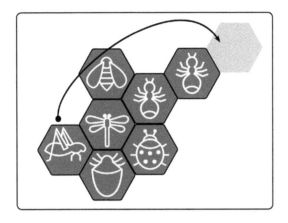

Description

The Pieces themselves compose the Map.

Discussion

These games blur the line between Units and Map, as the map is composed of the individual units themselves. Because of this, these games are typically played directly on the table surface without a board.

The two exemplar games for this mechanism, *Hive* and *Vortex*, use hexagonal tiles for units. Hexagons are a natural choice for this mechanism, as it gives more options for pieces to move.

Typically, pieces must be adjacent to other pieces, so there is one single connected block of units. Pieces are added to the other edge or moved around the outside. Pieces that are surrounded by others are usually locked in place, with only those on the outside of the block able to reposition.

Units may have intrinsic abilities (as in *Hive*) or gain special abilities based on adjacent tiles (*Vortex*).

Because all the pieces, both friendly and enemy, are in a connected block, these games are typically highly interactive, tactical, and quick.

Sample Games

Hive (Yianni, 2001)
Maelstrom (Hardy, Jolly, and Petersen, 2001)
Vortex (Hardy, Jolly, and Petersen, 2001)

MOV-22 Multiple Maps

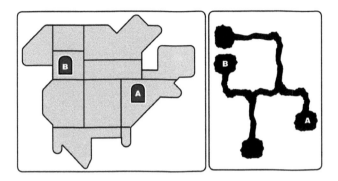

Description

The game takes place on Multiple Maps which are connected at defined points.

Discussion

This mechanism is implemented in *Iron Dragon*, a rail game set in a fantasy world. Trains may run through the main board or transition to a special Underground map. The two are connected at specific points, which can make for interesting route building.

Khronos has multiple boards, but these are connected in time rather than space. They represent three different ages of the same region, and actions that are taken on older boards, like building structures, can ripple through into the future boards.

Fische Fluppen Frikadellen is a trading game that may be played by up to 15 players on three maps placed at separate places in the room. Each board is played individually—turns are not synced between boards—and players may move from board to board under certain circumstances, taking their goods with them in an attempt to make better deals. When arriving at a new board, they are inserted into the turn order. Players move around each map visiting individual stores for buying and selling, and prices fluctuate independently (Illustration 10.10).

Having Multiple Maps forces players to approach the geometry of the situation in a different way. It may present shortcuts or advantages that need to be evaluated in the context of the cost to take advantage of them. It also allows the designers to create more complex structures.

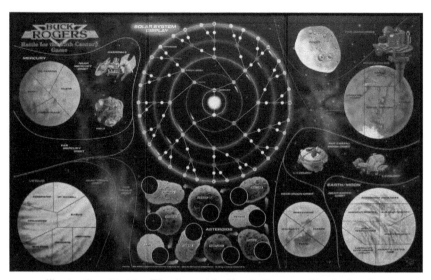

Illustration 10.10   The board in *Buck Rogers: Battle for the 25th Century*. Fleets and planets are moved on the solar system map in the upper center. When a fleet is in the same space as a planet or asteroid, ground forces may be landed onto the larger map for that object.

Sample Games

Buck Rogers: Battle for the 25th Century (Grubb, 1988)
Fische Fluppen Frikadellen (Friese, 2002)
Iron Dragon (Bromley and Wham, 1994)
Khronos (Urbon and Vialla, 2006)
World in Flames (Pinder and Rowland, 1985)

MOV-23 Shortcuts

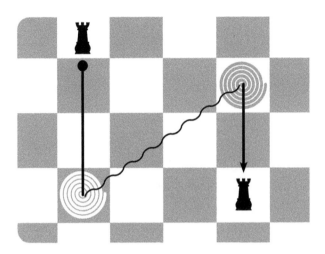

Description

A shorter or quicker route exists that may not always be available.

Discussion

Shortcuts are a way for designers to warp the geometry of the board, to give players other options. For example, in *Clue*, players may move directly between the diagonal corners of the board. This system reduces travel time, which is not a core feature of *Clue*.

Sometimes, shortcuts are only usable by certain characters or with certain equipment. This is commonly used in dungeon-crawl-type games, through the Secret Passage trope. Characters may need to use a skill to detect and be able to use them or need a special key.

Some games will have alternate paths that are shorter but more treacherous. This is a way to present tactical options to players in what is traditionally a basic Roll-and-Move format (MOV-02).

Sample Games

Clue (Pratt, 1949)
Dungeoneer (Denmark, 2003)

MOV-24 Hidden Movement

Description

Movement occurs that is not visible to all players.

Discussion

Hidden Movement is closely tied to many of the mechanisms discussed in Chapter 6, "Uncertainty," but there are specific considerations that are reviewed here.

Scotland Yard is a classic example of a game with Hidden Movement. One player, Mr. X, is trying to evade the other players for a set number of turns. Hidden Movement games require the hidden players to track their location somehow, and in *Scotland Yard*, it is done by recording it on a pad. This method is commonly used in these games, as it also allows for the players to review the hidden players' locations after the game is complete, both for the fun of seeing "close calls" as well as ensuring that the rules were followed.

This last item deserves to be emphasized. By its nature, Hidden Movement requires actions to be taken without the knowledge of the other players. So, typically the rules relating to this activity should be as simple as possible. In *Scotland Yard*, Mr. X uses Point-to-Point movement (discussed in Tessellation MOV-01) to move around the map, using different forms of transportation. The connections between the points are color-coded to match the transportation options, making it relatively simple to understand, and hopefully avoid mistakes. An error in a Hidden Movement game often cannot be found until after the game is over and can invalidate the entire experience (Illustration 10.11a).

There are games that have more complex movements and rules in general in order to support a specific play experience. *The Normandy Campaign* is the first entry in the Double-Blind trilogy. In these war games, each player has a map of the play area and keeps it hidden from the other behind a screen. The front line is represented by a chain of tokens. Any movement of pieces behind the front line (friendly territory) is not revealed to the other player. If a player wishes to move into enemy territory, they announce the coordinates of the spaces they moving into, one at a time. If there are enemy forces in a space, the movement is stopped and combat between the invaders and defenders is resolved. Any spaces the invading armies traverse are taken over by the invading player, and the front line is adjusted to reflect the transfer of ownership.

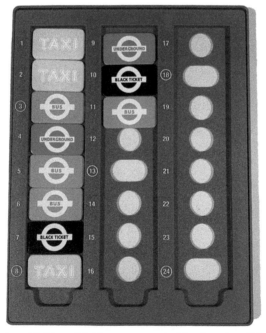

Illustration 10.11a Hidden movement in *Scotland Yard* is tracked with this component. A piece of a player is placed inside, and the Mr. X player writes their moves in the windows and covers it with the type of transportation that was used.

This procedure requires that both players be very familiar with the rules and relies on the honor system for following them (Illustration 10.11b).

The game *Flat Top* simulates carrier battles in World War II, and both players use Hidden Movement on private boards to track the location of their naval task forces to try to find the enemy players launch search planes on the main board. However, since simply placing search planes launched from carriers directly onto the board would reveal the carrier locations, players are allowed to use Hidden Movement for search planes until they want to reveal them on the main board. They can't search until they are revealed, but they can move to a different location far enough from their carrier to try to mislead the opponent about their origin point.

Since deception and deduction are typically part of the Hidden Movement experience, most of these games have defined points or reasons when players must reveal their location. *Scotland Yard* requires the player to surface on certain turns. *Specter Ops* requires the hidden player to commit crimes at certain

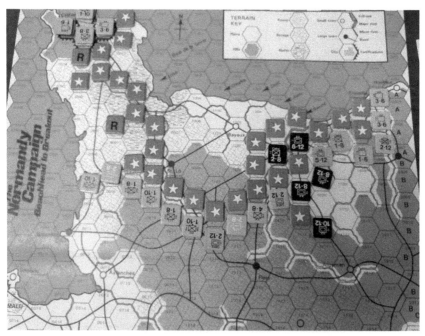

Illustration 10.11b   The Axis map in *The Normandy Campaign*. The Allied front line is indicated by the green star counters, but the actual Allied units may be anywhere within that area. Photo by Board Game Geek user oi_you_nutter.

locations, which reveal their location, as does moving in Line of Sight of a hunter (ARC-08). *Ghost Chase* does not permit the ghost player to enter the same room twice, gradually reducing their possible options for movement.

Another option for giving hints is used in *Captain Sonar*. In this game, each team announces what direction it is moving in (e.g., North or West). The other team records this information and, since subs cannot move through islands or off the map, can gradually figure out where the opponent is located.

The Fury of Dracula gives time-delayed hints to the hunters using an Action Queue system (ACT-06). Dracula plays a card showing the location he is moving to, but that card is added to a queue. Only the last card in the queue may be looked at by the hunters, so they see where Dracula was a few turns ago but not where he currently is. This has the benefit of not requiring any note-taking by the player conducting the Hidden Movement and helps detect rule violations.

Hidden movement games can take advantage of recording moves to force players to actually program movement in advance (Programmed Movement: MOV-10). In *Mind MGMT*, a one-vs-many game (STR-03), the single player begins the game by planning five turns of movement on a personal dry-erase board. Each turn they plan one more turn into the future. This combines future commitment for the hidden player with a "trail" system like The Fury of Dracula.

In the two-player *Duel in the Dark* about the bombing raids on Germany during World War II, the British player plans all of their movement before the raid begins, after targets and weather are determined. This is done by placing a series of "compass cards" in a stack indicating the direction the raid moves. During the raid, the Germans may move freely and try to predict what the British path and target are. In *Duel in the Dark*, the player using hidden movement has little chance to react to the "visible" movement player, so the need for information hints is minimized. It shifts more into a pure deductive exercise (UNC-12).

Pyramid of Pengqueen offers a unique approach to detecting hidden locations. Players place magnetized pieces on either side of a vertical center wall. When two pieces are on the same space, they repel and fall off of the wall.

Another way to implement Hidden Movement is what we call the Anchor/Distance mechanism. In this, the unit that is moving is revealed in a specific location. Then each turn, or as a result of an action, it moves one further away from that space, increasing the Distance. However, the exact location is not recorded or determined in any way. At some point, the movement is completed or the unit is revealed. At that time, it is placed on the map a number of spaces away from the Anchor space determined by the Distance.

This system is used by *War of the Ring*. The Fellowship hides, and then each time it takes a Move action, the Distance is increased by one on a movement track, but the Fellowship token itself does not yet move, and remains on its last revealed location. The opponent, The Shadow Armies, may try to hunt and reveal the location of the Fellowship, or the Fellowship may declare its position voluntarily. When the Fellowship is revealed, the Free Peoples player moves its token on the map by as many spaces as the Distance shown on the movement track. The Distance is then reset to zero. If the Fellowship selects a path through certain regions, like an enemy-controlled stronghold, consequences like taking increased corruption or damage will follow.

On a turn-by-turn basis, the Fellowship's exact location is undetermined. Interactions with the Fellowship are tied to its last known location, but an interaction which reveals the Fellowship also forces a declaration of its last few turns of movement. One important consequence of this system is that paper tracking of the Fellowship is not required and the experience is far less susceptible to human error.

In *4000 AD*, fleets move by "warping" from one location to another. This is done by placing them into a plastic tray and recording where it starts. Then each turn, it is advanced along the distance track, until the player decides to leave the warp. At this point, the fleet may be placed anywhere that is the current distance from the origin.

Sample Games

4000 AD (Doherty, 1972)
Captain Sonar (Fraga and Lemonnier, 2016)
Duel in the Dark (de Pedro, 2007)
Flat Top (Taylor, 1977)
The Fury of Dracula (Hand, 1987)
Ghost Chase (Haferkamp 2001)
Mind MGMT: The Psychic Espionage "Game" (Cormier and Lim, 2021)
The Normandy Campaign (Chadwick, 1983)
Pyramid of Pengqueen (Merkle, 2008)
Scotland Yard (Burggraf, Garrels, Hoermann, Ifland, Scheerer, and Schlegel, 1983)
Specter Ops (Matsuuchi, 2015)
Stop Thief (Doyle, 1979)
War of the Ring (Di Meglio, Maggi, and Nepitello, 2004)

11

Area Control

War-gaming is a thread that runs through much of board game design, and indeed, modeling conflicts through games remains a popular genre. At the center of games of conflict is the notion of controlling an area.

How a game represents this idea is tied to the overall scope of the conflict depicted. Theater-level games that deal with continents and countries tend to be more binary and abstract about control, while individual and squad-level games may not even define it, though the force projection capabilities of units will nonetheless enforce control over different parts of the board.

Area control games are more common in the American design school, but over time, European designers have brought indirect conflict and rapid resolution concepts into the space.

The term area majority is sometimes used in place of area control, and another term area influence is also used. There isn't a reliable definition for any of these terms. But here's one way to think of them: Area Influence is the highest-level category, which would cover all types of relationships between players, their tokens, and the specific areas they inhabit. Area Majority and Area Control would be two sub-branches of Area Influence. In practice, however, Area Majority and Area Control are the dominant mechanical forms we observe in games, and the distinction between the two is often ignored. Thus, we've chosen the name Area Control to stand for all the various mechanisms of control and influence that we'll discuss.

Many of the mechanisms discussed here are a subset of Chapter 10, "Movement." However, their use is specialized and common enough to warrant a chapter of their own.

DOI: 10.1201/9781003179184-11   485

ARC-01 Absolute Control

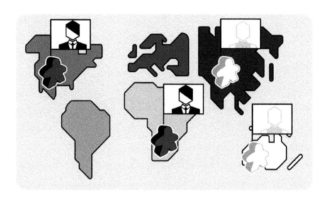

Description

One player has Absolute Control of an area.

Discussion

Absolute Control games, which are frequently referred to as Area Control games, have territories with a binary character: controlled by a single player or uncontrolled. Controlled territories typically only contain one player's units, and other players are barred from co-existing in that territory. This type of control can be seen in *Risk*, where attempting to move into enemy-occupied territories triggers a battle. This is as distinct from games like *Chess* or *Onitama*, where a piece might project force across other spaces but can never protect the space it occupies itself and is simply captured when another piece enters its space. This is further distinct from games in which multiple factions can share a territory without triggering a confrontation, like *Root*.

This observation leads us to another element of an area more generally, which is that it's important to know who controls the space, because the space occupied provides benefits, gives access to certain abilities, or produces resources. The reason to occupy the space is not simply tactical and positional. In *Axis & Allies*, spaces produce industrial production credits that can be used to buy new units. In *Small World*, territories may have different features like hills or mines, which may trigger specific effects or abilities, including bonus scoring.

Many games allow players to control a territory even though they have evacuated the units within it. Typically, these are marked with a "control

token" or something similar to indicate ownership of the area, like *Axis &*
Allies. However, some games, like *Diplomacy*, do not do this but rely on the
players to remember which spaces are controlled. In *Diplomacy*, this is not
much of a hardship because control only matters to special Supply Center
spaces, and there are few of those. The last player to control a non-Supply
Center space has no impact on the game.

Another consideration is how areas change control. The most common is
occupation by units. However, some games allow control to transfer without units, such as through diplomacy actions in *Pax Britannica* and *Divine
Right*. In the latter, neutral countries (composed of many spaces) may be per-
suaded to join a player's side, in which case, all the areas pass to the control of
that player. Similarly, they can revert to neutral status or control of another
player. *Diplomacy* only allows Supply Centers to change control every second
turn, which gives players more time and space to maneuver.

Sample Games

Axis & Allies (Harris, Jr., 1981)
Chess (Unknown, ~1200)
Diplomacy (Calhamer, 1959)
Divine Right (Rahman and Rahman, 1979)
Onitama (Sato, 2014)
Pax Britannica (Costikyan, 1985)
Risk (Lamorisse and Levin, 1959)
Root (Werle, 2018)
Small World (Keyaerts, 2009)

ARC-02 Area Majority/Influence

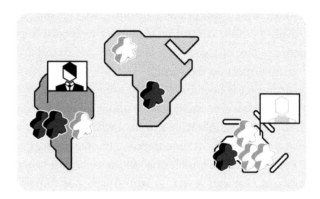

Description

Multiple players may occupy a space and gain benefits based on their proportional presence in the space.

Discussion

An elegant example of European design sensibilities applied to American-style conflict games is the area majority mechanism of *El Grande*. Each province is worth a different number of Victory Points (VPs) that will be awarded to the player with the most caballeros (soldiers) present in the province. Points are also awarded to the players with the second- and third-most caballeros in the region. Caballeros do not directly interact, and there is no conflict resolution mechanism of any kind. Instead, the game implements a Multiple-Lot simultaneous Auction (AUC-11) themed as a conflict game. The game is not won with tactical brilliance or a lucky streak of die-rolling but through efficiency in winning auctions for VPs.

This idea of efficiency is clearer in an even older game from the late nineteenth century, *Reversi*. In *Reversi*, both players will, in turn, play 32 double-sided tokens to the board, flipping tokens of their opponent's color when they lie in an orthogonal or diagonal line between the newly placed token and one or more anchoring tokens. The game is only scored after all tokens are laid down, with the player controlling the majority of the 64 spaces on the board being the victor. One could similarly envision *Go* as an area majority game, though it is strategically more of an area Enclosure game (RES-12).

In *Twilight Struggle*, players must not only have a majority of influence in a country in order to obtain control, but they must also have an edge over their opponent equal to the country's stability number. Stable countries with dependable governments, like Japan, have a stability number of 4, while war-torn, weaker nations who were pawns in the global contest, like Lebanon, have a stability number of 1. Controlling a country grants a few benefits, including doubling the cost of your opponent adding influence to the country through normal operations. However, being on the short end of that influence battle isn't all bad. As long as you had a presence in the country, you could spread influence to adjacent countries. This is a good example of how different levels of presence and domination of an area can offer different tactical and strategic advantages.

The notable distinction of Area Majority games is that troops of opposing factions can co-exist in the same territory. In *Inis*, not only can opposing clansmen co-exist in the same space, there is even a victory condition which calls for sharing spaces with factions in six different territories. Relatedly, the combat mechanism of *Inis* allows for players to participate in a round or two of combat and then mutually agree to stop fighting, without withdrawing any troops.

Civilization also allows for units from multiple players to co-exist in the same space as long as the total number of tokens does not exceed the food value. If it does, conflict occurs, but there is ample opportunity for peaceful co-occupation. Unlike *Twilight Struggle* and *El Grande*, there is no inherent benefit from having more tokens in a space in *Civilization*, unless combat breaks out. But it can serve as a base from which to expand.

While some games allow fluidity to the states of control a territory may exhibit, other games have moments where control must crystallize and resolve in some way. While turn-based approaches are common, in which scoring happens at the end of the round or at the end of some specific rounds, other games tie triggering resolution to the size of the forces present in the territory. In *Smash Up*, each base has a trigger number. Once the sum of forces played to that base equals or exceeds the trigger number, the base is scored. Similarly, in *Retreat to Darkmoor*, the legendary hero attacks a line of fleeing villains when the sum of the threat values of the villains breaches the hero's stability number. In *Darkmoor*, only those villains surviving the hero's attack are placed in the haven, whose victory points they will score based on majorities at game-end. For more on this topic, see Chapter 4, "Resolution."

It is worth noting that in a standard Area Majority game, where rewards are granted based on the ownership of a space, ties need to be considered by the designer. Some games use "friendly" ties, where all players tied for first, for example, receive first-place points. Other use "unfriendly" ties, where players tied for first are awarded second-place points. Other tie-breaking mechanisms (RES-18) are possible, such as priority tokens or simply not allowing players to create a tie.

Sample Games

> *Civilization* (Tresham, 1980)
> *El Grande* (Kramer and Ulrich, 1995)
> *Go* (Unknown, 2200 BCE)
> *Inis* (Martinez, 2016)
> *Retreat to Darkmoor* (Loomis and Shalev, 2016)
> *Reversi* (Mollet and Waterman, 1883)
> *Smash Up* (Peterson, 2012)
> *Twilight Struggle* (Gupta and Matthews, 2005)

ARC-03 Troop Types

Description

To compete for or establish control requires troops, inhabitants, influence, presence, or some similar metaphor for being in a place. Many games have a variety of unit types, with different abilities, and sometimes, different implications for area control.

Discussion

In some games, only certain units can exercise control over a territory. *Axis & Allies* requires infantry or armor units to take control of a territory away from an opponent. Fighter and bomber planes may not even land on newly captured territory, which can create some interesting decisions for players who are forced to decide between taking a valuable plane as a casualty of combat in order to capture a territory or having the more expendable infantry unit take the hit but be left with a plane that is unable to conquer the space. In *Kemet*, the powerful monsters and creatures summoned by the power tiles are not considered units and cannot even remain on the board if their accompanying troops are eliminated (Illustration 11.1).

In the context of area majority games, the simplest distinction between unit types is their power. Some units have the strength of one, and others are more powerful. *Dominant Species* has both a majority contest, based on the total population of a species, and a dominance contest, which is calculated by evaluating the types of food a species can eat and the quantity of that food that is available in the hex being scored. A single unit may lose the population battle but win the dominance battle. A more straightforward application of the idea of varying troop strengths is in *Belfort*, in which Elves and Dwarves start at a strength of one but can be promoted to count for two points of strength.

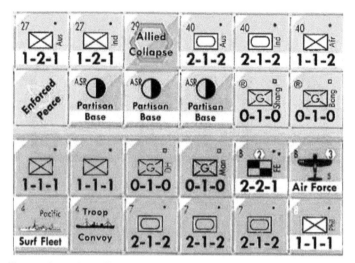

Illustration 11.1   Portion of a counter sheet from *Dai Senso!*
The symbol in the center indicates the type of unit (an X is
a type of infantry, while ovals are tanks), which impacts how
they move and fight. The three numbers on the bottom of
each unit are Attack, Defense, and Movement ratings.

The idea of different unit types is another foundational concept in game
design. It is both so old that it's hard to know where it first began and still a
regular feature of modern design. Units can vary in their movement abilities,
combat strength, cost, their ability to perform certain tasks or even to be
placed in certain spaces, and more. Whether we're dealing with space operas,
like *Twilight Imperium* and *Star Wars: Rebellion* or the highly simplified war
game-like system *Command & Colors*, we observe a broad variety of unity
types and methods for distinguishing them from one another.

In the context of absolute control, some differences in troop types are tied
to the uncertainty engine that resolves combat. Whether troops roll a die to
hit, or can only be hit by a certain die value, or all the other variations on this
core idea (Chapter 4, "Resolution"), the differences between troops are about
how they influence random outcomes. This is one of the means by which
designers moderate the impacts of output randomness. The types of troops
committed and the expected value they generate in terms of hits they can
inflict on the opposing side represent a wager, with the value of the territory
occupied representing the pot to be won.

In an area majority context, there is a narrower range of variation. There
are troops that are worth more than one point of strength, troops whose

value is hidden, troops who can override rules that restrict additional troops from being added, or troops that provide tie-breaker benefits. Rarely, a unit might actually eliminate existing units from an opposing player, as the T-Rex and Pterodactyl units do in *Triassic Terror*. In that same game, the Raptor unit also forces opponents to move units to another territory. *Cave Troll* is built entirely around the mechanism of special powers for units that influence the struggle for majorities in various rooms of a dungeon. Each player fields units that have abilities such as locking down a room in the dungeon to prevent other players from adding units there or swapping units between rooms. In *Glenn Drover's Empires: Galactic Rebellion* (which is only the latest iteration of a game once published under the *Age of Empires* license), a variety of units perform functions either related to or entirely additive to their roles in the majority contest. A Diplomat will let you bring another unit along to a planet to increase your strength there, while a Smuggler will let you get trade goods.

Sample Games

Axis & Allies (Harris, Jr., 1981)
Belfort (Cormier and Lim, 2011)
Cave Troll (Jolley, 2002)
Command & Colors (Borg, 2006)
Dai Senso! (Emrich, Prowell, Vasta, 2011)
Dominant Species (Jensen, 2010)
Glenn Drover's Empires: Galactic Rebellion (Drover, 2016)
Kemet (Bariot and Montiage, 2012)
Nexus Ops (Cantino and Kimball, 2005)
Star Wars: Rebellion (Konieczka, 2016)
Titan (McAllister and Trampier, 1980)
Triassic Terror (Hawes, 2013)
Twilight Imperium (Petersen, 1997)

ARC-04 Territories and Regions

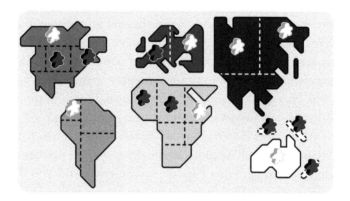

Description

Maps can exhibit hierarchical relationships among their constituent spaces such that a territory might exist in a region and various attributes and parameters may be tied to the control of these areas.

Discussion

The concept of Regions constituted out of a number of Territories is common in conflict games. One typical mechanism provides an additional reward to players who control a set of Regions that compose a territory. This mechanism, a kind of territorial Set Collection (Chapter 12) can be implemented based on absolute control, like *Risk*, or based on majority control, as in *Eight-Minute Empire: Legends* or *Twilight Struggle*. Setting regional control offers some natural hooks for designers to hang additional concepts off of. Making movement between Regions more difficult or expensive enhances the defensibility of a region, once it has been taken. Factions can be assigned "homeland" benefits when in their own Regions too, as in *Risk Legacy*. In essence, regionalizing Territories provides another dimension by which to differentiate Territories, much as the terrain does (Illustration 11.2).

Regional effects provide opportunities to bring a setting to life by providing narrative and mechanical events that differentiate the Territories from one another. For Intellectual-Property (IP)-based games like *War of the Ring*, regional parameters ensure that iconic moments in the original story can be recreated with greater fidelity. Strider can only be revealed as Aragorn and

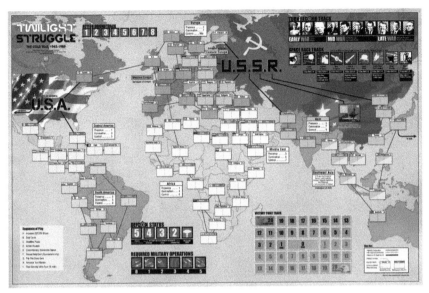

Illustration 11.2   The *Twilight Struggle* board is clearly broken up into regions, as indicated by the backgrounds of the territories. Each territory has a stability rating, and some are designated as Battleground spaces, shown by the dark purple banner.

crowned king if he reaches Minas Tirith or Dol Amroth. Similarly, the Corsairs of Umbar can only attack their historically hated enemies, Gondor, and cannot simply sail to any coastal region. *1960: The Making of the President*'s card-driven system helps the Nixon player carry the West and the Kennedy player, the Northeast. The contest is decided mostly in the South and Midwest. Though deviations are possible, the core identity and patterns of the 1960 election are reinforced by providing different regional strengths to the Kennedy and Nixon players, baked into the makeup of their unique decks.

Sample Games

1960: The Making of the President (Leonhard and Matthews, 2007)
Eight-Minute Empire: Legends (Laukat, 2013)
Risk (Lamorisse and Levin, 1959)
Risk Legacy (Daviau and Dupuis, 2011)
Twilight Struggle (Gupta and Matthews, 2005)
War of the Ring (Di Meglio, Maggi, and Nepitello, 2004)

ARC-05 Area Parameters

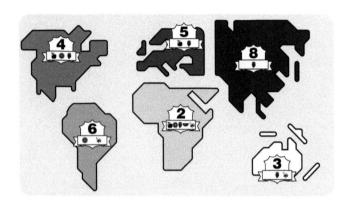

Description

In Area control games, Parameters are assigned to regions that impact why players might wish to control them and how they need to allocate resources to do so.

Discussion

The most common Area Parameters are the rewards gained for controlling areas. Those could be VPs, which are awarded to the majority owner in *El Grande* or to a single owner in *King of Tokyo*. Other common rewards include resources, like in *Nexus Ops*, and access to special powers, like in *Alien Frontiers*. As previously discussed, access to adjacent territories can also be considered a special ability. Exploration games like *The 7th Continent* and dungeon crawlers like *Descent: Journeys in the Dark* will pile on a variety of parameters onto the tiles that make up their game boards—though admittedly, this is stretching the notion of area control extremely thin, particularly in a co-op context. *Memoir '44* has various bonuses and penalties for attacking and defending in and out of certain types of terrain, as well as rules modifying movement for units moving through terrain. It is a good example of the flexibility of assigning Area Parameters (Illustration 11.3).

Carcassonne extends the notion of Area Parameters by assigning parameters to different features on each tile. These parameters include point values and rules for when and how they can be scored. Though we don't typically

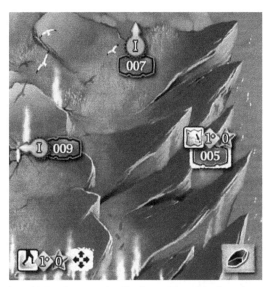

Illustration 11.3   A sample tile from *The 7th Continent*. The icons indicate actions that are available on the card, their costs, and other special features.

think of *Carcassonne* as an area control game or even a bidding game, both of those ideas find expression in its game engine. Placing a pawn takes control and represents a wager on the overall value of that feature when (and if!) it finally scores.

Another important Area Parameter is unit limits. These limits, sometimes called stacking limits because they defined how many counters could be stacked on top of one another in hex-and-counter war games, establish a limit to the size of armies. Sometimes these limitations are global, as in *Heroes of Land, Air & Sea*, which has a five-unit limit on territories. Other times, the stacking limit is expressed as a matter of control limits: in *Conquest of the Empire*, a general can lead a legion of up to seven units. Some limits are enforced based on terrain and unit type. The most common examples are that naval vessels can't enter land spaces, and conversely, land units can't enter sea spaces. *Advanced Squad Leader* and other war games often assign units a "stacking value," and each space can hold a maximum stacking total, which sometimes varies by terrain. Mountainous terrain often restricts mechanized unit movement, as in *Memoir '44*, where only infantry can move through mountains, but artillery can be emplaced on mountains at setup.

Line of sight is another Area Parameter, but one that is more connected to how units interact with one another across multiple areas, rather than being the quality of an area being occupied. We will address it in the section on Force Projection.

Sample Games

The 7th Continent (Roudy and Sautter, 2017)
Advanced Squad Leader (Greenwood, 1985)
Alien Frontiers (Niemann, 2010)
Carcassonne (Wrede, 2000)
Conquest of the Empire (Harris, Jr., 1984)
Descent: Journeys in the Dark (Wilson, 2005)
El Grande (Kramer and Ulrich, 1995)
Heroes of Land, Air & Sea (Almes, 2018)
King of Tokyo (Garfield, 2011)
Memoir '44 (Borg, 2004)
Nexus Ops (Cantino and Kimball, 2005)

ARC-06 Force Projection

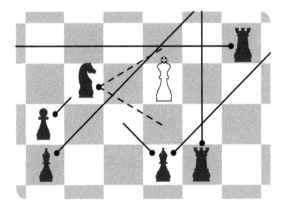

Description

Force Projection is the impact of the movement, attack, and other abilities of units on the decision-making of your opponent.

Discussion

Much of area control revolves around how units can claim and possess areas. However, achieving that control is a matter of how the various abilities and powers of units are arrayed and used in combination. *Chess* is a good example: in *Chess*, units occupy their own spaces, but the only relevant parameters tied to that are that pawn movement into the space is blocked, and bishop, rook, and queen units are blocked from passing through those spaces and must end their movements on capture. Where units are positioned in *Chess* matters much for where they project force. A bishop, knight, and rook may, from three different places on the board, train a withering triple attack on an opposing pawn. Similarly, a powerful queen piece might be harassed and forced off into a corner because all the spaces she could land on are being threatened by other units. Famously, a knight against the edge of the board can be corralled by a bishop in a position exactly three spaces away, orthogonally. In such a position, every space the knight may move to is threatened by the bishop. Force projection as a mechanism is strongly tied to Movement (Chapter 10).

   Onitama uses Force Projection almost exclusively. In each game, five random movement patterns are in play, and cards rotate in and out of the possession of the players. Skilled players will be able to look ahead several moves and predict the unfolding of the game board based on where units project force. Many capture-based abstract games exhibit this quality, from *Checkers* and *Chess* to *Elementos* to *Hive*. *Photosynthesis* has a unique implementation of this mechanism. Trees don't project force the way a spearman might. Rather, they project force based on the size of the shadow that they cast. As the sun rotates around the board, a tall tree will shadow others around it, preventing them from generating light points for their owners.

Force Projection is not uniquely related to area majority/control games. Enclosure games like *Blokus* exhibit this pattern, and auction games have a similar feeling in the way that each player's remaining money is a potential threat in every succeeding auction. The analogy between auctions and area majority games continues to resonate in this context as well. Force projection as we use it here is a spatial mechanism. The number of spaces an army can move, the range of an archer, the area of effect of a wizard's spell, or a sniper's line of sight mechanisms are what we'd call Force Projection mechanisms.

Sample Games

    Blokus (Tavitian, 2000)
    Checkers (Unknown)
    Chess (Unknown, ~1200)
    Elementos (Katz, 2015)
    Hive (Yianni, 2001)
    Onitama (Sato, 2014)
    Photosynthesis (Hach, 2017)

ARC-07 Zone of Control

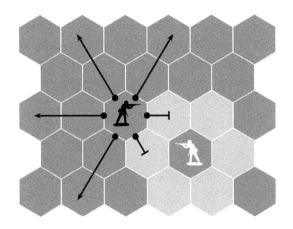

Description

Spaces adjacent to a unit impact the ability of opposing units to move or attack.

Discussion

The Zone of Control (ZOC) has been a staple of conflict games since the 1960s. It allows the designer to reduce the unit density and to still allow players to form lines with gaps that enemies cannot simply move through without consequence. It is a type of Force Projection (ARC-06), as it allows a unit to impact other areas of the board.

In the basic ZOC, units must stop when moving adjacent to enemy units and are required to attack. Typically all opposing units that are in a ZOC must be attacked, which can lead to one unit having to attack more than one opposing piece.

This type of ZOC is sometimes called a Hard ZOC. There are also Soft ZOCs, where pieces may continue moving after they enter the ZOC but have to expend more Movement Points (MOV-04). In some games, this is not permitted, but units that begin in a ZOC may leave the enemy ZOC by moving to a non-ZOC space or may move directly from one ZOC to another but must immediately stop.

Some games only assign ZOCs to certain types of units, such as Cavalry or Skirmishes, or deny it to units in a certain state, like Napoleonic units in a Square or unsupplied units.

ZOC can also be created more organically by allowing units to take opportunity attacks against units that move adjacent to them or past them or that begin a move next to them but move away. While not a ZOC in the classic sense, it does impose consequences for moving units and will shape the battlefield.

Sample Games

Blitzkrieg (Pinsky and Shaw, 1965)
Gettysburg (Roberts, 1958)
The Russian Campaign (Edwards, 1974)

ARC-08 Line of Sight

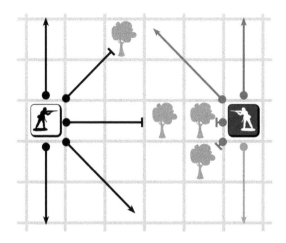

Description

Units may only see certain areas.

Discussion

Many tactical games need to determine if a unit can see another, typically for purposes of attacking. This is referred to as Line of Sight (LOS). A variety of mechanisms have been developed to deal with this situation, with different degrees of accuracy and complexity. LOS is a type of Force Projection (ARC-06) in that it controls which areas of the board a unit may impact.

The simplest LOS mechanism is to have a range of a certain number of spaces and to trace the shortest path of spaces (hexes or squares, typically) to the target. If there is any terrain that blocks LOS, the firing unit cannot see the target. *PanzerBlitz* uses this method.

There are almost always multiple ways to trace paths from attacker to target, so typically, the attackers may choose which path they prefer. While this has the benefit of simplicity, it also makes for some unusual situations, particularly on square grids. Its use is typically restricted to hex grids.

Games such as *Advanced Squad Leader* increase realism by having players lay a thread between the attacker and defender hexes. Dots are placed at the center of each hex to assist in this. If the thread touches any obstacles that block LOS, like buildings or forests, the LOS is blocked. The increased accuracy of this method comes at the cost of fiddliness in terms of moving pieces out of the way and adds the possibility of arguments, as the LOS may just graze certain obstacles and it isn't totally clear if it is blocked or not (Illustration 11.4a).

These systems need to deal with elevation changes as well, to account for hills, gullies, and multilevel buildings. All of these add both complexity and realism. Most games use a "layer cake" approach, with pieces being able to see all spaces on the same elevation as them and can only see lower levels if they are on the edge of their elevation (a "crest" hex). Some games even add rules for blind spots behind obstacles for observers at a height.

In *Nuns on the Run*, players are trying to avoid the nuns patrolling the grounds. Movement is Point-to-Point (MOV-01), and LOS is determined by placing a straight edge between the two points and seeing if it hits any walls. As a help to players, the spaces are numbered, and the rules include a table showing if two spaces (looked up by number) can see each other or not. *Nuns*

Line of Sight Example

The 4-6-7 can see 4-4-7a in yF3 because a string drawn from the center dot in I2 to the dot in F3 does not hit any woods depiction (it goes "down the road") and can see 4-4-7b in J5 with a +1 Hindrance due to the orchard in J4; it cannot see 4-4-7c in K4 due to the building in J3.

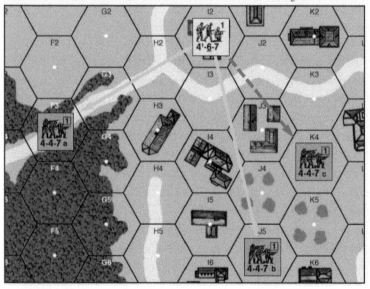

Illustration 11.4a   A Line of Sight example from *Advanced Squad Leader*. LOS is traced from hex center to hex center and uses the actual artistic rendition of terrain features to determine what is blocked.

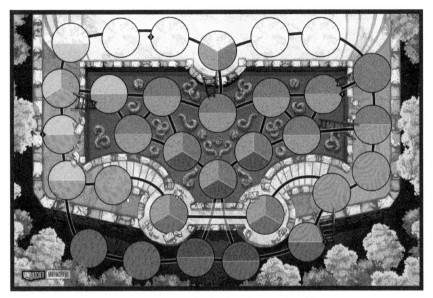

Illustration 11.4b   Line of Sight in *Unmatched* is
determined by space color. A piece can see pieces in
spaces of the same color.

on the Run also has facing. Nuns can only see 180 degrees in front of them. Other games like *Advanced Squad Leader* do not have facing.

Miniatures games often use a "model's eye" view to LOS. Players lean down to the table and check to see if they can see the opposing models. Laser pointers can be helpful here in making a determination. Yet, as with the thread method, this can often lead to player arguments. There may also need to be a judgment about whether some elements of the model don't count for LOS. *Warhammer Age of Sigmar*, for example, specifies that decorative elements added to a model like flowing capes and large crowns are not valid for LOS. This allows players to exercise their creativity when painting and decorating models. *Warmachine/Hordes* sidesteps this by having players use standard cylinders to represent models when checking for LOS.

The tactical battle game *Tannhäuser* takes a simplified approach to LOS. Spaces on the board are color-coded and grouped into "paths." Characters on the same path (same colored circles) can see each other. Some spaces between paths have two different colors—to represent that they can be seen from any space in either path (Illustration 11.4b).

LOS is a bedeviling aspect of game design. High-level conflict games don't require these rules at all, but squad-level combat games usually do, and these games often have some area control aspects to them. LOS usually interferes with force projection, so blocking LOS is a tool in the designer's toolkit for modifying the way in which certain units shape the battlefield and the options players have for navigating it.

Sample Games

Advanced Squad Leader (Greenwood, 1985)
Nuns on the Run (Moyersoen, 2010)
PanzerBlitz (Dunnigan, 1970)
Tannhäuser (Grosselin and Poli, 2007)
Unmatched (Daviau and Jacobson, 2019)
Warhammer Age of Sigmar (Uncredited, 2015)
Warmachine/Hordes (McVey, Snoddy, and Wilson, 2003)

12

Set Collection

Humans are pattern-seeking creatures, which perhaps explains why so many games incorporate some version of set collection. There's a nearly endless variety of types of sets to collect. Some sets are thematic, like Noah's pairs of animals, or the Three Little Pigs. Some are abstract, like Poker hands or melds in *Gin Rummy*, and some sets are arbitrary, like the compass, tablet, and gear science cards in *7 Wonders*. Even game concepts like contracts or tickets can be considered types of set. But no matter their variety and underlying commonality, all sets are built on the idea of synergy: the value or power of the set is greater than the sum of its parts.

The result of this characteristic of sets is that as players collect the components of a set, they will naturally diverge in their valuation of the remaining components. Picking up the fifth dumpling in *Sushi Go!* means much more than the first tempura—but for another player, that tempura completes their set and scores five points, while the first dumpling is worth only a single point. This value difference means that inter-player competition is no longer zero-sum. Players can set and achieve goals that are not in diametric opposition to their opponents, and the indirect conflicts that result engender a less aggressive dynamic that can appeal to players who may shy away from direct conflict.

Set collection can readily support multiple dimensions, and this is common to all but the simplest of games. Number-based sets can be collected in numerical order or in multiples of a single number. Add in colors or suits for yet another dimension. These orthogonal dimensions create choices and tension, as players consider which types of suits to collect based on their value, distribution of their components, and what their opponents might be trying to collect.

The rich math behind the set collection makes it a great tool for designers, but just as important for its popularity is the thematic consonance and

DOI: 10.1201/9781003179184-12

intuitiveness of the set collection. In *Ticket to Ride*, there's no imaginable reason why, at least from a simulation perspective, a set of four blue train cards can connect Chicago to Omaha, and also Helena to Winnipeg but not Winnipeg to Duluth, or Dallas to El Paso. Surely, the actual inputs of labor, capital, and raw materials are similar, and it's hard to think why, in practice, the blue tracks are any different from the green ones. And yet, through the set collection, these issues present no challenge to players, their understanding of the game, and their willingness to accept its conceits. Some tracks are green, and some are blue. Game on.

That's the real magic of the set collection. It is an incredibly versatile mechanism for abstracting a whole host of possible game activities. Sometimes, these sets feel richly thematic and representative of the activities being simulated, and other times, the sets are merely a veneer. But our human love for patterns and combinations means we'll accept quite a bit of abstraction in our set collection. Coupling this activity with clever scoring and collection dynamics, you have one of the fundamental building blocks of board game design.

While set collection can be implemented with many different kinds of components, by far the most common components are cards and tiles. For the sake of simplicity, we will refer to set elements generically as cards, unless referring to a specific game that uses some other component.

SET-01 Set Valuation

Linear		Triangular		Square		Triple	
🍎	⭐1	🍊	⭐1	🍓	⭐1	🍌	⭐0
🍎🍎	⭐2	🍊🍊	⭐3	🍓🍓	⭐4	🍌🍌	⭐0
🍎🍎🍎	⭐3	🍊🍊🍊	⭐6	🍓🍓🍓	⭐9	🍌🍌🍌	⭐3
🍎🍎🍎🍎	⭐4	🍊🍊🍊🍊	⭐10	🍓🍓🍓🍓	⭐16	🍌🍌🍌🍌	⭐3

Description

Set Valuation is the logic or underlying mathematical model by which designers assign values to sets of game elements. Set Valuation can be in terms of currency, resources, or victory points.

Discussion

To paraphrase Jerry Seinfeld, it's one thing to *collect* the set, but something else entirely to *value* the set. Many other chapters in this book, like "Economics" (Chapter 7), "Auctions" (Chapter 8), and "Card Mechanisms" (Chapter 13), discuss how resources are allocated and acquired, but in this section, we'll discuss what those resources are actually worth. Implicit in this framing is that sets are nearly always converted into some benefit and consumed, turned in, or otherwise removed from play, even if only at game-end. Sets are not typically semi-persistent: either you complete them, and spend or score them right away, or they persist and are scored at game-end. However, some sets may be held in hand, and scored when a player chooses to do so for maximal effect.

In the introduction to this chapter, we described sets as being worth more than the sum of their parts. A more precise way to say that is that sets do not increase in value in a linear fashion. However, there are many shapes that the value curve can take, and each of these shapes will incentivize different behaviors.

The simplest valuation is that set elements are worth nothing on their own, but the set, when completed, has a value. *Ticket to Ride*, and its traditional forebear, *Rummy*, value sets in this fashion. A card may fit into more than one set, but on its own, it has only potential value—and often, it may be a wasting asset too. In *Ticket to Ride*, routes will get claimed over time, and cards of matching colors therefore decline in their utility. In *Rummy*, cards left in your hand at game-end typically count against your score or contribute to your opponent's score, depending on the specific variant. This scoring system creates something of a push-your-luck dynamic as to when to cash in a set for a reward and when to hold cards to attempt to increase the set size and payout.

A less-punishing valuation provides that singleton cards have some basic value of their own. Cards may also have unequal values so that there are more valuable and less valuable cards. *Sushi Go!* has some cards that are worth points on their own but are worth more in a set, like the nigiri cards that have a point value that can be tripled when paired with a wasabi card.

Another aspect of Set Valuation is termination. Some games define sets strictly as some number of elements, after which the set terminates. *Catan* defines sets in this fashion: you need one wood and one clay to build a road. No further cards fit into the set in any way, though another set of wood and clay can build another road segment. Other games offer escalating sets that terminate so they have a minimum and maximum valid size, with different payouts based on the size of the set. A similar mechanism is found In *Ethnos*, where bands—sets of the same creatures—are awarded points and allow markers to be placed on the board for area control (Chapter 11). Bands of six or more all score the same amount, no matter how large they get, but larger bands still gain their full on-board placement benefits. In *7 Wonders*, there is no maximum set size or set score for science cards of the same type beyond the maximum number of science icons of the same type in the deck (Illustration 12.1).

When sets have a maximum size and/or score, players are incentivized to diversify and collect multiple types of sets. When sets are not limited, players are wiser to specialize. However, these base dynamics can be influenced both by the specific valuation curve and the existence of orthogonal sets. *7 Wonders* science scoring is a great example. In *7 Wonders*, there are three types of science cards: tablets, compasses, and gears. Cards of the same type

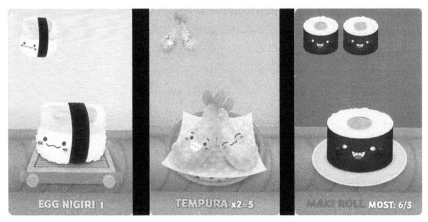

Illustration 12.1 Sample cards from *Sushi Go!* Each type
of sushi is scored in a different way, as shown on the card.
Egg Nigiri are worth 1 point each. Each set of two
Tempura is 5 points, and the player with the most Maki
Rolls scores 6.

score the number of matching cards raised to the power of two, which is a
sharply accelerating scoring curve that incentivizes collecting only one kind
of science. However, the orthogonal set—that is, one of each type of science—offers a counterbalance. A set of three compass cards is worth nine
points (three to the power of two), but a set of one of each science type is
worth a base of one point per card and a set bonus of seven, for a total of
ten points—actually outscoring the geometrically increasing set of the same
size. Only when the monotype set has four cards does it begin to outscore
diversity sets, 16 points to 13. Players leaning into a science strategy should
seek to specialize, but the most efficient scoring for three cards is a diversity
set. These varying incentives create interesting decisions and behavior patterns at the table—even aside from all the other types of sets and scoring in
7 Wonders.

When sets can increase in size and value, a designer can use a variety
of progressions to score increasingly larger sets. We had discussed squaring,
which is one common progression that accelerates sharply and is most useful either for smaller sets or for creating a shoot-the-moon or push-your-luck
dynamic, where a single large set can overwhelm other scoring strategies.
However, designers have overwhelmingly opted for a different sequence when
trying to preserve the greater balance among options: triangular numbers.

The triangular sequence, 1, 3, 6, 10, 15, 21, etc., has achieved nearly the
status of a mantra or a koan among game designers. It is featured in an

enormous number of games and proves incredibly versatile at providing escalating rewards for larger sets without overly incentivizing specialization to the exclusion of all other strategies. Triangular scoring also has a strongly intuitive property, which is that the second member of the set increases your marginal score by two points, the third increases that score by three, and so forth. If you're playing a game with triangular scoring and you're wondering how many additional points you'll score by adding the nth card to your set, the answer is n.

Not all scoring progressions slope up. Terminating sets are the most extreme example, but there are other possibilities too. In *Cacao*, players can move up a field-watering track. The track spaces are marked –10, –4, –1, 0, 2, 4, 7, 11, 16. Setting the track to start negative is mathematically uninteresting on its own. Instead, we will calculate the difference between values, which is to say, what is the actual point gain as you move from space to space. In this progression, the increase is 6, 3, 1, 2, 2, 3, 4, 5. As you can see, the first half is a declining sequence that scores well initially but yields sharply diminishing returns. The second half is a rising triangular sequence (you may notice that the 2, 4, 7, 11, 16 is our familiar 1, 3, 6, 10, 15, but with one added to each number). The marginal returns are highest at the beginning and the end of the curve, and the middle of the curve is least valuable. Players are incentivized to either water a little or a lot, but not a middling amount. This incentive is similar to the one in *Animals on Board*, in which players score a few points for singleton animals on their arks, and score maximum values for sets of three or more, but don't score anything for sets of two, which must be surrendered to Noah, who evidently holds the patent on pairing animals up.

Sample Games

> *7 Wonders* (Bauza, 2010)
> *Animals on Board* (Sentker and zur Linde, 2016)
> *Cacao* (Walker-Harding, 2015)
> *Catan* (Teuber, 1995)
> *Ethnos* (Mori, 2017)
> *Rummy* (Unknown, ~1850)
> *Sushi Go!* (Walker-Harding, 2013)
> *Ticket to Ride* (Moon, 2004)

SET-02 Tile-Laying

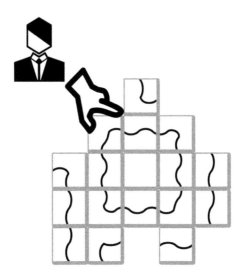

Description

Set-collection mechanisms with spatial elements. There are other aspects to Tile-Laying games like Area-Majority scoring (ARC-02) that we won't cover in this section.

Discussion

Tile-Laying is typically thought of as its own mechanism or family of mechanisms, and that perspective is reasonable. As we examine the patterns and relationships underlying Tile-Laying, set collection emerges as one of the foundational mechanisms of the genre, hence its inclusion in this chapter. *Carcassonne*'s city-completion scoring demonstrates the point: a completed city, which is a set of tiles arranged in a specific way, scores higher than the sum of the value of each tile. Tile-Laying introduces ideas of adjacency and spatial relationships to sets, either as new requirements for set validity or as buffs and nerfs to the valuation of sets.

 At its simplest, tile-matching of some kind defines whether a tile may be played at all. In *Kingdomino*, players must match at least one end of the domino played to one on the table in order to make a valid play. The actual value of the tiles is determined based on a secondary mechanism of accumulating crown tiles. *Latice* requires that a tile matches all of its neighbors by sharing a color or an animal type. Tiles played to match multiple tiles at the same time earn a player extra turns, a scoring mechanism, since the first player to lay all their tiles wins. Each of these plays is a set-completing play (Illustration 12.2).

Qwirkle requires players to place tiles such that they match either the color or shape (but not both) of the other tiles in their row or column. Players are, in essence, forming sets of either shapes or colors in a line. *Völuspá* has a variety of tiles, and each has its own placement and scoring mechanisms, often with set-collection features. For example, Fenris tiles are more powerful if in a line with other Fenris tiles, and no tiles may be placed adjacent to Troll tiles.

Alhambra has a light touch on tile placement but incentivizes players through other means. Tile edges can either have walls or be open. Wall edges may only be placed next to walls, and open to open, otherwise players are free to place tiles as desired. However, a bonus is given to the player who has the

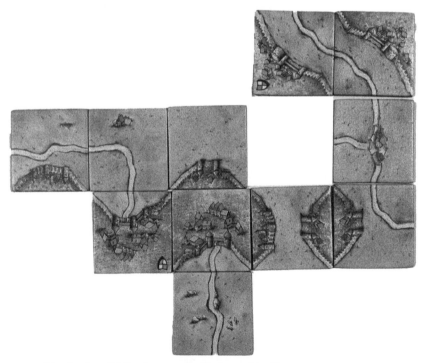

Illustration 12.2   A sample tile layout in *Carcassonne*. When tiles are placed, the features on the edges must match.

longest continuous wall running around the outside edge of their tiles, which can force players going for this bonus to change their valuation of certain tiles. Otherwise, *Alhambra* uses a basic area-majority system.

Isle of Skye: From Chieftain to King employs a large variety of possible sets that can be scored across the tiles that players collect. Some involve adjacencies, others look for region completion, while others are indifferent to spatial layouts. Some sets only score if they are the largest, a kind of Area-Majority concept (ARC-02) that is not uncommon to Tile-Laying games.

The idea of sets scoring regardless of spatial relationships, what we might call a global presence mechanism, is very common. *Suburbia* features buildings whose powers trigger or pay off based on adjacent tiles in some cases and on tiles in a player's city, or even in other players' cities. *Between Two Cities* and *Quadropolis* offer similar set-scoring rules for tiles of various kinds, based on their spatial relationships to themselves or to other tile types. Another type of set, an enclosing set, can be seen in *Rome: City of Marble*. Sets of tiles score based on enclosing and completing a hexagon, and the specific combination of colors, the flavor of the set, determines how well it scores, with sets of a single-color scoring the best. The aforementioned *Alhambra* allows players to score for same-color tile sets, regardless of their adjacency.

Sample Games

   Alhambra (Henn, 2003)
   Between Two Cities (O'Malley, Pedersen, and Rosset, 2015)
   Carcassonne (Wrede, 2000)
   Galaxy Trucker (Chvátil, 2007)
   Isle of Skye: From Chieftain to King (Pelikan and Pfister, 2015)
   Kingdomino (Cathala, 2016)
   Latice (Vincent, 2015)
   Quadropolis (Gandon, 2016)
   Qwirkle (Ross, 2006)
   Rome: City of Marble (Myers, 2015)
   Suburbia (Alspach, 2012)
   Völuspá (Caputo, 2012)

SET-03 Grid Coverage

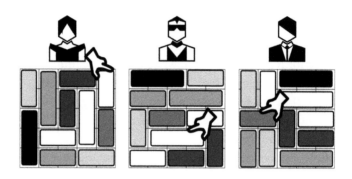

Description

A family of mechanisms in which players cover a grid or fill a space using a variety of shapes.

Discussion

There's a rich mathematical background to how different shapes can fill a two-dimensional plane or a three-dimensional volume and, as a result, many games operate on this basic framework. Undoubtedly, some of these are not really set-collection games, but many are. In *Patchwork*, players are trying to acquire the set of tiles that will allow them to fully tessellate their 9×9 grids. Tiles have a calculable valuation: each tile covers some number of spaces, and each uncovered space is –2 Victory Points (VPs). Tiles may also feature buttons, which are worth 1 VP per payout space that will be activated. However, simply adding up these values doesn't give the true value of the tile, because how well it fits on the board, and which other pieces it allows to still be placed is crucially important too. In this manner, the game is a set-collection game: the value of the tiles is greater than the sum of the parts.

The Princes of Florence has a similar mechanism, with players acquiring differently shaped tiles to fit into their palazzos. Since pieces can't be moved once placed, players are forced to plan ahead. It also changes the valuation of tiles for different players, as some shapes will be more valuable for certain players.

In *A Feast for Odin*, various-shaped goods and treasures are added to grids to try to cover as many spaces as possible. The way the tiles are laid also determines income, VPs, and bonuses. All are mediated through a variety of grids. Grid-Coverage games sometimes take advantage of the underlying grid itself to create another dimension of value. In *Bärenpark*, players lay polyominoes on top of icons in a grid made of a series of square tiles. These icons allow players to draw tiles of different sizes, shapes, and point values for future play. In addition, players are incentivized to fully cover each square grid tile sooner rather than later, since the value of completing a grid tile declines after each player completes one.

Admittedly, Grid-Coverage games don't always involve set-collection in any recognizable way, like *Blokus* and *Ubongo*. *Ubongo* is strictly a speed-puzzle game, where players are trying to solve Grid-Coverage puzzles using standard tiles faster than their opponents. *Blokus* has a placement rule that restricts where pieces may be placed: pieces of the same color may only touch at corners. Similar placement restriction rules underlie many spatial games. There may be other lenses through which to consider these games, like Area-Majority/Influence (ARC-02) (Illustration 12.3).

Illustration 12.3   Tetris-style pieces are added to the board in *FITS*, as players attempt to cover as many dots as possible while leaving the white bonus dots exposed.

Other examples of games about packing shapes into a defined space include *Pack & Stack* and *You Need Drew's Truck*. In these games, players are trying to pack Tetris-style pieces into trucks as efficiently as possible. *FITS*, *Brikks*, and *Rolltris* are more obviously based on Tetris, as players attempt to organize pieces that "drop" from the top edge of the grid. While typically leaving spaces uncovered is bad, *FITS* has special bonus spaces that score more when left open, similar to bonuses in *A Feast for Odin*.

NBMR9 extends Grid Coverage into three dimensions. Tiles are worth more as they are stacked on top of other tiles, but they may only be stacked if they are fully supported with no overhang.

Sample Games

Bärenpark (Walker-Harding, 2017)
Blokus (Tavitian, 2000)
Brikks (Warsch, 2018)
Cottage Garden (Rosenberg, 2016)
A Feast for Odin (Rosenberg, 2016)
FITS (Knizia, 2009)
NMBR9 (Wichman, 2017)
Pack & Stack (Eisenstein, 2008)
Patchwork (Rosenberg, 2014)
The Princes of Florence (Kramer, Ulrich, and Ulrich, 2000)
Ubongo (Rejchtman, 2003)
You Need Drew's Truck (Young, 2003)

SET-04 Network Building

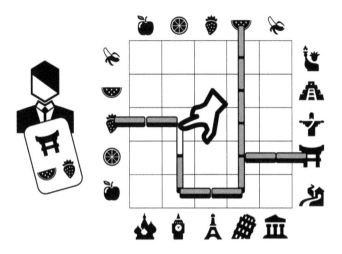

Description

Network Building is a specialized kind of set collection in which the sets collected represent ties between nodes, often represented as routes between destinations.

Discussion

Earlier in this chapter, we discussed *Ticket to Ride* as having a basic *Rummy-*like set-collection mechanism that allows players to build routes in specific places based on the color and number of train cards they collected. But there's another dimension, another kind of set that players collect in *Ticket to Ride*: the eponymous tickets themselves. A ticket can be satisfied by an enormous number of possible route combinations, or sets, that connect the two cities listed. The tickets represent a set of sets, or a super-set, a kind of telescoping set of set-collection mechanisms. *Brass* offers a similar concept in that not only are players seeking to connect certain cities but also they are seeking to ensure the availability of certain raw materials within the network created.

Considering sets in this way illuminates the issue of set element exclusivity. While some games require each set element to be part of only one set (as in *SET*, the pattern recognition game), route-building games typically make routes permanent and allow those routes to be reused as part of other sets or to be subsumed entirely into a larger set. The visual representation of the set as nodes and ties makes it really easy for players to understand why this mechanism works the way it does.

Route-building games have many other elements to them beyond set collection. Blocking other players, dealing with different types of terrain, and upgrading the vehicles that run on these routes are just a few of these elements. We will look at a few of those next. Yet, underneath all of that is the core notion that by linking together a few nodes into a contiguous relationship, you create a whole that is more valuable than the sum of its parts (Illustration 12.4).

There are several options available to the designer in terms of how the network is created. The three most commonly used are *Point-to-Point*, *Tile*

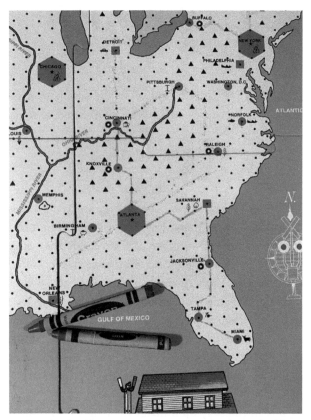

Illustration 12.4   Routes are drawn on the board with a crayon in *Empire Builder*. Each segment costs a different amount depending on the terrain that is being connected.

Placement, and *Existing Network*. In a *Point-to-Point* system, the map is a regular grid of dots or connections, and players may connect any two adjacent dots. Examples of this are *Empire Builder*, where the connections are drawn with markers on a dry-erase surface, and *Transamerica*, where players place wooden sticks to connect dots, similar to roads in *Catan*. Point-to-Point connections can either be owned by a particular player (*Empire Builder*, *Catan*) or be neutral and usable by all (*TransAmerica*).

In *Tile Placement* systems, players place (typically) square or hexagonal tiles onto a grid to form connections. *Streetcar* and *Tsuro* use square tiles, while *Age of Steam* and *1830* use hexagons. The requirement to form connections as tiles are placed can act as constraints on which tiles may be placed, as in Tile-Laying (SET-02), as edges need to match up. Tile Placement games allow for more complex tiles, including connections that go under or over each other, or branch off. It also allows for Upgrade systems (ECO-11), where tiles are replaced with more complex or valuable tiles. This is particularly used in rail games like *1830*.

The boards in *Existing Network* systems have the routes already printed on them. Players need to claim, construct, or activate them in some way. For example, in *Ticket To Ride*, all the possible rail lines are on the map but need to be claimed by players through the playing of sets of cars. In *Rail Baron* and *Power Grid*, players pay to control connections.

Point-to-Point systems work well when there are a lot of possible connections players may want to make. The random cities that need to be connected in *TransAmerica* or the wide variety of pick-up-and-deliver locations in *Empire Builder* make them well suited to give players ultimate flexibility on how to build their network. However, if there are stereotypical connections that are always made, an Existing Network system may work better. In *Power Grid*'s original incarnation as *Funkenshlag*, players drew power lines on the board with markers. However, build patterns were pretty standard, so when the game was released again, the switch was made to an Existing Network system, which earned a much better reception by players.

Network-Building mechanisms tend to dominate gameplay. Most games that use them do so as a centerpiece of the design. However, there are some games where the network construction is a sideshow in the main game. One example is the investigative game *Android*, where players may make connections between entities on a separate Conspiracy board which can give bonuses and impact victory points.

Because of the tactile nature of building networks, a variety of other physical media have been used besides those mentioned. Some examples include *Twixt*, which uses an ingenious peg-and-link system, *String Railway*, where players lay the string on the table to represent rail lines, and *Paperclip Railways*, which does something similar with paper clips, except that clips can be added to chains to represent additional rails being built.

Sample Games

Point-to-Point

Catan (Teuber, 1995)
Empire Builder (Bromley and Fawcett, 1982)
Paperclip Railways (Boydell, 2011)
String Railway (Hayashi, 2009)
TransAmerica (Delonge, 2001)
Twixt (Randolph, 1962)

Tile Placement

1830 (Tresham, 1986)
Age of Steam (Wallace, 2002)
Android (Clark and Wilson, 2008)
Streetcar (Dorra, 1995)
Tsuro (McMurchie, 2004)

Existing Network

Brass (Wallace, 2007)
Concordia (Gerdts, 2013)
Hansa Teutonica (Steding, 2009)
Power Grid (Friese, 2004)
Rail Baron (Erickson and Erickson, 1977)
Ticket to Ride (Moon, 2004)

SET-05 Combo Abilities

Description

A collection of Abilities that are acquired separately and synergize together.

Discussion

Earlier, in Set Valuation (SET-01), we discussed using sets as resources or as direct point-scoring elements. Here, we focus on sets as game verbs and adverbs, as elements that provide actions (verbs) or buffs (adverbs) to actions.

Combos are an emergent aspect of gameplay, in that they aren't explicitly explained in the rules, even though effective play usually requires finding strong Combos. For designers who wish to cultivate this kind of play in their games, there are some best practices to follow.

Games with Combo potential usually have a modular, black-box approach to actions, which tend to be direct and non-contingent. It also helps to have a few types of resources and a variety of domains within which game elements can exist. Finally, more open turn structures, with more options for how to play, help create a Combo dynamic. Card games like *Seasons* illustrate this well. Cards can exist in a deck, a hand, or in play. Actions that move cards from the deck to the hand create a chain that allows another play. Resources that can be converted into effects, or more resources, create the possibility of virtuous spirals. And the existence of dice opens up a whole dimension of possibilities for altering die faces and rerolling dice.

Combos exist in many games, perhaps most famously in *Magic: The Gathering*. However, when played in constructed formats, where players build their own decks before play, the set-collection aspect of the game exists largely in the purchasing of cards. In draft formats, however, players who can identify and select synergistic cards are in essence defining and collecting sets. What makes this type of set collection different from the set collection of a game like *Coloretto* is that the sets in *Magic: The Gathering* are not predefined or fixed. While the designers have certainly intended many of the powerful effects of certain card combinations, by not explicitly declaring these combinations as sets, they preserve the joy of discovery for players.

In *Kemet*, acquiring tiles that enhance your movement ability can synergize with a tile that forces your opponent to take casualties before a battle commences. Together, these two Abilities make for a potent combination that allows you to project force across the board. *Kemet* has many other synergies hiding among the power tiles that players can acquire.

Many games have these kinds of Combos, and identifying and assembling a Combo and then running it is the core of the gameplay. Many so-called engine-building games are precisely this: getting together a few elements that create a virtuous cycle of increasing productivity. Some games have you building actual engines, like *Steampunk Rally*, while in others, the engine is more metaphoric, such as the combinations of Abilities and scoring that you can build in *Race for the Galaxy*. In *Orléans*, a specific set of workers is required to trigger taking an action. *The 7th Continent* has a crafting system that allows players to combine cards, and *Evolution* features a similar system to provide creatures with traits and even to create multiple species with complementary Abilities that model symbiotic biological relationships. *Glory to Rome* and its spiritual successor, *Mottainai*, can best be described as games that challenge players to assemble a set of cards that add up to a game-breaking Combo.

We'll end by reflecting that set collection is dynamic, a pattern common to many games that are instantiated by a number of mechanisms, including those that define acquisition, usage, and valuation. Like with Auctions (Chapter 8), at some point, we begin to observe set-collection elements within nearly every game. That observation, though interesting, may not be useful to the working designer. The set collection as a concept may be everywhere, but the set collection as a mechanism exists in fewer places.

Sample Games

The 7th Continent (Roudy and Sautter, 2017)

Coloretto (Schacht, 2003)
Glory to Rome (Chudyk, 2005)
Kemet (Bariot and Montiage, 2012)
Magic: The Gathering (Garfield, 1993)
Mottainai (Chudyk, 2015)
Orléans (Stockhausen, 2014)
Race for the Galaxy (Lehmann, 2007)
Seasons (Bonnessée, 2012)
Steampunk Rally (Bishop, 2015)

13

Card Mechanisms

Card games go back to the first millennium CE, possibly as early as the 800s in China, and by 1400, variations on the now-familiar 4-suit, 52-card deck are attested to in Persia, the Middle East, and Europe. All of this is to say that card games and their attendant mechanisms have been around for a long, long time.

Core concepts in card games include a face-down draw deck from which players can draw cards privately into a hand; the public table where all players can see and interact with cards; the tableau, a private, but visible play area; and the discard pile, which has varying rules for interaction. The various types of runs and sets, predicated on the ranks and suits of cards, have different implications for different games, as does the existence of "joker" or wild cards in a variety of flavors.

Overall goals of card games might include shedding cards from a hand, capturing or avoiding specific cards, collecting a larger number of cards than the opponent, winning a specified number of hands, defeating attacks from other players, and aligning outcomes to bids. Card games have rules about hand limits, how cards may be acquired, used, and discarded, how turn order may be manipulated, and what the specific composition of cards in the deck must be.

Broadly, we can speak of *trick-taking games*, *shedding games*, and *hand-comparison games*, though there is substantial hybridization. *Trick-taking games* focus on card comparison in card-by-card and turn-by-turn play, often tied to some contract or bid that players seek to make. *Shedding games* are games in which players seek to get rid of their cards first, as in *Rummy*-style games. Ladder-Climbing games, a hybrid type, are a combination of trick-taking games and shedding games that are especially popular. Players shed their hands by laying down a valid set, as in *Rummy*, but compete for the right to lead a new ladder by playing the highest-ranked cards of that set. *Hand-comparison* games often involve betting, like *Poker* and *Blackjack*, where players compare hands based on some standard ranking of hands. The action in these games is in acquiring the set, rather than grouping an existing hand into a few sets and playing them out.

Modern card games sometimes follow these models fairly closely. There are many *Rummy*, trick-taking, climbing, and even *Poker* variants, from the *Mystery Rummy* series to *Tichu* to *Pyramid Poker*. However, there is a new school of modern card games that shares basic ideas about decks and hands with classic card games, but little about the nature and meaning of the cards themselves.

It will take a better work of history to properly trace the evolution of card games and to disentangle the influence of collectible card games from the emergence of card-based versions of middleweight European-style board games. However, the modern design embraces cards as flexible game elements that function almost as rulebook additions. Cards carry a small payload of additional rules that define how they may be used, while possibly also sharing broader characteristics like suits, costs, prerequisites, bindings to other game elements, and more.

We cover many mechanisms throughout this book that are often implemented with cards, and there's probably no truly satisfying definition for the category of card games. Nonetheless, in this section, we'll explore some of the major concepts and mechanisms that feature regularly in card games and games played mostly with cards, which we haven't already addressed elsewhere in this volume.

CAR-01 Trick-Taking

Description

Players play cards from their hand to the table in a series of rounds or "tricks," which are each evaluated separately to determine a winner and to apply other potential effects.

Discussion

Trick-Taking games are about 1,000 years old, and as such, there are many games, variations, and scoring rules. Covering all those possibilities is beyond our scope, and we will instead focus briefly on the core concepts.

Trick-Taking games begin with dealing cards out. In classic games, like *Bridge* and *Spades*, all cards are dealt out evenly to the players. Some games have a betting phase in which players declare the number of tricks they intend to take. After this, players play in turn order, starting with the first player, called the lead. Many games require that players "follow the lead" or "follow suit," which means playing a card of the same suit as the lead, if possible. The player playing the highest card of the lead suit wins the trick and becomes the lead for the next round. Often, one suit is the "trump" suit, and cards of that suit outrank cards of the lead suit, no matter their numerical value. Finally, players score for the number of tricks they've won.

Designers have created variations of all of these core rules. In *Diamonds*, rather than dealing the entire deck, a subset of the deck is dealt out, which creates uncertainty and lowers the impact of memory and card counting. In

Sticheln, players do not have to follow the lead suit, and unlike most games, where off-suit cards are disregarded when determining the winner of the trick, here, they are considered trump! In *The Bottle Imp*, trump isn't tied to suit at all. Instead, only a single card may be trump at any given time: the card closest to, but not exceeding, the value of the bottle, which begins at 19. As lower numbers are played, the bottle takes on the value of those cards. A related approach is featured in *Little Devils*, where the second card played to the trick will set the rule for the trick: if the card is lower, all proceeding players must play lower, and if it is higher, they must play higher. The game also features the variation that winning tricks is a negative outcome. Going back to *Sticheln*, players want to win tricks, but every round, all players choose a "pain" suit whose cards will count against them and try to win tricks while avoiding taking cards from their pain suit.

Betting can also feature variations. In *Bridge*, for example, the bid for a contract includes the right to determine which suit will be trump. Only the team that wins the bidding can score points for making its contract. Trick-Taking games are often played in partnership, and the bidding phase will typically have players taking turns bidding, alternating between the two teams. In some games, like *Wizard*, the sum total of tricks that players bid cannot equal the number of tricks in the hand. This guarantees that at least one player or partnership will miss their bid. Another common variant is the impact of "over-booking" or "over-tricking," which is collecting more tricks than the contract called for. Whether over-booking is more valuable, equal in value, or less valuable than the tricks contracted for varies from game to game. In "exact bid" games like *Sluff Off*, over-tricking may even be penalized.

Trick-Taking games share many features and dynamics with both Once-Around Auction (AUC-07) and Sealed-Bid Auction (AUC-04), as unintuitive as that may sound. Readers curious about this should study *Trick of the Rails*, a card game that models *18xx*-style games and uses Trick-Taking in place of auctions. A Trick-Taking game is similar to an auction in that players hold a hand of currency and bid that currency to win the trick. The currency is not consistent in relative value, because the exact same trick might be won by different cards depending on which card was led and what suit is trump. In addition, the lot up for bid—the cards of the trick—is also what's being used to bid. This kind of dynamic is how a wager usually works; you commit money to the pot, hoping to win the pot, which is composed of all the bids. Trick-Taking games may be described as highly specialized auctions, at least mathematically speaking. From a game-design perspective, however, Trick-Taking games typically emphasize hand-management and planning skills, rather than valuation skills, and the experiential difference between a series of auctions and a hand of tricks is substantial as well.

Sample Games

18xx (Tresham, 1974)
The Bottle Imp (Cornett, 1995)
Bridge (Vanderbilt, 1908)
Diamonds (Fitzgerald, 2014)
Little Devils (Feldkotter, 2012)
Sluff Off (Dorra, 2003)
Spades (Unknown)
Sticheln (Palesch, 1993)
Trick of the Rails (Hayashi, 2011)
Wizard (Fisher, 1984)

CAR-02 Ladder Climbing

Description

Players play one card or a set of related cards. Subsequently, players must play cards of an equal or higher value of the same set already played. The last player to successfully play wins the right to start a new round of Climbing.

Discussion

Ladder-Climbing games, or simply Climbing games, are closely related to trick-taking games. The two began to differentiate geographically, with Western games in Europe developing around winning tricks and trump suits, and Eastern games in China, Korea, and Japan developing around shedding hands and playing sets.

The simplest Climbing games, like *President* (also known as *Scum, Bum, Landlord,* and *Capitalism* among many others), have players playing single cards, doubles, triples, or quads. Subsequent plays must follow the set but be of an equal or higher rank, for example, following three 8s with three 10s. More complex sets, as in *Haggis*, include runs or sequences of consecutive cards or runs of paired cards. Bombs, unbeatable combinations that can be played no matter what set preceded them, are another wrinkle in this genre.

Shedding all your cards, also called "going out," is generally a goal in Climbing games, and in many classic shedding games, it is the win condition. In some games, like *The Great Dalmuti*, play continues until all but one player has gone out, and players are ranked in order of going out. Going out isn't necessarily the win condition. Some games, like *Tichu*, reward the player who goes out first with points for doing so, while also granting points for the specific contents of tricks won.

Climbing games offer many of the same kinds of variations as trick-taking games. Bidding, partnerships, and wild cards are all common. Another popular variation is the pyramidal deck, as in *The Great Dalmuti*, which is a deck of ranked cards with a number of cards in each rank equal to the value of the rank. Thus, there are eight 8s, nine 9s, etc. Taking this idea even further, *Custom Heroes* introduces plastic cards that are placed in sleeves. Adding more cards to a sleeve can change the card's value or introduce special abilities to the card.

Sample Games

    Custom Heroes (Clair, 2017)
    The Great Dalmuti (Garfield, 1995)
    Haggis (Ross, 2010)
    President (Unknown)
    Tichu (Hostettler, 1991)

CAR-03 Melding

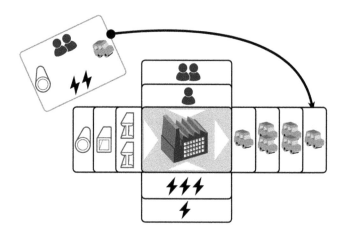

Description

A set of cards in a specific relationship to one another that allows them to be played to a table or scored is a meld. When laying these cards down, the way the cards splay, or overlap one another, may sometimes reveal or conceal certain abilities or attributes.

Discussion

Melds are a kind of Set Collection (Chapter 12) that are very common in card games. Classic card games typically allow melds of identical cards, sometimes called a set, or melds containing cards in a fixed series, for example, ascending by one, usually called a run. *Rummikub* is one example of a game that includes both types of melds. *Go Fish* is a very simple example of a single meld—the group of four.

Commonly, players must assemble a meld in their hands and only then play the melds out onto the table. In *Rummy* and its many variants, melds played out on the table can be added to by other players, sometimes called "laying off"—but only if they have already played a meld themselves. In *Rummikub*, players may disassemble and reassemble any melds on the table, as they seek to lay off more tiles from their hands into these new arrangements.

Melding is not limited to cards. The very popular *Mahjong* uses tiles and takes advantage of their tactile nature in a variety of ways, such as being used to form a wall at the start of each round which defines the play area.

An important design consideration for melds is that each element (card or tile) should belong to more than one possible grouping. For example, in *Rummy*, legal melds include groups of the same values as well as sequential values. Melds with overlapping elements give more nuanced and textured gameplay. Conversely, each element being a part of only one possible meld simplifies the game and decisions and is typically used in children's games such as the aforementioned *Go Fish*.

Melding often involves Splaying, which is discussed thoroughly in ACT-20 Layering.

Sample Games

...*and then, we held hands* (Chircop and Massa, 2015)
Circle the Wagons (Aramini, Devine, and Kluka, 2017)
Go Fish (Unknown)
Honshu (Malmioja, 2016)
Innovation (Chudyk, 2010)
Lotus (Goddard and Goddard, 2016)
Mahjong (Unknown, ~1850)
Rummy (Unknown, ~1850)
Rummikub (Hertzano, 1977)

CAR-04 Card Draw, Limits, and Deck Exhaustion

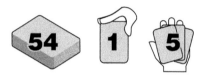

Description

Games frequently limit the number of cards that may be held in a given container, whether that is a hand, a deck, or something else. Similarly, various game effects trigger when a deck, draw pile, or hand becomes exhausted.

Discussion

Hand Limits are a critical part of the superstructure of a game. Cards represent options, and the more cards are held in hand, the more choices a player must consider. In modern games, where cards are not simply members of a set, but instead provide actions or other benefits, more cards mean more power.

In many games, there is no possibility of card advantage because card plays and Card Draws are symmetrical and metered. In *Diamonds*, as in most trick-taking games, all the cards that will be in play are dealt at the beginning, and players each play one card per turn. In *Mystery Rummy: Jack the Ripper*, as in most *Rummy*-style games, players draw a card into their hands at the start of their turns and discard one card to end their turns. Similarly, cooperative card games tend to tightly limit card economies because of how closely coupled those economies are with game difficulty. *Forbidden Island*, for example, if played without a hand limit of artifact cards, is a substantially easier game. Whenever a game involves collecting sets of cards, it will be easier for players to collect sets when they can draw and keep larger numbers of cards. Cooperative games can tweak these settings to change the challenge level presented to the players.

This one-in-one-out static card economy is overturned by many modern designs, and players routinely have more agency over their draws and discards. In *Memoir '44*, scenario-specific rules set the draws, discards, and hand limits for each faction, which allows the designer to model military concepts like surprise, supply lines, and operational capacity. Individual cards, like "Recon," allow players to draw additional cards, at the cost of taking a less powerful action on the map. In *Evolution: The Beginning*, players always receive the same number of cards each turn, but they may play as many or as few cards as they wish and carry over all their cards from turn to turn. Intentionally or not, this evokes the idea of punctuated equilibrium, in which long periods of limited speciation are punctuated by moments of great activity, evolutionarily speaking.

Ticket to Ride similarly doesn't encumber players with a hand limit but imposes a draw limit of two (one if you draw a face-up wild train from the display). Players may lay down melds of any size though, so long as a matching route in size and color is available on the board. Thus, player hand-size fluctuates throughout the game, and skilled players will consider the potential moves their opponents can make based on the number of cards in their hands. *Bohnanza* requires players to draw, and either plant or trade, a fixed number of cards from the deck each turn. These cards can then be supplemented by any number of cards in hand.

Some games treat Card Draw as similar to any other resource. In *Deus*, players choose to either play a card or discard some number of cards. Players may discard any number of cards, but one discarded card, and its suit, determines which discard ability is triggered. The discard abilities include gaining money, resources, buildings, or additional card draws. In *Race for the Galaxy*, players must explicitly choose whether to convert goods, represented by cards, into victory points or additional card draws.

At the other end of the spectrum, from this more permissive approach to card economies is *Through the Ages*, which sorely restricts card movement from the market row into the hand. Players must spend precious actions to acquire cards from the market row and may never exceed their hand limit—unlike many other games that allow players to temporarily exceed hand limits and then discard down at the end of the phase or turn. In fact, *Through the Ages: A Story of Civilization* has no player-triggered discard mechanism at all, and taking a card into hand comes with an enormous opportunity cost. The hand limit is itself determined by a civilization's government type, and more advanced governments increase the player's hand size and thus, fairly directly, the power and possibilities of that player's civilization.

Sample Games

Power Grid (Friese, 2004)
Bohnanza (Rosenberg, 1997)
Deus (Dujardin, 2014)
Diamonds (Fitzgerald, 2014)
Evolution: The Beginning (Crapuchetts, 2016)
Forbidden Island (Leacock, 2010)
Memoir '44 (Borg, 2004)
Mystery Rummy: Jack the Ripper (Fitzgerald, 1998)
Race for the Galaxy (Lehmann, 2007)
Through the Ages: A Story of Civilization (Chvátil, 2006)
Ticket to Ride (Moon, 2004)

CAR-05 Deck Building

Description

Players play cards out of individual decks, seeking to acquire new cards and to play through their decks iteratively, improving them over time through card acquisition.

Discussion

Deck Building isn't a single mechanism, and throughout this book, we discuss mechanisms that are also present in Deck-Building games. Nevertheless, a core structure has emerged in deck-building games that we'll consider here. Though Deck Building is a relatively new mechanism and genre, having appeared first in 2008's *Dominion*, follow-ups have often mimicked *Dominion*'s basic structures. The basic idea is that cards can provide actions, currency for use only in the current turn, or victory points. In base *Dominion*, nearly all the cards provide only one of each of these uses, but many deck builders that followed combined these and offered players a choice for how to use each card. Some games have also expanded beyond these boundaries, like the bases that persist in players' tableaus until they are destroyed in *Star Realms*.

In many deck builders, players will dispose of their whole hand of cards each turn. Commonly, players have a limit on the number of cards they can play as actions, but no limit on the cards that can be played as money, though not all cards will have a money value. While *Dominion* limits the number of buy actions that players can take, most follow-ups limit players to what they can afford. Some cards allow players to draw, and then play, even more cards. At the conclusion of their turn, players will draw back to the full hand, usually five cards. While *Dominion* provided for a static, open market for cards, later deck builders like *Ascension: Deckbuilding Game* and *Star Realms* offer players a market row that is replenished from a randomized deck.

Acquisition methods are a good place to evoke a theme, while also addressing the inherent variability of laying out cards for purchase at random. *Valley of the Kings* has a pyramidal market that allows players to buy only the three cards at the base, after which higher-level cards will drop down into lower levels as the pyramid crumbles. This mechanism gives players foresight, and a bit of control, over which cards will be available to their opponents. In *Eminent Domain*, basic cards are acquired at no cost from a central display, but powerful tech cards are acquired by being able to play the requisite number of technology icons. Though there are no dependencies and prerequisites as in an actual Tech Tree (ACT-16), the effect of making players show a greater number of technology icons for the more powerful cards offers a similar scaling effect. The synergies of certain combinations of cards create more viable and powerful branches through this tiered collection of technologies.

For readers interested in fully exploring Deck-Building mechanisms, *Dominion*'s expansions are an instructive journey. *Intrigue* introduces negative player interactions like forced discards. *Alchemy* introduces a second currency type, and cards which can only be purchased with that currency. *Seaside* introduces the ability to carry over cards from turn to turn. *Prosperity* adds treasures, a new kind of resource that can be spent to trigger abilities without using up actions. *Dark Ages* focuses on interactions with the discard pile, while *Adventures* adds persistent cards that can be played in a future hand. *Cornucopia* rewards players for collecting varieties of cards, while *Guilds* introduces persistent money and reasons to spend it.

Dominion represents one approach to Deck Building, which is part of a larger category called pool building, which includes pools built from items other than cards. This can be entirely isomorphic to Deck Building, as in *Puzzle Strike*, in which cards are replaced with custom *Poker* chips that are drawn from a bag. The *Poker* chip component is easier to shuffle as often as deck builders require and is more durable when subjected to frequent shuffling. *Orléans*, on the other hand, has players drawing workers out of a bag, who can then be assigned to a variety of actions on a player's board.

Andy Parks, the designer of the deck builder *Core Worlds*, describes the distinction between these games as being between drafting verbs, that is, actions, as in most deck builders, and drafting nouns, as in *Orléans*. In a deck builder like *Dominion*, most cards represent an action that players can take simply by playing the card, which is what Parks means by drafting verbs. In *Orléans*, players pull workers out of a bag and assign them to different actions. However, actions require some specific combination of worker types in order to trigger—a kind of Set Collection (Chapter 12)—rather than each worker type having a specific type of action associated with it. Parks refers to this as drafting nouns. His own *Assault of the Giants* game features drafting adjectives—modifiers that provide bonuses and additional abilities, but that must attach to existing cards and characters—out of the pool, presenting yet another possible way to construct a pool builder.

Pools work well as resolution mechanisms, where they're called chit-pull systems. There are also games that don't have true pool-building mechanisms but come very close.

In *Machi Koro*, players purchase numbered cards whose abilities are triggered based on die rolls. Players can buy cards, representing the pool, and they can buy cards that trigger on the same numbers, to increase the payouts of specific numbers. However, players have a limited impact on the overall probability of numbers being rolled. They can choose to roll one die or two dice, but that's all. In a deck builder, players can assure themselves of a zero probability of not drawing certain cards, simply by not acquiring them. *Machi Koro* doesn't provide quite that level of control to players.

Going farther out on this mechanical limb, we can consider the placement of settlements in *Catan* as a pool-building-adjacent mechanism. Even the selection of runners in *Can't Stop* shares something of this flavor. In *Roll for the Galaxy*, players acquire worker dice that have different faces and different values as goods. Players may shape their overall pool both based on which dice they acquire and which dice they place back into their pool each turn. As deck builders and collectible card games show, there is an enormous amount of design space outlined by cards and some tokens. In addition to the games discussed above, cooperative deck builders like *Shadowrun: Crossfire*, *Gloomhaven*, and *Pathfinder Adventure Card Game* continue to blur the line between card, board, and role-playing games. There are also variants like no-shuffle deck builders like *Aeon's End* and build-the-enemy's deck games like *Tiny Epic Defender*.

Sample Games

Aeon's End (Riley, 2016)
Ascension: Deckbuilding Game (Fiorillo and Gary, 2010)
Assault of the Giants (Parks, 2017)
Can't Stop (Sackson, 1980)
Catan (Teuber, 1995)
Core Worlds (Parks, 2011)

Dominion (Vaccarino, 2008)
Dominion and Expansions (Vaccarino, 2008)
Eminent Domain (Jaffee, 2011)
Gloomhaven (Childres, 2017)
Intrigue (Dorra, 1994)
Machi Koro (Suganuma, 2012)
Orléans (Stockhausen, 2014)
Pathfinder Adventure Card Game (Selinker, Brown, O'Connor, Peterson, and Weidling, 2013)
Puzzle Strike (Sirlin, 2010)
Roll for the Galaxy (Huang and Lehmann, 2014)
Shadowrun: Crossfire (Elliot, Heinsoo, Lin, Marques, McCarthy, Schneider, and Watkins, 2014)
Star Realms (Dougherty and Kastle, 2014)
Valley of the Kings (Cleaver, 2014)

CAR-06 Drafting

Description

Drafting is a means of distributing cards or other game elements to players through an ordered selection process.

Discussion

Many games can be described as a process of acquiring, manipulating, and spending resources. One of the main distinctions between modern and classic card games is the move away from random deals and draws and towards more agential means of acquiring cards. Auctions are one popular method (Chapter 8), but they can be cumbersome, mathy, and intimidating to many players. Drafting represents a quicker alternative. One way to think of a draft is that instead of precisely valuing each lot and bidding accordingly in an auction, players can instead ask *What do I want most right now? Do I have to take it now, or will it be here for me next turn too?*

Drafting cards is closely related to Action, Drafting (ACT-02), and Worker Placement (Chapter 9). The core concept is the same in all of these: players select, in turn order, something for their exclusive use. What makes card Drafting different is the variety of design options afforded by the physicality of the card.

The draft variant most similar to worker placement is the Rochester draft, as exemplified in *The Networks*. All available cards are laid on the table, and players each take one card on their turns. Play continues until all the cards have been taken or all players pass their turn. Like a worker placement game, Rochester drafts make all options visible and available at the same time. This can be overwhelming for players and can lead to analysis paralysis, just like in a worker placement game. By physically removing cards from the display, Rochester drafts simplify visually as the draft continues. Consequently, each card is also exclusive to the player who selects it, though designers can include multiple copies of a card if they wish for an action to be available to multiple players. In addition, for games in which cards are taken in hand and played in a later phase, Rochester drafts test the players' ability to recall what cards their opponents took. In a worker placement game, the players' pawns encode that information visually, and everyone can see where each pawn was played.

Another simple draft mechanism is pick-and-pass. In *Lords of Waterdeep*, a game effect calls for the active player to draw a hand of cards equal to the number of players at the table, select one to keep, and pass the rest. Each player does this in turn, until the last player is left with the last card. Some games call for drawing one more card than the number of players, so the last player also has a choice. This mechanism is tightly coupled to turn order. *Lords of Waterdeep* leverages this coupling to provide the greatest return to the player who triggered the effect, but designers should take care not to overly advantage players based on turn order when using this mechanism.

To mitigate turn-order imbalances, designers can implement a snake draft, in which the order of Drafting in round 1 is inverted in round 2, so that the last player in the first round becomes the first player in the last round. Snake Drafting mitigates but does not resolve turn-order imbalance. Assuming a level drop-off in the values of cards, the value of the first choice in round 1 and the last choice in round 2 is greater than the value of the last choice in round 1 and the first choice in round 2. In cases where values don't drop off in a level fashion, the problem remains: some positions are superior to others. Games where the difference in value is negligible, or in which different selections have different values for each player, may be the best place to implement snake drafts. Most games will use a snake draft as part of some larger system, or in setup, as in *Catan*'s placement of initial settlements.

One game to cleverly address this issue is *Kingdomino*, in which players draft dominoes with two terrain squares on them and add them to their kingdom. Some squares feature crowns, which make all connected squares of the same terrain worth one point per crown in the combined region. The tiles are numbered, with the lowest-numbered tiles being the least valuable. To draft the tiles, they are laid out in numbered order in a vertical display. The player who chooses the most valuable tiles, the bottom tile in the display, will claim that tile, but will go last in the following turn. Conversely, the player selecting the least-valuable top tile will go first in the next round. While the tiles have some absolute value, they will differ in relative value to each player based on the exact terrains featured on them and what is in each player's tableau already. In some cases, a player will gladly take a weaker tile, and its better place in turn order, because of how well the tile fits in his or her own board.

Another approach to balancing the turn-order issue of Drafting is to have parallel pick-and-pass drafts happening simultaneously. This method, featured in *7 Wonders*, *Sushi Go!*, and *Among the Stars*, is executed by dealing each player a hand with a number of cards equal to or greater than the number of players playing. Each player picks a card from his or her hand to keep, then passes the hand to the left, and receives a hand from the player to the right. Play continues until all cards are selected. This kind of draft accelerates gameplay because all players are choosing at the same time. However, unlike a Rochester draft, where all choices are visible at all times and where players have nearly equal access to every card, in a parallel draft, each player will only see some fraction of the cards—as few as half in a 7-player game of *7 Wonders*—and will simply not ever have the option of taking those cards. Another consideration is if one player is particularly slow, he or she can create a bottleneck, which often leads to confusion about which player is up to which round of Drafting.

As mentioned earlier, Drafting, in nearly all its formats, presents two questions. The first is what does the player value most. Many players will stop their analysis here and select the card they like best. But, more skilled players will ask whether they need to take that card right away or when turn order wheels back around to them, that card will still be there. This technique, called "wheeling," adds tension and skill to Drafting.

Wheeling is particularly important to booster drafts of *Magic: The Gathering* and other Collectible Card Games (CCG). What's unique about these styles of the draft is that the pool of cards in the draft is unknown to any player, since they come out of sealed booster packs. Moreover, in many CCGs, card synergies are tightly coupled such that once you begin drafting toward some strategy or deck type, other cards drop to little or even negative value. The extremes in valuation for cards between players make wheeling much more likely to succeed, since the card that one player values the most may have little use to the other players. When that disparity is large enough, it might make sense to take a card that's useless to you, simply to deny it to other players, a move called hate-drafting.

Wheeling and hate-drafting are not mechanisms, but they are behaviors that emerge from the Drafting mechanism and the underlying card distributions and overall game system. They are part of what makes the Drafting mechanism so engaging, and designers should evaluate their prototypes with these behaviors in mind.

A few other variants on the parallel Drafting structure include whether cards are played immediately after Drafting, as in *Best Treehouse Ever*, or in turn order during a play phase, for example, in *Medieval Academy*. Sometimes, not all cards drafted are played, as in *Fairy Tale*, where only three of the five cards drafted each round are played and the other two are discarded. Another variant is to allow players to mix their hand with the hand of cards being passed. In this kind of setup, players may take as many cards as they wish from the new hand, as long as they pass the correct number of cards to the next player. Having players play a card immediately after drafting can also help keep the draft on schedule and avoids bottlenecking and confusion by forcing all players to play at roughly the same cadence.

Drafting games can sometimes be played at 2 players, as in *Seasons*, but they tend to be a little flat. *Tides of Madness* is a drafting game limited to 2 players only, and among its innovations is that players can be forced to collect cards with madness symbols on them and can even lose the game if they collect too many.

7 Wonders Duel is a 2-player drafting game with quite a few mechanical twists to ratchet up the tension. Players can only draft cards on the bottom-most revealed level of a structure, but by taking a card, they can reveal face-down cards higher in the structure that become available for drafting. Cards can be used for multiple purposes, including selling off for money, which incentivizes hate-drafting. In addition, there are three possible win conditions, including two in-game sudden-death wins. One win condition is tied to a tug-of-war contest that requires both players to take enough military cards to prevent being overrun by the other player. Another instant-win condition is subject to a set-collection contest in which players must draft wisely to at least prevent their opponents from assembling the winning set. These during-game concerns, and the possibility of forcing certain lines of play because of them, add richness to the Drafting choices.

Sample Games

7 Wonders (Bauza, 2010)
7 Wonders Duel (Bauza and Cathala, 2015)
Among the Stars (Bagiartakis, 2012)
Best Treehouse Ever (Almes, 2015)
Catan (Teuber, 1995)
Fairy Tale (Nakamura, 2004)
Kingdomino (Cathala, 2016)
Lords of Waterdeep (Lee and Thompson, 2012)
Magic: The Gathering (Garfield, 1993)
Medieval Academy (Poncin, 2014)
The Networks (Hova, 2016)
Seasons (Bonnessée, 2012)
Sushi Go! (Walker-Harding, 2013)
Tides of Madness (Čurla, 2016)

CAR-07 Deck Construction

Description

Prior to a multiplayer game session, players select the cards that will make up the decks they use during the multiplayer session. The game provides rules governing how decks may be constructed that typically covers the number of cards in the deck, required cards, restricted cards, and limits on copies of the same card. This mechanism is isomorphic to force-building or list-building in miniatures games and can more generally refer to any game that requires players to assemble private pools of game elements that they will use during play.

Discussion

Deck construction is a retronym, a term that is only required because of the emergence of a later mechanism that creates ambiguity about what we may be referring to. In deck-building players build decks and play them as an integrated part of the core play experience (see CAR-05). Deck construction, on the other hand, refers to games where players typically prepare a deck in advance.

The most familiar implementation of deck construction is common in trading card games (TCG), from competitive dueling games like *Magic: The Gathering* to cooperative ones like *Arkham Horror: The Card Game*. Players sit down with a pool of cards and build a deck to suit their play style and objectives, within the rules set forth by the game.

Perhaps the most important rule of all in deck construction is defining the pool of cards available to players. In competitive TCGs, there might be many sanctioned play formats, each with its own rules about available cards. Official tournaments might be limited to cards from a specific cycle or set of expansions, and within that pool, there may be cards that are banned entirely or limited to fewer copies than the normal limit.

In collectible games, another key limit is which cards players own and thus have access to. Even in non-collectible formats, such as the Living Card Game® format introduced by Fantasy Flight Games, players may not have as many copies of a card as they wish and may need to acquire multiple sets to construct a deck to their exact specifications.

Other types of limits include limiting players to selecting cards of a particular faction and to selecting cards with a total cost that falls under some budgeted amount. These limits are frequently found in miniatures and skirmish games. Both present useful opportunities for designers. Faction identities emerge from the abilities assigned to their cards, and players might prefer factions that support their desired play style. Buying a deck or army within some point limit ensures that players have roughly balanced sides, even as they select units from large and varied pools.

Rules about deck construction are critical to ensuring playability, balance, and limitation on exploits. In games where deck exhaustion is a loss condition, the maximum number of cards in the deck determines how appealing and successful a "milling" strategy, which forces opponents to discard from their decks, might be. A required minimum number of cards in the deck, coupled with limits on copies of cards, sets the variability range for a deck. Without those rules, a deck might contain one particular combo of a couple of cards over and over again, ensuring the combo is present in every hand. This might be quite efficient, but it undermines the conceit of the genre, in which players seed effective combinations into a deck that is large enough to output variable draws.

While deck construction is usually a mechanism intended to give players a lot of agency, choice, and self-expression within a game system, it can also be a barrier to entry. Building a deck in advance of a game takes time, and building an effective deck takes experience. Many games offer preconstructed starter decks that let players jump into the game and only later engage in the deck-construction elements. In cooperative and solo games, decks will typically have to be rebuilt to optimize deck contents for each scenario, making the meta-game activity of deck construction a key aspect of engagement with the game.

An alternative to pregame deck construction is a draft format. CAR-06 goes into detail about draft options. Rather than having rules about deck size, numbers of copies of a single card allowed, and other restrictions, drafting naturally constrains players by only allowing them to select from the pool of available cards, a pool which is shared by all players.

At the other end of the spectrum of agency and engagement lies *Smash Up*. *Smash Up* invites players to select two different faction decks and shuffle them together to produce one integrated deck. These faction decks are all preconstructed and so players are not selecting individual cards at all. This is the most extreme version of the limitations of deck contents, and it completely removes the barriers of deck construction, though at a high cost to the player agency in the design of the deck.

Deck construction is part of a larger design pattern in which players choose the kinds of power-ups, abilities, and characteristics they want to play with. One axis of differentiation is whether the choices happen in the meta-game, as in a TCG, or in a pregame selection format. While *Smash Up* does technically have rules for drafting the available factions, players often simply just decide to play with some pair of factions without formally engaging in that process. In *Seasons*, on the other hand, players use a pick-and-pass drafting format (CAR-06) that is very much the first stage of the game itself, precisely because players are responding to each other's choices as they move through the selection process.

Notable marginal examples straddle a broad range. In *Baseball Highlights 2045*, players begin with preconstructed decks and draft new cards in between rounds. This is a kind of midpoint between deck construction, deck building, and preconstructed decks. In the solo scenario-based game *Israeli Air Force Leader*, players choose a squadron of pilots for each mission. One might even see *Galaxy Trucker* as an example of deck construction, albeit as loosely construed as possible. These examples demonstrate the wealth of possibilities available to designers in designing a meta-game selection experience for players.

Sample Games

Arkham Horror: The Card Game (French and Newman, 2016)
Baseball Highlights 2045 (Fitzgerald, 2015)
Galaxy Trucker (Chvátil, 2007)
Israeli Air Force Leader (Verssen and Verssen, 2017)
Magic: The Gathering (Garfield, 1993)
Seasons (Bonnessée, 2012)
Smash Up (Peterson, 2012)

CAR-08 Multi-Use Cards

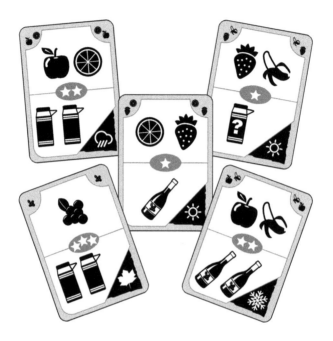

Definition

Multiple actions are shown on a card, but only one can be used.

Discussion

In this mechanism, the cards are typically broken up into clearly defined areas, each of which presents the player with a different option. Note: We use "cards" throughout this entry, as that is the most common implementation. Tiles may also be used, although this mechanism can also be used on tiles or other components. However, it does require a certain amount of real estate to make the choices clear, so cards tend to be the component of choice.

This mechanism presents the players with two or more choices, and they can select only one to perform. For example, in *La Granja*, each card has four different abilities that can be used, each of which is arranged on the edge of a card. The clever player mat allows for cards to be tucked under any of its four edges, so only the operative section of the card is showing. Once the card is placed it cannot be moved—the player forgoes the other options (Illustration 13.1a).

Sometimes, the cards can only be used one time, as in *La Granja*. In others, however, they are recycled so that players may select different options each time. In *Gloomhaven*, for example, each action card has two abilities, and the player can choose which to execute each time the card returns to their hand.

A positive feature of this mechanism is that it presents the players with clear and focused options. It also naturally leads to difficult decisions, particularly when only one option may be chosen the entire game. This feeds into players' feelings of decision anxiety, which may or may not be a design goal.

A key consideration for the designer is which abilities to combine on the same card. One option is simply to randomly assign them to cards. However, this may result cards where one choice is generally superior to the others, which can reduce the decision space.

A better approach is to match the power levels of the different options. This will maximize the difficulty in the player deciding which option to use.

A final consideration is whether to thematically tie the elements together for each card. In *Gloomhaven*, the two halves of the cards are frequently thematically connected.

A subset of this mechanism is Action/Event (ACT-04). In this system, players can choose from a set number of action points or an event. Since one element of the card is a number, balancing is simplified. See that mechanism for more details about specific implementation considerations.

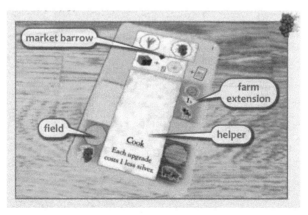

Illustration 13.1a The cards in *La Granja* are placed under the player mat at different edges, only showing the chosen section of the card.

An alternative approach to Multi-Use cards is to allow the cards themselves to be used as physical objects, typically as a discard. For example, in *Race for the Galaxy*, cards must be discarded to pay to play other cards. In *The Ares Project*, cards can be played either face up, typically creating a structure that can create units, or face down on those structures where they represent the resources required for the units to be built.

The Multi-Use cards in *Combat Commander* have six functions in the game; however, only two are options for the players. At the top of the card is an Order that players can issue on their turn. Next, there is an Action, which can be used either on their own or on their opponent's turn. Below the Action is an Event. Randomly, the players may be required to flip the top card of their deck and perform the Event. Finally, at the bottom left is a Random Hex, which can be used for some events and other game functions, and at the bottom right a series of die rolls, which are used to resolve actions. Additionally, the die rolls may be in a special "trigger" box which can generate events, sniper attacks, or jam guns (Illustration 13.1b).

Illustration 13.1b   The cards in *Combat Commander* serve many purposes. Players use Orders and Actions to command their units. The other features are various types of randomizers.

All of this allows a compact way to present a wide range of information. It also gives savvy players the ability to track which die rolls have been used, for example, to modulate their play accordingly.

Sample Games

Andean Abyss (Ruhnke, 2012)
The Ares Project (Engelstein and Engelstein, 2011)
Ceylon (Zinsli and Zinsli, 2018)
Combat Commander: Europe (Jensen, 2006)
Gloomhaven (Childress, 2017)
Glory to Rome (Chudyk, 2005)
La Granja (Keller and Odendahl, 2014)
We the People (Herman, 1993)

CAR-09 Tags

Description

Game objects, typically cards, have icons or other identifiers that identify them as belonging to specific categories. These tags may trigger special effects and/or have values and meaning that can vary, even within the scope of a single play. Tags are additional parameters on top of the base meaning of the game element, so tags represent a means of coupling the game element with more mechanisms and systems. Tags are also bookmarks that can reference a variable set of possible rules that are encoded elsewhere, so they are also a means to modularize, or uncouple, game triggers and game effects.

Discussion

Tags sit quite close to the boundary between a mechanism and a graphical representation, and they are among the most common and useful approaches to creating interconnections between game elements and categories. A card or similar game element is a collection of parameters. Some parameters have specific game meaning, such as the speed or strength of a unit, or the color of a pawn. Other parameters may have no game meaning at all, as is often the case with the size of a pawn or marker. Some parameters have a variable meaning based on other cards, game conditions, scenario rules, and more.

Tags indicate that a card has additional implications and parameters. Suits of cards in traditional card games are a kind of tag that puts cards into one of four categories. This is an Ur-mechanism that one can find in an enormous number of games. Viewed in this way, card colors, suits, and types can all be considered tags.

There is not a substantial distinction between using a card color, icon, or keyword to differentiate cards from one another, and the choice of which visual representation to use is largely a matter of usability. Color is a favorite primary method of distinguishing card categories, but as the number of parameters a card needs to store increases, tags are a handy solution. Tags are also somewhat more amenable to storing multiple values. While it is possible for a card to belong to several colors, it can be a strain to represent this clearly. Multiple tags on a card are more legible when representing a handful of parameters.

Tags are useful for a few different purposes: as an additional fixed dimension of categorization of a card, creating a variable that can be defined differently in different scenarios.

Tags as an additional fixed dimension are familiar features of many card-driven games. Costs for playing a card from hand are often represented with icons, as in *7 Wonders*. These could be viewed as a kind of tag. *Terraforming Mars* builds on this idea by presenting category tags, such as Space, Plants, and Science. Some tags, like Space and Building tags, allow players to pay the cost of the associated card with an alternate resource, like titanium and steel. These are fixed attributes of these tags, which apply to all players at all times.

Tags are also used in *Terraforming Mars* in a contingent way. Space tags have no fixed meaning on their own. However, in some games, they may contribute towards achieving certain milestones, they may be themselves the subject of a majority competition, playing a card with a Space tag may trigger some effect, and some cards may require a certain number of Space tags to be in a player's tableau as a prerequisite. The various other tags in the game operate similarly using this consistent pattern as a language for the game's mechanisms. This consistency in functional relationships makes it easier to grasp the rules as a system, while the sheer variety of tags and possible effects provides a large toolbox of possible effects. The combination of tag types, mechanisms that key off of the tags, and the effects themselves create a highly expressive system that can describe many different kinds of projects, from hurling asteroids at a planet to nurturing plants under a dome to searching for microbial life in the red dust of Mars.

Scenario-based games often use tags to create a similar variability from scenario to scenario. In *Horrified*, the symbol "!" is used to indicate that a monster's special ability should be triggered. Each game is played with a selection of different monsters, each with its own special ability. The trigger simply says to trigger a monster's special effect. The effect that occurs depends on the specific monsters that happen to be in the game.

This type of modularity is part of the toolkit of object-oriented programming, which seeks to uncouple inputs, mechanisms, and outputs in order to create many little machines that accept a defined input, perform some basic function, and produce a defined output. The machines, or modules, can then be strung together in different ways to produce complex interactions. The game design leverages these ideas, but in many cases, the goal of the designer is to retain certain couplings and to create interesting decisions based on those couplings.

The examples above demonstrate how the same method, tagging, can be used for either coupling or uncoupling. The first method, of adding parameters to a given entity, couples that new parameter with all the previous parameters, uses, and values of the entity. It is one more element to consider in how to use that element to the best advantage. The last example shows how to uncouple triggers and effects, so that the designer can include greater variety and content, within a smaller set of rules and components. The second example is a masterful use of tagging for both coupling and uncoupling and demonstrates the enormous power and flexibility of the mechanism.

Magic: The Gathering makes extensive use of tags. There are several varieties. "Evergreen" keywords are abilities that are common and players are expected to know, like Flying and First Strike. These typically do not include explanations of what they do on the cards. "Set" keywords are new keywords introduced with new sets, such as the Morph ability that was introduced in the Onslaught block. Set keywords are explained on each card. The keywords in this case are a shorthand for players who are familiar with them. Finally, "Reminder" tags are keywords that are generally consistent in when they trigger, but the precise effect varies from card to card. Morbid, introduced in *Innistrad*, is an example of this (Illustration 13.2).

Illustration 13.2 Abomination of Gudul card from *Magic: The Gathering*. In addition to the CREATURE and HORROR tags, the ability section includes the Evergreen FLYING keyword and Set MORPH keyword. Note that FLYING does not include an explanation, while MORPH does.

Sample Games

7 Wonders (Bauza, 2010)
Horrified (Uncredited, 2019)
Magic: The Gathering (Garfield, 1993)
Terraforming Mars (Fryxelius, 2016)

Game Index

Note: This Game Index shows what mechanisms used a particular game as an example. It is not intended to be a full cross-reference of all mechanisms that each of these games includes.

Index

Milton Keynes UK
Ingram Content Group UK Ltd.
UKHW051532141024
449569UK00002B/61